DANGEROUS
SEATS

DANGEROUS SEATS

PARLIAMENTARY VIOLENCE IN THE UNITED KINGDOM

EUGENE L. WOLFE

AMBERLEY

Front of jacket: 'The dagger scene, or the plot discover'd' by James Gillray, 1792. Edmund Burke throws down a dagger in the House of Commons in front of terrified members as a warning about the danger of the French Revolution. It was a theatrical flourish rather than an actual threat to life and limb.

Back of jacket: Edward Orde under Creative Commons 4.0.

First published 2019

Amberley Publishing
The Hill, Stroud
Gloucestershire, GL5 4EP

www.amberley-books.com

Copyright © Eugene Lewis Wolfe III, 2019

The right of Eugene Lewis Wolfe III to be identified as the Author of this work has been asserted in accordance with the Copyrights, Designs and Patents Act 1988.

ISBN 978 1 4456 8982 1 (hardback)
ISBN 978 1 4456 8983 8 (ebook)

British Library Cataloguing in Publication Data. A catalogue record for this book is available from the British Library.

Typesetting by Aura Technology and Software Services, India.
Printed in the UK.

CONTENTS

ACKNOWLEDGEMENTS

Whether it was brave or foolish for an American political scientist with a background in Russia and Japan to undertake a history of parliamentary violence in the United Kingdom will be left for the reader to decide. It seemed like a good idea when the project began more than a decade ago. What is beyond dispute is that the pages that follow would have been significantly poorer had not the author received extensive help from many quarters.

The debt begins with the published works listed in the bibliography and, especially, the invaluable History of Parliament series, the *Oxford Dictionary of National Biography* and the online archives of *The Times* and *The New York Times*. Scholars, including Art Cosgrove, Philip Cowley, Emma Crewe, Michael Chwe, Coleman Dennehy, Vic Gatrell, Julian Goodare, Phil Gyford, Tim Harris, Geoffrey Haywood, Maija Jansson, James Kelly, Mark Kishlansky, Gillian MacIntosh, Brid McGrath, Charles McGrath, Mark Ormrod, Derek Patrick, Philip Robinson, Nick Rogers, Philip Salmon, Paul Seaward, Bob Shoemaker, John Stevenson, Richard Toye, David Underdown, Alison Wall and John Walter, kindly responded to a stranger's emails with helpful insights, suggestions and advice. The staff of the House of Commons Information Office patiently answered numerous queries. University librarians Lisa Rose-Wiles and Alan Delozier (at Seton Hall) and Jeremy Darrington (at Princeton) helped with access to documents, as did staff at the British Library, the National Library of Ireland, the Library of Congress and the Cobham (Surrey) and Mendham (New Jersey) public libraries. The cover illustration, 'The dagger scene, or, the plot discover'd', by James Gillray, 1792, is courtesy of Yale University's Lewis Walpole Library. Kristen McDonald, at the Library, helped me obtain both that image and most of the artwork in the Plates section. Michael Healy at the Copyright Clearance Center provided guidance on the selection of images. Sammy Sturgess at the History of Parliament assisted with citations. Alastair Mann and an anonymous reviewer provided helpful feedback on sections of the manuscript. Connor Stait at Amberley Publishing patiently helped me bring this book to fruition. Jenny Davis, Hamish Lochhead and Steven Roy at Parkside School educated an outsider in some of the basics of parliamentary politics. None of the above, of course, bears responsibility for any errors, omissions or infelicities in the ensuing pages.

Closer to home, the lads at Old Wokingians FC provided a refuge for a visiting Yank, all the while (largely) resisting the urge to tell him just how rubbish he was at their beautiful game. My mother, Mary Wolfe, and her friend Kittie Beyer pored over candidates for the Plates section. My sons, Levering and Clinton, (mostly) resisted snide comments about what must have seemed a never-ending project. However, by far my greatest debt is to my 大好きな wife, Cathy. Without her love, support, patience and six-year posting to Kingston upon Thames, the tale that follows surely would have remained untold.

ILLUSTRATIONS

Plate 10. 'The Mob Destroying & Setting Fire to the Kings Bench Prison & House of Correction in St Georges Fields', published by Fielding and Walker (London, 1780). (Courtesy of The Lewis Walpole Library, Yale University)

Plate 11. 'The Irish Patriots', James Gillray (London, 1783). (Courtesy of The Lewis Walpole Library, Yale University)

Plate 12. 'Paddy O Pitts Triumphal Exit!!', published by S. W. Fores (London, 1785). (Courtesy of The Lewis Walpole Library, Yale University)

Plate 13. 'Quarrel & Reconciliation', William Dent (London, 1788). (Courtesy of The Lewis Walpole Library, Yale University)

Plate 14. 'The Meeting of Parties, or, Humphreys & Mendoza Fighting for a Crown', William Dent (London, 1788). (Courtesy of The Lewis Walpole Library, Yale University)

Plate 15. 'Guy-Vaux Discovered in his Attempt to Destroy the King & the House of Lords', James Gillray (London, 1791). (Courtesy of The Lewis Walpole Library, Yale University)

Plate 16. 'The Republican-Attack', James Gillray (London, 1795). (Courtesy of The Lewis Walpole Library, Yale University)

Plate 17. 'A Specimen of Light Horsemanship', Isaac Cruikshank (London, 1795). (Courtesy of The Lewis Walpole Library, Yale University)

Plate 18. 'The Duel: Oh! What a Pity Twas that he Did not Hit his Waistcoat', Richard Newton (London, 1798). (Courtesy of The Lewis Walpole Library, Yale University)

Plate 19. 'We Come to Recover your Long Lost Liberties', James Gillray (London, 1798). (Courtesy of The Lewis Walpole Library, Yale University)

Plate 20. 'Don't you Remember the 5th of November', William Heath (London, 1829). (Courtesy of The Lewis Walpole Library, Yale University)

WHAT IS PARLIAMENTARY VIOLENCE?

The United Kingdom's parliamentary seats long have been inherently dangerous. Those who have held them over the centuries thereby have risked physical injury from irate monarchs, vexed colleagues, disgruntled soldiers, angry mobs and aggrieved activists. They have endured imprisonment for their parliamentary activity, duels arising out of debate, brawls on the floor, forcible removals from the chamber and personal assaults on the streets. At least twenty-one parliamentarians have died as a result.[1] Threats to seat holders have prompted the expansion of parliamentary privilege and changes to institutional procedure, legislation, public policy and popular opinion. So regularly have political controversies been punctuated by such perils that their history serves as a useful, if rather unusual, window into development of the parliamentary system over the past seven hundred years. Yet the fascinating, incredible, and often faintly absurd story of parliamentary violence in the United Kingdom has yet to be told.

Terminological Exactitude

The neglect is surprising and undeserved for parliamentary violence often has been quite consequential. There is a reason Guy Fawkes's attempt to blow up Westminster Palace in 1605 is remembered every Fifth of November. Other incidents, though less well known, also have left important legacies. A savage attack on Sir John Coventry for an impertinent 1670 Commons allusion to the king's mistresses prompted a change to the penal code that endured for over a century.

A duel between erstwhile cabinet colleagues George Canning and Viscount Castlereagh in 1809 had a lasting impact not only on British politics but also on the shape of the post-Napoleonic European order.[2] Even incidents that were obscure and inconsequential on their own occasionally have had a significant cumulative effect. Repeated assaults on politicians by militant Suffragettes in the early twentieth century proved counterproductive, strengthening parliamentary resistance to extending the franchise to women.[3]

This is a saga of delicious contradictions. Start out with an existential irony: parliament was created to reduce conflict but often has served to foment it; add in lawmakers repeatedly flouting their own laws by seeking to fight duels and elected representatives occasionally being pressured to adhere to popular opinion by baying mobs. Savour the thought of personal violence, often regarded as the instrument of the weak and dispossessed, being employed by some of the most powerful individuals in the kingdom. Six of the fourteen prime ministers in office between 1779 and 1846 fought, or sought to fight, duels.[4] As did a number of cabinet ministers, dozens of aristocrats and scores of parliamentarians. It is no wonder parliamentary violence has been a minor cultural sensation, inspiring the satiric illustrations of Gillray, Hogarth and others in the eighteenth century (some of which are found on the cover and in the Plates section), the sardonic prose of Dickens in the nineteenth and even the rock music of the present day.[5]

The denizens of Westminster Palace dominate our story, so much so that unless otherwise specified, the parliament in question is the English/British institution. This is partly because they have been studied more than their cousins in other parliaments. It also may reflect the predilections of the predominant nationality: according to Jeremy Paxman, 'thuggery is something the English do'.[6] Indeed, foreigners long identified a penchant for violence as an important characteristic of Englishness.[7]

Yet, parliamentary violence hardly has been an English monopoly. The members of the two assemblies absorbed into Westminster, namely the (pre-1707) Scottish and the (pre-1800) Irish parliaments, also were involved in quite a bit of hurly-burly. Often, it was connected to English/British politics, so it makes sense to consider violence in Dublin and Edinburgh along with that in Westminster. By the same token, devolution of power to the Parliament of Northern Ireland a century ago effectively transferred some disorder from Westminster to Belfast, so violence involving those with seats in Stormont should not be ignored. (However, violence in the Irish Republic's Dáil, although created by those elected to Westminster, is omitted.) The same logic demands scrutiny of the recently devolved Scottish Parliament and Welsh Assembly, although both seem unsullied by violence, at least so far.[8]

How important, interesting and pervasive parliamentary violence has been depends on how the term is defined. From early on, it has been recognised that parliamentary deliberations should be free from intimidation; force of argument rather than force of arms was to be decisive. Physical threats that might change how members behave politically undermine parliament as an institution. Focusing on such menaces seems to require that 'violence' be construed rather broadly while 'parliamentary' is understood more narrowly.

There is quite a bit of ostensible violence that reaffirms rather than subverts the established political order. Before the monarch travels to Westminster Palace for the State Opening of Parliament, a Member of the House of Commons is sent to Buckingham Palace as a 'hostage' to ensure the sovereign's safe return from her perilous journey. The Gentleman Usher of the Black Rod is then dispatched to summon Members of Parliament (MPs) to listen to the Queen's Speech at the bar of the House of Lords. As he approaches the Commons, the doors are slammed in his face to demonstrate the institution's independence. To gain admittance, he strikes the doors with his staff, the marks from which 'would be seen as evidence of vandalism in a different context'.[9] When MPs return from the Lords, they choose a Speaker. It was long traditional for a newly elected Speaker to be dragged physically to the chair, feigning reluctance and professing incapacity for the tasks ahead. 'See him in the seventeenth century: wriggling his shoulders, as if he were struggling against captors leading him to the dungeon or the stake!'[10]

Even violence that is not part of the traditional script is often nothing more than theatre. In mid-1930, for example, Lady Astor, frustrated that the Commons debate on a bill was delaying consideration of legislation dear to her heart, first pretended to pull the coattails of a colleague to prevent him from rising to speak and then, when this did not work, shook her fist at him in mock indignation.[11] Such sham or ritual violence poses little threat either to parliamentarians or political institutions, so it will be ignored.

So, too, will injuries sustained accidentally. Perhaps the most famous victim of this sort was William Huskisson, killed by a train at the 1830 opening of the Liverpool–Manchester railway line. Six decades later, Walter Powell disappeared, presumed drowned, after being carried out to sea by a balloon. After his clothes were discovered on a Miami beach in 1974, it was feared that John Stonehouse had suffered the same fate, at least until the former MP was discovered living in Australia under an assumed name.[12] Lord Thomson perished in the 1930 crash of the dirigible that the minister was promoting as a new mode of long-distance travel. Equally awkward, if less serious, was the fate of Colonel Sir Harwood Harrison, chair of the All-Party Parliamentary Road Safety Group, who was hospitalised after being 'run over by a bus in Whitehall'.[13] Only slightly less embarrassing was the experience of Immigration Minister Mark Harper, who broke his foot after falling off a table while dancing in a Soho bar.[14] Lembit Opik's fall was more spectacular: the Liberal Democrat plunged 40 feet in a 1998 paragliding accident that left him with a fractured vertebra and other injuries.[15] David Blunkett suffered a broken rib after being 'hit by a stampeding cow', while walking with his guide dog and his son in the Peak District.[16]

Stampeding MPs can be only slightly less parlous. Benjamin Disraeli once sent thanks to F. Hugh O'Donnell, after the young MP protected the frail elder statesman from 'a rather ugly rush' of colleagues desperately seeking to escape the confines of the House following the end of a sitting.[17] This seems to have been a perennial problem. In 1561, Members were enjoined 'always at the rising of the House [to] depart and come forth in comely and civil sort', rather than 'so unseemly and rudely to thrust and throng out' as sometimes had been the case.[18]

Equally hazardous could be the sovereign's speech at the opening of parliament. Under Elizabeth I, some MPs sought to squeeze themselves 'with great thrusting' into the crowded space behind the bar in the House of Lords.[19] A similar situation was described almost three centuries later, 'The Speaker of the House of Commons answers the summons of his liege lady the Queen, as if he were a schoolmaster with a mob of unmannerly boys at his heels; and is propelled to the bar of the House with the frantic fear of being knocked down and trampled upon by the rush of MPs.' One Member reported that he had been able neither to see nor hear the monarch, but 'was knocked against a corner; my head was knocked against a post, and I might have been much injured if a stout member, to whom I am much obliged, had not come to my assistance'.[20] Similarly, 1901 witnessed 'a thick crowd' of MPs 'hustling and jostling each other', as they hastened from the Commons to seek a place in the Lords from which to watch the new king open parliament. In the 'undignified scramble', an 'old Parliamentary hand was so badly hustled that only the intervention of the police saved him from serious bodily injury'. Two other MPs 'had their hats battered out of shape in the struggle to get to the front'.[21]

A throng of admirers could pose a similar menace. When Ramsay MacDonald returned to London from his constituency following the 1929 general election, a huge crowd turned up at King's Cross station to cheer the man who would soon lead Labour's second government. He was 'mobbed' and 'literally swept off his feet' by jubilant supporters and was 'saved from personal injury only with the greatest difficulty'.[22]

Even injuries intentionally inflicted upon politicians do not merit consideration here, provided the motivation is not actually malicious. In June 2012, for example, Labour MP Austin Mitchell allowed a fishmonger to hit him in the face with a fresh, 5lb cod to raise money for charity.[23] More than a century earlier, the Earl of Chesterfield, desirous of the vote of a colleague who considered himself 'skilful in physic', went to the peer and, after some conversation, complained of a headache. As expected, the medic *manqué* offered to bleed the earl, who thereby won his trust and his vote.[24] More modern medical treatments also are excluded, even if they occasionally prove fatal.[25]

Confining ourselves to acts that are animated by hostility does not fully delimit violence, which often has been understood to include not only the use of physical force but also emotional incontinence. According to *The New York Times*, for example, a 'violent disturbance broke out in the House of Commons' in September 1950, after Brigadier Terence Clarke demanded that the government 'look into the credentials' of War Secretary John Strachey. Clarke's assertion that soldiers should not be asked to fight Communism in Korea under a minister who, Clarke alleged, had admitted to being a Communist in the past, led to 'shouts, whistles and the stamping of feet. Arguments broke out on all sides of the House and the Deputy Speaker, Sir Charles MacAndrew, was unable to quell them for some time'. Clarke's subsequent statement that he hoped the prime minister would 'shuffle the pack' [i.e. replace Strachey], produced 'a long and continued uproar' and 'verbal jousting' that continued for ten minutes.[26]

If such scenes are violent, then Westminster Palace long has been a war zone. The Victorians considered displays of great passion, extreme ardour and a lack of moderation almost as distasteful as physical altercations.[27] Yet intemperate and indecorous behaviour in parliament was not all that rare in their era (and earlier). Today, it seems almost commonplace.

According to the authority on British legislative norms and procedures, 'good temper and moderation are the characteristics of parliamentary language'.[28] In practice, as a former speechwriter for William Hague points out, when the Commons is at least half full, 'MPs simply bellow and heckle each other', making it hard for the Speakers to be heard above the din. What is more, 'the things MPs shout are not very nice, either. Sexist, rude, slanderous, irrelevant, childish'.[29]

This sort of verbal harassment can be intimidating. In mid-2013, Julian Huppert complained that those on the benches opposite were bullying him by yawning, groaning and pulling faces whenever he rose to speak, a reaction perhaps related to the Liberal Democrat's penchant for expostulating upon the merits of wind farms and bicycles.[30]

Even less boisterous demonstrations of dissent can be fatal to those of weak dispositions. In 1822, intense public criticism, combined with the onset of mental illness, is thought to have prompted the suicide of the Foreign Secretary, the Marquess of Londonderry. Sixty-five years later, George Goschen agreed to join the Marquess of Salisbury's cabinet, but only on condition that Lord Iddesleigh be removed from the Foreign Office. The prime minister sought to shift the peer to the Privy Council, but news of the plan leaked out, prompting Iddesleigh's resignation. Soon thereafter, the indignant ex-minister 'visited 10 Downing Street to protest about his discourteous treatment, only to drop dead at Salisbury's feet'.[31]

The nursery rhyme assertion that 'names will never hurt' may not be entirely accurate, but insults, barracking and foot-stomping do not explicitly threaten anyone's physical well-being. This kind of intimidation long has been condoned, if not celebrated, in the parliamentary context. The use of sticks, stones, fists and other weapons is another matter altogether. It is only when the use of such means seems imminent that we arrive at situations here considered violent.

Crucially, this conception of violence does not require that physical injury result. A crowd seeking to force its way into parliament, or pelt a politician with rocks or demolish his residence can be quite intimidating, even if unsuccessful. A duel is traumatic, even if it ends bloodlessly. Indeed, the credible imminent threat of force, rather than its actual use, is all that is necessary for an episode to be deemed violent.

Sending a challenge to fight a duel, or merely taking the preliminary steps to do so, here are considered violent acts. So, too, is the Serjeant-at-Arms' placement of his hand upon the shoulder of an MP who is resisting the Speaker's order to leave the Commons, for this action clearly threatens that further recalcitrance will result in the individual's forcible removal from the chamber. Arrest and imprisonment, likewise, are classified as violent because the threat of force is implicit. And when the Commons is suspended due to 'grave disorder', this is deemed a violent episode; such is the latent danger of an altercation.

'Violence', then, is defined here fairly broadly, to include not only instances in which force has been used against parliamentarians but also those in which it clearly has been threatened. To be sure, such clarity is not always present, particularly in these polarised times. For example, some fellow Tories were persuaded by Mark Field's explanation for his June 2019 assault on a Greenpeace activist who crashed a banquet he was attending at Mansion House, 'I was for a split-second genuinely worried she might have been armed.'[32] But many who did not share the MP's partisan affiliation saw it as an attempt to rationalise an unjustified attack on a peaceful protester. So when is violence sufficiently interesting to be considered 'parliamentary'?

To merit this designation, a violent episode must involve a parliamentarian. Typically, this is someone who holds a seat at the time of the incident. In a few cases, it is a former seat-holder, targeted for their activities while in parliament. And in three instances, those who did not have seats are considered parliamentarians because they were attacked under the mistaken belief that they did. The monarch, also, is considered part of the club, but only when acting in a parliamentary capacity, such as during the State Opening.

To be deemed parliamentary, moreover, violence must stem from activities associated with a seat: speaking in debate, participating in divisions, sitting on committees, addressing constituents, etc. This puts quite a bit of activity deleterious to the health and safety of parliamentarians beyond the ken of the present study.

The two World Wars, for example, each claimed the lives of roughly two dozen MPs. Numerous other parliamentarians died in bloodshed of a more personal nature. Thomas Thynne was slain in 1682, apparently on orders from a Swedish count with designs on his child bride.[33] In 1613, Sir Edward Sackville slaughtered Edward Bruce, 2nd Lord Kinloss, in a duel over a woman. Peter Legh was fatally injured in a 1642 affair of honour, which arose out of some horseplay at the theatre.[34] Sir Henry Belasyse perished in a 1667 duel that followed a 'drunken quarrel with a friend'.[35] That same year the Earl of Shrewsbury lost his life in a duel with the Duke of Buckingham, who was having an affair with Lady Shrewsbury. Sharington Talbot was killed in a 1685 duel with a fellow officer of the Wiltshire militia, after an argument over whose troops had performed better in the Battle of Sedgemoor.[36] Sir Cholmley Dering expired as a result of a 1710 duel that followed a brawl in tavern.[37] In 1720, Owen Buckingham was sent to meet his Maker in a duel with a man whose birthday party he had been attending.[38]

More recently, politicians often have found themselves in harm's way for reasons unrelated to their seats. When John Bennett rode out to confront some of the 'Swing' rioters in 1830, the MP was pelted with stones and brickbats, 'very much wounded' and only saved by the arrival of a troop of cavalry.[39] In 1993, Trade Minister Neil Hamilton suffered a broken nose after he intervened to protect the owner of a shirt shop (an ex-MP), who was being attacked.[40] Tobias Ellwood received minor injuries in 2009, after being assaulted by four youths, whom the MP had asked to stop throwing a ball in Boscombe High Street.[41] Three years later, Stewart Jackson was hurt after he tried to make a citizen's arrest of a man who allegedly had damaged a Peterborough bus shelter by throwing a beer bottle at it.[42] In 2008, Anne Moffat was knocked unconscious and robbed while walking along a coastal path by youths she later characterised as 'the scum of society'.[43]

Parliamentarians sometimes have been targeted for activities connected not with their seats but with other hats they wore. John Byng, for example, had the unenviable distinction of becoming, in 1757, the only English admiral executed on his own ship. Although the MP for Rochester seems to have been a victim of politics, specifically a government attempt to create a scapegoat for a military defeat, his fate was not tied to his actions in the Commons. Rather, as Voltaire famously argued, he was hanged *'pour encourager les autres'*, to prod other British admirals to behave more courageously in battle.

Similarly, when in 1897 a young man with a horsewhip attacked Henry Labouchere, declaring his intention to murder the MP for Northampton, the cause was not the latter's activities in the Commons but his work as editor of *Truth*, a journal that previously had exposed the youth's father as the author of numerous fraudulent 'begging letters' to prominent figures.[44] When James Thomas was blinded momentarily in 1912, after a man threw red ochre in his face, the motivation for the attack was not the Labour MP's parliamentary behaviour but rather his position as an official in the Amalgamated Society of Railway Servants, which, somewhat embarrassingly, was facing a strike by its headquarters staff.[45] And when, almost a century later, a bomb was sent to Trish Godman, a Member of the Scottish Parliament, this was not, apparently, for her activities in Holyrood but instead due to her prominent support for Celtic Football Club, whose manager also received a perilous parcel.[46]

In many cases, particularly those from the hoary past, the documentary record provides too little evidence to determine the motivation for violence. For example, Robert Galbraith, who represented Edinburgh in the Scottish parliament in 1544, 'was murdered in Greyfriars churchyard because of a dispute with a fellow burgess'.[47] In 1606, there was a 'street tumult caused by a quarrel' between two Members of the Scottish parliament, then meeting in Perth. In 1698, Lord Tullibardine, another Scottish MP, was arrested partly for the purpose of 'preserving the peace and preventing bloodshed while the parliament was sitting'. Two years later, yet another Scottish MP, Lord Bellenden, 'did beat' a man named 'Gibsone' in 'the room next to the Parliament House'.[48] In 1700, a 'cashiered officer' was ordered taken into custody for assaulting a Member near Westminster.[49]

In 1737, the Irish House of Commons ordered the arrest of three 'gentlemen' who, 'with several other persons unknown', did 'forcibly enter the dwelling-house' of MP Sir James Somervell, 'break open several inner doors ... and in a violent manner assault and wound him and his servants'.[50] Six years previously, the Irish Commons ordered taken into custody two men, one for assaulting MP John Bourke 'in a violent and notorious manner ... by presenting a pistol to his breast, and threatening to shoot him', and the other, Alexander Graydon, for encouraging this attack.[51] Graydon may be the man of this name who, between 1703 and 1723, was MP for the Borough of Naas, the constituency Bourke represented from 1727. If so, the dispute could be parliamentary, but the evidence in this case, as in those immediately preceding it, and quite a few others, is insufficient to make a definitive determination.[52]

Discerning a motive can be difficult, even with incidents that are much more recent. In 1997, for example, an inebriated part-time bouncer head-butted and broke the nose of Ian McCartney at a Labour club in Manchester. The MP had been pushing for a national registration scheme for doormen and bouncers.[53] It is possible that the bouncer targeted McCartney because of the latter's parliamentary activities, but absent clear evidence of such a motivation, this, and similarly ambivalent cases, will be ignored.

Lacking clear evidence that it is connected to a seat, violence will be assumed parliamentary only if it originates in parliament. Even then, some episodes do not make the cut.[54] In 1727, John Ward was left bleeding from the mouth and rendered senseless for several hours after being made to stand at the pillory in the Westminster Palace Yard. Although many members of both Houses gathered to watch the humiliation of someone who, until his recent expulsion from the Commons, had been a colleague, the violence was not parliamentary because it stemmed from Ward's conviction for forgery, rather than anything connected with his former seat.[55]

This highlights a final caveat. Criminal behaviour generally is not considered parliamentary unless it is directly connected to a seat. Activities that today are standard parliamentary practice – such as organising before the start of a session, criticising government policies or proposing measures unwanted by the ministry – once were unlawful. Numerous MPs have been imprisoned for daring to do such things. To ignore as not parliamentary illegal acts aimed at strengthening the Commons as an institution seems perverse.

Punishment for other transgressions is another matter entirely. In the mid-seventeenth century, MP Lionel Copley was accused, at the age of 57, of 'assaulting a neighbour, Richard Firth, and having "put a bridle into his mouth, got on to his back, and ridden him about for half an hour, kicking him to make him move"'.[56] More recently, not a few other parliamentarians have faced similar, if less colourful, accusations of criminal misconduct.[57] Like forgery, however, such behaviour hardly seems parliamentary.

Perhaps more controversially, neither is illegal speech, provided it is outside of parliament. In September 1887, for example, MP William O'Brien was arrested in Ireland for inciting people to 'assault, obstruct, and intimidate' law officers in the execution of their duties.[58] The following year, at least seven other MPs were incarcerated for similar transgressions in Ireland.[59] In 1920, the Communist Cecil Malone earned six months in prison for making a seditious speech in the Albert Hall, in which he said, 'What are a few Churchills or a few Curzons on lamp posts compared to the massacres of thousands of human beings?'[60]

Had those who were not parliamentarians said similar things they presumably would have faced the same sanctions. Like volunteering to be hit in the face with a dead fish, such episodes shed little light on the intrinsic dangers of a parliamentary seat. Accordingly, they will be ignored.

Occupational Hazards

The 815 documented instances of parliamentary violence considered below, then, constitute only one facet of the peril faced by those who have occupied seats over the centuries.[61] (Another element, the danger inherent in seeking a seat through election, will be considered elsewhere.) It may be true that assassination 'has never been the English vice'.[62] Or that revolutions only happen across the Channel.[63] But mayhem on a much smaller scale clearly long has been endemic in the British Isles, with those from the very top to the very bottom of society enthusiastically participating. The sheer volume and diversity of the danger is all the more astounding given that none of it is supposed to happen. Violence against those who hold seats almost always is contrary to parliamentary procedures, against the law, and socially condemned.

On the other hand, what perhaps is surprising is not how much parliamentary violence there has been, but how little. If one considers the tens of thousands of people who have occupied seats over the centuries, and the countless interactions they have had with colleagues and outsiders, the several hundred instances in which violence did occur is but an infinitesimal fraction of the possible outbreaks.[64] Politics is a high-stakes, emotional game; one that creates winners and losers. Surely such a stressful environment could have been expected to average more than about one violent incident a year.

Perhaps it did. It seems likely that seats were, at least somewhat, more dangerous than depicted below. For one thing, as mentioned, it can be hard to determine if long-ago incidents were parliamentary. For another, politicians generally have not publicised their scrapes. Silence and a stiff upper lip typically won them more sympathy and respect than whinging. Even today it seems probable that parliamentary violence could occur without becoming public knowledge.

Going back in time only increases the likelihood that incidents will escape the historical record. Both official sources, such as House Journals and Hansard, and newspapers disappear. Literacy falls, meaning that those who witness a violent incident may not be able to record it for posterity. And, perhaps most importantly, culture changes. Medieval society was far more violent than today. Relatively minor incidents, which now seem remarkable, might have been considered unworthy of mention centuries ago. Episodes lost in the mists of time, in short, may help explain why the first half of the history of parliamentary violence requires only two chapters while the second needs twelve.[65]

An even more important reason parliamentary violence has been relative exiguous is that quite a bit of effort has been devoted to preventing it. When the spread of the code of honour made debate more dangerous, parliament responded not only by changing its rules to prohibit the use of 'reviling or nipping words' but also by spending lots of valuable time mediating quarrels between Members so they did not escalate into potentially fatal duels.[66] As parliament's power grew, so too did the privileges it demanded to protect its Members from outside threats.

Disorder on the floor replaced the danger of individual combat as democracy increased and political parties became more disciplined and cohesive. Again, procedural changes ensued. However, the limited effectiveness of these reforms prompted the development of informal mechanisms, dubbed 'the usual channels', by which party leaders have sought to resolve conflicts that might otherwise bring parliament to a disorderly standstill.

Parliamentary efforts to reduce violence have even become the stuff of legend. According to popular myth, the lines on the floor of the House of Commons separate the government and opposition benches by two sword lengths to prevent Members from fighting. The demarcations hardly were a response to an obvious problem. There are no known instances of sword fights breaking out in the Commons. This is not because, as an influential textbook asserts, 'there is no record of a time when members were permitted to bring swords into the Chamber'.[67] Parliamentarians have worn swords on the floor and, on a number of occasions, partially unsheathed them during quarrels. Had the lines then existed, it is unlikely they would have deterred swordplay, particularly as nobody ever has been punished for crossing them. However, by the time the lines appeared, after Westminster Palace was rebuilt following a fire in 1834, gentlemen had not worn swords for many decades. The lines are purely decorative.

That is a pity, for the notion of MPs requiring physical separation lest they fight like lions over matters of high principle has a certain appeal. Occasionally, this has not been far from the truth. Many of the dramatis personae have behaved commendably, choosing to risk possibly serious physical injury rather than compromise their beliefs. The bravery and character displayed by quite a few parliamentarians may not be enough to perform the peculiar alchemy of transmuting the reputations of the political class from lead to gold, but it does provide a bit of an antidote to current cynicism.

That said, most parliamentary violence seems childish rather than chivalrous, tawdry rather than noble, closer to farce than tragedy. It is often politics in microcosm. As such, an examination of parliament's dirty little secret is more than an exercise in institutional voyeurism or political pornography. Parliamentary violence may titillate, but it also provides a window into the soul of the body politic. It therefore deserves (mostly) serious attention.

That parliamentary seats occasionally have been dangerous may not be a revelation to most readers. What a systematic and thorough examination of parliamentary violence reveals is not only the astonishing scope and diversity of the phenomenon but also trends that otherwise might remain obscure. For example, while it might be thought that the peril was greatest long ago, in fact, in terms of both frequency and lethality, the occupational hazard of a seat was greatest in the twentieth century, with the twenty-first on pace to be even worse.

The pages that follow are more than a litany of violent episodes. They collectively show how the practice of politics in the United Kingdom has evolved. They reveal the impact of democratisation both inside and outside parliament. And, because the perils of a seat often have been greatest at moments of political controversy, parliamentary violence serves as an interesting, innovative and entertaining interpretive lens through which to view British political development. From struggles between kings and barons in the thirteenth century to conflict over Brexit today, parliamentary history becomes a drama in eight hundred violent acts.

I

CHILDHOOD TRAUMA

It is unclear exactly when in the medieval era the parliaments of England, Scotland and Ireland came into being.[1] The forms and functions of the institutions were in such flux during the thirteenth century that opinions differ as to when proper parliaments can be said to exist. Even the term 'parliament' was vague initially, used to describe three very different sorts of meeting: an informal gathering of barons, a judicial session of the king's court and an assignation between a French king and queen in a palace stairway, far from the prying eyes of the queen mother.[2] What is unambiguous, however, is that the gestation, parturition and early childhood of the English, and to a lesser extent the Scottish, parliament was marked by considerable violence, making it all the more remarkable that by the end of the fifteenth century both assemblies were poised to make the transition from bullied children to assertive teenagers. Ireland's colonial parliament, by contrast, suffered considerably less mistreatment, at least partly because its autonomy and influence diminished over the same period.

A Violent Birth

Even before the establishment of what would come to be the House of Commons, English monarchs were forced, practically at sword's point, to acquiesce to reforms aimed at strengthening an inchoate parliament. At Runnymede in 1215, barons forced King John to sign Magna Carta, central to which was an assertion that taxation required consent.[3] In 1258, concerned that Henry III was encroaching on the terms of the agreement, barons turned up to a meeting of the

Grand Council in full armour to demonstrate their willingness to fight, literally, for their rights.[4] Evidently cowed, Henry subsequently agreed to a series of changes known as the Provisions of Oxford in an ensuing parliament. The next year, the king and parliament agreed to an expanded list of measures known as the Provisions of Westminster. This document sought to address some of the excesses not only of the king but also of the barons. Most notably, to prevent the sort of intimidation that had occurred previously, it 'forbade anyone to "come to parliament with horse, armour and weapons unless specially required by the king and council to do so for the common needs of the realm"'.[5]

A few years' later, rebellious barons led by Simon de Montfort sought to bolster their legitimacy by summoning to a parliament the first elected representatives of the shires and boroughs.[6] This innovation, along with the Provisions of Oxford and Westminster, was abandoned following the barons' defeat at Evesham in 1265, but only temporarily.

The Crown's desire to keep armed men as far away as possible from parliament in order to prevent intimidation raised other dangers. The right of Members (and their servants) to go to and from parliament unmolested was one of the earliest parliamentary privileges. Yet, it could not be enforced always. In 1292, while passing through London unarmed and under the King's protection on the way to parliament, Roger de Dreiton, the Earl of Cornwall's treasurer, and other members of the noble's household, were attacked and killed on a public street by a group armed with swords and knives.[7]

A similar, if even more politically consequential incident had occurred three decades previously in Ireland. On 6 December 1264, Richard of la Rochelle, the Justiciar (chief minister of the king), and a number of other magnates were taken prisoner near Castledermot. They were not armed, suggesting that they had assembled for a parliament. 'The outrage gave the signal for civil war.'[8]

In any event, those determined to confront the king were unlikely to abide by his restrictions. This was made clear in 1310, when, despite a royal order prohibiting the bringing of weapons to the English parliament, earls arrived for the conclave armed and in full armour. As before, the king was sufficiently concerned to agree to concessions. Although the Ordinances of 1311 eventually met the same fate as the Provisions, there were two important lasting effects of their passage.

First, despite their evanescence, the Provisions and the Ordinances contributed to a sense that important decisions should have parliamentary consent. The most dramatic illustration of this role came when parliament was used to legitimate the depositions of Edward II in 1327 and Richard II in 1399. The notion that parliament could exist once the king who summoned it was dethroned was dubious constitutionally, but as a means of signifying that the new rulers had the support of the realm, the assembly of lords and representatives was indispensable.[9] (The related fear that an Irish parliament might confer legitimacy upon a pretender led, in 1494, to the passing of Poynings' Law, which gave the Crown control over the summoning and legislative output of the colonial assembly.[10])

Second, subsequent rulers took even greater steps to avoid the menace faced by Henry III and Edward II. Thus, fearing opposition to a peace treaty with Scotland that would require lords to relinquish their claims to land north of the border, Roger Mortimer imposed a variety of restrictions leading up to the meeting of parliament in Northampton in April 1328. Those summoned were forbidden to bring men-at-arms. Tournaments were banned to deny armed opponents a pretext for assembling.[11] And, in a move that would set a precedent that would be followed repeatedly, a proclamation was read out prohibiting the wearing of weapons in and around the building in which parliament was meeting. Although lords were exempted, they were not allowed to wear swords in the king's presence or in the council.[12]

Likewise, when parliament met in Leicester in 1426, the Duke of Gloucester, regent to the infant King Henry VI, forbade Members to wear swords, apparently concerned that his plans to sideline Henry Beaufort, a powerful rival, could meet violent resistance. That did not happen, but some Members hid clubs in their clothing, just in case, earning the assembly the designation the 'Parliament of Bats'. And when bats also were prohibited, Members reportedly 'had recourse to stones and leaden plummets'.[13]

Those attending parliament were not the only danger. The large retinues that typically accompanied lords might be used to intimidate the assembly, which is why Mortimer banned them in 1328. The presence of hordes of armed men also could produce chaos in the surrounding area, which helps explain why parliament moved around quite a bit early on.[14] In 1317, for example, Edward II felt compelled to relocate a parliament that had been summoned to Dublin, out of fear of clashes between the citizens and the retinues of the parliamentarians. Tellingly, he instructed magnates not to house 'their men within the city against the will of the community, nor to cause victuals within the city to be taken without their consent'. Less than a decade later, another Irish assembly passed a provision that not only prohibited bearing arms in parliament but also required that armed followers be kept outside of the town where it was meeting.[15]

Although sometimes honoured in the breach, measures of this sort helped make medieval parliaments virtual oases of tranquillity. Indeed, when the English parliament finally found a permanent home in Westminster, the restrictions on weapons and prohibitions against brawling led to the area being called 'the freest place in England'.[16]

At first glance, this might seem rather strange. Medieval and early modern England was a violent place. The murder rate, adjusted for population size, was fifteen to twenty times that of today, with less serious violence apparently even more prevalent.[17] The problem was hardly confined to the socially marginalised. On the contrary, 'homicide was as common among the upper classes as among the lower in the sixteenth and seventeenth centuries.'[18] In this period, gentlemen 'grew up in a culture in which violence was endemic: casually inflicted upon servants, spouses, children, and animals, it was often the first resort of a frustrated or angry man'.[19] Nor did widespread religious beliefs necessarily deter such behaviour; 'medieval Christians, knowing the other cheek would be bloodied, did not turn it.'[20]

That they wore weapons and were surrounded by armed retainers meant that gentlemen were often prepared to avenge any slight, real or perceived. In a milieu in which self-control was seen almost as a character flaw, provocations were not hard to find. 'The language used by men of breeding and high social standing is often so intemperate as to be almost deranged, and this petulant childishness of language was matched by a childishness of deed.'[21]

Given that violence was endemic outside the parliamentary walls, surely quite a bit should be expected inside them as well. After all, early parliaments were comprised almost exclusively of these highly strung, high-status men, who tended to owe their position, at least in part, to their martial prowess. Yet, even allowing for the relative paucity of historical sources for much of this era, the number of incidents of parliamentary violence recorded seems exceedingly small. 'In an age of such tremendous energies, long swords, and short tempers, it is surprising that parliaments functioned as smoothly as they did.'[22]

One explanation for the relative lack of violence is institutional: the duties of early parliaments reduced the risks of conflict between Members. The knights and burgesses typically were summoned to consent to taxes.[23] They were expected to arrive with full and sufficient power to agree to these and other matters on behalf of their communities.[24] Once assembled, however, parliaments could engage a wide variety of other activities. It received petitions, the sending of which the crown seems to have encouraged in the late thirteenth century as a means of learning of official misconduct.[25] It played a role in legislation but could not initiate bills. Parliament also had a judicial role, about which more anon. Yet it rarely had the only or last word on matters. Moreover, parliament was organised to foster agreement about the advice given to the king rather than to make decisions in his stead.[26] Both of these attributes made fights in parliament less likely than would be the case later, when procedures became more adversarial and matters increasingly were decided in Westminster Palace.

Another reason why Members so rarely fought each other in parliament was that doing so outside it was preferable. Drawing a sword in the king's presence was a capital offence. It was much better to pursue the dispute outside the parliamentary walls, where the chances of detection and punishment were lower. Moreover, until disarmed by the Tudors, many who sat in parliament had servants, retainers, tenants, and friends who could be called upon to help in a fight that took place outside the walls of parliament. Indeed, some of the great lords had small armies, meaning that disputes between them could lead to actual wars.

Preventing this was a priority. The parliament that met in November 1381, for example, was postponed for a few days to give Richard II time to resolve a quarrel between John of Gaunt, the Duke of Lancaster, and the Earl of Northumberland, both of whom had arrived for the session with 'a great force of men-at-arms and archers, arrayed in warlike manner'.[27] The king subsequently forbade supporters of the two from coming to parliament armed.[28]

Instead of generating the sorts of disputes that could turn violent, as would be the case later, medieval parliaments often served as a forum for resolving differences that had arisen elsewhere.

For example, Richard Leatherhead, Bishop of Ossory, was so fearful of his life owing to a feud with Arnold le Poer that he went to the Irish parliament that met in May 1324 by 'a devious and difficult route', arriving late. Le Poer entered the hall 'accompanied by a band of followers clad in his livery', relaying a message from the council regarding the topics parliament was to discuss. He then 'delivered a pointed and offensive exposition' on the first of these matters, an assertion that the king wished that the Church should enjoy the liberties set forth in the Magna Carta. Leatherhead, at the instigation of his fellow bishops, delivered an extensive and eloquent rejoinder to Arnold's comments, prompting 'a further altercation' between the two, after which Arnold and his followers left the hall. Evidently fearful that the quarrel could escalate to violence, the assembled prelates pushed for reconciliation between the men, which eventually led to le Poer begging Leatherhead's forgiveness and the two exchanged kisses of peace.[29]

There was a much different outcome at the English parliament that met at Lincoln in 1316. John of Roos had angered the younger Hugh le Despenser by arresting one of his knights. When the two men were brought together in parliament, Despenser struck John of Roos 'with his fist until he drew blood and inflicted other outrages upon him', in contempt of the king, who was present, and 'to the harm of his peace and the terror of the people present at the said parliament'.[30]

The limits of parliamentary peacemaking were again on display fifteen years later. Meeting in September 1331, parliament ordered Sir William la Zouche not to 'devise any ruse to do wrong' to Sir John de Grey, with whom he had a dispute.[31] When parliament reconvened six months later, however, it was reported that, despite this order that each man not 'commit any wrong, molestation or crime against the other' Zouche and Grey subsequently had exchanged 'heated words' in the presence of the king and council. Grey 'placed his hand upon his dagger and began to draw it, though he did not entirely remove it from its sheath'. Both men were sent to prison, but Zouche was released after providing a surety.[32]

Not every violent incident between Members early on was the result of an extra-parliamentary dispute. After Roger Mortimer engineered parliamentary approval for the deposition of Edward II and his replacement by his son in January 1327, most of those in attendance sang 'Glory, Laud and Honour' to celebrate the occasion. The Bishop of Rochester, one of the few who refused to join in, later was assaulted for his omission.[33]

Even in the medieval period, parliamentary business did not always proceed calmly. At the Irish parliament meeting at Kilkenny in 1310, for example, 'great discords arose between certain magnates', according to a chronicler.[34] When matters were particularly contentious, the prospects for a violent explosion grew, as demonstrated at the so-called Merciless Parliament of 1388.

Having been appointed regents to young Richard II in response to anger over military setbacks, the Lord Appellants sought to have parliament condemn for treason many of the king's advisors. One of their targets was Simon Burley, a friend of the Duke of York. On 27 April 1388, York told parliament that Burley had served the king loyally. York further promised to meet anyone who disputed this in personal combat. This led a furious Duke of Gloucester, one of the Lords Appellant, to assert that Burley had been 'false in his allegiance', a contention Gloucester offered to prove 'with his own sword-arm'. The brothers proceeded to call each other liars and 'would have hurled themselves upon each other' had not the king intervened.[35]

The activities of the Merciless Parliament are interesting not only for this incident but because they illustrate another facet of parliamentary violence that distinguishes the medieval and early modern eras from later periods, namely the judicial role of the assemblies. To be sure, the Lords' role in trying peers for felony or treason would endure into the twentieth century, which is why the Lords spiritual were exempted from sitting when parliament was making judgments 'concerning life and limb'.[36] It also is true that legislators in later eras, such as those in the eighteenth century who turned minor property crimes into capital offences, might be responsible indirectly for more bloodshed. But when it came to ordering violence, quite often against colleagues, early parliaments were unmatched.

A conclave held in Shrewsbury in 1283, for example, found David, brother of the Prince of Wales, guilty of treason for his role in a Welsh rebellion. For thoroughly despicable conduct, David was condemned to be executed thoroughly. According to the Annals of Osney, 'First he was pulled asunder by horses, secondly he was hanged, thirdly he was beheaded, fourthly his heart and entrails were drawn out for burning, and fifthly his body was divided into four parts to be hung up separately in the four quarters of England, whilst his head was carried away to London by the citizens who were present, to be placed, as a notable spectacle, on the Tower of London next to the head of his brother Llewelyn.'[37]

Although Tudor and Stuart monarchs eventually would be discomfited by parliamentary demands for retribution, summarily dispensed justice was not unwelcome early on. Edward III made sure Roger Mortimer was given no opportunity to defend himself before parliament ordered his execution in 1330. Edward IV used a packed parliament in 1478 to convict of treason his brother, the Duke of Clarence, who subsequently was drowned in a butt of malmsey wine.

Richard III sought to reinforce his claims to the throne by using a meeting of parliament in early 1484 to pass sentence on scores of people implicated in a recent rebellion.[38]

It may be that during this period 'intrigue thickened every princely court, liquidation of enemies was tolerated among all social classes'.[39] Yet, the extent to which some parliaments took to vengeance with a vengeance raised even contemporary eyebrows, as indicated by the designations affixed to some of the sessions. The Merciless Parliament earned its sobriquet by authorising the destruction of not only a handful of Richard II's leading allies but also many secondary figures. The Parliament of Devils, held in the Lancastrian stronghold of Coventry in 1459, was so named because it condemned for treason many of the leading Yorkists.

Not all those condemned by these parliaments actually were executed. Kings often found it expedient to suspend sentences, like a sword of Damocles, to ensure good behaviour in the future.[40] Still, early parliaments proscribed their Members en masse to an extent that would be all but inconceivable following the end of the Wars of the Roses in 1485.

Ultimo Ratio Regis

In justice, as in other matters, early parliaments largely did what they were told. This was by design. Kings convened assemblies on their own initiative and for their own purposes – typically to raise money – not because their subjects sought an institutional voice.[41] By summoning parliament, the king 'was exacting a response to his own power of command and seeking his own ends, rather than consciously providing a channel of communication for the nation's will in answer to a demand from below which it would have been imprudent to resist'.[42] If parliamentarians did not follow the script, they could face intimidation or worse. Parliamentary violence was the last argument of not a few Plantagenet kings and their minions.

Toward the end of the Long Parliament of 1406, for example, Henry IV became frustrated at the assembly's refusal to provide the funds he desired without insisting upon reforms he did not. 'Only the king's angry threats of violence, the refusal to co-operate of the lords and the compelling desire of Members to get home for Christmas at last produced a most reluctant grant after darkness on 22 December.'[43]

There was a similar incident across the Irish Sea around the same time. The Earl of Ormond had been accused of packing parliaments and employing intimidation in his protracted feud with

Sir John Talbot, a struggle that left the Irish government in disarray.[44] So it perhaps is not surprising that, shortly after the feud's denouement, a parliamentarian abandoned (albeit only temporarily) a claim to precedence rather than incur the earl's wrath.

The stage was a 1450 meeting of the Irish Grand Council, an assembly slightly less formal than a parliament. Ormond, presiding in place of the absent lieutenant, 'haughtily, without lawful deliberation, commanded' Sir Robert Preston, Lord of Gormanston, 'upon great and hazardous penalty, and under terms of dangerous and evil menace', to take his place below the Baron of Slane. Sir Robert objected, asserting that his title enjoyed pre-eminence over Slane's. Rejecting repeated requests to examine the issue, Ormond commanded Sir Robert to sit where directed 'in such terrible manner and form' as to cause the knight to obey 'solely from fear and compulsion'.[45]

Explicit threats of this sort were not always necessary. Not long after the Merciless Parliament exterminated some of his most trusted courtiers, Richard II sought to coerce other assemblies to deliver his revenge. In 1397, parliament sentenced to death the Earls of Arundel and Warwick, two prominent former Lords Appellant, although the king saw fit to pardon the latter. It may have been no coincidence that Richard had turned up to parliament with a bodyguard a contemporary described as 'a savage crowd of Cheshire men, armed with axes, bows and arrows'.[46] When parliament next met in Shrewsbury in early 1398, it annulled measures passed by the Merciless Parliament. Members again were confronted with *force majeure*: Richard surrounded the roofed, but sideless, structure in which parliament was meeting with 4000 archers.[47]

Three decades earlier, William of Windsor, Edward III's lieutenant, unsuccessfully resorted to similar techniques in an effort to compel Irish parliaments to consent to taxes to fund his military operations. One parliament was 'starved into submission' after being summoned to meet in an inhospitable and remote location where Members had little access to food or lodging. Another saw some recalcitrant Members thrown in prison. But while Irish parliamentarians resisted and complained to Edward about these coercive methods, they were unable to prevent Windsor's subsequent re-appointing as lieutenant, a decision apparently influenced by his wife, who was the king's mistress.[48]

Soon thereafter, in 1375, the Irish parliament refused to vote a subsidy. Sixty representatives of the colony were ordered to go to England in order to consent to taxation before the king and council. Any unwillingness to provide such consent was likely to be insalubrious. The order prompted assertions that the representatives were not obligated to make such a journey, though they expressed willingness to do so out of reverence for the monarch. In the end, the colonists seem to have won this first significant political and constitutional struggle with the home government as many communities refused to give their representatives full power to agree to taxes in London. At least partly due to the growing assertiveness of the Commons, the government began inviting representatives of Ireland's lower clergy to come to parliament to give their consent to taxation.[49]

Royal intimidation typically was more selective, aimed at particular Members rather than parliament as a whole. From the outset, the Speaker of the Commons proved a frequent target of the crown's wrath. Peter de la Mare, the first man designated to speak for the English Commons, discovered this to his cost. After playing a prominent role in the unprecedented impeachment proceedings against some of Edward III's corrupt officials in the Good Parliament of 1376, de la Mare was imprisoned following the end of the session. The Bad Parliament of early 1377, which undid the reforms of the previous session, featured calls for his release, but it was not until Edward's death in June that the prisoner was freed, pardoned, and compensated, enabling him to return as Speaker in the next parliament.[50]

De la Mare was not the first parliamentarian to fall afoul of Edward III. In 1341, the king's agents had physically prevented John Stratford, Archbishop of Canterbury, and two of his relatives, also lords spiritual, from sitting in parliament as part of a dispute stemming from the prelate's criticisms of royal policy. After more than a week of parliamentary complaints about this exclusion, Edward backed down and allowed the three men to take their seats.[51]

Still, de la Mare's fate was ominous. How could one chosen to express the views of the Commons do so if this were to result in unhealthy attention from the throne? It was not for nothing that future Speakers would often, upon taking office, beg the sovereign's pardon for anything objectionable they said in the course of their duties.

This hardly indemnified them, although the perils of the speakership often are exaggerated. One respected parliamentary textbook claims that 'between 1471 and 1535, six Speakers were executed'.[52] The top job in the Commons might seem a position to die for, but matters were not so simple. Unlike de la Mare, most early Speakers were the king's men. They obtained the post because of royal support. They behaved in office as active politicians and were therefore 'subject to all the hazards of politics'.[53] Those that served loyally as Speaker could often expect promotion to bigger and better things. For at least five of the six, it was their behaviour in subsequent offices, rather than their performance as Speaker, that proved to be their undoing.[54]

The perils of the speakership early on nonetheless were real. If the head wearing the crown was uneasy, so too were those close to it. Sir John Bussy, for example, was beheaded in 1399, partly for his efforts as Speaker to punish those deemed insufficiently loyal to Richard II. When one of these men, Henry Bolingbroke, became king, Bussy paid with his life.

Perhaps the best illustration of the fickleness and potential lethality of the turning of fortune's wheel is the experience of Sir William Oldhall, elected Speaker in 1450 on the strength of his ties to Richard, Duke of York, whom he served as chamberlain. Not coincidentally, Oldham's election followed the entry into London of the duke and his allies, the Earl of Warwick and the Duke of Norfolk, all at the head of large bodies of armed men.[55] However, when his patron's star waned the following year, Oldhall was forced to flee for his life. He subsequently was indicted for treason, outlawed for not showing up for trial, and attainted, that is, his life, property, and hereditary titles were declared forfeit. Following York's victory at St Albans in 1455, however, Oldhall's attainder was reversed. He was attainted again after York's military setbacks in 1459, although this was reversed once more the following year.

Other parliamentarians found the political waters around the time of the Wars of the Roses to be equally treacherous. The wrath of the king was not the only danger. The public could be a threat too. The year 1450 alone saw the murder of three who sat in the Lords, though in none of the cases does the violence seem attributable to their parliamentary activities. When Adam Moleyns, Bishop of Chichester and Lord Privy Seal, arrived in Portsmouth to pay soldiers about to go fight in France, he was accused of betrayal for military setbacks and hacked to death.[56] A few months later, the Duke of Suffolk was murdered on his way to exile. And in the summer, rebels led by Jack Cade captured London and executed Baron Saye and Sele, the Lord High Treasurer. Still, parliamentary activism clearly could be unhealthy. John Morteyn, nine times MP for Bedfordshire in the early fourteenth century, created so many enemies from his strong partisanship that the king gave him permission to ride always armed.[57]

Claims that parliamentarians were entitled to other protections rang somewhat hollow in light of the bullying they suffered early on. The most ancient privilege, tracing its origins back to the sixth-century laws of King Ethelbert of Kent, prohibited the arrest for debt or trespass of those going to, serving in, or returning from parliament, as well as the detention of the servants and horses necessary for them to make the journey.[58] From almost the beginning it also was recognised that parliamentarians could only advise the monarch effectively if they could speak freely in debate. In time, parliament would grow strong enough to back up its claims of privilege. In its infancy, however, parliament depended on others for enforcement. As a result, these protections at times were more theoretical than real.

In 1397, for example, a bill condemning extravagant expenditures in the royal household was introduced in the Commons. Enraged, Richard II demanded to know who had done this. Bussy fingered Thomas Haxey, who was not an MP. Declared a traitor by the Lords and sentenced to death, Haxey only was spared by the intervention of some of the lords spiritual, including Thomas Arundel, Archbishop of Canterbury and Chancellor. Three months later he was granted a full pardon.[59] Richard's successor, Henry IV, subsequently annulled the Lords' ruling against Haxey and promised never to pay attention to unauthorised accounts of parliamentary proceedings.[60] Yet this hardly ended the danger.

Indeed, little more than five decades later furious Lancastrians sent Thomas Yonge to the Tower for proposing in the Commons that the Duke of York be named heir presumptive to the childless Henry VI. Despite making one of the first recorded pleas for parliamentary freedom of speech, Yonge remained locked up for a year, until the Lancastrians and Yorkists managed a temporary détente.[61]

Two years later Speaker Thomas Thorpe, an ardent Lancastrian, was imprisoned for debt after being fined as the result of a lawsuit that began when he ordered the seizure of some property belonging to the Duke of York. Although Thorpe had been arrested between sessions, the Commons claimed breach of privilege. However, the Lords, disregarding the recommendation of judges that Thorpe be released, ordered the Commons to elect a new Speaker, which the lower house was forced to do.[62]

The Parliament of Scotland

Medieval parliamentary violence was somewhat less common north of the Tweed. A meeting of Scotland's three estates, more so than the English parliament, was a gathering of the most powerful men in the kingdom. Its influence was derived primarily from the stature of its Members. A medieval Scottish parliament effectively was the body politic, rather than simply a representation thereof.[63] Such conclaves were intended, and structured, to resolve disputes and foster consensus in order to prevent violence outside the parliamentary walls. When they failed to do so, it typically was because their consultative function had been subverted.

The infrequency and limited duration of meetings of the estates also militated against parliamentary violence. So, too, did their business: early on, the Scottish parliament's primary function was juridical, namely the determination of legal disputes. It was only by the dawn of the sixteenth century that parliament became almost exclusively concerned with legislation, a potentially more contentious matter.[64] Indeed, in Scotland, as in England and Ireland, one of the biggest struggles for early parliaments was not to prevent Members from fighting but to ensure that sufficient numbers turned up in the first place.[65]

The influence of the Scottish parliament tended to wax and wane. When the king was a minor, the estates often wielded considerable power; when an adult wore the crown parliament could be marginalised. There were exceptions, of course. David II was bullied by his nobles in parliament, and by others: when, in 1357, he sought to hold his first council after returning to Scotland after more than a decade in English captivity, the king 'had to beat back suitors with the ceremonial mace as they pressed in on him with demands'.[66] Yet it was another Scottish monarch, albeit one with a similar background, who was involved in some of the most notable parliamentary violence of the medieval period.

Returning to Scotland in 1424 after almost two decades of English captivity, James I needed funds to pay his ransom. The Scottish parliament provided one instalment. However, there was considerable opposition the following year to granting a second levy. Nine days into the parliament, James ordered the arrest of the Duke of Albany, who had governed Scotland in the king's absence and, apparently, was one of the leading parliamentary critics of the additional taxes. Albany and his sons subsequently were executed, but even before this happened parliament, unsurprisingly, became more willing to provide funds.

In 1428, James travelled north to demand submission from Alexander, Lord of the Isles, with whom relations had deteriorated. A parliament was convened at Inverness Castle. During this time, Alexander, his mother, and other leading northerners were invited to meet individually with the king in the castle's tower. Each was arrested in turn. This abuse of parliament only added to James's reputation for ruthlessness.[67]

The monarch was not alone in manifesting the limits of parliamentary privilege. In an effort to convince a 1433 general council – similar to a parliament but without judicial powers – of the merits of a marriage alliance with the English, James sent the Abbot of Melrose, John Fogo, to argue his case. Not only did the effort fail spectacularly but the unfortunate abbot soon discovered the limits of parliamentary free speech. 'Laurence of Lindores, inquisitor into heresy in Scotland, so disliked the theological elements which Fogo had employed that he forced him into recanting his ideas during an appearance in St Andrews.'[68] If even the king's personal confessor could be bullied in this manner for something said in support of the monarch at a meeting of the estates, how could parliamentarians question, let alone criticise, royal policies?

It was precisely this concern, that the estates were unable to constrain James by conventional means, which produced a dramatic confrontation at another general council two years later. The king sought the October 1436 meeting in order to raise money to continue an unsuccessful attempt to recapture Roxburgh castle from the English. This endeavour enjoyed little parliamentary support. In any case, there was considerable distrust of the king in the estates: in the past, he had shown few scruples about diverting to other uses funds that had been raised for a particular purpose, such as paying his ransom. To prevent the king from riding roughshod over the estates yet again, some of his opponents gathered before the meeting to prepare a surprise. It did not go as planned.

Soon after the assembly convened, Sir Robert Graham dramatically announced that he was arresting the king in the name of the three estates. The conspirators presumably expected there to be strong support for this move, for which there was recent precedent: both James's father and grandfather had been stripped of power at meetings of the estates. When the time came, however, Graham's declaration was greeted with a rather awkward silence. James, quickly recovering from his shock, summoned troops to arrest the hapless Graham and intimidate the estates into passing the legislation the king desired.

The monarch's escape was only temporary: frustrated in their attempt to remove James by lawful means, Graham and his allies resorted to the ultimate illegality – regicide – five months later.[69] However, soon thereafter a general council oversaw Graham's torture and execution.[70]

Partly as a result, by the middle of the fifteenth century, the Scottish parliament had become 'a place of danger' to the extent that many of the king's critics felt it was safer not to attend.[71] Indeed, the powerful and much disliked Boyd family 'probably deliberately avoided calling parliament in the latter part of the minority of James III, fearing what would happen when the hostile estates were gathered in one place'.[72] Once he came of age, James III suffered a fate not dissimilar to that of his grandfather: opponents, despairing of their ability to check the king in parliament, used meetings of the estates to plan his seizure at Lauder Bridge in 1482.[73]

Growth and Abuse

The parliaments of England, Ireland and Scotland developed along roughly similar lines during the medieval era, but the part violence played in this process varied considerably. The parliament that had established the strongest institutional position by the end of the fifteenth century (England's) had witnessed the most violence to get there, while the assembly least touched by disorder (Ireland's) also was the most etiolated. This pattern would only continue as religious schism raised the political stakes in the sixteenth and early seventeenth centuries. In England, and to a lesser extent Scotland, parliament's political role, and the physical dangers that parliamentarians faced, increased further. Yet even in Ireland, where parliament's autonomy and influence decreased in the wake of Poynings' Law, Members still were not fully insulated from the threat associated with a seat.[74]

2

ADOLESCENT CHALLENGES

Adolescence is a challenging time. So, it proved for the parliaments of England, Ireland, and Scotland. The sixteenth and early seventeenth centuries saw the growth of religious controversies that enhanced parliament's stature and fostered greater assertiveness. In all three countries monarchs who preferred to keep their assemblies in childlike subservience challenged parliament's attempts to forge greater institutional independence. Far more threatening to the health and safety of parliamentarians in the long run was another sort of challenge, for this period also saw the advent of a code of conduct that demanded men risk their lives to expunge the merest hint of a stain upon their personal honour. As a result of both of these changes, parliamentary debate began generating violence like never before.

Tudor Tutoring

When Henry VII became the first Tudor monarch there was little to suggest that parliament would soon develop teenage rebelliousness. Its legislative role recently had been supplanted.[1] Impeachment, an institutional innovation that had allowed the Commons to hold some of the king's more incompetent officials to account, had fallen into desuetude.[2] Most importantly, while the Commons had carved out for itself a vital role in taxation, it had greatly undercut this leverage by repeatedly granting monarchs subsidies for life, allowing them to avoid calling parliament for long periods.[3]

When they did summon parliaments, the Tudors generally proved quite skilful in managing the Commons, helped by the fact that quite a few MPs had sworn obeisance to the king as members of his household or as royal officials. Yet even Henry VII found that the institution was not always quiescent.[4] In an effort to draw a veil of secrecy over its proceedings, and thereby prevent undue pressure being placed on MPs, the Commons apparently had one of its Members sent to the Tower for daring to apprise the king of its deliberations.[5] Still, by the end of Henry VII's reign, 'the Commons had not even begun to assert the claim to determine matters concerning their own privileges'.[6] This would change under his successors, who found parliament increasingly resistant to traditional methods of persuasion.

Henry VIII's break with Rome was a watershed. To legitimise his Reformation, Henry elevated statute law, made by the king in parliament, above common law, which had been seen as supreme in medieval times.[7] And with resistance to his changes most likely in the Lords, where the bishops sat, the king found it expedient to initiate the legislation he desired in the Commons. As the influence of the lower house increased, so too did the allure of a seat. Demand from country gentlemen led to the enfranchisement of more boroughs. As these individuals came to dominate borough representation, the independence and self-confidence of the Commons was enhanced.[8] This hardly was the intention of the 'architect of parliament': Henry wanted the institution to have more power to better do his bidding. When it did not do so, the strong-arm tactics of the past were sometimes employed, though not always with great success.

Upon his election as Speaker in 1523, Sir Thomas More made the first recorded claim of free speech as a parliamentary privilege. This assertion was quite narrow: only that MPs were free to vote against bills before the House and that the words they used in debate should be interpreted as favourably as possible.[9] Although rather limited, this innovative claim of privilege should have served as a warning to tread somewhat carefully around parliamentary toes. Thomas Wolsey, the Lord Chancellor (and Archbishop of York), paid no heed. Instead, he went himself to the Commons to pressure MPs to pass a subsidy. The Commons greeted with a stony silence both his explanation of why the funds were needed and his call for a motion to grant the subsidy. He asked a few MPs to respond to his remarks, but none would do so. He then requested that the Speaker explain the feelings of the House, but Sir Thomas More replied that it was neither expedient nor agreeable to the ancient liberties of the Commons for MPs to answer such a noble personage. Wolsey departed in a huff, his effort to bully the Commons having failed.[10]

Sir Thomas then proceeded to employ a slightly more subtle form of the same tactic, directing those who supported the grant to stand on one side of the chamber while those opposed gathered on the other. The intention of what some see as the first parliamentary 'division' seems to have been sinister: 'to identify opponents to a measure so they could then be dissuaded of their recalcitrance'.[11]

Nine years later, in 1532, the king took the lessons of both Wolsey and More to heart. To ensure passage of an act diverting to the royal treasury annates previously paid to the Pope, Henry VIII travelled to the Commons himself, rather than leaving the matter to a minion. He then employed More's innovation to expose opponents of the bill to his 'basilisk eye'. Henry commanded all MPs who 'wished for the King's welfare' to stand on one side of the chamber while those who opposed the measure were to congregate on the other. Unsurprisingly, most sided with the monarch.[12] Four years afterwards, when the Commons did not pass with sufficient alacrity his bill for the suppression of lesser monasteries, Henry employed less subtle coercive methods. First, he made it known that further delays could be fatal for some MPs. When the Commons continued to dither, the king 'sent for the influential Edward Montague, who knelt before him. "Ho man! Will they not suffer my Bill to pass?" He took Montague by the ear. "Get my Bill passed by tomorrow, or else tomorrow this head of yours will be off!" The Bill duly was passed'.[13]

Henry resorted to similar tactics with the Irish parliament of 1536–7, which was manifesting the first signs of the independent opposition that would grow under his Tudor successors. Coming in the wake of a rebellion by the Earl of Kildare and the Dublin administration's efforts to manage parliamentary elections, MPs did not resist the king's religious reforms, but they did demur to provide the financial assistance he requested. After a session was prorogued, two MPs were sent to London to explain their opposition. Henry then wrote to two bishops, commanding them to support the government or risk replacement. In response to continued resistance, the king sent a commission to Dublin 'to issue a solemn warning that if the members continued to resist the king's wishes they would do so at their peril'. This, plus a few timely policy concessions, had the desired effect: not only did parliament become more tractable but it agreed to exclude from the Commons the clerical proctors who had been some of the most vocal critics of the ecclesiastical bills.[14]

If Henry was unwilling to grant MPs the freedom to vote as their consciences dictated, he would have dismissed as absurd the notion that MPs should be able speak their minds freely in debate. Even the Commons was not asserting the latter at this time. So, when Sir John Gostwick accused Thomas Cranmer, Archbishop of Canterbury, of heresy in parliament in 1539, the message he received from the king represented a personal rather than a constitutional threat, 'Tell that varlet Gostwick that if he do not acknowledge his fault unto my lord of Canterbury ... I will sure both make him a poor Gostwick and otherwise punish him, to the example of others.'[15]

The above notwithstanding, Henry was not opposed to parliamentary privilege. Provided the Commons did what he wanted, he was happy for it to be better able to defend itself. Thus, he was far from disappointed when the Commons was able to respond more forcefully, and successfully, to a challenge similar to the fiasco with Speaker Thorpe.

In 1543, George Ferrers was imprisoned for debt. The Commons sent the Serjeant-at-Arms, carrying the mace, to secure the MP's release. A struggle ensued during which the mace was broken. After sheriffs from London came and sided with the jailers, the Serjeant was compelled to return to Westminster empty handed. MPs then 'rose up wholly' and went to the Lords, protesting that, in view of the contempt with which Ferrers had been treated, the Commons would work no more until he was released. The Lord Chancellor offered to provide a writ to secure Ferrers' freedom, but the Commons, anxious not to depend on outsiders to defend its own privileges, insisted that the mace, symbolising the authority of parliament, should be all that was required.

The Serjeant was sent to try again. This time he was able to secure Ferrers' release. Those responsible for treating parliament with contempt then faced the wrath of the Commons: the sheriffs and the plaintiffs who had brought the suit against Ferrers were sent to the Tower; five jailers were dispatched to Newgate; and the clerk deemed most responsible for the fight that damaged the mace was confined to the Tower's Little Ease dungeon. Henry was sufficiently impressed by this episode to commend parliament publicly for the defence of its privileges, although he vitiated the effect of this praise somewhat by implying that the Commons enjoyed these privileges only to do the king's business and not as a source of any institutional independence.[16]

One way to consolidate claims of privilege was for parliament to demonstrate that it would use its powers responsibly. This could mean punishing wayward Members before the monarch had a chance to do so. The first instance of this came during debate in January

1549, two years after Edward VI had assumed the throne at the age of ten. When John Story exclaimed, 'Woe unto thee England when the king is a child', his colleagues wasted little time in sending the MP to the Tower, from whence he was not released for more than a month.[17]

Not everyone in the Commons was so eager to please the sovereign. The first stirrings of physical resistance came during the reign of Mary, as the Catholic queen sought to reverse her father's religious reforms. In the parliament elected in 1555, the crown managed to win passage of legislation renouncing revenue from a clerical tax only because a vote on the bill was delayed long enough for sufficient supporters to be found to outvote its many foes. Having been outmanoeuvred once, some of these opponents were determined to avoid a similar fate on a second bill, which sought to confiscate the property of Protestant exiles (many related by blood or friendship to those in parliament). A group led by Sir Anthony Kingston managed to obtain the keys to the Commons chamber, locked its door when their allies had a majority, and voted down the bill. Kingston's audacity was punished with a stint in the Tower.[18]

Two years later resistance of a more serious character was threatened. When it became known that Mary wanted to rebuild the monasteries and restore their lands, thereby dispossessing those to whom the estates had been given, this 'created such warmth of debate in the Commons that several of the members laid their hands on their swords, saying, "They knew how to defend their own properties." This put a stop to the intentions of the court'.[19]

Mary's successor faced even more obstreperous parliaments. The tension was partly ideological: Elizabeth envisioned a traditional, limited, role for parliament, but many MPs, already frustrated that some of the institution's customary functions were being usurped by other bodies, wanted to enhance the political influence of the Commons.[20] Religion raised the stakes of the struggle from conditions in this life to eternal salvation. Moreover, the zeal of some MPs to persecute Catholics and purify the established church of its 'popish' elements was inimical to a monarch committed to religious tolerance. Although the influence and organisation of the Puritan MPs should not be overstated, they played a disproportionate role in the escalating parliamentary violence of the Elizabethan era.[21]

The first incident of note came in 1566. In response to a proposed subsidy to the queen, some MPs called for linking the grant to the resolution of the issue of her succession. This was an emotive issue for, should she die without an established heir (preferably one endorsed by parliament), civil war likely would ensue as various claimants sought the crown. After extensive debate, some MPs, either hungry for dinner or mindful of courtier warnings that the succession was a royal prerogative, sought to leave the chamber, postponing the discussion. Others, however, shut the chamber's doors to keep them in. The Spanish ambassador, admittedly not always the most reliable source, claimed that the two sides came to blows.[22]

Several weeks later there was conflict of greater constitutional moment. After the queen expressly forbade further discussion of the matter, Paul Wentworth rose in the Commons to ask whether this command represented a breach of privilege. This was an astonishing suggestion. The queen clearly was justified historically in asserting that the succession fell within her prerogative, and therefore was none of the Commons' business. Moreover, parliamentary freedom of speech hitherto had meant that MPs had some latitude to express their feelings in debate, not that they were at liberty to discuss any topic they desired.

The next day's sitting was delayed because the Speaker had been summoned to meet the queen. He returned to the Commons with a commandment from the sovereign repeating her prohibition of further talk of the succession. The queen's order added, ominously, that any MP who was not satisfied could take the matter up with the Privy Council. Evidently stunned by the threat, MPs eventually responded by sending a message to the queen requesting a meeting to discuss the liberties of the Commons. Such a chat was unlikely to be advantageous to the monarch. Dissolving parliament also was not an attractive option. Elizabeth chose to back down, revoking her commandments on the pretext that they were unnecessary.[23]

There were somewhat similar scenes when the Irish parliament met in early 1569. Amid complaints that some Members had not been duly elected, the government suffered not only almost unprecedented legislative defeats but also the real prospect that the session could degenerate into actual violence. Again, the executive felt compelled to respond with a mixture of concessions and threats.[24]

When a new English parliament met in 1571, the Speaker-elect's petition for freedom of speech elicited a royal reminder that MPs should not concern themselves with matters of prerogative. However, less than two weeks later, William Strickland proposed, and the Commons gave a first reading to, a bill for reforming the Book of Common Prayer. This was a clear violation of the queen's instructions because the monarch's prerogative included religious affairs. Consequently, when parliament recessed for Easter shortly thereafter, Strickland was summoned before the Privy Council. His continued sequestration when parliament resumed provoked another challenge.

Not only did MPs denounce Strickland's confinement under house arrest as a breach of privilege, but some also supported the novel assertion that only the House should discipline its Members. The Commons discussed sending for Strickland, and thereby creating a constitutional confrontation, at least until the Speaker prevailed upon Members to drop the matter. The danger, however, was clear. Once again, Elizabeth, who apparently was behind the sequestration, beat a tactical retreat: the next morning Strickland returned to the Commons.[25]

He was not the only MP to face official chastisement in the parliament of 1571. During discussion of supply, Robert Bell supported a subsidy for the queen, but argued it should be tied to the redress of particular grievances, some of which touched on both the perquisites of courtiers and the royal prerogative. Bell was summoned to the Privy Council, where he was given a severe tongue-lashing. 'The intimidation of Bell was a warning to the commons.' MPs evidently got the message for it several days before they dared discuss any matters of importance.[26]

Realising that 'the Commons might become as stubborn as a mule, should members be imprisoned for speeches only', Elizabeth tended towards tolerance.[27] Yet this relatively gentle treatment seems to have fostered among Members, who were increasingly well educated, a greater commitment to privileges such as free speech.[28] In any case, as the Commons grew in influence MPs found that they had more to fear than the wrath of the prince. Both colleagues and outsiders were coming to pose a greater danger, as the sad tale of Arthur Hall attests.

When parliament met in May 1572, the country was digesting news of the Ridolfi Plot, a scheme to bring about, with Spanish military support, an insurrection that would depose Elizabeth, free Mary Queen of Scots, marry her to the Duke of Norfolk, and restore Catholicism to England. Hall struck a discordant note to the chorus of MPs baying for the execution of Mary and Norfolk. His colleagues were not amused. According to an anonymous diarist, 'The House misliked so much of his talk that with shuffling of feet and hawking they well nigh barred him to be heard.' Although another MP called for Hall to be allowed to speak freely, this sentiment does not seem to have been widely held. Indeed, over the next several days the House was asked repeatedly whether Hall was fit to be a Member.

In the extensive debate that ensued, some of those who previously had claimed most vociferously that the queen should respect parliamentary freedom of speech now averred that MPs should not be permitted to speak their minds without restraint. Eventually, the House decided that Hall should be brought to the bar to answer 'for sundry lewd speeches, used as well in the House as also abroad elsewhere'. After first claiming that he had been so angered by the interruptions that he had not known what he was saying, Hall eventually expressed contrition and was reprimanded by the Speaker.[29] This, however, was only the prelude.

As was the case with the monarch's other councils, the deliberations of parliament were supposed to be secret. In practice, given the many royal officials who sat in the Commons, it was always unlikely that the monarch would not hear of the most controversial remarks. The best MPs could hope for was that their speeches would not become public knowledge. Indeed, until well into the eighteenth century the Commons would seek to shield its debates from the eyes of those it claimed to represent. It was a futile effort, for even in the Elizabethan era parliamentary affairs were widely discussed. If they had not been, Arthur Hall might have avoided considerable additional misfortune.

A year after his reprimand by the Speaker, Hall's parliamentary conduct was used against him during an argument over a game of dice in a tavern. Melchisedech Mallory 'called Hall a fool, who had had to eat his words in the last parliament'.[30] Although 'Etna smoked, daggers were a drawing', the pair did not fight on this occasion. A year later lingering animosity between the two resulted in an affray in which Edward Smalley, Hall's servant, wounded Mallory in the face. This set in motion a train of events that established a number of important precedents.

Mallory went to court, winning damages from Smalley, who contrived to get himself arrested so he could avoid paying by claiming immunity as the servant of an MP. The Commons backed his assertion of privilege, ordering Smalley's release from prison, but then instructing the Serjeant-at-Arms to arrest him again for fraudulently avoiding a debt. Smalley still refused to pay, ending up in the Tower. The House sought to pressure Hall to assume the debt, on threat of expulsion. In the end, Smalley capitulated, substantiating the House's claim to a right to both discipline and protect the servants of its Members.

This did not spell the end of the matter. An aggrieved Hall subsequently wrote a letter criticising the behaviour of some of those involved in the affair, including the Speaker. Copies of the missive, and a tract by Hall claiming that the Commons had aggrandised itself as the third member of the Trinity, were published. The Privy Council summoned Hall before it. When parliament next met in 1581, Hall's writings were brought to the attention of the Commons. Called to the bar to answer for a variety of offences, Hall did not help his case by showing contempt for the House. He accordingly was treated harshly: sent to the Tower until he apologised seven weeks later, heavily fined, and expelled from the Commons, earning the ignominious distinction of being the first MP to suffer this fate at the hands of his colleagues. Again, an important (if not necessarily positive) precedent was set as far as the Commons controlling its membership.[31]

Hall was hardly the only Elizabethan parliamentarian to suffer for what he had dared to say on the floor of the Commons. By the time parliament met in 1576, Elizabeth repeatedly had shown a willingness to intervene to dissuade MPs from discussing matters she claimed (rightly) fell under her prerogative. Anticipating more of the same, and mindful of discipline to which Bell and Strickland had been subjected, Peter Wentworth rose early in the session to argue that both messages from the queen indicating her views on matters under consideration in the Commons and commands from her that the House cease discussing particular issues were 'wicked' and a violation of the privilege of free speech. If his colleagues were uneasy at his novel claim that the sovereign could not legitimately intervene in deliberations, an assertion that flew in the face of precedent, they were positively unnerved by what Wentworth said next. Alluding to frustrated parliamentary efforts to push Elizabeth to execute Mary Queen of Scots, Wentworth asserted that 'there is none without fault', including the queen. Such personal criticism of the monarch was intolerable. Wentworth was interrupted, ordered to leave the chamber, and then committed to the custody of the Serjeant-at-Arms, while a committee investigated the incident. Eventually the Commons sent Wentworth to the Tower, where he remained for over a month.[32]

Almost a decade later the assassination of the Protestant Dutch ruler and revelations of similar plots directed against Elizabeth had greatly heightened fears for the queen's safety. Many MPs argued that she would be better protected through greater persecution of Catholics. On 17 December 1584, Dr William Parry rose in the Commons to denounce a bill providing measures of this sort, claiming that it savoured of treason and would bring nothing but misery to English subjects. What really angered MPs, however, was Parry's assertion that many backed the legislation not out of concern for the queen's safety but from baser motivations. The House immediately moved that the Serjeant-at-Arms take Parry into custody. He was released the following day, after he told the House he meant no offence and the Queen sent a message requesting clemency. Several months later, Parry would be expelled from the Commons and executed for allegedly plotting to assassinate Elizabeth. His former colleagues helpfully suggested that, if found guilty, Parry should suffer tortures even more terrible than a traitor's death, but the queen, while thanking MPs for their concern, insisted upon 'the ordinary course of law'.[33]

In early 1587, weeks after parliament finally managed to induce Elizabeth to execute Mary Queen of Scots, Anthony Cope presented to the Commons a Bill and prayer book aimed at transforming English religious practice. The queen, now even more sensitive to infringements of prerogative than usual, immediately demanded that the Speaker provide her with both Cope's documents and similar materials proposed in the Commons by Dr Peter Tanner two years earlier. This prompted Peter Wentworth to move that his colleagues discuss a number of matters concerning their privileges, including whether MPs should be free to say or propose anything they thought beneficial to the realm, whether it was contrary to parliamentary rules to inform the sovereign or others of matters discussed in the Commons, whether the Speaker could interrupt a Member or rise without the consent of the House, and whether it is contrary to their liberties for the prince or the Privy Council to send for and punish an MP for what he said in the Commons.

Implicit in these questions was a radical expansion of the scope of parliamentary freedom of speech, one that threatened to undermine many of the traditional means by which monarchs had sought to influence Commons' deliberations. Rather than put these questions to the House, as Wentworth demanded, the Speaker placed the paper on which they were written in his pocket. He was summoned to meet the queen on another matter before his actions provoked debate. Nevertheless, by the end of the day Wentworth was in the Tower. Within twenty-four hours he would be joined there by Cope and three other MPs who had supported the latter's bid to discuss religious reform. In case anyone failed to get the message, Elizabeth ordered the Commons to meddle no further in matters of her prerogative.[34]

Religion was not the only dangerous topic of discussion. At around the same time, another MP found himself in the Tower for complicating Elizabeth's foreign policy. In mid-February 1587, during debate on providing a subsidy to the queen, Job Throckmorton averred, 'A Frenchman unreformed is as vile a man as lives, and no villainy can make him blush.' This allusion to the French king, with whom Elizabeth was trying desperately to remain on good terms, was awkward. Much worse were Throckmorton's 'lewd and blasphemous' criticisms of James VI of Scotland, a monarch already rather peeved at Elizabeth for the execution of his mother. Throckmorton initially was admonished for his unwelcome comments, a sanction evidently supported by the queen. However, as it became clear that his remarks threatened a diplomatic rupture with Scotland, it was deemed expedient to punish the unfortunate MP more severely, with extended imprisonment.[35]

Incidents such as these helped stiffen parliamentary spines. The Commons had appointed committees to defend its privileges in 1585 and 1587, but in 1589 this became its first order of business. (The Lords would not follow suit until 1621.) In time, this institutional innovation would not only help protect MPs from royal intimidation, but, as it became involved in election disputes, give the Commons greater control over its membership.[36] In the short term, however, the new committee afforded only limited protection, as Peter Wentworth soon discovered to his detriment.

In the twilight of her reign, Elizabeth sought to maintain a degree of uncertainty about the succession in order to induce better behaviour from James VI of Scotland, the leading claimant. Wentworth, by contrast, feared calamity should the queen die without settling who would replace her. During the 1589 parliament, he had sought to persuade a senior courtier to deliver to the queen a tract Wentworth hoped would convince her to summon parliament to examine the competing claims to the throne and determine the rightful heir. He continued these efforts even after Elizabeth dissolved parliament. This was risky, for discussing matters of state outside of parliament was forbidden. When the authorities got word of what he was doing, Wentworth was summoned before the Privy Council. He was committed close prisoner to the Gatehouse prison for four months, followed by almost ten weeks of house arrest.[37]

Shortly before a new parliament opened in February 1593, Wentworth met with several other MPs to discuss plans to push for settlement of the succession. In an era before organised parties were considered legitimate, Wentworth's efforts were suspect. When the Privy Council learned of them, he was committed to the Tower and three other MPs were sent to the Fleet prison. Although several other parliamentarians had been involved in the discussions, they did not share the fate of their colleagues, partly because they confessed their sins but also, apparently, because of apprehension about the Commons' reaction should so many of its Members be incarcerated during a session. Most of imprisoned MPs were released after the end of parliament, but the unrepentant Wentworth remained in the Tower until his death nearly five years later.[38]

Concern about the Commons' reaction also may have inspired relative leniency in the treatment of two other transgressive MPs in the same parliament. After James Morice presented two petitions aimed at the Archbishop of Canterbury's persecution of Puritans, the Queen summoned the Speaker to provide details. She ordered him to tell the Commons to focus on ensuring her safety and defending the realm, rather than meddling in matters of royal prerogative. Morice was summoned before the Privy Council and confined to the residence of a councillor. Although 'honourably received and indulgently treated', he remained in custody for more than eight weeks. Robert Beale, an MP allied to Morice, apparently received a similar punishment.[39]

The seventh and final MP to be imprisoned or confined to private custody during the 1593 parliament was Sir Edward Hoby. His offence was to have insulted a Privy Councillor during a committee meeting. Although the scale of parliamentary detentions was unprecedented for the Elizabethan era, the Commons raised barely a peep of protest.[40] Perhaps, after pushing to expand their privileges for much of the period, and often suffering for it, MPs felt the need to pause and catch their breaths.

In any event, while the wrath of the prince remained fearsome, other threats to the health and safety of parliamentarians were looming larger. As the influence of the Commons grew so too did the attention its Members received from outsiders. The quarrel between Hall and Mallory was one manifestation of this trend. Another was the growth of lobbying, a practice that could be pursued with an aggression that bordered on violence. In 1589, for example, Thomas Drurie, who opposed a private bill, was brought to the bar of the House and charged with making 'great threats' to some Members and offering others 'great sums of money to speak … for him and not against him'.[41]

Others were suspected of even more dangerous designs. Such were the fears for the queen's safety in 1584 that, when it was discovered that a 'stranger' named Richard Robinson had been sitting among them listening to the day's debates, MPs had his pockets searched, stripped him to the shirt and committed him to custody. Robinson, a skinner by trade, evidently was just curious, but the Commons' unease made his inquisitiveness rather costly: he 'was censured, made to take the oath of supremacy, sworn to secrecy, and imprisoned in the Serjeant's ward for a week'.[42]

As the House increasingly filled with independent-minded gentlemen and ideological divisions deepened, the danger grew that debate could spark a physical confrontation. To reduce the risk that Members would engage in the sort of *ad hominem* verbal attacks that could lead to physical confrontations, parliament adopted rules limiting freedom of speech by prohibiting the use of certain types of expressions. The earliest extant account of Commons' procedure, written by Sir Thomas Smith in the 1560s, indicates that speakers were required to address the House, rather than individual members, and that they were supposed to avoid referring to each other by name or circumlocution and refrain from 'reviling or nipping words'.[43] These rules did not prevent 'excited, even stormy, sittings of the Commons' during Elizabeth's reign.[44] Indeed, in 1589, the Speaker saw fit to complain during a disorderly sitting that members frequently delivered 'very sharp and bitter speeches' that were unduly offensive and vehement.[45]

If some parliamentary procedures during the Tudor era were intended to decrease the likelihood of violence at least one innovation had the opposite effect, contributing to a rather notorious incident.

For the first few centuries, the will of the Commons was discerned in much the same manner as winners were chosen in early elections: MPs voiced their support or disapproval of the measure and the presiding officer adjudged which side predominated. This method gave significant discretion to the Speaker, who, with few exceptions, was nominated by the Crown. Opponents of Mary's contentious policies found this procedure unbearable. Consequently, they began to insist on 'divisions', a technique that provided a precise tally of the 'ayes' and 'noes', making it difficult for the Speaker to fudge the result.[46]

Divisions made the vote of a single MP potentially decisive. Early on, they also had a built-in bias against innovation: those supporting a measure went out into the lobby, while those opposed remained in the chamber. The chamber often had insufficient seats to accommodate all MPs, so those who left their places to vote for a bill risked having to stand upon their return. In these circumstances, it may not have taken all that much force to convert an 'aye' vote into a 'no'.

This is just what happened in 1601. The last parliament of the Tudor period was particularly turbulent: 'speakers were interrupted, cried, or coughed down'.[47] The nadir apparently was reached when a bill for the Stricter Observance of the Sabbath was defeated by a single vote. It subsequently was revealed that an MP who had desired to support the measure had been pulled back and held in his seat by an opponent of the Bill. Those in the Commons upset by this violent incident were hardly mollified by the comment of Sir Walter Raleigh, 'Why, if it please you, it is a small matter to pull one by the sleeve, for I have done it myself often time.'[48] Still, the controversy died down when it became clear that 'on this occasion two wrongs did make a right': counterbalancing the MP forced to vote against the bill was another compelled to do the opposite by similar means.[49]

Stuart Stewardship

Of all the episodes of parliamentary violence, that which occurred early in the reign of the first Stuart monarch was easily the most infamous and audacious. In 1605, Guy Fawkes and others sought to destroy not only King James I, who had greatly disappointed Catholics by being less tolerant than anticipated, but also parliament, which was responsible for legislation penalising those who did not conform to the practices of the established Church.[50] Had the Gunpowder Plot played out as the conspirators planned, a huge explosion would have obliterated virtually the entire government, Westminster Palace and much of the surrounding area.

Unfortunately for James, it was not just some Catholics who became disillusioned with the new king. The king's relationship with parliament got off on the wrong foot partly due to violence, although this was not his fault. Desiring to witness James open his first parliament, many royal officials and other 'strangers' gathered at the bar of the House of Lords in March 1604. This apparently created the impression that the Commons, the Members of which normally occupy this position at the state opening of parliament, had arrived. In fact, it had not yet been summoned. When some MPs did try to take their place behind the bar, they were 'roughly repelled' by Brian Tash, a yeoman of the guard, with the words, 'Goodman Burgess, you come not here.' It was only near the end of James's quite extended oration that the mistake was recognised and rectified.[51]

After this inauspicious start, the king's relationship with the Commons did not improve much. Tensions between the Scottish monarch, intent on using patronage to win friends and influence people in order to secure his hold on the English crown, and parliaments exasperated by the free-spending king's requests for funds, were to persist for much of James's reign. Like many of his predecessors, James sought to do without parliament as much as possible. Between 1610 and 1621, the Commons sat for a total of just two months. Largely as a result, the volume of parliamentary business fell substantially, leading to fears about the institution's future.[52]

James's heavy-handedness toward parliament did not assuage these concerns. Largely spurning the Tudor practice of seeking to manage the Commons through agents among its membership, the king instead relied on intimidation. Soon after Christopher Piggott bitterly denounced the planned union with Scotland in particular and Scots in general in February 1607, the Commons was informed of the king's displeasure both with the speech and the House's failure to interrupt it. Piggott's chastened colleagues quickly sent him to the Tower and expelled him from the Commons.[53] When the dyspeptic Addled Parliament of 1614 disdained to provide the funds he sought, James dismissed it after only eight weeks, sending four of its Members to the Tower for good measure.

Despite its name, England's Addled Parliament could not hold a candle to its equivalent across the Irish Sea. As in the sixteenth century, Irish parliamentary contumacy stemmed from concerns by members of established (Catholic) families that their political and economic position was threatened by new (Protestant) arrivals. Had James I and his officials not been so flagrantly insensitive to Old English apprehensions it is likely that one of the most extraordinary, and farcical, incidents of parliamentary violence could have been avoided.

In the wake of the 1607 'Flight of the Earls' of Tyrconnell and Tyrone, the Irish administration had confiscated the lands of the seemingly rebellious aristocrats and initiated the wholesale 'plantation' of Protestants into Ulster, previously a Catholic stronghold. This, in turn, allowed the government to engineer a Protestant majority in the Irish parliament by adding 84 seats to Commons, which had only 148 previously. In vain did Catholics complain that many of the newly enfranchised boroughs were nothing more than collections of 'beggarly cottages' undeserving of parliamentary representation.[54]

Parliament met on 18 May 1613 in Dublin Castle, for security reasons. Although Catholic peers stayed away in protest, trouble was expected from recusants in the Commons. Armed guards searched assembling MPs. The Lord Deputy, worried that Catholics MPs might combine with defeated candidates to occupy the floor of the Commons, ordered all those who had been elected to present themselves to him for scrutiny and forbade any but those duly returned from coming to the chamber. Yet these precautions proved insufficient.[55]

Soon after the sitting began, a senior royal official nominated Sir John Davies, the Attorney General, to be Speaker. Catholics objected, arguing that before a Speaker was elected their complaints that some (Protestants) in the chamber had not been duly elected should be investigated. A division on Davies' nomination was called, nonetheless. Protestant MPs began to leave the chamber (and thereby vote in favour of the nomination). Catholic MPs refused to assign tellers to the division, so two senior crown officials offered to count those remaining in the chamber (and thereby voting 'no'). But when the officials sought to tally those opposed to the nomination, Catholic MPs 'gathered themselves into a clump to the end they might not be numbered'. The officials left in frustration.

No sooner had the door closed behind them then arose the shout of 'An Everard!' The officials returned to find Sir John Everard, who had been forced to resign as a senior judge for recusancy in 1607, sitting in the Speaker's chair. Protestant MPs rushed into the chamber shouting that Davies was the rightful Speaker. They threatened to 'pluck' Everard from his seat if he did not depart voluntarily. He refused to budge. Then 'diverse knights and gentlemen of the best quality' sought to hoist Davies onto Everard's lap, a task made more difficult because the Protestant was a 'distinctly corpulent individual'. They managed to get Davies onto Everard's knee, where he perched absurdly and precariously. A scrum then ensued as Protestant MPs sought to eject Everard from the chair, while their Catholic counterparts endeavoured to prevent this. Eventually Everard was deposed, though the two sides disagreed greatly on how much force was used in the process.

Catholic MPs sought to depart the chamber en masse, only to find that the doors had been locked. It was at least an hour before they were able to escape, during which 'many words of hate' reportedly were exchanged. It would take sixteen months and a number of political concessions, including the disqualification of (Protestant) MPs returned under the most dubious circumstances, before Catholics were willing to return to both the Lords and the Commons.[56]

The choler persisted even then. On 4 November 1614 a delegation of peers informed the Irish Commons that one of its Members had used 'scandalous words' in relation to the Upper House. Specifically, John Fishe, the Knight of the Shire for County Cavan, was alleged to have asserted that the Lords 'had no care for the Common-wealth or their own consciences'. The Lords' request that the MP be sent to the Upper House for punishment was rejected in a division, but the Commons did order that Fishe be committed prisoner to Dublin Castle four days later. On 10 November, despite an abject written apology from the MP to the Lords, the Commons resolved that he should remain a prisoner, which he did for more than a week afterward.[57]

Bitterness again was evident a few months later when, on 3 May 1615, the Irish House of Commons ordered two of its number taken into custody for words spoken in debate. In response to a motion that recusant attorneys be allowed to resume practicing law, Thomas Crooke asserted that such men, 'being so corrupt in judgment, are not fit to corrupt others'. Outraged Catholic MPs demanded he explain himself at the bar. When the Protestant MP refused to apologise, he was censured and committed to Dublin Castle. Another MP, John More, who had made the disputed motion, received the same punishment after comments interpreted as implying that the Lords had provided a subsidy less willingly than the Commons. Both MPs were released two days later. Perhaps not surprisingly, given the tensions, it would be almost two decades before another Irish parliament met.[58]

Tensions were not quite this high in Westminster, but they slowly were moving in that direction. When parliament met again, seven years later, the disposition of MPs had not improved. In response to a spat with the king over the scope of his prerogative and the nature of parliamentary privilege, the Commons made the Grand Protestation of December 1621, which asserted (inaccurately) that its liberties were not only both ancient and an Englishman's birthright but also that parliament was free to discuss matters of government and state religion. Realising that the king would reject such a claim, MPs did not send the Protestation to him but instead had it entered into the Commons' journal. Declaring himself 'justly offended', James pronounced the Protestation invalid. To emphasise the point, the king sent for the journal after parliament had been dissolved and personally ripped out the pages containing the Protestation. For good measure, five of the MPs responsible for the offending document were imprisoned, while four others were 'exiled' by being compelled to serve as commissioners in Ireland.[59]

Parliament itself was becoming increasingly violent. According to one, perhaps exaggerated, claim, 'Swords were still occasionally drawn in the House of Commons. If the motion for candles in the evening was opposed (effectively supporting adjournment), the resulting scrimmage might produce a situation in which the Speaker feared for his life.'[60]

Minor violence there certainly was. A case in point were the deliberations of a committee appointed by the Commons in 1614 to investigate claims that 'undertakers' had offered to manage the House on the Crown's behalf. During one meeting, Sir William Herbert, accused the chair, Sir Robert Owen, of being partial. Another MP, Sir Robert Killigrew, grabbed Owen by the hand and threatened to pull him from his chair, 'that he should put no more tricks upon the House'.[61]

As the code of honour spread, so too did the fear that minor incidents of this sort could escalate into bloodshed. Consequently, those in both Houses felt compelled to devote precious parliamentary time to mediating in quarrels to prevent them from escalating into potentially fatal duels. This proved harder than might have been expected, as three incidents from 1621 attest.

In February the Lords ordered the Earl of Berkshire to be taken into custody after it was revealed that he had 'violently thrust' Lord Scrope, while near the Bar of the House.[62] Three months later, MPs Clement Coke and Sir Charles Morrison fought in a Westminster Hall stairway, 'occasioning a terror to the people assembled in Parliament'. In response to a blow from Coke, Morrison, reportedly, 'catched at a sword then in his man's hand, to strike with it'. After a detailed examination of the affair, the Commons sent Coke to the Tower for striking first.[63] That same year, Thomas Howard, 14th Earl of Arundel, was sent to the Tower briefly for refusing to apologise to Lord Spencer of Wormleighton, after taunting the newly made baron with the claim that his ancestors had been sitting in the Lords when Spencer's still were herding sheep.[64]

Both Houses responded to episodes of this sort by changing their rules to encourage more civil behaviour. In 1626, the Lords introduced a ban on 'asperity of speech' after an episode in which two aristocrats treated each other less than peerlessly in a committee.[65] Yet well-intentioned reforms of this nature were insufficient to counter the spread of an ethos that required gentlemen to respond violently to the hint of a personal affront. Moreover, in a time of rising political tension, incivility was hardly the only spur to violence, as events were to demonstrate just a few years later.

When Charles I ascended to the throne in 1625, his disdainful attitude toward parliament, and his latitudinarianism at a time of rising Puritan sentiment, soon led to conflict with an increasingly assertive House of Commons.[66] It could be dangerous to become caught in the middle. In 1626, the Commons initiated impeachment proceedings against the Duke of Buckingham, the royal favourite and the leader for an ill-fated naval expedition. Soon thereafter, Sir Dudley Digges and Sir John Eliot, the MPs who led the effort, were arrested at the door of the Commons' chamber and sent to the Tower. Two years later, Sir Edmund Sawyer suffered the same fate, and was expelled from the Commons, for raising customs rates to provide additional (extra-parliamentary) revenue for the crown.[67]

By 1629, the conflict had put the Speaker, Sir John Finch, in a tight spot. Like most of his predecessors, he was expected to do the king's bidding. On the other hand, there were signs that MPs were growing increasingly upset at Speakers who did not put the interests of the Commons first. Fear that the presiding officer would help manufacture a majority for the queen's bill in 1555, led to Sir Anthony King's subterfuge. Similar concern prompted the Commons to create a 'committee of the whole', a device by which it could temporarily elect its own chair and thereby evade the rule of the Speaker.[68] And in 1621, after he had tried to cut off debate critical of the king's conduct, MPs reminded Sir Thomas Richardson that 'Mr Speaker is but a servant to the House, not a master, nor a master's mate'. To emphasise the point, Speaker Richardson was stripped of some of his power to set the agenda, and the Commons passed a motion calling for him to be silent for a day to allow Members to get on with business.[69] Finch, in short, had been warned.

He paid insufficient heed, as a result of which, on 2 March 1629, there occurred an episode of parliamentary violence reminiscent of a notorious Irish precedent. In response to repeated attempts by the Commons to investigate Crown revenue collection that had not been authorised by parliament, Charles instructed Finch to adjourn the House until 10 March. When the Speaker told the Commons of his orders, MPs, who believed that the House itself should decide when to rise, responded with angry cries. Sir John Eliot, who wanted to debate a remonstrance critical of royal policy, stood to speak, but Finch told him that the king had ordered the Speaker to vacate the chair should anyone seek to prolong the sitting after the order to adjourn had been read. As Finch sought to leave the chair, however, several MPs rushed to stop him. A group of courtiers then surrounded the Speaker, allowing him to descend to the floor. Denzil Holles and Benjamin Valentine then grabbed the hapless Finch, dragged him back to his chair, and held him in it. Another MP,

Sir Miles Hobart, locked the door. Some privy councillors tried to rescue Finch, leading to a scrum in which punches were thrown.

Eliot's remonstrance was read, but Finch refused to put the question to the House. This prompted MPs to ask the Speaker whether he was the servant of the House. He famously replied, 'I am not the less the King's servant for being yours.' Soon thereafter, there was a knock on the door. A messenger from the king instructed the Serjeant-at-Arms to bring the mace from the Commons. The House allowed the Serjeant to depart, but without the symbol of parliamentary authority. Then Black Rod knocked on the door. He was denied admittance and his message went unheard. As it became known that the king had ordered his Captain of the Guard to force his way into the Chamber and disperse the Commons by force, MPs quickly passed Eliot's remonstrance by acclamation, voted to adjourn, and allowed the Speaker to depart.[70]

Although Charles, like his predecessors, was not averse to using violence to control parliament, he could not abide by a group of his subjects doing the same. To tolerate such a manoeuvre would be to condone a program that was thoroughly revolutionary.[71] Eight MPs involved in the rebellion against his Speaker were imprisoned, with one, Sir John Eliot, kept in the Tower until his death in 1632. (Finch was promoted to Lord Chief Justice of the King's Bench for his loyalty. However, when parliament again met in late 1640, he was summoned before the bar to answer for his conduct as Speaker. Fearing impeachment, Finch fled abroad.)

This harsh response was added to the litany of parliamentary grievances against the king. Moreover, when some of the prisoners sued for habeas corpus, a peeved monarch prevented them from being brought to court, an illegal move that did his reputation no good. To be sure, the stature of the Commons hardly was enhanced by the incident. And this, combined with what Charles described as the anarchy and confusion engendered there, seems to have prompted him try to do what many in Westminster feared was his plan all along: to rule without parliament.[72]

Scottish Echoes

The religious ructions unleashed by Martin Luther's calls for reform of the Catholic Church precipitated considerable political strife in Scotland, although markedly less parliamentary violence than in England. This was first evident in conjunction with the so-called Reformation Parliament of 1560, which provided for the reorganisation of the Scottish Kirk along Protestant, if not quite yet Presbyterian, lines (although the monarch would not ratify the changes until seven years later). Despite a previous agreement that all those who had cause to could attend, fear of mob violence and the armed retainers of Protestant lords caused a substantial portion of the Catholic clergy to stay away from the sitting. The prospects for Protestant reform were improved still further when almost 100 barons, who traditionally had not attended parliament in great numbers, turned up to support it.[73]

Even more hazardous were some of the parliaments held during the civil war that erupted a few years later, following the forced abdication of Mary, Queen of Scots. Both her supporters and those who backed her son, James VI, sought to use meetings of the estates to legitimise their actions and condemn their rivals. This made attending such conclaves potentially perilous, something that became painfully obvious when, in May 1571, the king's party sought to hold an assembly in the Canongate despite their opponents occupying the high ground at Edinburgh Castle, not far away.

Preparations for the sitting were the source of some embarrassment: replicas of the Honours of Scotland had to be procured because the originals were held by the queen's party, which would soon use them in its own parliament in Edinburgh's Tolbooth. The meeting itself quickly degenerated from the not-quite sublime to the more-than-faintly ridiculous. 'To the amusement of onlookers, the king's men faced the indignity of ducking to avoid the cannon fire from the castle, earning themselves the sobriquet of the "creeping parliament".' The session lasted all of ten minutes.[74]

Efforts by the king's party to hold another parliament in Stirling a few months later fared even worse as Mary's supporters attacked the town and killed the Earl of Lennox, the regent. Undeterred, James's allies quickly convened a convention of the estates, which chose a new regent. The parliamentary session then continued.[75] However, the young king's presence, intended to solemnify the assembly, probably did the opposite. 'Bored with the proceedings, James spotted light coming through the roof and, with more accuracy than he realised, announced in the penetrating voice four-year-olds use, "Thair is ane hole in this parliament."'[76]

Disputes considerably less momentous than the state's religious or constitutional order also could produce parliamentary violence. While the Scottish court generally was more informal than its English counterpart, Scotland's parliament was considerably more hierarchical and status conscious than Westminster Palace, at least partly because it was unicameral.[77] Sittings of the Scottish parliament began with a 'riding', a ceremonial procession to the place of meeting. It was organised by rank, with the lowliest burgh commissioners in the front and the most exalted participants, the monarch or his representative, in the back. Parliamentary seating also was hierarchical: the higher the status of a Member, the closer to the throne he sat. Voting also was by rank, but this time in reverse order, so that the burgh commissioners would have an opportunity to learn from the example set by their 'betters'.[78]

All this emphasis on status meant that issues of precedence could become quite contentious, even for those at the bottom of the hierarchy. The riding of the parliament of 1567, for example, witnessed a 'tumult' as representatives of Perth and Dundee struggled to occupy the coveted position of second burgh, after Edinburgh. The two burghs continued their battle for pre-eminence, albeit by less violent means, until 1602.[79]

Status anxiety was particularly acute among the nobility. This was nowhere more apparent than the July 1587 parliament, the business of which was delayed to allow the privy council to rule on a precedence dispute between the Earls of Bothwell and Crawford. The council found for Crawford, but insult subsequently appears to have been added to injury for '[g]reat words passed betwixt Bothwell' and the Earl of Angus, before the former abandoned parliament in a huff.

A contemporaneous dispute almost produced bloodshed. Lord Fleming told Lord Hume that the latter should not be placed ahead of him in precedence, 'except he won it with the sword'. Accordingly, the two men prepared to settle the matter on the duelling ground. Ultimately, however, Edinburgh magistrates prevented the meeting and the king then reconciled the pair.[80]

Perhaps not surprisingly, the 1587 parliament adopted regulations aimed at preventing similar indignities in the future. One obliged Members not to disrupt proceedings by disputing the place they were assigned by the Lord Lyon King of Arms. Another established a commission to adjudicate status controversies.[81] Yet repeated demands that Members come to parliament 'in quyett manor without armour' and not to 'persew truble or offer injurie' to anyone, suggest considerable concern about the possibility of parliamentary violence during Scotland's fractious late sixteenth century.[82]

Fellow parliamentarians were not the only danger during this period. When a convention of the estates, similar to a parliament, authorised a debasement of the currency in 1575, its Members 'had to walk to Holyrood through a gauntlet of abuse from angry townsfolk'.[83]

Those who assembled for a parliament in mid-1592 also apparently did so with some trepidation. The previous year, the Earl of Bothwell, who had earlier sought to raise a rebellion, had been arrested on charges of consulting witches in an effort to harm the monarch. Bothwell escaped from confinement in Edinburgh Castle and, several months later, invaded the royal chambers in Holyrood Palace, evidently intent on killing the chancellor, who he presumably held responsible for the witchcraft charge, and seizing the king. Security concerns led to the postponement of the parliament that was to sanction the rebellious earl. When it did meet, 'such was the apprehension that Bothwell might perform another of his daring raids that, for the duration of parliament, the council of Edinburgh mounted a watch at Holyrood and on the spire of St. Giles'.[84] (Similar steps were taken two years later for a parliament that was expected to try three earls for treason.[85])

The Lords of the Articles, parliament's steering committee, found Bothwell guilty of treason for invading the king's chambers, attainting both the earl and his allies. These actions may have contributed to a physical confrontation between two of the lairds who sat on the committee. The encounter culminated in Sir John Murray of Tullibardine striking James Edmundstone of Duntreath 'with the hilt of his sword, breaking his face foully'.[86]

When James VI of Scotland moved south in 1603 to become James I of England, his influence in the Scottish parliament actually increased, due to both the indelicacy of criticising the absent monarch and a massive increase in royal patronage.[87] Nevertheless, the means he employed in 1621 to push through parliament measures aimed at making his kingdoms more ecclesiastically homogeneous (by Anglicising the Scottish Kirk) greatly rankled. However, James's success encouraged his successor to employ even more heavy-handed tactics to ram additional ecclesiastical changes through another Scottish parliament. This time the victory proved pyrrhic.[88]

Charles I went to extraordinary lengths to ensure that the Scottish parliament of 1633 would pass legislation that included controversial ecclesiastical reforms. The most objectionable steps came on the last day of parliament. Instead of discussing and voting separately on each item, Members were given the choice of supporting or rejecting the entire package, with little opportunity to debate. Still worse, the king, personally present in the chamber, conspicuously recorded each vote in what was viewed as an attempt to intimidate potential opponents. Moreover, when it was announced that the legislation had passed, the Earl of Rothes, a leading critic of the changes, stood to express the pervasive (but probably unfounded) view that the Clerk Register deliberately had miscounted the votes. The king commanded that the nobleman be silent or else, in the words of one account of the incident, 'upon the peril of his life, make that good which he had spoken'. Unable or unwilling to try to corroborate his claim, the dissentient 'sat down and was silent'. Yet such was the scandal surrounding the incident that six years later it was deemed expedient to publish, in the king's name, a denial that any manipulation of parliamentary voting had occurred.[89]

The intimidation did not end with the meeting of the estates. The day after parliament ended, 'the privy council turned a royal audience with Highland chieftains into a general mustering of the clans, thereby indicating that the military use of the Gaels as part of the British expeditionary force in continental Europe since 1626 might usefully be deployed for domestic purposes'. This did not deter William Haig, a former crown solicitor, from drawing up a supplication complaining about what had transpired in parliament, but also professed loyalty to the king.

Although the king refused to receive the document, possession of the supplication subsequently became dangerous. When Rothes and Lord Balmerino, another leading disaffected noble, were suspected of having copies, both were called in for questioning. Rothes was released, but Balmerino was charged with lease-making, convicted, and sentenced to death. He would eventually be pardoned, but his treatment, and the crown's management of parliament, played important roles in the emergence a few years later of a movement that would constitute a serious challenge to royal authority in Scotland.[90]

Irish Intimidation

Efforts to bully the Irish parliament also produced short-term success at substantial long-term cost. Thomas, Viscount Wentworth, had been appointed Lord Deputy in the expectation that he would use the position to secure sufficient financial support to allow the king to rule without having to summon an English parliament. To this end he turned the Irish parliament 'into a mere instrument of government policy', partly by playing Protestants off against Catholics.[91] This triumph ultimately would cost Wentworth his life and contribute to yet another Irish rebellion.

Wentworth's aggressive efforts to pack parliament provoked hostility, and almost violence, when it met in mid-1634. Instead of following the government's lead, MPs engaged in a sustained debate about whether to exclude from the Commons those not duly elected because they were not resident in the constituencies from which they were returned. This was an issue of considerable political significance because many of the non-residents were Protestant supporters of the Lord Deputy. When one MP expressed support for such a purge, Captain Charles Price, a close Wentworth ally, told those sitting near him that his colleague 'understands it not'. This prompted Sir John Dungan, who was sitting behind Price, to tell him, 'As well as yourself.' Price then called Dungan 'a saucy fellow', to which the latter responded, 'You lie.'

The Commons ignored the quarrel. Soon after the parliamentary session ended, however, Wentworth, fearing that the dispute might again 'brake [sic] out into some distemper', had Price and Dungan taken into custody. When parliament resumed on 4 November, the Lord Deputy informed the Commons of his actions. Price evidently was allowed to resume his place quickly but Dungan, identified by Wentworth as having given the 'first provocation', was kept in Dublin Castle until 15 November, at which time he was allowed to return to his place, having first apologised on his knees at the bar of the House.[92]

Dungan was not alone in being punished for his actions in the Irish parliament of 1634. On 30 July, 'exception was taken' to words spoken by an MP named Netervill. Exactly what he said is unclear, but his utterances apparently led not only to his expulsion from the Commons but also to Wentworth's efforts to prosecute the son of Viscount Netervill in the court of castle chamber, on the grounds that the erstwhile MP had, in the Lord Deputy's words, 'most barbarously and insolently demeaned himself this last session of parliament, expressing upon all occasions wondrous ill affections towards his Majesty's affairs and towards his ministers'.[93]

Another Wentworth critic, Catholic lawyer Sir Robert Talbot, received similar treatment. On 1 August 1634, he was expelled from the Commons and committed to the custody of the Serjeant-at-Arms until he made a 'humble submission on his knees' to the Lord Deputy for committing 'an offence, which tended to the dishonour of his lordship and of this Houses'.[94]

Despite, or perhaps because of, these efforts to intimidate critics, the next parliamentary session was considerably stormier. By now it was clear that, promises to the contrary notwithstanding, Wentworth was not disposed to make concessions to Catholics. Members of the aggrieved 'Popish party' became even less tractable, to the extent that the government temporarily lost control of the Irish Commons. The Lord Deputy responded without subtlety, ordering the imprisonment of Sir Edward FitzHarris, one of the party's leaders. When this did not have the desired effect, Wentworth turned his baleful attention to another leading Old English MP, Geoffrey Barron. On 2 December the House declared itself satisfied with the explanation provided by the Member for Clonmel for an unspecified offence. However, the next day, under pressure from Wentworth, the Commons expelled Barron for the previous day's 'misinformation' and committed him to Dublin Castle for contempt.[95] The Commons did not order his discharge from custody for more than a week, and then 'for so much only as belongs to this House', a tacit acknowledgement that other forces also were behind his imprisonment.[96]

If these moves were not sufficient to establish Wentworth's 'complete dominance' over parliament, his subsequent efforts would be. When, in April 1635, poor Protestant attendance allowed Catholic MPs to defeat one bill and block the progress of two others, Wentworth converted the defeated measure into an act of state, issuing it while parliament still was in session. Then he sent Lord Robert Dillon, a Protestant with extensive family ties to the Old English, to the Commons with a warning that the Lord Deputy 'would take revenge on them for showing so little regard of all things recommended unto them by me'. Presumably mindful of the fates of those who previously had stood in the way of Wentworth's designs, his opponents quickly capitulated.[97]

Three Kingdoms, One Strategy

In England, Scotland and Ireland, then, Charles I and his agents adopted ham-handed, menacing and ultimately counterproductive tactics in an effort to control parliaments. Some English MPs sought to resist this contemptuous treatment physically, with violence against Speaker Finch, a provocation that prompted the monarch to try to rule without parliament. Thanks in part to Wentworth's efforts to intimidate the Irish parliament, the king was able to avoid summoning English MPs for over a decade. In the end, however, the king's scheme proved unfeasible, in no small part because his bullying of the Scottish estates convinced many of his northern subjects that his policies only could be resisted by extra-parliamentary means. The ensuing civil wars would cost the king his head and, while greatly enhancing the institutional position of parliament, also increase and expand the perils of a seat.

3

UNCIVIL WARS

Up to the mid-1630s monarchs generally had been successful in using force, or the threat thereof, to bring recalcitrant parliamentarians into line. This was about to change. Growing disaffection with the personal rule of Charles I, combined with a sense that corruption was becoming pervasive, enhanced the stature of critics of royal policy, and also of parliament, an institution many pinned their hopes on to solve these and other problems.[1] The ensuing struggle would mark parliament's coming of age. Before it could stand independently on its own two feet, however, it would have to survive both civil war and an unprecedented volume and variety of parliamentary violence. Much of the action, at least as far as parliamentarians were concerned, took place in England, but the trouble began in Scotland and Ireland.

Overcrowded

King Charles's extended efforts to rule without parliament were undone by military defeats at the hands of Scots angry at an attempt to impose an Anglicised prayer book on their Kirk. Thomas Wentworth, by now Earl of Strafford and Lord Lieutenant, persuaded the king that the Scottish problem might have an Irish solution: if the parliament in Dublin provided troops and funds, its counterpart in Westminster might be more inclined to do the same. But while Dublin largely cooperated, Westminster refused to follow the script, resulting in the abrupt dissolution of the Short Parliament. A desperate monarch soon was forced to try again, but the Long Parliament proved even more contumacious. From almost its beginning there were calls for Strafford's impeachment for his anti-parliamentary activities.

And when, on 11 November 1640, he went to parliament to confront his accusers, he was first ordered to withdraw and then committed into custody.[2]

By this point, a similar attitude had overtaken the Irish parliament. The lord lieutenant's return to England in April 1640 'had removed the slender principle of cohesion in the government party which, though it included a few men who supported [Strafford] wholeheartedly, was principally composed of men who supported him because it was to their advantage to remain close to power and patronage'.[3] A dramatic signal of the change came just two days before Strafford's own arrest, when Edward Lake, one of his close associates, was expelled from the Irish Commons for obstructing (while serving as its chair) a parliamentary committee investigating the administration's finances. When informed of the sanction, while on his knees at the bar of the House, Lake uttered 'contemptuous and peremptory words', as a result of which his former colleagues committed him 'to the Constable of the Castle of Dublin, there to remain during the pleasure of this House'.[4]

Three months later the Irish Commons moved against two other Strafford allies within their ranks. Joshua Carpenter and Thomas Little were summoned to testify about the tobacco monopoly, which they had operated as part of the lord lieutenant's efforts to provide the king with extra-parliamentary funding. After providing 'cunning evasions' instead of truthful answers to parliamentary questions, both men were expelled from the Commons and ordered into custody, from which Carpenter was not released until mid-May.[5] The Irish parliament also initiated impeachment proceedings against several Strafford allies in the Dublin administration, but these were not completed before the session ended.[6]

If this period's first episodes of parliamentary violence came at the hands of colleagues, however, much of what followed came from a new, and quite disturbing source: the populace. Large crowds are first recorded coming to Westminster Palace to press for redress of grievances in the late Elizabethan era.[7] By 1641, however, the 'mob' (short for *mobile vulgus* or excitable crowd) effectively had become weaponised.[8] That is, the Puritans dominating the lower ranks of the City of London's administration used their positions to mobilise popular support for their views.[9]

One of the first hints of the new danger came in February 1641, when, concerned about overly enthusiastic public participation in its committee meetings, the Commons ordered the Warden of the Fleet and court ushers to ensure that their staff 'do attend the committees to regulate and prevent such disorders as are committed by disorderly multitudes that press in'.[10] Two months later, parliament faced considerably more serious disturbances.

At issue was the fate of Strafford, who, rightly or wrongly, 'came to personify the apparently lawless defence of the King's interests in the face of all political difficulties; a willingness to subvert the constitution in defence of otherwise indefensible policies'.[11] While many inside and outside parliament wanted to punish the earl, with some believing that his downfall was a prerequisite for other changes, the king was determined to protect Strafford. After all, how could a man acting with the king's support possibly be guilty of treason?

To help parliament decide what to do, on 21 April a crowd of people, said to number 10,000, accompanied the delivery to the Commons of a petition calling for the execution of justice against Strafford. That same day, a bill of attainder against him was carried 204 to 59. Many MPs avoided voting rather than incur the public's wrath by opposing the bill. Those who had the temerity to vote against Strafford's attainder soon found their names listed as 'enemies of the Commonwealth' on placards posted on the doors of parliament and elsewhere.[12] After this, 'the first exercise in parliamentary history of the coercive use of publicity about members' votes in the chamber', attendance in the Commons began to fall.[13]

The bill of attainder then went to the Lords, where Strafford had many friends. The beleaguered earl's prospects began to look even better when the king informed the Lords that he was inclined to exile Strafford rather than consent to his execution. To ratchet up the pressure on the peers, Puritans began to organise demonstrations outside parliament. On 3 May, 5,000 respectable merchants and tradesmen, some reportedly quite wealthy, 'began to line the approaches to Westminster Hall so that Members of both Houses had to pass between two columns of belligerent citizens shouting for Strafford's execution'.[14] When the Lords rose, most of the peers opted to return home by water to avoid the crowds. Opponents of the bill who left Westminster Palace by coach were threatened, but so far only verbally.[15]

There was another demonstration the next day, although the crowd's composition was different and comprised of many who were both of lower social rank and armed with swords and staves. As peers sought to make their way through the throng, those present were accused 'with great rudeness and insolence pressing upon and thrusting these lords whom they suspected not to favour that bill'. The Lords complained to the Commons that, because its Members 'were so encompassed with multitudes of people' the peers 'might be conceived not to be free'. The Commons sent someone to try to calm the crowd, which eventually dispersed but only after apparently warning that there would be violence unless Strafford was condemned to death within a week.[16]

By now rumours were rife that the king was seeking to use the military against parliament in order to rescue Strafford. On 5 May, John Pym informed the Commons of what came to be called the 'First Army Plot', a scheme to use the military to intimidate parliament. Four MPs later were implicated and expelled.[17]

With Members on the verge of panic at Pym's news, a loud cracking sound was all that it took to push them over the edge. One MP shouted that he smelled gunpowder. Some ran around with swords drawn while others fled the House, leading to rumours that parliament had been attacked by Papists or set alight. The truth, it eventually emerged, was more prosaic: 'a fat member leaning over between the gallery and the window to pick up a piece of paper, "with his weight broke a few laths, which made a sudden noise"'.[18]

While those in the Commons feared the army, those in the Lords quailed at the mob. The threat of popular disorder led peers to pass the bill of attainder against Strafford on 8 May. As in the Commons, many in the Lords chose to absent themselves rather than incur the hostility of the street by voting against the execution of their friend. Faced with the prospect of public violence if he refused, Charles consented to Strafford's destruction, which was carried out on 12 May amidst great celebrations.

The costs of this popular victory were substantial. The crowd's barely concealed threat of violence against parliament was profoundly disturbing to many. 'Not the law, not the parliament, not the king, had decided this issue, but the mob: it seemed that power had passed to the rabble in the streets.' This could portend anarchy and the destruction of the social order. Such fears, combined with a suspicion that some MPs were stirring the populace to intimidate parliament, led more than a few to rally to the royalist cause.[19] This trend would only intensify as a result of another wave of public pressure on parliament later in the year.

Before this commenced there was a particularly strange and sinister incident. In late October, a letter was delivered to John Pym as he sat in the Commons. It reportedly had come from a gentleman on horseback who had given it to the City Guard along with a shilling and instructions to deliver it with great care and speed. When Pym opened the letter, something fell onto the floor. He took no notice but, after reading a few words of the letter, pronounced it a scandalous libel and passed it to John Rushworth, an assistant clerk. The latter calmly read to the House the letter's abuse of Pym and its 'asseveration that if he should escape the present attempt, the writer had a dagger prepared for him'. At this point Rushworth lost his composure, quickly reading the next few lines, which indicated that what had dropped from the letter was a rag that had come from a plague wound and which was intended to infect the opener of the letter. 'Whereupon Rushworth, having read so far, threw down the letter into the house, and so it was spurned away out of the door.'[20]

Pym survived, but soon he and his colleagues came under popular pressure to deal with what some viewed as a plague of a very different sort. Abolition of the episcopate had been a central demand of the 'Root and Branch' petition presented to parliament in December 1640. Partly because many MPs did not support this and partly because they had other priorities, parliament dithered over the petition for quite a while before rejecting a bill based on in it in August 1641. Two months later, news of the Irish rebellion, complete with lurid tales of atrocities against Protestants, fuelled fears of resurgent popery, of which the bishops were alleged to be agents.

Those in the Commons had particular reason to be alarmed: the leader of the rebellion claimed that his actions, justified as protecting the king from Puritans and Parliament, enjoyed Charles's support. This seems to have encouraged the Commons to pass, on 22 November, the Grand Remonstrance, a litany of grievances that attributed many of the nation's ills to bishops and papists.

The Remonstrance was less a request for the king to redress particular grievances than a means to rally the public to support parliament in its power struggle with the monarch. 'The only possible aim of this document was to appeal to the people at large by making propaganda against Charles.'[21] Such a radical step was divisive, to say the least. In the Commons, Geoffrey Palmer repeatedly sought to have recorded his protest against the decision to have the Grand Remonstrance 'published', that is, circulated in manuscript form. If, as some speculated, Palmer hoped to start a fight on the floor and thereby prevent the document's publication, he nearly succeeded.[22] His efforts produced tumultuous scenes in which those of similar views waved their hats over their heads and some took their swords, still in their scabbards, from their belts. Violence, it was thought, was averted only narrowly.

Two days later, Palmer was sent to the Tower for inflaming the temper of the House. That same day Radical John Venn asked his wife to send armed men to Westminster to prevent 'the worser party' from getting the better of the 'good party'. The fear that force would be used in the Commons against the radicals was, in this instance at least, unwarranted, but by the time the House rose there were a thousand armed apprentices outside Westminster Palace.[23]

On 28 November hundreds of armed citizens came to parliament to call for the end of episcopacy. Four of their number were brought before the Lords for allegedly threatening that, if they were not heard on that day, they would come back with many more on the next. The four, who denied the charge, ultimately were dismissed 'with a sharp rebuke for flocking about parliament'. However, the following day hundreds of citizens gathered in the court of requests, making movement between the Houses difficult. Those in the crowd 'were undoubtedly intimidatory for they came armed with swords, staves and clubs and their lobbying of MPs was robust'.

Another armed crowd gathered outside parliament, shouting 'No bishops' at passing Members. Demonstrators surrounded Sir John Strangways, who had opposed the Remonstrance, demanding that he vote to eliminate bishops. As he extricated himself from the throng, Strangways heard some demonstrators refer to him as 'one of the greatest enemies we have'. After calls for the crowd to disperse went unheeded, the commander of the troops guarding parliament set demonstrators to flight by ordering his men to fire on them (they did not do so, but their weapons were charged only with powder in any event).[24]

Strangways subsequently complained to the Commons that parliamentary privilege was utterly broken, if Members could not come in safety to give their votes freely. This hinted at twin fears. First, there was concern that anything that the Long Parliament did could be nullified if it were seen to have acted under threat of mob violence. By this point, Charles already had consented to the redress of many grievances from the 1630s. Moderates, and even many of his staunch supporters, did not want to give him a justification for backtracking. Second, public pressure might intimidate individual Members, leading them to support more radical policies than otherwise would have been the case. Many suspected the Radicals in the Commons of deploying mobs for precisely this purpose. Not only was this objectionable on policy grounds but allowing the 'lower orders' to influence parliament was a threat to the established social and political hierarchy. Fear of ochlocracy, rule by the mob, was beginning to drive supporters of order into the royalist camp.[25]

Even the more radical Members of parliament had reservations about popular pressure. However, as the crowd seemed the only defence MPs had against a king suspected of planning to use military force against parliament, those in the Commons did not dare to discourage demonstrations. The Lords was a different matter.

On 1 December, after another large demonstration, peers called for steps to end the 'tumults' in Westminster. The Commons, anxious not to alienate its supporters, not only declined to join the Lords in this endeavour but denied that there had been any tumults. As a result, the Lords unilaterally authorised writs to implement various security measures. However, when, on 10 December, constables and several hundred halberdiers 'stationed themselves outside parliament, a greatly perturbed Commons ordered the chamber door to be shut, and the MPs to remain in the House', fearing another attempt to overawe parliament with military force. In fact, the halberdiers had been deployed in response to a rumour that ten thousand people were going to try to petition parliament. The Commons sent the justice of the peace deemed responsible for the scare to the Tower for breach of privilege, namely hindering citizens from petitioning parliament.[26]

After a hiatus of several weeks, during which more petitions were delivered to the Commons, tensions began to build again on 21 December, a day on which Puritans made substantial gains in London municipal elections and the king replaced as Lieutenant of the Tower a man seen as sympathetic to them with Colonel Thomas Lunsford, reputed to be relatively ungodly.

On Sunday, 26 December, Puritan pulpits thundered with denunciations of Lunsford's appointment. The next day, a large crowd gathered at Westminster Palace to demand his removal. Learning that the Privy Council already had done this, the crowd began to chant 'No bishops'. When a number of prelates tried to enter the Lords, some accounts claimed that they were assaulted and their robes torn while others, more sympathetic to the crowd, contended that they met only verbal abuse.

Certainly, there was serious violence in Westminster Hall, where Lunsford and a group of other ex-servicemen went to seek back pay and Irish commissions. They drew their swords and tried to clear the demonstrators from the Hall, only to be met with a storm of stones and other projectiles. News of this confrontation brought more armed people to the area, where they remained until late at night despite attempts to disperse them. The bishops, although advised to remain in Westminster Palace for their own safety, eventually managed to leave, although not without considerable trepidation.[27]

On the following day, 28 December, the crowd returned. 'The stairs from the river to Palace Yard were blocked by citizens who refused to let the Bishops land to attend a sitting of the Lords.'[28] As a result, only 'very brave or foolhardy bishops tried to take their seats that day'. Two prelates did manage to enter Westminster Palace, but this news so angered the crowd that both quickly departed in the interests of personal safety.[29] The situation prompted Lord Digby to move that, given that parliament was besieged by a tumultuous multitude, it was not free. The king earlier had promised not to dissolve parliament without its consent. However, if it was not free, it could not provide such consent. Supporting Digby's motion effectively would have authorised the king to terminate his troublesome parliament. After a lengthy debate, the Lords narrowly adopted a resolution stating that parliament was 'at present' free. The peers also sought a joint declaration with the Commons forbidding crowds to assemble outside parliament. However, a majority of the Commons, while apprehensive about the crowds, did not want to discourage the public from protecting parliament from the king's troops.[30]

On 29 December, large groups of armed citizens again gathered outside parliament. The Lords ordered local sheriffs and justices of the peace to deal with the crowd. It also called for the drafting of an order prohibiting any but Members of Parliament from wearing swords or other weapons near the two Houses. The king, meanwhile, had instructed all courtiers to wear their swords. That afternoon there was a clash between apprentices who had been demonstrating outside parliament and soldiers guarding Whitehall. Many in the Commons now viewed the king's troops (and those the Archbishop of York was reported to be assembling) as much more of a threat than the mob. Accordingly, the Commons backed the demonstrators and complained to the Lords about the incident, which marked the genesis of the term 'Roundhead' – a derisive reference to the short hair of the apprentices at a time when gentlemen typically wore longer locks.[31]

Meanwhile, in the Lords, twelve bishops, led by the Archbishop of York, asserted that they had been so threatened and assaulted that they had been unable to sit and vote. They further argued that all votes taken in the Lords since 27 December should be considered nullified. This transparent attempt to challenge the Lords' earlier decision that parliament remained free prompted a furious response from the Commons, which immediately impeached the bishops. The Lords sent them to prison the next day. Gratified that their main foes had been vanquished, and exhausted after three days of marching and shouting, the demonstrators lifted the siege of parliament.[32]

The next move was the king's. He muffed it badly. His failure was all the more egregious because he learned nothing from a similar blunder committed only a few months earlier.

In late 1641, Charles went to Scotland to sign a peace treaty that would provide for the departure from English soil of the Scottish army. The meeting of the Scottish parliament soon became contentious. Royalists were particularly upset with the Marquess of Hamilton, who sought to find a middle ground between their positions and those of the men who had signed a covenant to protect the Scottish Kirk. Lord Ker, the heir to the Earl of Roxburgh, called Hamilton a traitor and 'juglar with the King', before sending his (intoxicated) second, the Earl of Crawford, to challenge the marquess to a duel. An indignant parliament forced Ker to apologise, one of the first times it sought to bring an outsider to book for a violation of privilege. Yet other royalists, 'more loyal than wise', began to consider how they, too, might use violence to aid the king's cause.

A plot quickly formed to seize three nobles seen as the king's most important enemies: Hamilton, the Marquess of Argyll and the Earl of Lanark. As the conspirators sought to recruit mercenaries to carry out the operation, the scheme became public knowledge. Charles then went to parliament to disclaim any involvement in the nefarious conspiracy 'but stupidly let himself be accompanied by some hundreds of armed and aggressive royalists'. The three noblemen, fearing that the king was coming to arrest them, fled. With them escaped any chance that Charles might realise his hope of winning Scottish help against the pesky English parliament.[33]

A more sagacious ruler might have learned something from what became known as 'The Incident'. Charles did not. In early January 1642, while sparring with the Commons over security measures for parliament, the king received reports that a committee of MPs was planning to impeach the queen. In response, five MPs and one peer (Viscount Mandeville) were accused of treason.[34] More provocatively still, Charles decided to go to parliament, at the head of a large body of troops, in order to arrest personally the offending MPs. As in Scotland, this was a significant miscalculation.

The king's evident contempt for parliamentary privilege, and the growing mood of defiance in the Commons, helped Speaker William Lenthall decide on which side his bread was buttered. On arriving in the Commons to arrest the five members on 4 January, Charles asked the Speaker for help securing them. Lenthall replied that he had 'neither eyes to see nor tongue to speak in this place but as the House is pleased to demand of me'. For the first time, a Speaker openly declared that his primary institutional loyalty lay to the Commons, not the Crown. Charles quickly realising that, forewarned, 'all the birds are flown', departed amidst mutterings of 'Privilege!' (Some birds flew more readily than others. William Strode, the last of the five to leave, was determined to stay, arguing that he was innocent and would prove this with his blood if need be. Soon before the King arrived, Sir Walter Erle grabbed Strode by the cloak and dragged him from the chamber.[35])

The five wanted MPs took refuge in the City of London. The next day, Charles, this time accompanied by only four peers and a small escort, went there to try to persuade the local authorities to hand over the fugitives. As the king's intentions became clear, shouts of 'Privilege!' filled the Guildhall. Charles then went to dine with a sheriff, whose house soon was surrounded by thousands of people chanting 'Privilege of Parliament'. There were fears for the king's safety. One of his dining companions, the mayor, was pulled off his horse and roughed up to such an extent that his chain of office was broken and his gown ripped. The king's plans to visit the Tower had to be abandoned when it became clear that a large crowd had blocked the road.[36]

Fearing for their safety in the wake of the king's attempt to arrest five of their colleagues, MPs had first denounced the effort as a gross violation of parliamentary privilege and then adjourned the Commons until 11 January. Following the king's unsuccessful foray into the City, popular mobilisation in defence of parliament increased. Plans were laid for the five MPs to make a triumphal return to parliament, escorted by a large crowd of supporters. Rather than be present for this humiliation, and concerned about the safety of his own family, Charles fled the capital on 10 January.[37] Before long, the king and his parliament literally would be at war.

This did not happen right away. Instead the populace, so recently the Commons' protector, became its menace. As the immediate threat to parliament receded, popular attention returned to economic grievances. Petitions seeking various sorts of redress began to pour into parliament, often accompanied by large crowds. Some also sought action against the bishops and popish lords who were believed to be blocking the reforms that would improve popular welfare. Much of this petitioning transpired without appreciable parliamentary violence. There were, however, some notable exceptions.

On 31 January 1642, for example, members of a large crowd of artificers delivering a petition allegedly assaulted or ill-treated a number of MPs on their way to parliament.[38] That same day witnessed an even more unusual spectacle, as a group of women presented to the Lords a petition calling not only for the help on the economic matters (such as cheap bread) but also for the exclusion from the Lords of bishops and popish peers. The next day, 400 women returned to parliament to demand an answer to their petition. The Duke of Lennox met them, only to dismiss the intervention of the fairer sex with the words, 'away with these women'. A scuffle ensued in which Lennox's staff was broken, an event, perhaps, of some symbolic significance. Lennox and the Lord Keeper 'were both mobbed by a crowd of women and porters', when they left Westminster Palace that evening.[39]

On the following day, 2 February, a petition signed by 15,000 'poor labouring men' was delivered to the Commons. Denzil Holles was sent to tell the Lords that, unless it joined with the Commons, Members of the latter body would bear no responsibility for whatever 'mischief or inconveniency' might befall the peers. Under the implicit threat of the mob, the Lords capitulated, not only agreeing to support a Commons proposal to the king that a number of military assets be put under the command of those recommended by parliament but, on 5 February, agreeing to exclude bishops from the Upper House.

From this day on, those who might have resisted the popular party in the Lords increasingly retired to their country homes rather than expose themselves to danger from 'tumultuary assemblies'. 'The royalists always maintained that a majority of the peers, and many of the Commons, were driven away from the parliament by fear of their lives; and that many of those that remained were overawed by the mob.'[40] While there was more than a little truth to this accusation, by early 1642 the point largely was moot. In any case, even in the Commons support for demonstrators was waning as the military threat receded: on 5 February, MPs appointed a committee to consider how 'to hinder the people from gathering together to come hither'.[41]

Preventing Quarrels

As the external threat to parliament abated an internal danger began to loom larger. In both the Lords and the Commons concerns were growing about violence between parliamentarians. Physical confrontations of this sort were not, as we have seen, unprecedented prior to 1640. Starting in that year, however, they proliferated. Or, more precisely, those in parliament became acutely sensitive to the sorts of quarrels that could lead to a breach of the peace. As a result, during a period when parliament was fighting for its very life, it also devoted quite a bit of its time to trying to prevent its Members from murdering each other over trivialities.

The most obvious reason for the growing danger was the spread of the code of honour, which encouraged parliamentarians to respond with violence to slights they might previously have overlooked. A political crisis that shortened tempers did not help. Nor did structural change, as a parliament originally organised to foster consensual advice to the monarch had to transform itself, in the midst of civil war, into an adversarial body capable of making decisions on its own.[42] That this meant operating more continuously than ever before provided increased opportunities for the sorts of disagreements that could escalate into violence.

Countervailing the increasing pressure to fight was the growing influence of Puritanism, an ethos quite inimical to the code. The tension between the two philosophies helps explain the extraordinary parliamentary peacemaking during the Civil Wars. According to the journals of the Commons and Lords, the two Houses interrupted their business in order to 'interpose to prevent a quarrel', in what became the standard marginal notation, more than twenty times in the 1640s, at least twice the rate of all subsequent decades.[43]

Indeed, in contrast to almost all subsequent periods, both Houses sometimes interceded in disputes that did not even involve their Members. In April 1642, for example, the Lords intervened in two separate quarrels of this nature.[44] On Christmas Day of the following year, a Commons committee met to broker peace between two men, neither an MP (though both would become one in the future).[45]

To be sure, many of the disputes that both Houses sought to mediate did involve their Members. In November 1640, the Commons referred a quarrel between MPs Harbottle Grimston and Robert Hunt to the Speaker for resolution.[46] In June of 1641, the Lords ordered that the High Constable of Middlesex be sent for to answer for an assault upon the Earl of Cleveland.[47] Two weeks later, the Lords ordered

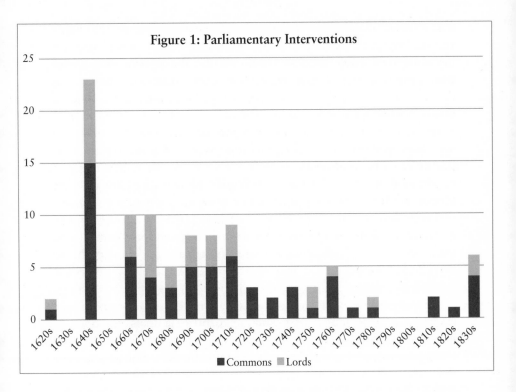

Figure 1: Parliamentary Interventions

Commons ■ Lords

that Thomas Payne be taken into custody for giving 'ill language' to the Earl of Thanett. When Thanett accused the attorney of making certain comments, Payne repeatedly had claimed the earl's statements were 'false and a lye', an accusation that could lead to a duel.[48]

Parliamentary intervention in personal disputes may have prevented them from escalating to bloodshed, but such efforts could be quite time consuming, particularly since determining who did what to whom, and why, was not always easy. The exact reasons for violence in a Commons committee in January 1641, for example, are hard to discern, even if the sources of antipathy between the two disputants are not. Sir John Littleton, who had long represented Worcestershire, previously had challenged the return of his replacement, John Wilde. When Sir Henry Herbert, who had supported Littleton's petition, was appointed chair of the committee investigating controverted elections, Wilde cried foul and forced him to stand down. Herbert and Wilde had clashed before, and would take different sides in the Civil War, so there seems to have been ample cause for animosity. Still, it is unknown what precipitated their encounter in the committee. Nor is it clear what exactly happened. There was an exchange of abuse and then, according to Wilde, Herbert struck him. In Herbert's version, Wilde threatened to kick him, prompting Sir Henry to push his antagonist away in self-defence. The Commons evidently found the episode too murky to apportion blame and punishment so, despite considering the matter more than once, apparently took no action beyond trying to reconcile the pair.[49]

Religious fervour was not the only impetus for parliamentarians to act as peacemakers. Both Elizabeth and the first two Stuart monarchs had acted to prevent duels. In 1628, for example, the Commons was informed that one MP, Henry Stanhope, had sent a challenge to the son of another. The king intervened, ordering Stanhope to remain in his lodgings. The MP refused, declaring that 'his honour was above his body'. The Privy Council then had Stanhope committed to the Marshalsea.[50] Defending parliamentary privilege, the Commons brought the keeper of the prison to the bar of the House to secure Stanhope's release.[51]

Yet the crown's actions had not been entirely unwelcome. Once Charles I was no longer in a position to prevent duels, the onus of doing so fell upon parliament. There really was little alternative: to allow quarrels to fester and possibly degenerate into violence not only would have had a chilling effect on debate but also would prove an invaluable gift to the king's propagandists.

Further stoking the Long Parliament's enthusiasm for preventing quarrels was the existence of alternate means of reputation rehabilitation. Duels generally were fought to defend or restore a gentleman's honour. There would come a time when only the risk of life and limb was deemed sufficient to remove a stain on one's reputation, but this point had not been reached by the 1640s. On the contrary, in early Stuart England, a 'lawsuit was regarded as an acceptable alternative to violence in defence of one's good name'.[52] Peers were encouraged to take those who defamed them to court for *scandalum magnatum* rather than fight duels.[53] Whether lawsuits prevented duels by allowing tempers to cool, fomented them by delaying the resolution of a dispute, or the two processes represented potentially complementary means of vexing opponents is the subject of some dispute.[54] What does seem clear is that as long as viable legal remedies to affront existed, parliament had more of an incentive to try to prevent illegal means to the same end.

This helps explain why parliament might intervene even after the monarch had dealt with an incident. On 17 July 1641, for example, Baron Mowbray and the Earl of Pembroke came to blows in a parliamentary committee. The fracas culminated in Pembroke, the Lord Chamberlain, breaking his staff of office across the head of his aristocratic colleague. After receiving a complaint about this unseemly episode, the king confined both peers to their lodgings. The affair also gave Charles the pretext he had been seeking to demand Pembroke's resignation as Lord Chamberlain. The House of Lords, however, was not satisfied. It sent both Mowbray and Pembroke to the Tower, where they remained for a week.[55]

The Long Parliament's efforts to prevent duels were not confined to intervening in individual squabbles. It also adopted procedural changes to facilitate the resolution of disputes and legislation aimed at preventing duels. Tellingly, each of these initiatives seems to have been a direct response to violent incidents involving parliamentarians.

Not long after Mowbray's fight with Pembroke, and on the same day that Sir Richard Wiseman was ordered detained for 'miscarrying himself toward a peer', the Lords appointed a committee 'to draw up an order to prevent quarrels in this House'. This led to the amendment to the standing orders to include a provision aimed at 'avoiding all mistakes, unkindnesses, or other differences, which may grow to quarrels' and lead to a breach of the peace. Those who believed they had received an 'affront or injury' from another peer while in parliament were required to seek reparation through the Lords or be subject to 'severe censure'.[56]

The Commons took a similar step a few months later, ordering that the Speaker 'shall have a warrant to stay, at any time, to apprehend and stay, such members of this House as he shall be informed do either send challenges or receive and entertain challenges'. It presumably was no coincidence that immediately afterwards, the House questioned MP John Griffith about whether he previously had sent a challenge to a colleague. Griffith acknowledged that six months earlier he had requested 'a meeting', having received 'some ill words' from Lord Herbert. However, Griffith testified that, after Herbert gave him 'very honourable satisfaction', he had not sent him any challenges.[57]

That same day the Commons appointed a committee to investigate an incident involving Gervase Holles and Thomas Ogle. As Holles was passing through Westminster Hall on the way to dinner, Ogle 'jostled him with his elbow'. Ogle confessed to the House that he had used 'reviling words' toward the MP, but claimed 'he was provoked by such terms as he could not endure'. The committee was still considering the matter more than a month later.[58]

Westminster's parliament was not the only assembly to face such problems. The 1640s saw the Scottish parliament meet more often, and for longer periods, than ever before, passing a great volume of legislation in the process.[59] The Covenanters also took steps to ensure parliamentary privilege, particularly freedom of speech.[60] Nevertheless, there seems also to have been some concern that greater licence meant an enhanced risk of violence.

In July 1641, for example, the estates passed articles for the 'ordering' of parliament. One provision stipulated that only Members be permitted to remain with the estates in the parliament house. Another authorised only Members and specified parliamentary officials to wear swords in the building. Members were enjoined not to speak without permission or to interrupt others. Furthermore, 'for eschewing of contest and hate', they were to direct their comments to the presiding officer rather than to the previous speaker.[61]

These restrictions notwithstanding, Scotland's parliamentary scene seems to have been considerably less dangerous than in England, where, in early 1644, MPs were asked to draft a declaration 'to prevent the drawing of swords or quarrels in Westminster Hall or the Palace Yards'.[62] It may be no coincidence that two days earlier the Commons had sent word to the Upper House that Lord Willoughby had sent a challenge to the Earl of Manchester. The Lords ordered Willoughby to be taken into custody and appointed a committee to 'examine this whole business thoroughly'.[63]

Several months later, it was the Lower House's turn to mediate. On 6 December 1644, informed 'that some words of heat passed between Sir Martin Lister and Sir Arthur Heslerigg in the House, tending to a quarrel', the Commons sought assurances from both MPs that they would not pursue the matter further.[64]

The most glaring shortcoming of the steps taken so far was that they authorised action only while parliament was sitting. The Commons sought to rectify this in 1645, while investigating a dispute in Westminster Hall between Sir William Andrewes and Colonel Tirrell, by ordering 'that if any quarrel happen between any gentlemen, or others, in any place within the cities of London and Westminster' while the House is not sitting, the Speaker 'shall have the power to send for the parties, and secure their persons, till the House be acquainted with it and take further order'.[65]

In May 1646, the Lords appointed a committee to attempt to reconcile a quarrel between Viscount Campden and Lord Chandois. For good measure, the committee also was instructed to try to settle two other 'differences', neither of which involved peers. Furthermore, one of the members of the committee was ordered present to the Lords 'an ordinance for to [sic] prevent challenges'.[66]

Several months later the Lords commanded that John Griffith be arrested for affronting Lord Philip Herbert in order to prevent 'further danger and the shedding of blood'.[67] In March 1647, informed of 'a falling-out' between Lord Howard of Charlton and Thomas Howard that resulted in challenges, the peers ordered both men to keep to their lodgings. That same day the Lords gave its Speaker the authority to prevent 'mischief in the like cases' when the House was not sitting.[68]

Despite this evident parliamentary enthusiasm for reconciling quarrels, doing so did not always prove easy. When Lord Strafford, the Viceroy of Ireland, expressly forbade Members from entering either Irish House with a sword, all apparently complied except for the young Earl of Ormond, who told the usher that the only way he should have the peer's sword was through the latter's body.[69] Yet even without such outright resistance family ties sometimes made it difficult to stamp out quarrels.

In January 1643, Sir Edward Hungerford became involved in a bitter feud with fellow MP Sir Edward Baynton after the latter was appointed military leader of Wiltshire, where the former had an estate. In the course of the dispute, each had the other arrested for treason before parliament finally ruled in Hungerford's favour.[70] This did not end the matter.

Over the next few months the Commons had to intervene at least three times to prevent related quarrels. In February 1643, it sought to prevent a duel between Giles Hungerford, brother of Sir Edward, and MP Edward Baynton, son of the other Sir Edward. The cause was words spoken by the son about the brother, and the latter's response of striking the former with a cane.[71] (Baynton junior was no stranger to the duelling ground, having been wounded in an encounter with fellow MP, Richard Rogers, several months earlier.[72]) In May, the Commons sought to prevent another duel after Colonel John Fettiplace, a relative of Hungerford, sent a challenge to Sir Edward Baynton.[73] And two months later, the Commons ordered that three MPs, Sir Edward Baynton, Edward Baynton and Sir Edward Hungerford, 'be enjoined and required not to give or receive any challenge, or do any thing that concerns any of their own private affairs, that may tend to the disturbance of the peace of this House or of the Kingdom'.[74]

A dispute around the same time occupied almost as much parliamentary time. Following a conference between the two Houses in April 1643, the Earl of Northumberland struck Henry Marten with a cane after learning that the MP had intercepted and opened a letter to the peer's wife, presumably in an effort to learn about the aristocrat's negotiations with the king. This prompted both Houses to decry the breach of privilege involving their Members and to demand reparations from the other. A conference was arranged to discuss the matter.[75]

A few months later Marten was involved in another incident that showed that a duel was not the only danger that could arise from an incautious choice of words in debate. Speaking in support of Puritan Divine John Saltmarsh, who had written a pamphlet advocating the deposition of the king, Marten told the Commons on 16 August 1643 that it was better for one family to be destroyed than many. When interrupted to ask what he meant, Marten replied that he was referring to the royal family. This prompted his colleagues to send him to the Tower. He was imprisoned for two weeks but barred from the Commons for almost three years.[76] It was a rather impressive display by MPs of loyalty to a king with whom they were at war.

Two years later, another violent incident led the Commons to bring (ultimately abortive) impeachment charges against the Earl of Stamford. The Parliamentarian military leader, who had been strongly criticised for surrendering Exeter to Royalist forces in 1643, was accused of assaulting, 'without injury, offence or provocation to them given, and for matters and things done in parliament', Sir Arthur Heslerigg. The MP had been travelling home on the highway when Stamford and two of his servants 'did suddenly and unexpectedly, several times, thrust and strike the said Sir Arthur Heslerigg with a drawn sword and other offensive instruments', actions which constituted a high breach of the privileges of the Commons and inflicted 'great damage' on its Member.[77]

As parliament's conflict with the king wore on, political competition within the Commons increased. Both the radical Independents and the moderate Presbyterians began to organise to win both elections and divisions. Some innovations introduced as part of this effort elicited complaints. The ability of Denzil Holles to dominate carefully packed committee meetings was a case in point. So, too, were the tactics of Presbyterian Walter Long, perhaps the first party whip. Long's habit of leaving the chamber to round up allies when a vote appeared imminent hardly seems egregious by modern standards, but some colleagues criticised it. His predilection for physically assaulting opponents is harder to defend.[78] According to one account, in early 1645, the Commons discussed two incidents in which Long was accused of striking one MP so hard he made him stagger and shaking another by the shoulders so violently that he was almost thrown from his seat.[79]

Had political differences been the only requirement, fights between parliamentarians presumably would have been quite a bit more common, not only during the civil war but both before and afterwards. As it was, violence typically required more of a spark, often in the form of a personal insult, even if such differences provided the accelerant.

In April 1647, for example, Henry Ireton, a military leader, addressed the Commons in support of an army petition that sought assurances that a number of grievances would be addressed. This put him on a collision course with Denzil Holles, who deemed anyone opposed to plans for promptly disbanding the army to be an enemy of the state. In the course of heated debate Ireton made some rude comments about Holles, who persuaded him to leave the House. The Commons intervened to prevent a duel, but it probably need not have bothered; Ireton not only refused to 'go over the water' to fight but continued to do so even after Holles resorted to the extreme provocation of pulling his adversary's nose.[80]

Two months later, informed that Colonel Thomas Ceeley and Colonel John Bingham 'were gone out, expressing some great distaste between them', the Commons ordered the Serjeant to bring the two MPs back to the House. When this was done, the Speaker enjoined them 'not to act any thing, by word or deed, that shall violate the peace that is due, and ought to be preserved, by all Members of the House'.[81]

In November 1647, the Commons intervened in a quarrel that could have had important repercussions. MPs ordered William Murray taken into custody after a 'letter by way of challenge directed to Colonel Whalley' was read in the House.[82] Five days earlier, Charles I had escaped from Hampton Court while under the guard of troops commanded by Colonel Edward Whalley.

Parliamentary intervention generally seems to have been quite successful in preventing duels. There were, however, exceptions. On 17 February 1648, for example, the Lords were informed that there was a quarrel between Lord Savage, John Mordant and Thomas Howard. All three were ordered to keep to their lodgings while efforts were made to resolve their differences. This did not end the matter, for a month later, the Lords ordered that Mordant be brought to the bar 'to answer for his contempt in not keeping the peace with the Lord Savage'.[83]

Meanwhile, in Scotland, the Engagement, an agreement negotiated with the king, was extremely contentious. Disputes about the desirability of this accord prompted a number of duels, at least one of which was parliamentary. It involved the Marquess of Argyll, a leading opponent of the Engagement, and the Earl of Crawford-Lindsay, a prominent supporter. During debate in the Scottish parliament in March 1648, Argyll became convinced that Crawford-Lindsay had claimed to be a better man than him. The earl subsequently 'refused to explain what he had said but stated that "whatever it was, he would make it good with his sword"'. The two aristocrats soon found themselves on the duelling ground, but friends prevented them from fighting. Nevertheless, some feared the episode was part of an effort to intimidate opponents of the Engagement.[84]

Perhaps appropriately, given the diminished status of parliament by this time, the last relevant affair of honour prior to the Restoration was a much more tawdry affair. In January 1659, on the day before a committee met to investigate controverted elections, Lewis Audley got into a contretemps with MPs Edward Bishe and Thomas Turgis. Audley, a former Knight of the Shire for Surrey who recently had stood unsuccessfully for Gatton, had gone to parliament to deliver a petition seeking to be returned for the borough. In Westminster Hall, he accosted Bishe and Turgis, the men who had been elected for Gatton, unfairly according to Audley. The frustrated former candidate called Bishe a 'base rascal' and invited him to 'come over the hedge', that is, to fight a duel. Audley then pronounced Turgis a 'base stinking fellow and a Shit-breech'. The Commons sent Audley to the Tower for giving 'contumelious and provoking language' to the two MPs.[85]

Threats from Without

If parliament enjoyed considerable success in protecting its Members from each other, it proved less efficacious in safeguarding them from outsiders. The first manifestation of the external threat after the outbreak of civil war came in a form of a throwback to the early days of the Long Parliament.

On 5 August 1643, concerned that parliament might accept an accommodation with the king, Lord Mayor Isaac Penington organised a crowd that physically threatened a number of peers outside parliament in an effort to arrest Lord Northumberland and other leaders of the Peace Party.[86] Two days later, Penington followed up by having the City government petition the Commons urging it to reject the accommodation proposed by the Lords.[87]

Unfortunately for Penington, the Radicals no longer had a monopoly on popular pressure. On 8 August, a group of women gathered outside the Commons seeking to present a petition calling for peace. 'When a committee went out to try to appease them, they beat on the door of the committee-room to force it open and threatened to cast Pym, Strode and others into the Thames. They threw brickbats too.' Leaders of the parliamentary Peace Party were suspected of being behind the incident, since, of course, the females could not possibly have organised themselves. Still, the women were back a few days later. This time the violence escalated: 'from words they fell to blows – troopers were called in, many were injured, and a woman was killed'. *Newsbook* reports of the clash denigrated the women as 'oyster wives and dirty tattered sluts', but their actions suggested popular support for the Radicals was waning.[88]

Crowds again besieged Westminster Palace at the end of 1646, as those who wanted to conclude a rapid peace (and Presbyterian church settlement) mobilised Londoners to put pressure on parliament.[89] However it was not until the following year that parliamentary violence became a serious concern.

March 1647 saw the publication of the 'Large Petition', a document that advocated popular sovereignty as the best means to restrain royal power and hold parliament accountable. The Commons condemned this 'seditious paper' while Penington requested that the Lords suppress it. At a parliamentary committee investigating the matter, Nicholas Tew spoke out so forcefully in favour of having the petition considered that he was restrained. This provoked an altercation sufficiently violent that the committee ordered the room cleared. When Major Tulidah, a petition supporter, seemed disinclined to comply, MP Sir Philip Stapleton, a leader of the Peace Party, grabbed him by the throat and forcibly evicted him. The Commons subsequently ordered the Serjeant-at-Arms to take into custody both Tew and Tulidah.[90]

This incident foreshadowed the conflict between parliament and the military that would play out over the coming months. With the king in custody and the prospects of further military engagements seeming to recede, there were calls to disband the New Model Army. This raised the hackles of soldiers who were becoming increasingly assertive in pushing for radical political changes. The army, approaching London, called for the impeachment of eleven 'corrupt' MPs, all Presbyterians. The Commons demanded to see the evidence against the Members but, as the army drew ever closer, the eleven withdrew. On 6 July, the army presented articles of impeachment against the MPs, the first time such had been moved from outside parliament. Two weeks later, unable or unwilling to contest this action, the Commons authorised the eleven to leave the country to prepare their defences. This apparent capitulation infuriated many Londoners, who 'swarmed around Westminster in such a tumultuous way that the Commons ordered 100 halberds be brought in for their defence'.[91]

Worse was to come on 26 July, when angry demonstrators invaded parliament. Going first to the Lords, they terrified the eight peers present into repealing an ordinance – passed days before – transferring the militia to Independent control. The crowd then sought similar action from the Commons, only to be told that MPs would give serious consideration to their petition. 'For six hours they brawled in the lobbies, shouting "Vote, Vote", and pounding at the doors.' Eventually the mob forced its way into the Chamber. The Commons, then, was pressed to return the militia to Presbyterian control. Afterwards, MPs voted to adjourn until 30 July. As they were departing, the crowd grabbed Speaker Lenthall, carried him back to the Chamber, put him back in the chair, and then forced him to put, and declare carried, a resolution calling for the king to come to the capital to negotiate a peace treaty.[92]

By the time parliament reconvened, fifty-eight of its Members, including the presiding officers of both Houses, had fled to army protection. Speaker Lenthall had released a statement asserting that he himself had done so because the demonstrators who earlier had invaded parliament had threatened to 'destroy' him on 30 July. No matter. Both (now diminished) Houses quickly chose new leaders. The Commons, after borrowing a mace to replace the one taken by the departing Independents, voted to restore the eleven MPs. It also ordered the army not to approach within 30 miles of London. However, on 6 August, the troops entered the capital, ostensibly to defend parliament. The eleven impeached MPs were forced to flee once again as colleagues who had sought military protection were escorted back to Westminster Palace.[93]

The Radical victory soon proved incomplete. By late 1648, as negotiations with the king appeared to be making some progress, public support for a settlement became so strong that those that those perceived as opposing it risked harm. As MP Bulstrode Whitelocke recalled, 'It was dangerous for any member of the House or of the army to walk without company, for fear of being assassinated.' Rumours of attacks on or plots against MPs were rife. Royalist toughs certainly assaulted at least one MP, Miles Corbet. Thomas Rainsborough, a former MP and leading Leveller in the military, was killed in a bungled abduction attempt in late October 1648.[94]

Many in the army watched the growing momentum for a treaty with deep unease. Concerns grew after the Commons agreed that Charles's land and revenue would be restored after a settlement. Such an outcome was unconscionable to the many in the military who held the king personally responsible for the second phase of the Civil War. Army leaders sent the Commons a Remonstrance demanding that the king be brought to justice. When parliament refused to discuss it, troops again began marching on London.

Soon after they arrived, the axe fell. On 6 December, Colonel Thomas Pride mounted the steps leading to the House of Commons holding a list of Members to be detained. Most of those listed went quietly; some, such as William Prynne, had to be dragged down the stairs. The forty-one MPs arrested on the first day eventually were sent to Hell, the name of an alehouse next to Westminster Hall. By the end of 7 December, around a hundred MPs had been arrested or secluded, with many more voluntarily staying away. Only those MPs who had opposed a 5 December resolution in favour of a settlement with the king were deemed sufficiently loyal to continue to sit in the Commons. When additional Members were purged in the following days, the Rump, with only a few dozen now in attendance, found obtaining a quorum problematic.[95]

From the standpoint of parliamentary violence, Pride's Purge brought the Civil War to a pleasingly symmetrical conclusion. 'A war that had begun when Charles had tried to remove unruly MPs ended with the Army deciding to do the same.'[96] Yet victory in the war did not mean that those in the Commons or the Lords immediately became much safer.

The purged parliament, acting under the baleful eye of the military, managed to try, sentence and execute the king, and abolish both the House of Lords and the monarchy in a matter of months. A very real threat of force helped the Radicals act with such dispatch. When Lady Fairfax, sitting in the gallery, interrupted the sentencing of the king by shouting that the court did not speak for the people of England and that Oliver Cromwell was a traitor, the soldiers present levelled their muskets at her as their commanding officer shouted 'down with the whores'. Bloodshed was averted when her friends removed Fairfax from the room. This may not have been the most important violent act of the drama: Richard Ingoldsby claimed after the Restoration that Cromwell physically had forced the MP to sign the warrant for the king's execution, an assertion that presumably needs to be taken with copious quantities of salt.[97]

Military intervention also did not preclude further attempts by crowds to influence parliament. The Radical minority of the Rump was compelled to reach out to more moderate Members.[98] The compromises this entailed angered those who sought political and social revolution. Criticism of the government's moderation led to the arrest of leading Levellers in March 1649. In response, a large group of supporters, many of them women, went to parliament to present a petition for the release of the leaders. Revealing just the sort of patronising and patriarchal attitudes that made the egalitarian Leveller movement so appealing to women, MPs told them that they should stay at home and wash dishes rather than petitioning. Perhaps not surprisingly, the women had to be dispersed by troops, although they returned a few days later with a more strongly worded petition.[99]

An even less acceptable expression of dissent came in November 1652, when a man threw bricks at Speaker Lenthall as he was on his way to parliament. The first projectile narrowly missed the head of the Serjeant-at-Arms, striking his mace instead. The second hit the Speaker in the face. The Commons subsequently ordered that the perpetrator 'be committed to Bridewell, London, there to be kept to hard labour, and daily corrected [i.e. beaten], until the Parliament take further order'.[100]

These incidents notwithstanding, the main threat to MPs in the wake of Pride's Purge would come from the military, not the populace. Soon after the execution of Charles I, the Scottish parliament, itself purged of supporters of the Engagement, proclaimed his son King not only of Scotland but also of Great Britain, Ireland and France. This prompted the invasion of an English army under the command of Oliver Cromwell. In late August 1651, the army captured many members of the committee of estates, set up by the Covenanters to govern between parliamentary sessions. A rump committee managed to meet but, harassed by English forces, it dissolved in mid-October. There was an attempt to convene a parliament the following month, but only a few nobles, and no members of the other estates, turned up. Scotland's parliament, politically supreme for a decade, henceforth would be suppressed for almost as long.[101]

Two years afterwards, in England, the body created by the sword perished the same way. On 20 April 1653, Oliver Cromwell went to the Rump to listen to debate on a bill for parliamentary reform, which was expected to pass that day. When MPs showed a disinclination to approve the measure desired by the army, Cromwell told them, 'I will put an end to your prating.' He continued, 'You have sat too long here for any good you have been doing lately. You shall now give place to better men. Call them in.' With that, twenty to thirty musketeers entered with loaded guns. Cromwell then announced, 'you are no Parliament', adding that some Members were drunkards and others were 'living in open contempt of God's commandments'. He told the MPs to depart and, lifting the mace, asked, 'What shall we do with this bauble? Take it away!' giving it to a musketeer. Then, of the Speaker, Cromwell ordered, 'Fetch him down!' Although Speaker Lenthall declared he would not come until forced, he was eventually persuaded to leave the chair and parliament was dissolved.[102] Londoners celebrated the dismissal of the dregs of the Long Parliament by roasting rump steaks in the streets.[103]

Later that year, the (unelected) Barebones Parliament generated such fears of Radical domination that, on a morning in which moderates comprised a majority, they voted for dissolution. Upon coming to clear the House, a colonel encountered a few Radicals determined to remain. When he asked what they were doing, they told him they were 'seeking the Lord', to which he replied, 'then you may go elsewhere, for to my certain knowledge He has not been here these twelve years'.[104]

Under Oliver Cromwell's Protectorate, efforts to create tractable parliaments drew unfavourable comparisons to both Charles's attempt to arrest the Five Members and Pride's Purge. The Instrument of Government gave members of the executive council authority to vet, and exclude, those returned by voters. This power was employed sparingly in the First Protectorate Parliament (1654), when only a handful of Members were prevented from taking their seats. The council showed much less restraint with the successor to this obstreperous assembly, excluding almost a quarter of the Members elected to the Second Protectorate Parliament two years later. Another fifty MPs stayed away in protest.[105]

After the military overthrew the Protectorate, the Rump was recalled. On 9 May 1659, a dozen of those MPs originally excluded by Colonel Pride sought to enter the Commons, only to be turned away by troops once again. In October, however, the army expelled the Rump again, before inviting it back after the failure of its replacement, the Committee of Safety. The praetorian impulse was not exhausted until February 1660, when General George Monck entered London at the head of an army and restored the excluded Members to parliament, a move that paved the way for the Restoration of the Stuarts.[106]

This marked the conclusion of a period in which parliamentary seats were particularly precarious. It has been estimated that perhaps half the MPs elected between 1640 and 1660, 'at one time or another found themselves excluded from the House by executive order or barred by novel tests, withdrew under varying degrees of duress, were voted out by their colleagues, fled to or from the army or were detained or expelled by soldiers'.[107] The reputation of the people's tribunal sunk so low that according to Samuel Pepys, many said 'kiss my parliament' instead of 'kiss my arse'. News that Monck had instructed parliament to dissolve itself and call elections was greeted with celebratory bonfires throughout London. It also led to the era's final act of parliamentary violence. 'The Speaker of the Rump, returning home late, was affronted by a crowd, his men beaten and his windows smashed. A rump in a chair was then roasted at his gate and bonfires made there.'[108]

4

RESTORATION AND REVOLUTION

The Restoration did not bring a return to the *status quo ante*. True, many of the institutional changes of the previous two decades – the elimination of the monarchy and the House of Lords, revisions to the franchise, and ecclesiastical reforms – were rolled back so that, by 1661, 'hardly a trace of the upheaval remained'.[1] Yet the dangers MPs and peers faced were quite different under Charles II and his immediate successors than they had been during the reigns of the earlier Stuarts. The threat from the military was banished, seemingly forever. The wrath of the prince was slightly less fearsome. And the menace of the mob temporarily had receded. At the same time, the peril posed by the code of honour grew substantially.

Subjugation and Demobilisation
The difficulty of re-establishing royal authority varied substantially among Charles II's parliaments. The Irish assembly was least problematic: although Protestants and Catholics remained bitterly divided, few of the latter took their seats.[2] Scotland proved a somewhat tougher nut to crack. Although the estates acceded to legislation in early 1661 that augmented Crown control, Charles never dominated parliament as his father had in 1633.[3] It was not for lack of trying.

In September 1661, the Scottish Privy Council, acting on the king's instructions, ordered the imprisonment of Lord Tweeddale, whose apparent offence was to have spoken and voted in a recent parliament against the execution of James Gutherie, a Presbyterian minister.

Although Tweeddale averred that freedom of speech was both a parliamentary right and a benefit to the king, it was several weeks before he was released.[4]

The wrath of the monarch was not the only peril to Scottish parliamentarians. In 1662, they passed an act intended to promote internal order. One clause sought to insulate the estates from outside pressure by prohibiting from staying in parliament any but Members and various officials. Others – forbidding Members from interrupting or making 'reflections' on each other – hinted that incivility was seen to pose a threat.[5]

However, a decade later, another Scottish MP found himself in Tweeddale's shoes. In July 1672, William More 'was sent to prison for proposing that draft acts should be read in the House on two separate days before being passed'. He was released five days later. His apology to parliament suggests that his imprisonment may have been based on a misunderstanding: he had been suspected (wrongly) of advocating that the three estates meet separately, something that previously had helped parliament resist Crown control.[6]

English MPs seem to have avoided similar treatment perhaps because they devoted more effort to insulating themselves from popular pressure than to resisting royal influence. In 1661, parliament sharply limited the number of people who could present a petition.[7] The following year saw a bid to reintroduce pre-publication censorship, although this attempt to limit the political news available to the populace proved ineffective.[8] A move in 1675 to suppress coffeehouses, cornerstone of the emerging public sphere, was quickly abandoned in the face of widespread disapproval.[9] Most importantly, the 1641 Triennial Act was repealed, allowing the king to extend the life of the Cavalier Parliament, elected in 1661, until 1679, without the bother of an appeal to voters.

If the assembly's long tenure suggested its actions were amenable to the monarch, there was one conspicuous exception, which resulted in one of the most notorious and consequential episodes of parliamentary violence to date. In late 1670, around fifteen people attacked Sir John Coventry in the street. Wrapping the MP in his cloak to immobilise him, the assailants then slit his nose to the bone. To add insult to injury, they also stole his periwig.

The Commons' Journal's assertion that Coventry was attacked 'without any provocation offered or offense given' was more than a tad disingenuous. In the House, not long before, he had proposed a tax on theatres. When a colleague pointed out that these had been of great service to the king, Coventry asked him whether he meant the men or women players, a snide reference to the Charles II's romantic involvement with actresses Nell Gwyn and Moll Davis. This minor act of *lèse-majesté* prompted retaliation by troops of the Duke of Monmouth, the king's illegitimate son, an action apparently supported by the monarch himself.[10]

If Charles thought such a crude form of retribution would terrify MPs into greater deference, he soon was disabused of this fantasy. News of the assault on Coventry elicited outrage in the Commons. Although parliament had risen for Christmas hours before the attack, the incident was seen as a breach of privilege because it prevented the MP from attending when the Commons resumed sitting. After taking up the matter on 9 January, MPs resolved to do no other business until it had been dealt with. This resulted, on 14 January, in a bill that provided for the banishment of Coventry's assailants and their disqualification from a royal pardon. More broadly, it made 'malicious wounding' a felony without benefit of clergy, that is, a capital offence.[11] The Coventry Act was not repealed until 1828.

The Danger Within

The sensational attack on Coventry had lasting implications, but it was unusual. In the first two decades after Charles II took the throne, the main threat to the physical safety of English parliamentarians came not from outsiders but from colleagues. The return of the monarchy coincided with renewed enthusiasm for aristocratic mores, most notably duelling. Increased sensitivity to slights did not mix well with another contemporary fashion, heavy drinking.[12] Royal ambivalence (or hypocrisy) did not help either: although Charles II repeatedly indicated his opposition to duelling, he greatly vitiated this message by pardoning some of the most notorious practitioners.[13] As a result, the Cavalier Parliament devoted quite a bit of its time to extricating its Members from potentially deadly affairs of honour.

On 1 July 1661, for example, informed of a quarrel between Edward Seymour and Jonathan Trelawney, the Commons ordered the Speaker to send for the MPs and 'endeavour a reconciliation between them'.[14] Five months later, it followed the same approach toward another MP who had been detained by the king to prevent him from fighting a duel.[15]

Mediation was not always easy. In early 1662, efforts to bring together two squabbling MPs provoked a bit of resistance. The Speaker ordered that Andrew Marvell, who had given the 'first provocation', should apologise first, after which Thomas Clifford would follow suit. Marvell refused to comply. Such defiance often led to incarceration, but in this case the Speaker merely delivered a 'grave reprehension' to both MPs, who then apologised and promised not to renew their quarrel.[16]

Two months later, informed 'of a difference and a mischief like to ensue' between Lord Ossory and Philip Howard, the Commons ordered both MPs to be taken into custody. They were subsequently released after promising not to 'prosecute the old or begin any new difference'.[17] Less than two weeks after this, the House ordered that another three Members be detained for the same reason.[18]

Around the same time, after taking notice of 'a quarrel' between Randolph Beresford and Sir John Rowley, the Irish House of Commons ordered its Serjeant-at-Arms to take into custody both MPs 'for prevention of any further mischiefs and inconveniences'.[19]

It was not just parliamentary time that was consumed by efforts to prevent bloodshed. After the Earl of Middlesex sent a written challenge to the Earl of Bridgewater, the king consulted with a number of other peers to propose an accommodation. When this failed to resolve the dispute, the commissioners for the office of Earl Marshal were ordered to propose a plan of reconciliation. The king sent for both earls and apprised them of the plan. Bridgewater accepted it but Middlesex did not, giving 'His Majesty great offense thereby'.

On 12 June 1663, the king sent the matter to the House of Lords, which promptly sent Middlesex to the Tower and had Bridgewater taken into custody. Although both were later transferred to confinement in their homes, they are not released until 2 July, after the House's 'resentments' to each were read and both apologised. Perhaps not coincidentally, the Lords discussed a bill to prevent duelling on 1 July.[20] Two days later, informed of an intended duel between the Earl of Sunderland and MP William Russell, the Commons ordered the latter 'not to receive, send or prosecute any challenge' from, of, or with the former.[21]

Without greater documentation, it is impossible to say for certain whether any of these disputes arose out of parliamentary business. One that clearly did, took place in 1665. As they left a meeting of the committee of privileges, Henry Seymour quarrelled with Lord St John over the political record of a third MP, Edward Nosworthy, with whom Seymour was involved in litigation. Seymour and St John both 'were ordered to attend the House to prevent a duel'.[22]

The vast majority of parliamentarians in this era managed to avoid becoming embroiled in such political affairs of honour, although doing so apparently was becoming more difficult. A few, by contrast, were involved in multiple quarrels. Perhaps the most notorious serial offender of the era was George Villiers, 2nd Duke of Buckingham. His 1668 duel with the Earl of Shrewsbury was the most infamous of the Restoration era, not only because of the rank of those involved but because the latter was twice victimised: cuckolded and killed by his rival. Parliament's response to this encounter was limited to a forlorn proposal (made on the day of Shrewsbury's death) by Puritan William Prynne that the estates of the duellists be confiscated.[23] Two years earlier, however, the Lords had acted more forcefully, intervening twice in as many months to prevent Buckingham from fighting duels that arose out of his legislative conduct.

In late October 1666, Buckingham spoke in support of a measure banning the import of Irish cattle, telling the Lords that whoever opposed the bill 'had either an Irish interest or an Irish understanding'. Lord Butler, who held the Irish title of Earl of Ossory, took this aspersion upon the wisdom of his countrymen as a personal affront. He sent the duke a challenge. Buckingham accepted but then 'outmaneuvered his opponent by going to the wrong field, by accusing him of not turning up at the appointed place, and by informing the House of Lords of Ossory's challenge'.[24] When questioned in the Lords, Butler admitted he wanted to fight Buckingham but denied this was due to anything the latter had said in the House. The Lords had Butler sent to the Tower and Buckingham taken into custody until 31 October, when both were ordered released on condition 'that they shall forbear any occasion of quarrelling in the future'.[25]

In late December, Buckingham was in another scrape, this time with the Marquess of Dorchester. At issue was the duke's intrusive elbow in a parliamentary committee. According to Samuel Pepys, who witnessed the incident, Buckingham leaned 'rudely' over Dorchester, who removed his elbow. The marquess asserted that the duke would not dare to behave in such a manner anywhere else. Buckingham replied that he would, adding that he was a better man than Dorchester. This prompted the marquess to call Buckingham a liar, the reddest of flags for a bull-headed duellist. Buckingham proceeded to knock off Dorchester's hat, pull aside his periwig, and grab hold of him before others intervened.[26] The Lords sent both men to the Tower, ordering their release three days later on the condition that each 'forbear any further proceedings or provocations' with the other.[27]

Over the next eight years, the Lords intervened at least four times to prevent duels involving peers. John Wilmot, 2nd Earl of Rochester, twice was compelled to promise not to fight: in 1669 with the Earl of Mulgrave and in 1673 with Viscount Dunbar.[28] Although neither of these disputes appears to have been parliamentary, attributable more to the poet's sharp wit and penchant for drink, the other two quarrels that occupied the Lords' time clearly were.

In early 1671, a petition to the Lords by the mother of the Earl of Peterborough challenging his claim to an estate led to 'some words of provocation' between him and Lord Lucas and an order from the House that both aristocrats promise not to prosecute the quarrel any further.[29] Four years later, after 'some unusual words in a debate passed between' Viscount Mordant and Lord Mohun, the Lords demanded of the two 'that there should be no remembrance of what had passed, and that they should acquiesce from any further proceedings concerning this business, as they will answer the contrary to this House'.[30]

Parliamentary intervention typically was quite successful in preventing quarrels from escalating into a 'war between two', the literal derivation of the Latin *duellum*.[31] Yet even MPs and peers determined to mediate did not always manage to do so. On 3 December 1669, for example, Roger Vaughan fought a duel with Henry Seymour, who had claimed the other MP has misrepresented one of his speeches to the Duke of York.[32]

Part of the problem was that resentment could build slowly and imperceptibly into anger, making it difficult for those in parliament to realise that colleagues were on the brink of violence. Such seems to have been the case with MPs John Morton and Henry Brouckner. In debate in early 1668, the former impugned the latter's courage for behaviour in a military engagement three years previous. The extent of the ill will generated by this exchange did not become evident until the following year when, following a chance encounter on the streets, the two MPs ended up facing each other with drawn swords. Brouncker followed this up by sending a challenge, 'which Morton referred to the King's bench under the Duelling Act of 1666 which he had helped to draft', but nothing was done on instructions from the government.[33]

It was not just wars between two that those in parliament had reason to fear. On at least one occasion in the seventeenth century, something closer to general warfare erupted on the floor of the Commons. While meeting in Grand Committee on 10 May 1675 to discuss a resolution demanding the recall of British troops serving the

French king, there was a dispute over voting that led to great disorder in which 'hot and provoking discourse and gestures passed on both sides'. At the centre of the fray were William Lord Cavendish and Sir John Hanmer. By one account Cavendish drew his sword halfway out of the scabbard before being stopped by a colleague. There were claims that Cavendish spit in Hanmer's face, though others asserted that spittle flew only from 'eagerness of speech'. Sir James Smyth set his arms at his side and rudely made his way to the table, jostling several MPs, one of who apparently responded with a challenge.[34] 'This disorder continued for near half an hour, the standers by, on the upper benches, expecting very fatal consequences', especially after some 'young gallants' leaped over the seats to join Cavendish. Another source reported, 'The Members ran in confusion up to the table, grievously affronted one by the other, every man's hand upon his hilt, and all ready to decide the question by the sword.'

In the end, and not for the last time, parliamentary disorder was quelled by a calculated violation of the rules. The Speaker took the chair, something that is not done when the Commons is meeting in committee. The mace, which several men sought, with their feet, to keep under the table (to signify that the House remained in committee), was 'forcibly laid' upon it after some resistance. When several MPs objected to this procedural irregularity, the Speaker defended his conduct by saying 'that to bring the House into order again, he took the Chair, though not according to order'. All MPs then were required to stand and promise 'to proceed no farther in any thing that had happened in the unfortunate disorder' for fear that 'as soon as the House had risen the thing might be recriminated and ill consequences ensue thereupon'.[35]

Despite the Speaker's efforts, the emotive issue at the heart of the dispute nearly produced more parliamentary violence several months later. Cavendish, who had supported the recall of British troops, again was in the middle of the action. Upon learning that some Englishmen had died fighting for the French king, he and fellow MP, Sir Thomas Meres, indicated that the soldiers got what they deserved for serving abroad despite the parliamentary resolution. This prompted Thomas Howard, whose brother had been killed fighting for the French, to publish and post a pamphlet denouncing Cavendish and Meres. When the Commons was informed of the pamphlet, Cavendish, 'seeming much surprised by it[,] went out of the House in heat'. Both he and Meres were enjoined not to prosecute further the quarrel with Howard or with anyone else.

The affair was given further impetus after Howard insinuated that Cavendish had welcomed the House's action because it relieved him of the burden of having to respond to the accusations made in the pamphlet. Cavendish replied with a publication of his own, copies of which he posted around Westminster. For this, the Commons sent Cavendish to the Tower for two days. Three days after his release, Cavendish was challenged by Francis Newport, related to Howard by marriage. On 25 October, the same day it sought to stifle this encounter by summoning Newport, the Commons ordered the drafting of a bill to prevent duels.[36]

Less than two years later, continued divisions over relations with France almost prompted a repeat of one of parliament's more notorious scenes. Upset at their resistance to a cross-Channel alliance he sought, the king summoned MPs to the Palace of Whitehall on 28 May 1677 to chastise them from encroaching upon his prerogative. He ordered the Commons adjourned until 16 July to give its Members time to reconsider their behaviour. Back in Westminster Palace, Speaker Edward Seymour formally reported the king's command. Instead of adjourning, MPs sought to debate whether they should decide when to suspend the session. In the face of this resistance, Seymour simply declared the House adjourned and left the chair.

Some MPs sought to prevent this, as had been done half a century earlier, but they were thwarted when the Speaker leapt from his perch 'very nimbly'. Rebellious Members than attempted to seize the mace, with which they intended to authorise another to take Seymour's place. This constitutionally dubious scheme also was frustrated as 'the retainers of the Court formed a guard around the [mace-bearing] Serjeant-at-Arms, and the Speaker went away amid shouts of reproaches and threats'. This did not deter Seymour from subsequently adjourning repeatedly the Commons on the king's command, without the consent of the House.[37]

MPs made no further efforts to challenge these moves by force. As the 1629 precedent suggested, any victories they could achieve by such means were likely to be pyrrhic. Consequently, the violence of the final year of the Cavalier Parliament was of a more personal nature. Specifically, the Commons and the Lords each intervened twice in order to prevent spats from leading to bloodshed.

In May 1678, informed that 'upon a division of the House a quarrel had happened between the Lord [Ibrakan, Henry] O'Brien and Sir Thomas Chicheley and that blows were given', the Commons ordered both MPs taken into custody.[38] Six months later, after 'words' passed between the Marquess of Winton and the Earl of Clarendon, the Lords demanded both peers 'not to resent any thing further of what passed now between them'.[39]

The following week 'a breach of the peace' occurred in the Commons between Sir Jonathan Trelawney and William Ashe. Both MPs were taken into custody until the House could discuss the matter. It transpired that, during a discussion of religious toleration, Trelawney interjected that he would not tolerate 'Presbytery'. Ash expressed similar sentiment toward 'Popery'. This reportedly led Trelawney to call Ash a 'rascal' and a 'rebel' before striking him. Both men were required not to prosecute the quarrel further. As the aggressor, Trelawney was committed to the Tower for the duration of the session; a vote to expel him from the Commons failed 110 to 130.[40]

Finally, on 27 November, informed that a quarrel had occurred between the Earls of Pembroke and Dorset, the Lords ordered both peers confined to their lodgings and prohibited them from sending messages to each other. Pembroke claimed that Dorset earlier had 'laid violent hands upon him'. Dorset acknowledged that he had asked Pembroke to visit his house to discuss 'business' but denied any intention of fighting.[41]

Exclusion and Revolution

By the time the Cavalier Parliament was dissolved in early 1679, the political temperature had increased considerably. The previous year had seen the sensational (but unsubstantiated) claims of a 'Popish Plot' to assassinate the king. In the ensuing hysteria, parliament attainted Viscount Stafford, although the king exercised a degree of clemency by restricting the peer's punishment to mere beheading, sparing him the hanging, castration, and drawing and quartering that typically result from the sentence.[42] It also passed the Test Act, which effectively barred Catholics from sitting in parliament. Even more controversially, it sought to exclude from the succession Charles II's brother, a Catholic.

The three-year crisis that ensued was notable partly for the legacy it left to political nomenclature. Those who sought to exclude James from taking the throne included many dissenters. Accordingly, they were derided as 'Whigs', a term derived from the name of radical Presbyterians. They responded by calling supporters of James's succession 'Tories', from the Irish *toraidhe*, or 'raider', after Catholic bandits who had preyed on English settlers in Ireland.[43]

Such was the antipathy between the two that 'a climate of intimidation ... [was] created, in which doing the King's business or supporting him in public was clearly seen as dangerous'.[44] The three short Exclusion parliaments managed to generate as many violent incidents.

After the Commons passed an Exclusion Bill in 1680, discussion of the highly contentious measure passed to the Lords, where the king himself was present. 'The debate was long, earnest, and occasionally furious. Some hands were laid on the pommels of swords', before the peers rejected the bill by a great majority.[45]

A year later, Edmund Webb 'wounded and disarmed' fellow MP Gilbert Gerard 'in a political duel arising out the exclusion debates'.[46] Gerard was not the only MP elected in 1681, whose blood was spilled on the field of honour: Thomas Howard and Walter Norborne were killed in separate duels, although it is unclear whether either incident was parliamentary.[47]

No such ambiguity exists regarding the third violent affair. In 1680, Sir Robert Peyton was expelled from the Commons for treasonously bargaining to support York's claims to the throne. In pronouncing the House's decision, Speaker Sir William Williams told Peyton, 'You are absolutely the worst man and have committed the greatest of offenses for which you deserve to be obliterated from the knowledge of all ... you are become nauseous to this house and therefore they now spew you out.' It was only after this speech was published in February 1681 that Peyton went to Williams's chamber and demanded a public disavowal. When the Speaker refused, Peyton delivered a challenge. Williams reported this to the Privy Council, which sent the hapless former MP to the Tower.[48]

After the third Exclusion Parliament proved to be no more complaisant than its predecessors, Charles II sought to strengthen his political position by appealing to help from the North. The Scottish parliament duly obliged, legally guaranteeing James's path to the throne, making a treasonable offence any attempt to change the succession, and providing such a generous supply of funds that Charles would not need to call an English parliament again for quite some time.[49] Yet, the August 1681 session hardly passed without menace.

During debate on the Test Act, Lord Belhaven remarked that, while the legislation had some merits, it would not 'secure our Protestant religion against a Popish or fanatical successor to the Crown'. His colleagues promptly had him imprisoned in Edinburgh Castle. The king's advocate ominously declared that Belhaven could face treason charges. A point having been made, Belhaven was allowed to resume his seat a few days later, but only after getting on his knees at the bar of the House to beg the pardon of both the Duke of York and of parliament.[50]

This was not the only potentially fatal excitement. Cromwell Lockhart of Lee sought to depart during a prolonged sitting. 'A macer, following strictly the rule of the House, refused to open the door, and Lockhart "gave him a thrust".' The macer sought to press charges of treason against the commissioner for Lanarkshire. An act of 1593 had made striking a man in the presence of the king's commissioner during a sitting of parliament a treasonable offence. Having already displeased the Duke of York by his oppositional voting, Lockhart evidently felt sufficiently vulnerable to pay off the macer to settle the matter.[51]

There was even a third minatory incident. The Earl of Breadalbane complained to the king's commissioner and the Lords of the Articles that the Earl of Caithness recently had threatened him in the House by saying, 'If you do not quit any interest you have in those lands that were my father's, by God's wounds, I will be even with you.' Caithness, called to respond to this allegation, 'denied he spoke these words'.[52]

The Scottish parliament's largesse, combined with a mixture of repression, propaganda and purges of local government, allowed Charles to temper support for exclusion in the last years of his reign. His death in 1685 forced James II to summon both an English and a Scottish parliament. Neither behaved to the new monarch's liking.

At the opening of the English parliament in November 1685, James conceded that, in response to rebellions against his accession, he had increased the size of the standing army and given some military commissions to Catholics. This admission produced an uproar. The Commons sent him an address stating that officers who had not taken the Test only could be employed by act of parliament. James angrily responded that he 'did not expect such an address' from the House. In seconding a motion that a day be set aside to consider a reply to the king's answer, MP John Coke told the Commons, 'I hope we are all Englishmen, and are not frightened out of our duty by a few high words.' On a motion by a colleague, Coke was sent to the Tower. The Commons eventually agreed to supply some of the funds demanded by the king but, angered by some comments he had heard while attending debate in the Lords, he quickly prorogued parliament, thereby depriving himself of much-needed financial assistance.[53]

James then summoned a Scottish parliament, hoping that it might pass measures endorsing greater toleration of Catholics. This precedent, in turn, might be used to secure something similar from an English parliament. Yet the Scottish parliament of 1686 proved no more amenable to the king's designs than had its English counterpart the previous year.

It did not help that the meeting of the estates was preceded by riots in Edinburgh that saw the coach of the (Catholic) Lord Chancellor surrounded by a hostile mob.[54] When the Scottish parliament met in April 1686 it soon became clear that tolerance was in short supply. An MP quickly moved that those who had not taken the Test should not be allowed to take their seats. This apparently was aimed at James's high commissioner, the Earl of Moray, a suspected crypto-Catholic. Although Moray managed to prevent a vote on the motion by threatening to have anyone supporting it thrown in prison, the Scottish parliament resisted other attempts at intimidation and was dismissed.[55]

Despite his 'popish' beliefs, James had come to power with considerable public support. In three years, he squandered much of it by aggressively pursuing a policy of absolutist state-building and Catholicisation that discomfited even many of his co-religionists. Growing disaffection with James's rule encouraged a Protestant ruler with a claim to the throne, William of Orange, to lead the first successful invasion of England since 1066. The change of regime that ensued was considerably less Glorious and more of a Revolution than often imagined, but little of its rather extensive violence was parliamentary in character.[56]

One important exception was England's Convention Parliament of 1689. Bitterly fought elections, featuring at least 80 contests, had created a House of Commons in which the political forces were evenly balanced. On 28 January, this assembly adopted a resolution declaring the throne vacant, an assertion that elided over the divisive issue of how it had become so. The Lords proved unwilling to agree to a similar measure. The impasse prompted a public petition calling for William and Mary to be declared king and queen. Petitioners descended on Westminster Palace, with some managing to enter the building. The Lords capitulated on 6 February. Although this development probably owed something to William's lobbying efforts, 'it is hard to imagine that the angry crowds demonstrating in Westminster, claiming to have the support of thousands more, did not powerfully persuade the lords. In a revolutionary crisis that had already had its fair share of political violence, the threat posed by the Whig crowds must have been intimidating indeed'. Still, almost forty peers protested against the decision to declare the throne vacant.[57]

A Scottish Convention also was held to adopt legislation paving the way for William and Mary to assume the throne. As in England, this happened only under some duress: troops and armed volunteers often surrounded the assembly to protect it from 'papists'.[58]

The Glorious Revolution was a milestone. It led to passage of the Bill of Rights, which, by providing various protections against outside interference, reinforced parliament's claims to privileges as a matter of right, rather than a gift from the sovereign.[59] An institution originally summoned to do the king's bidding now could more effectively assert its autonomy, a radical claim.[60] The concomitant passage of the Mutiny Act in response to the desertion of troops loyal to James II, and the need to renew the legislation annually, further bolstered parliamentary independence. For a monarch to rule without parliament became virtually impossible.[61]

Parliament's enhanced stature meant that physical threats by monarchs to its Members, already rare after 1642, now became inconceivable. Yet the potency of other means of royal influence soon became apparent. Less than a decade after the Revolution, John Toland bemoaned the dangers of 'mercenary parliaments', whose Members allegedly did not stand up to the king and act in the interests of the people because 'their eyes [are] blinded with the dust of gold, and their tongues lock'd up with silver keys'.[62] He was upset by the crown's use of places and pensions to win friends in the Commons. Whatever the merits of his complaint, it implies a degree of progress, at least from the standpoint of parliamentary violence. Such corruption, as Sir Lewis Namier pointed out, was 'a mark of English freedom and independence, for no one bribes where he can bully'.[63]

The Rage of Party

Some have argued that, by resolving major sources of elite conflict, the Glorious Revolution paved the way for a settlement that eventually would lead to democratisation.[64] This was hardly evident at the time. Indeed, the immediate result of the Revolution in Ireland effectively was to purge parliament of Catholics, clearing the way for the imposition of a wide range of disabilities upon members of the religious majority.[65] Even in England, the post-Revolutionary decades saw an exacerbation rather than an amelioration of the divisions that had developed over the exclusion of James a decade before, so much so that it was said to be the era of the 'rage of party'.

Quite a bit of this antipathy was manifest inside Westminster Palace. 'So violent were the political passions, wrote one of Sir Ralph Varney's friends, that some members almost "fought in the Parliament house".'[66] In 1689 alone, the Commons interrupted its business three times, and the Lords twice, in order to prevent tiffs between colleagues from escalating into duels.[67]

Parliamentary peacemaking was not always easy. On 21 March 1690, the Commons was informed 'that a quarrel had happened in the lobby of the House' between two Members, Sir Thomas Mompesson and William Okeden. Both were ordered not to prosecute the matter further until the House had a chance to investigate. When it did so, four days later, there were claims that Mompesson had assaulted Okeden, but such was the conflicting evidence that 'a difference' arose between two other MPs. The Commons, 'fearing some inconveniences might, by reason thereof, ensue between them', required these two to promise not to pursue their quarrel. Only after sorting out this complication, did a 'very indulgent' House require its 'ancient member', Mompesson (born sixty years earlier), to ask Okeden's pardon for the initial incident.[68]

There was a similar intervention by the Lords later that year.[69] In 1693, each House acted to reconcile a quarrel involving their Members.[70] The Commons did so again, once in each of the next three years.[71] In December 1697, the House intervened to prevent a duel between Henry Holmes and Lord John Cutts. The latter had been seeking to control the Isle of Wight's three parliamentary boroughs. In the general election of 1695, however, Holmes and an ally had been returned for Yarmouth, defeating John Acton, Cutts's brother-in-law. When Holmes accused Cutts in the Commons of discharging from the militia officers who had voted against Acton, the quarrel looked set to become violent.[72]

Incautious words in debate produced other dangers in these highly partisan times. When it became clear in late 1696 that insufficient evidence could be mustered to convict of treason in a court of law the Jacobite conspirator, Sir John Fenwick, the government opted to push through parliament a bill of attainder against the former MP. This prompted John Manley to exclaim that 'it would not be the first time that people have repented their making their court to the government, at the hazard of the liberties of the people'. His colleagues responded by sending Manley to the Tower, but his sentiment ultimately was vindicated: the use of such dubious methods was discredited sufficiently that Fenwick was to be the last person executed for treason as a result of an act of attainder.[73]

Manley's fate notwithstanding, the period's greatest threat to parliamentary free speech came from the code of honour. During a 1698 debate on Crown grants, John Granville caused to be revealed that one of these, though ostensibly intended for someone else, actually was destined for Chancellor of the Exchequer, Charles Montagu. The two had history: a year before, Montagu had responded to Granville's opposition to increasing the civil list by alluding to the vast sums that had been granted to the latter's kin during the reign of Charles II. Granville's criticism of Crown grants led another MP to pick up where Montagu had left off. William Norris expressed wonder that Granville could be so angry at the grants, 'when his own family had had so many, and was thereby raised from a mean estate to what they are'. Sensing danger, the House interposed to prevent a duel, and Norris apologised, 'in case it had been thought that he had reflected on Granville's family'.[74]

There were at least two similar incidents the following year. In one, the Lords summoned three earls to promise that they would not pursue a dispute.[75] In the other, a quarrel in an elections committee led to a challenge, but the difference was composed.[76] The Commons also was drawn into a dispute that, while not strictly parliamentary, illustrates the potential costs of refusing to follow the code of honour.

Simon Harcourt was married to the widow of the brother of fellow MP John Philipps. The two had become embroiled in a lawsuit over the brother's estate, leading Harcourt to challenge Philipps to a duel. On 21 December 1699, Philipps complained to the Commons of this, adding that when he refused to fight, Harcourt had become verbally abusive and struck him repeatedly with a cane. The Commons ordered Harcourt taken into custody. The Society for the Promoting Christian Knowledge, of which Philipps was a member, passed a resolution praising the MP for refusing to fight despite suffering the highest provocation.[77]

Almost a decade later, another Society member, Sir Humphrey Mackworth, brought before the Commons a complaint of breach of privilege after being challenged by the servant of a family with which he was embroiled in a bitter dispute in Glamorgan.[78]

Protecting its Members from bloodshed was becoming almost commonplace for parliament. The journals of the two Houses record thirteen interventions to prevent quarrels between 1701 and

1714.[79] Indeed, judging only from the journals, such intervention averaged slightly more than one per year (twenty-eight times between 1689–1714) during the period designated the 'rage of party'. Yet these numbers understate the danger of parliamentary politics in at least three ways.

First, the tally does not include all parliamentary efforts to prevent duels. Such interpositions typically came only when an MP was thought at risk of sending a challenge. When a parliamentarian was challenged by an outsider, as Mackworth was, the matter was dealt with as a breach of privilege. This was not characterised as an interposition or included in the tally even though some of these disputes clearly were parliamentary. For example, in 1711, a Lieutenant Colonel Fitzpatrick was ordered taken into custody for challenging Major General Thomas Pearce for words the MP had used in debate.[80] Moreover, entirely absent from the journals are instances in which the Speaker interceded between the disputants without involving the Commons.

Second, parliament had little cause to intervene if one side declined to fight and the other did not pursue the matter. In March 1700, for example, Thomas Coningsby supported a proposal in the Commons to dock half-pay officers a quarter of their salaries to make up a budget shortfall. This led one such officer to send the MP a challenge. Coningsby declined, citing parliamentary privilege. This may have been easier to do given that he had been 'out' with Lord Chandos a few years earlier, a background that may have been expected to deflect accusations that he was afraid to fight.[81]

Third, parliament did not need to intervene if others did so instead. On 2 April 1711, for example, Charles Eversfield nearly provoked a duel with Robert Walpole. When the MP for Sussex rose to speak in the Commons, Walpole watched him intently. Eversfield reproached his colleague for being 'very impudent'. Walpole immediately left the chamber, with Eversfield following in his wake. It seemed likely that a duel would ensue, but their friends interposed to prevent it.[82]

It was not just 'friends' who might relieve parliament of the need to prevent a duel between its Members. In debate in the Lords in May 1712, the Duke of Ormond was criticised for failing to fight in a war in the Netherlands. The Earl Poulett defended Ormond's courage, adding that the duke was not like 'a certain general', who led his troops to the slaughter so that he could fill his pockets by selling the commissions of fallen officers. This was widely seen as an allusion to the Duke of Marlborough, then under investigation for mismanagement of military funds. Poulett soon received a visitor who informed him that Marlborough desired that the earl 'go and take a little air in the country' in order to explain some expressions he had used in the debate. Poulett told his wife of his intention to fight Marlborough. Alarmed, she informed the Earl of Dartmouth, who took steps to keep both principals in their houses and then told the queen. Anne then sent for Marlborough and made him promise not to pursue the matter, thereby terminating the affair.[83]

Finally, and perhaps most obviously, the journals of both Houses do not reflect fully the danger of parliamentary life because not all duels involving Members were prevented. In 1692, Sir Bourchier Wrey broke his sword in a duel with fellow MP, Thomas Bulkeley. Two years later, he was 'run through the body, but supposed not mortal', in a fight with another, James Praed. Although subsequent reports that Wrey had died of his wounds proved false, he apparently never fully recovered.[84]

In late April 1695, John Beaumont complained to the Commons of an insult he had received from fellow MP, Sir William Forrester. 'Before the House could properly investigate the incident, the two men met again, and on reopening their quarrel, proceeded to St. James' Square where in a duel Forester was "disarmed".'[85] In January 1698, Lord William Powlett fought a duel with Anthony Hammond 'after a quarrel in committee over the Cambridgeshire election'.[86] Not long thereafter, the Commons intervened to prevent Powlett from fighting another MP, Francis Gwyn.[87]

An angry exchange between MPs, Lewis Oglethorpe and Sir Richard Onslow, led to a duel in early 1703 in which the former was disarmed and slightly wounded.[88] In 1707, there were at least two duels in which the principals were MPs. In one, Robert Wroth was slightly injured fighting George Woodroffe.[89] In the other, John Manley fatally wounded Thomas Dodson.[90]

The causes of some of these encounters are obscure. Considerably better documented are the particulars surrounding the 1711 duel that proved fatal to MP Sir Cholmley Dering. Although the affair was not parliamentary, it is worth considering, both because of its consequences and because it is illustrative of an era in which words could easily lead to shocking violence.

At a late-April meeting of the 'Board of Brothers', held at the Toy Tavern in Hampton Court, Richard Thornhill 'affronted' Lord Scarsdale, one of the founders of the Tory drinking club. Dering suggested that Thornhill apologise. When he declined to do so, a scuffle broke out, during the course of which Dering broke Thornhill's jaw with a bottle and kicked out several of his teeth. Soon thereafter, Thornhill responded with a challenge. Dering was wounded mortally in the duel that followed, one of the first to be fought with pistols rather than swords.

The law's response was predictable. As invariably happened when the principals observed accepted duelling procedures, the jury rejected the prosecutor's call to convict Thornhill of murder. That he was found guilty even of manslaughter may have had something to do with the fact that he had been only four yards from Dering when they discharged their pistols. It seems likely that he effectively escaped punishment, presumably by pleading benefit of clergy, a wheeze that effectively pardoned (literate) first-time offenders. Thornhill did not, however, long survive his day in court: shortly after his trial, two men with whom he had quarrelled stabbed him to death.[91] According to Jonathan Swift, as they did so, the pair 'bid him remember Sir Cholmley Dering'.[92]

Equally predictable was parliament's response. Days after the Dering's death, MPs introduced a bill to prevent duelling. As with most such legislative efforts, it went nowhere. So, it was not entirely surprising that, a little more than a year later, more parliamentary blood was shed on the field of honour.

At first sight, the 1712 duel that claimed the lives of both the duke of Hamilton and Lord Mohun was not parliamentary; the proximate *casus belli* was a property dispute. The estate in question, however, was crucial to the economic and political fortunes of both men. Its loss would likely significantly reduce the parliamentary influence of one of the peers. That Hamilton was a leading Tory and Mohun a prominent Whig exacerbated their differences, which came at a time in which the two factions were locked in a bitter struggle for dominance. The aristocrats' mutual destruction was a fitting metaphor for the 'take-no-prisoners' politics of era that was fast drawing to a close.[93]

This was not, of course, the way the encounter was perceived at the time. On the contrary, the duel was seen through a partisan lens with the Tories accusing the Whigs of political murder. It also elicited more than the usual hand wringing about duelling. Opening parliament in 1713, Queen Anne alluded to the frequency of duelling and called for the speedy adoption of an effectual legislative remedy. A bill was brought in, but it failed to survive a second reading, 'to the very great regret of all the sensible portion of the community'.[94]

The following year, another parliamentarian was killed in a duel. The September 1714 death of Charles Aldworth also was not, strictly speaking, parliamentary, but it illustrates perils of political activity and the flexibility surrounding the notion of honour. Previously, Aldworth had drunk the Pretender's health publicly, so it was rather brazen of him to go to St James's Palace. There he encountered an officer of the foot guards whom he previously had berated for drinking to the health of the Duke of Marlborough. The duel that followed did not reflect well upon the code. In fact, it was positively unsporting: the officer apparently was aware that Aldworth had a congenital disability that prevented him from fully stretching out his arms, a rather serious disadvantage in a sword fight.[95]

A Violent End to Scotland's Parliament

The 'rage of party' had Scottish reverberations. The Lords of the Articles, responsible for drafting legislation for the Scottish parliament's consideration, was abolished after the Glorious Revolution. The Estates' ability to resist Crown management grew, but so too did the political temperature.

In July 1695, Alexander Gedd complained that fellow Member, John Dick, had breached privilege by 'menacing him for his vote' on a bill altering the malt tax. After a witness testified that the MP indeed had threatened to make Gedd 'smart for his vote', the House expelled Dick.[96]

By 1703, partisan animosity had grown to such an extent that bloodshed on the floor was feared. As Sir John Clerk of Penicuik later recalled, the various 'factions rubb'd upon one another and with great severity, so that we were often in the form of a Polish Diet, with our swords in our hands, or at least our hands on our swords'.[97]

On at least one occasion, violence actually erupted. During a debate on a disputed election, 'some hott words' passed between Lord Belhaven and Sir Alexander Ogilvie. The pair 'went out together with a design to have fought', only to find that the parliament doors would not open. Belhaven then kicked Ogilvie, who hit back in retaliation. 'This caused mayhem and parliament was adjourned.' Both men were taken into custody but, after apologising for 'unbecoming expressions and other undutiful behaviour', were allowed to return to their seats, leniency probably attributable to their familial connections.[98]

Several weeks later, during a dispute about the allocation of commissions to 'inferior officers', Lord Blantyre called the Duke of Queensberry a 'base and impudent liar'. Blantyre did not make the remark in parliament, which may explain why, when the matter was brought before his colleagues, they did not arrest him. However, given that his comments about Her Majesty's High Commissioner could be seen to reflect upon the queen, Blantyre took the advice of the presiding officer (and 'friends') and placed himself in the hands of the Lord Constable, who confined him to his chambers. He was released after agreeing to pay a fine of £5,000 Scots and apologise to Queensberry, who graciously waived a requirement that Blantyre do so on his knees.[99]

Scotland's most dangerous parliamentarian of this period was Andrew Fletcher of Saltoun, a Nationalist pamphleteer who became increasingly frustrated as his colleagues ignored his (often sound) policy suggestions. In 1704, parliament intervened to prevent Fletcher from 'fighting duels with the Duke of Hamilton and Lord Stair, among others'.[100] The following year he demanded that two individuals be called before the House to explain their economic proposals, which Fletcher characterised as 'gibberish'. When the Earl of Roxburghe replied that parliament could not do so, Fletcher took this as a slight and challenged his erstwhile ally. A duel was averted only when soldiers arrived as the men were preparing to fight.[101]

It was not just colleagues that Scottish parliamentarians had to fear at the dawn of the eighteenth century. Technological advances, including improved means of communication, afforded the Country Party greater opportunity to mobilise public opinion against the government. The political potency of this weapon was revealed in May 1700 as the Country Party leveraged popular support to capture effective control of parliament, forcing the royal commissioner to adjourn the session after only nine days.

A month later, the darker, more menacing side of popular mobilisation became apparent. Country Party leaders called for supporters to put candles in the windows of their houses. This prompted some 'to throw stones a dark windows, targeting in particular those belonging to Court party figures'. A mob tried, unsuccessfully, to break into the home of the king's secretary. It had more luck at the home of the Lord Advocate, who was forced to sign a warrant for the release of two prisoners held in the Tolbooth. This document proved somewhat superfluous as another crowd burned down the Tolbooth door and released all the prisoners held behind it.[102]

The popular threat to parliamentarians reached a crescendo as the estates began to deliberate on a treaty of Anglo–Scottish union. Indeed, despite Robert Burns' claim that the estates only acceded to this measure because many Members had been 'bought and sold for English gold', parliamentary violence seems to have been an important element of the transaction.

Prior to November 1706, the Scottish parliament did not publish vote totals, much less the choices of individual Members. With the beginning of divisions on the articles of the treaty, however, it began to do so.[103] As it became easier for the public to discern how Members voted, supporting an unpopular accord became riskier. 'Pro-union court politicians were jeered and jostled' as they went to and from parliament. Three earls were so apprehensive that, when they learned that their votes in favour of the Union would be recorded in the parliamentary minutes, they sought (unsuccessfully) to rescind them.[104]

There were ample grounds for concern. The Country Party mounted a campaign to demonstrate popular antipathy to the agreement, as a result of which over a hundred anti-treaty addresses came flooding into parliament.[105] But some such efforts were more menacing.

The Duke of Hamilton encouraged a crowd of apprentices and young people to escort him home each evening after parliament rose. On 22 October 1706, one such crowd, after seeing the aristocrat to his lodgings, returned to the High Street to throw stones and call treaty supporters 'traitors'. The following afternoon, a crowd pressing against the doors of Parliament House forced the commissioner to adjourn the sitting. After conducting Hamilton home, a mob attacked the house of Sir Patrick Johnston, a negotiator of the treaty. A detachment of town guards intervened before protesters could carry out their threat to 'massacre' the Edinburgh MP.[106]

The subsequent deployment of troops in Edinburgh, including a guard outside Parliament House, temporarily calmed matters. However, disorder resumed on 1 November, when the estates debated whether to begin voting or recess to allow Members to consult with their constituents. Such was the 'clamour' outside parliament that many inside feared the 'rabble' would force their way in, armed guards notwithstanding.[107]

The threats did not flow in just one direction. The Court Party sought to stem the tide of petitions both by putting pressure on local magistrates not to authorise them and, in parliament, by outright intimidation. When, on 6 November, Sir John Houstoun tried to present an address from Renfrewshire, he was abused in 'gros and scandalous' terms. This hostile treatment dissuaded a colleague, William Baillie of Lamington, from presenting any of the Lanarkshire petitions he possessed. 'The duke of Hamilton took the Hamilton parish petition from Baillie to present himself and the duke of Atholl presented the address of the burgh of Falkland, but few others had the courage to present addresses that day.'[108]

On 15 and 16 November crowds, taking advantage of the cover of darkness provided by a late adjournment, pelted with stones the coach of the royal commissioner as it left parliament. On the second of these occasions, the attack injured one of Queensberry's servants and made the duke's horses 'gallop off at an undignified speed'.[109] Queensbury, who also was subject to frequent assassination threats at this time, was hardly the only target. 'Late sittings of Parliament and the consequent uncomfortable journeys home were viewed by government ministers and officers of state with considerable trepidation.'[110]

Violence did not, of course, prevent adoption of the treaty. However, it did suggest that a failure to heed opinion could produce significant public disorder. As a result, the government made concessions that made the union more palatable. This dynamic, perhaps more than the employment of 'English gold', was crucial to the passage of an accord that led to the demise of the Scottish parliament.[111]

English Mobs

Goaded by a growing, and increasingly intemperate, partisan press, England's populace also occasionally mobilised to an extent rarely witnessed since the 1640s. In January 1697, there were 'great tumults' at the door of the Commons as a 'multitude' of weavers pressed for legislation curtailing the wearing of imported silks and calicoes.[112] Two months later, when a bill prohibiting the import of silk from the Far East was defeated, a large crowd, including many silk-weavers who had supported the legislation, directed their ire at the man they held responsible: George Bohun, MP and Governor of the East India Company. They went to Bohun's house and, 'with iron bars, pick-axes, and other instruments, broke the same, and threatened to kill him and his family'. The MP's household fought back, firing shots that killed two and wounded others before several companies of militia arrived to restore order. The next day, apprehensive that a crowd was reassembling, Bohun reported the incident to the Commons, which sought militia protection for the MP's residence.[113]

There was even greater public disorder in 1710 when the government foolishly sought to make an example of Dr Henry Sacheverell for criticisms some saw as seditious. The clergyman came to Westminster Hall for the trial each day accompanied by large crowds. In addition to destroying several Dissenters' meeting houses, pro-Sacheverell mobs targeted government parliamentarians. A number of Whig peers were insulted and threatened as they returned home from Westminster. John Dolben had a much narrower escape: the MP, who had characterised Sacheverell as the devil's emissary from Hell, 'would have been hanged had he not successfully denied his own identity' to the mob.[114]

It was to prevent a recurrence of such disorder that the Riot Act would be passed four years later. Yet, the popular threat to parliamentarians came not just from crowds. Robert Harley, the Earl of Oxford, escaped two assassination attempts in as many years. In 1711, the queen's chief minister was stabbed by the Marquis de Guiscard, a French refugee appearing before the Privy Council on charges of treason. The following year, Oxford was sent a hatbox containing two pistols arranged to fire when the container was opened. Jonathan Swift, who detected and disarmed the trap, used his pen to ensure that the Tory politician reaped the maximum public sympathy, and political advantage, from the incidents.

Growing partisanship, then, marked the waning years of the Stuart dynasty in England, Scotland and even Ireland.[115] Politics became more expensive, and more dangerous. With the advent of the Hanoverians, the rage of party abated.[116] Parliamentary violence did likewise, but it did not disappear completely.

5

FROM WALPOLE TO WILKES

Tory support for a Jacobite rebellion against the 1714 Hanoverian Succession led to the party's exclusion from ministerial office for half a century. This, plus a government that sought to eschew controversial issues, tempered partisan passions. Parliamentary violence fell accordingly. However, before long, as growing popular political involvement helped create 'the most riotous century in London's history', the peril associated with a seat rose.[1]

Walpole's Tranquilliser
Many Tories were bitter that the Act of Settlement had given the Crown to the Protestant ruler of Hanover in favour of more than fifty Catholics with better hereditary claims. Voicing such misgivings, even in the Commons, a supposed sanctuary of free speech, was unsafe. When William Shippen lamented in 1717 that the new king was 'unacquainted with our language and constitution', his colleagues responded by sending the Jacobite MP to the Tower.[2] This occurred not long after Irish MPs showed similar intolerance, expelling colleague John Leigh for 'his notorious disaffection to the Protestant Succession'.[3]

Such xenophobic rancour always was likely to fade over time, but much of the credit for calming the political waters belongs to Robert Walpole. He dominated the political scene for decades, becoming in the process the country's first and longest-serving prime minister. He did this, in part, by circumventing issues that were likely to inflame political passions. However, he also was adept at some of the darker political arts.

Since at least the Revolution, a growing state had allowed governments to create sinecures that could be used to reward friends or co-opt enemies.[4] Walpole proved particularly adept, ruthless and blatant in employing these levers of power. 'There had been places and placemen before, but Walpole was the most systematic and unfastidious player of that game electorally and inside the House of Commons itself.'[5]

One measure of the success of Walpole's tranquillisation of politics is the drop in the frequency of quarrels prompting parliamentary intervention. Initially, this was similar to that of the era of enraged partisanship. Between 1715 and 1719, the Commons and Lords interceded to mediate potentially violent differences between their Members at least five times, or an average of once per year. Once, intervention followed a challenge sent in the House.[6]

Over the next four decades, however, issues that had divided parties before, and would do so in the future, virtually disappeared.[7] Indicative of the diminished partisan temperature was a fall in parliamentary intervention to prevent Members from fighting. Where such mediation had been an annual occurrence during the rage of party, from 1720 to 1760 there were only three such incidents per decade.[8] And in the 1760s, there were only four.[9]

Despite such efforts, parliament was not always able to protect its Members. Owen Buckingham, MP for Reading, was killed in a rather irregular affair in 1720. The dispute was not parliamentary, arising out of birthday celebration given by a good friend of Buckingham. 'They quarreled "after having drank too freely" and fought in the dark.'[10] Even defenders of duelling might have had qualms about this sort of affair. In response to the death of one of its own in such circumstances, the Commons did manage to pass an anti-duelling bill, but it was defeated in the Lords on the first reading. Almost a century would pass before parliament again considered legislation aimed at curbing duels.[11]

The effectiveness, and egregiousness, of Walpole's methods made them controversial, so much so that he occasionally risked violence. In a financial debate on 20 May 1717, for example, James Stanhope told the Commons that, as the recently appointed First Lord of the Treasury, he would make up with honesty what he lacked in capacity for the position. He then proceeded to list a number of questionable practices from which he would refrain. This was an obvious insinuation about the conduct of his predecessor, and former ally, Walpole, who had been unburdened by such scruples. Stanhope's comments led to an altercation so heated that the House unanimously passed a resolution forbidding the two men from carrying the dispute any further.[12]

Similar aspersions were at the heart of another dispute in early 1730. Shortly before Lord Townshend resigned from the government led by his brother-in-law, Walpole, the two had a physical confrontation at the home of Colonel John Selwyn, MP for Whitechurch and a confidant of both men. At the crux of the disagreement was a foreign policy initiative that Townshend, the Northern Secretary, wanted to drop and Walpole desired to pursue. Since it was to be taken up in the Commons, the peer gave way, but asserted that 'upon my honour' the course he supported seemed the most advisable. Walpole scornfully replied, 'My lord, for once there is no man's sincerity which I doubt so much as your lordship's; and I never doubted it so much as when you are pleased to make such strong professions.'

In response, Townshend rushed forward and grabbed Walpole by the collar. The two government ministers then 'were not ashamed to resent their wrongs by a personal struggle, which might have been approved of by the frequenters of a village taproom, but which was certainly out of place when we remember the high position of the combatants, and that the scene was laid in the house of a friend, and in the presence of a lady'. Following this scuffle, 'the rival ministers laid their hands on their swords, and prepared for an immediate duel. Mrs. Selwyn, in terror, was on the point of summoning the guards, but was prevented' by another guest, Henry Pelham, brother of the Duke of Newcastle. Friends then interposed, rather belatedly, to effect 'a cold and hollow reconciliation', but the incident remained a source of bitterness for both forever afterwards.[13]

The following year saw another clash between parliamentarians. Although Walpole was not directly involved this time, his shadow loomed large over the proceedings.

In the Commons, the manifestly constitutional motivations of the Tories, combined with their claim to represent interests ignored by Walpole's government, helped legitimate the notion that sustained and organised opposition to the king's ministers could be 'loyal' rather than inherently treasonous.[14] Outside parliament, they sought to put pressure on the government by swaying public opinion through an extensive propaganda campaign that employed not just squibs and pamphlets but also the burgeoning medium of indigenously produced graphic satire.[15]

Perhaps the most influential voice warning that Whig corruption threatened not only the independence of parliament but also aristocratic predominance, belonged to Henry St John, Viscount Bolingbroke.[16]

Barred from doing so in the Lords after being implicated in the 1715 rebellion, Bolingbroke attacked the administration with a printing press. Walpole's allies responded in kind. In 1731, the exchange of invective became so personal that it produced a duel that can almost be seen as an encounter by proxy of Walpole and Bolingbroke.

William Pulteney was Bolingbroke's chief confederate in the pamphlet war with the government. Fellow MP, John Hervey, had been a close friend of Pulteney before switching sides and joining Walpole's team. When an anonymous publication attacking Pulteney and Bolingbroke appeared, it seemed clear who was to blame. Pulteney's printed riposte referred to Hervey in insulting terms. Both MPs were wounded in the ensuing duel with swords but, had not Pulteney's foot slipped before the seconds intervened, it is likely he would have killed his opponent.[17]

The following year an old scandal produced a new quarrel that forced the Speaker to intervene to prevent a duel between two MPs. Edward Vernon claimed in a Commons speech that the directors of the South Seas Company had behaved contrary to their oath and in a manner hurtful to the firm. Sir John Eyles, the company's leader, took this as a personal affront and a fight seemed imminent.[18]

Considerably more dangerous were the ramifications of one of Walpole's rare political miscalculations. In an effort to reduce the tax on land, he decided to introduce an excise on tobacco in 1733. This meant that the poor would pay to lower a tax that fell mainly on the rich. It also threatened powerful vested interests, particularly traders who fraudulently evaded customs duties. City leaders mobilised citizens by portraying this measure as symptomatic of much broader problems. 'Walpolean Whiggery was increasingly identified with the cultivation of private interests, sycophancy, jobbery, the exploitation of public office, and overweening, opportunistic politics.'[19]

As had been the case following the collapse of the South Sea bubble, large crowds surrounded parliament as the excise tax was discussed. The speeches of two of the London Members, Sir John Barnard and Micaiah Perry, 'were accompanied by a large and noisy demonstration at the doors of the House, and Walpole, in an unguarded moment, called the demonstrators a gang of "sturdy beggars"'. Although the House does not appear to have been intimidated by the tumult, support for the bill diminished to the point that, to prevent its defeat, Walpole felt compelled to push for postponement of further consideration of the measure for two months.[20] It was then that the excitement really began.

As Walpole walked through the lobby of the Commons with a few other MPs, 'he was surrounded by a clamorous mob, not of rabble, but of well-dressed people'. Near the steps leading to Alice's Coffee House, 'some individuals seized Sir Robert's cloak, and, as the collar was tightly fastened, nearly strangled him'. Henry Pelham, who was accompanying Walpole, 'attacked the assailants', pushed the prime minister into a passageway leading to the coffee house and, 'drawing his sword, stationed himself at the entrance, exclaiming in a firm and determined tone, "Now, gentlemen, who will be the first to fall?" This spirited defiance overawed the assailants, who quietly dispersed'.[21]

Walpole's biographer dismisses the incident as 'a scuffle, crowd noise, some jostling and police brutality'.[22] Walpole himself lost no time in depicting it as tantamount to an assassination attempt. In the face of this alleged outrage, even Walpole's most strident critics were forced to condemn the crowd. The following day, the Commons unanimously resolved 'that the assaulting, insulting, or menacing, any member of this House, in his coming to, or going from, the House, or upon the account of his behaviour in Parliament, is an high infringement of the Privilege of this House, a most outrageous and dangerous violation of the rights of Parliament, and an high crime and misdemeanour'. Assembling, or causing to come to parliament 'in a riotous, tumultuous, and disorderly, manner', to promote or hinder a matter before the House was similarly censured.[23]

This episode did not exactly allow Walpole to turn defeat into victory; he later abandoned the excise bill. Yet the actions of the anti-Walpole crowd clearly backfired. The canny politician exaggerated the peril he had faced to strengthen his position. The King was persuaded to dismiss some courtiers who supported Walpole's opponents. The prime minister followed this up by purging a number of placeholders who were deemed insufficiently loyal.[24]

There was a violent coda to the story. Many in London wanted to commemorate the defeat of the hated excise by holding a celebration on the anniversary of its demise. The Lord Mayor, Sir William Billers, was too well disposed toward the Walpole administration to permit such an affront. He therefore ordered a special watch and the arrest of anyone who sought to light a bonfire or create a disturbance. This did not go down well with would-be celebrants. A riot ensued, during which 'Billers had his windows broken and, as he patrolled the streets, was pelted with dirt and stones. Moreover, as he went out of office shortly after, crowds pelted him again and tried to smash his coach'.[25]

Walpole might have found himself in even greater peril had another bit of legislation been more effective. Responding to a petition from Middlesex justices, parliament passed the 1736 Gin Act, which aimed to tax out of existence the cheap spirit seen to be at the heart of a variety of social ills. Walpole and Sir Joseph Jekyll, Master of the Rolls, sat on the committee that drafted the legislation. Whatever salubrious effects the act might entail, it was unpopular with both the consumers and producers of 'Mother Gin'. London authorities mobilised opposition in the hopes that the act would be repealed before it came into force. That did not happen, but the potential for violence was clear. In early September, 'a government informant wrote that "it is the Common Talk of the Tippling Ale houses and little Gin Shops that Sr Robert Walpole and the Master of ye Rolls will not outlive Michaelmas long"'.[26] As it turned out, the Gin Act was not the tonic supporters had hoped. The poverty of small gin shops made prosecution uneconomical and, after a number of informers were lynched, information about violations of the law became scarce.[27] As a result, dipsomaniacs had little reason to try to exact revenge upon Walpole or Jekyll.

Others with a grudge were less restrained. That same year, Thames boatmen, fearing the effect on their livelihoods of a planned bridge nearby, left 'a packet of gunpowder in Westminster Hall'. It exploded harmlessly, perhaps because it was damp.[28]

So contentious were Walpole and his methods that they continued to provoke parliamentary violence even after he left office. In March 1743, William Chetwynd, a Bolingbroke ally, told fellow MP, Horatio Walpole, that both he and his older brother should be hanged for their actions while in power. This led to an exchange of 'hot words' behind the Speaker's chair, after which Chetwynd led Horatio into the lobby to fight. Although Walpole sought to avoid an immediate clash in such a public place, Chetwynd insisted. They drew their swords at the bottom of the stairs. 'After a couple of passes Walpole had driven Chetwynd against a post and might have run him through had not a clerk arrived to beat down their swords. Chetwynd, slightly wounded, went off to find a surgeon, while Walpole, apparently unruffled, returned to the Chamber to speak in a debate.'[29] Perhaps shutting the barn door firmly after the horses had departed, the Speaker then sought assurances from both men that they would pursue the matter no further.[30]

Across the Irish Sea, the growing importance of parliament, rising nationalism, and, perhaps, the example set in Westminster, helped make similar encounters more common. During an impassioned speech by John Hely-Hutchinson in the early 1760s, for example, Radical MP John Lucas interjected, 'Rest, rest perturbed spirit.' The always prickly Provost of Trinity College chose to interpret this as a personal affront rather than standard parliamentary bantering. A challenge was sent and accepted. Although Lucas was so incapacitated by gout that he would have to fight sitting down, he was determined to do so, selecting an especially long sword for the purpose. (His second, presumably concerned that combat of this sort might not be in accordance with the code, prevailed upon Lucas to take a brace of pistols too.) The two principals duly took the field, but the arrival of several Privy Councillors provided an opportunity for their seconds to adjust the matter.[31]

A more conventional intervention took place in early November 1773, after Benjamin Chapman exchanged invective of a personal nature with John Scott during a committee meeting on public expenditure. The former was a leading Patriot while the latter was a prominent Castle supporter. Sir William Mayne subsequently was observed shuttling between the two men, apparently making arrangements for a hostile encounter. When the Speaker, Edmund Sexton Pery, was informed of this, he cleared the House of 'strangers', locked the doors and ordered Scott and Chapman to remain until they pledged not to pursue the matter any further.[32]

Pery himself had been on the other side of mediation efforts twice in the 1750s. On one occasion, he had been challenged by fellow MP Arthur Rochfort, only to see his mentor, Primate Stone, intervene to prevent a duel. In 1759, Pery questioned the motives of Lord Drogheda and others in raising regiments to support the Crown's war effort with France. Drogheda's demand that Pery provide an explanation in the Commons 'provoked a furore'. Pery promised colleagues that he would not send a challenge but refused to pledge that he would decline to receive one. The matter was only settled when the Speaker, John Ponsonby, who was Drogheda's uncle, apologised on behalf of his nephew and promised that the latter would not challenge Pery.[33]

Not all Irish political quarrels were resolved peacefully. In 1773, the Earl of Bellamont was wounded seriously in a duel with Viscount Townshend. The Irish peer had taken offence after Townshend, then Lord Lieutenant of Ireland, repeatedly (and publicly) had refused to meet with him, fed up with Bellamont's requests for favours. An extensive exchange of letters followed, during which Townsend apologised, but when this was deemed insufficient, sent a challenge.

The duel was a sensation not only due to the rank of the participants but because, while previous lord lieutenants had been threatened with challenges, this marked the first time one actually was forced to fight over his official conduct. Yet, a sequel was not long in coming: three days later, Townshend's successor, Sir John Blaquiere, fought a duel with Beauchamp Bagenal, MP for County Clare, over perceived slights connected to a request for official favours.[34]

Wilkes and Liberty I

If the Irish largely followed Westminster's lead in regard to duelling, they blazed trails in another respect. While Walpole had tried to demobilise the populace, others subsequently took the opposite tack. John Wilkes was to be the most famous and successful politician of the age in this respect, but his triumphs in London were adumbrated by events in Dublin, where the second half of the eighteenth century saw 'a growing public interest in political affairs, and pressure of public opinion on parliament'.[35]

In 1748, several years after trying unsuccessfully to reform the Dublin Corporation from within, apothecary Charles Lucas sought to represent the city in parliament. In support of his candidacy, he unleashed a torrent of publications on matters ranging from accusations of nefarious procedural irregularities by the Corporation to assertions of Irish parliamentary independence. Alarmed both by Lucas's message and his popularity, the lord lieutenant used the speech opening parliament on 10 October 1749 to condemn those who would create jealousy between the two kingdoms. A parliamentary committee soon demanded that Lucas admit authorship of some offending documents, something he was disinclined to do. Lacking proof positive of his authorship, the committee concluded that Lucas 'appear[ed]' to have written works slandering the lord lieutenant and promoting sedition and insurrection. Lucas fled before an order for his arrest could be carried out, but the MPs deemed responsible for hounding the popular champion into exile received death threats. And the lord lieutenant's popularity suffered so much that when he departed office, 'bonfires were made and thousands of insults offered him'.[36]

In the decade that followed, the popular nationalism Lucas had championed grew stronger. Increased interest in parliamentary proceedings 'manifested itself in the thronging of people to the House of Commons ... in ovations for members who were on the patriotic side and in hostile demonstrations against members who took the unpopular side'.[37]

By late 1759, Dublin was awash with (unfounded) rumours about plans to effectuate a union between Ireland and Great Britain. When, in response to the threat of a French invasion, the government drafted legislation that would allow it to assemble parliament more expeditiously, some saw this as the first step toward increased Irish subservience. On 22 November, the day the bill was to be introduced, the crowd that gathered outside parliament expressed such hostility to the measure that Chief Secretary Richard Rigby felt obliged to drop it.[38]

In response to MP complaints of mistreatment at the hands of a 'riotous and disorderly mob', the Commons summoned the lord mayor and sheriffs, instructing them 'to prevent the like indecencies for the future'.[39] Yet worse was to come a week later.

On 3 December, a crowd, summoned by the beating of a drum, headed to parliament. By the time it reached College Green, it had grown to around 3,000 strong. Some were armed with swords and bludgeons. As parliamentarians arrived for the sitting, around fifty, 'regarded with suspicion by the mob[,] were obliged to swear to oppose a union'. A number of MPs were 'abused, struck and otherwise ill-treated'. Hercules Langford Rowley, an MP and privy councillor, 'was dragged the length of the street'. Attorney-General Warden Flood was 'wounded in his coach and obliged to take refuge in Trinity College'. The Earl of Inchiquin was de-wigged.

Parliament House soon was invaded. The Speaker and several MPs were permitted to enter the chamber and adjourn the sitting but persuaded the mob to allow them to depart only with some difficulty. Assured by the Speaker that there would be no union, the crowd dispersed after a show of force by the military, but not before placing an old woman, complete with a clay pipe, upon the throne in the House of Lords, an indictment of those prepared to give away Irish liberties.

Preparations to create a bonfire out of the Commons' journals were averted when, as a diversion, it was suggested that it would be more efficacious to hang Rigby. The rioters proceeded to his residence, having constructed a gallows for their purpose but, evidently forewarned, the MP was nowhere to be found. However, for at least a week after the riot ended, Rigby's servants felt it prudent to arm themselves whenever he was out late at night.[40]

By this time, the London mob was terrorising politicians once again. In 1753, parliamentary approval of a measure providing for the naturalisation of Jews provoked an outcry at what was depicted as an attack on the Church of England. The Bishop of Norwich, who had supported the legislation, 'was attacked by mobs in his diocese and Dr Josiah Tucker, who had remarked that the real cause of the clamour was merchants' fears of Jews breaking their monopoly, was attacked in the streets of Bristol, burned in effigy and dubbed Josiah ben Tucker ben Judas Iscariot'.[41] Such scenes help explain why the government repealed the measure only a few months after it became law.

Two years later, the Duke of Newcastle felt the wrath of the crowd. In September 1756, the prime minister, blamed for recent military setbacks, was 'mobbed. His carriage was pelted in Greenwich and, while he retreated to the Observatory, the mob enjoined his coachman to deliver him to the Tower'.[42] Although he escaped serious injury, widespread rioting prompted Newcastle's resignation, even though he retained the backing of the King and a large parliamentary majority.

The 1761, the Lord Mayor's banquet witnessed similar scenes. When the popular William Pitt travelled to the Guildhall, supporters thronged him, clinging to his carriage, hugging his footmen, and, if reports are to be believed, kissing his horses.[43] Embarrassingly, the crowd's reception for the new monarch was considerably less enthusiastic. Worse still was the reaction to the arrival of the Earl of Bute, the prime minister, who 'was pelted with mud and hooted and might, it was believed, have suffered serious injury if he had not hired a force of "butchers and bruisers" to protect his carriage from direct assault'.[44]

As a Scot, a rival to Pitt, and a man who was rumoured to owe his rise to an illicit relationship with the king's mother, Bute was so widely despised he 'could hardly walk the streets in safety without disguising himself'. One such effort failed when he was recognised in Covent Garden, 'muffled in a large coat, and with a hat and wig drawn down over his brows'.[45]

On his way to the opening of parliament in November 1762, Bute was 'very much insulted, hiss'd and abused in every gross manner, and a little pelted'.[46] The arrival of the Guards saved him, but to avoid similar treatment on his way home, Bute abandoned his coach for a more anonymous hackney chair. 'However, the mob spotted him anyway, smashed the glasses of his chair and put him, it was reported, "very reasonably in great fear" of being "demolished"'.[47] To add insult to near injury, Pitt was cheered warmly all the way to the Commons when he returned to parliament a fortnight later.

Opposition to the unfortunate Bute already was creating another popular hero. In June 1762, MP John Wilkes and a colleague sought to counter the pro-government scribes by (anonymously) publishing the *North Briton*, a weekly that criticised the administration for, among other things, an allegedly pro-Scottish bias. Bute was not the only target. After Lord Talbot's efforts to demonstrate his equestrian skills at George III's coronation went embarrassingly wrong, Wilkes mocked the 'dexterity' of the Lord Steward of the Royal Household, provoking a (bloodless) duel between the two. Having literally dodged a bullet with Talbot, Wilkes then used the threat of another rencontre to deter legal action by a different victim of his satirical quill.[48]

The ministry found the *North Briton* sufficiently irksome to offer Wilkes bribes (including the governorship of Canada) to abandon it. He refused but, following Bute's April 1763 resignation, suspended publication. *North Briton*'s work, it seemed, was done. However, when the king's speech at the close of parliament a week later revealed the concessions made to secure peace with France, Wilkes felt compelled to respond with another issue, No. 45. It offended the monarch and his ministers, while making the provocative (some said revolutionary) claim that legal resistance to government searches for 'dangerous' publications in private houses was constitutionally justified.[49]

In response to the king's demand that Wilkes be arrested, ministers issued a general warrant, a document that specified the crime, in this instance the writing and publishing of *North Briton* No. 45, but gave the crown messengers wide discretion over whom to detain. It was precisely this instrument, previously used by the government against other critics, which Wilkes had railed against. With good reason: under its authority, messengers were to arrest forty-nine men, four of whom, Wilkes included, would have their homes broken into and ransacked in the search for evidence related not only to the *North Briton* but to other suspicious activity as well.

After a week in the Tower, Wilkes was released on the basis of parliamentary privilege. He promptly took legal action against the government, not only winning damages for himself and others but also effectively preventing the future use of general warrants. These triumphs for 'liberty' at the expense of an unloved ministry boosted the MP's already considerable popular support.[50]

Not everyone was impressed. A few months later Wilkes found himself in an (abortive) affair of honour with a Scot who resented disparaging remarks about his compatriots in the *North Briton*.[51] More importantly, the king, despairing of bringing Wilkes to heel through the courts, pushed his ministers to do so in parliament.

This they did, winning Wilkes's expulsion from the Commons and conviction for 'seditious libel' even though his authorship of the offending material never was established definitively.[52] By the time this happened, Wilkes's controversial behaviour and treatment already had generated violence.

In No. 40 of the *North Briton*, responsibility for rampant embezzlement in the army was attributed to Secretary of the Treasury Samuel Martin, who was characterised as 'the most treacherous, base, selfish, mean, abject, low-lived and dirty fellow that ever wriggled himself into a secretaryship'. In the Commons, on 15 November, Martin complained, rather belatedly, that he had been libelled. Looking directly at Wilkes, Martin continued that whoever had written the anonymous article, 'thereby stabbing another in the dark, is a cowardly rascal, a villain, and a scoundrel'.[53]

Wilkes was wounded seriously in the ensuing duel. That Martin waited eight months to complain of libel, reportedly had used the intervening period to practice his marksmanship and had received from the government £41,000 for 'secret and special service', all fuelled suspicions that the ministry had resorted to extra-legal means to remove a persistent thorn.[54]

A little more than a week after this duel, another potentially was averted. During debate about whether parliamentary privilege should extend to the publication of 'seditious libels', and therefore protect Wilkes, 'some words' were used that led to fears that 'a quarrel might ensue'. After Richard Rigby accused Lord Temple of instigating Wilkes and the mob, James Grenville rose to defend his brother. He not only, in the words of Horace Walpole, 'vomited out a torrent of invectives' directed at his colleague but also gesticulated so forcefully and aggressively at Rigby, who was seated nearby, that the latter had to crouch down to avoid being struck. In response, the Speaker required both MPs to assure the House that they 'would not prosecute the matter'.[55]

The Wilkes controversy fomented danger outside of parliament too. Soon after the Commons' condemnation of No. 45, someone recognised MP Sir Alexander Grant at the Royal Exchange and shouted, 'He voted for it. Pelt him.' The Wilkesite mob proceeded to do just that.[56]

The same location saw a similar scene when the common hangman sought to carry out parliament's order to burn the offending publication on 3 December. A 'tumultuous' crowd chanting 'Wilkes and Liberty' rescued the condemned document from the flames.

Alderman Thomas Harley, MP for London, had come to supervise proceedings in his capacity as sheriff. He was afraid to leave his carriage, which was pelted with mud. Before it was driven off, a window was smashed, cutting Harley's forehead.[57]

A few days later, Wilkes's servants struggled to contain a Scot who arrived at the MP's residence intent on killing the man who had traduced his countrymen on the pages of the *North Briton*. The would-be assassin later was arrested and subsequently sent to a lunatic asylum.[58]

As it became clear that parliamentary privilege would not protect him, Wilkes fled to France. Thus, ended the first chapter of his saga, but such was his popularity and presumed influence that he was suspected (no doubt baselessly) of engineering from abroad one further violent episode.

In May 1765, 8,000 weavers marched on parliament in support of a bill prohibiting imported silk. Arriving Members 'were jostled and roughly treated'. The coach of the Duke of Bedford, who not only had negotiated the peace treaty that reopened English markets to French silks but also was a leading proponent of freer trade, was destroyed. Bedford himself was hit on the head by a stone. This did not prevent him from blocking the bill temporarily. As a result, when the sitting ended, the crowd pursued the duke as he returned home and tried to demolish his residence. A few days later, the mob again sought to destroy Bedford's house, but were chased away by troops after the Riot Act was read. The bill passed soon thereafter.[59]

Wilkes and Liberty II

The second act of the Wilkes tale begins not with the end of his four-year self-imposed exile but rather with a parliamentary duel he almost triggered from France in 1766.

To put pressure on the government to induce the king to grant a royal pardon, Wilkes published a letter that he had written following his duel with Talbot several years before. The earl, furious at his portrayal in the epistle, confronted, in the lobby of the House of Lords, Lord Temple, Wilkes's patron, the original recipient of the letter, and the man Talbot deemed responsible for its publication. Talbot's invective became so insulting that Temple actually drew his sword before others intervened to broker peace.[60]

Less than two years later, pursued by creditors and cognisant that MPs could not be imprisoned for debt, Wilkes returned to England and sought to re-enter parliament. After unsuccessfully standing in London, he was returned for Middlesex. It was now time to face justice. Turning himself in to authorities, Wilkes was sent to King's Bench prison, arriving only after eluding a crowd intent on 'rescuing' him.

Fervent support for Wilkes, particularly among the lower and middle classes, fostered apprehension, even if the ostensible popular champion repeatedly sought to discourage mob violence. Such fears only grew after events on 10 May 1768, the day parliament opened.

Up to 40,000 assembled outside prison in anticipation of escorting their hero to Westminster Palace to take his seat. As it became clear that the MP for Middlesex would not be released, growing frustration gave way to disorder and eventually bloodshed by soldiers in what came to be known as the Massacre of St George's Fields. Meanwhile, outside the Houses of Parliament, magistrates were finding it difficult to prevent 'the hallooing of the common people' in the Palace Yard, and there was a riot outside the House of Lords amidst cries of 'Wilkes and Liberty'. The violence grew worse as news of the massacre spread. 'London was in a state of virtual civil war ... George III threatened to abdicate.'[61]

Although the rioting soon died down, Wilkes would not be at liberty for quite a while. In June, he was sentenced to twenty-two months imprisonment and fines totalling £1,000. While incarcerated, he was expelled again from parliament for libelling a minister who he claimed had 'planned' the massacre. Middlesex voters again returned Wilkes, prompting more embarrassing behaviour from his colleagues.

On the day after his election, the Commons resolved that Wilkes was 'incapable of being elected a Member of the present Parliament'. Debate on the matter was so heated that it produced a motion (ultimately rejected) to censure the Speaker, who had stated that he could 'expect no candour' from a particular MP, thereby implicitly questioning his honour.[62] When Wilkes was returned again a month later, the Commons not only declared the election void, in a blatant violation of the law, but ministers also considered expelling two Members who had signed the writ.[63]

Wilkes's repeated victories prompted a group of the king's 'friends', led by Charles Dingley, his opponent in the most recent contest, to collect signatures on an address decrying the by-election results and lauding the monarch. They set out to present it to the king on 22 March, a day Wilkes's supporters had chosen for their own demonstration. When the two groups met, the loyalists, who included 'many gentlemen in their finery', were pelted with 'urban mud, largely made up of horse and human faeces'. Of the 130 who accompanied the address, 'a mere mud-bespattered dozen' made it to St James's Palace. They were greeted by some courtiers, one of whom, the Duke of Northumberland, was reported to have been 'severely pelted'. His 'chariot', and that of the Duke of Kingston, were said to have been demolished. The humiliations faced by Wilkes's foes did not end there. The last indignity was self-imposed: ushered into the royal presence, Dingley was forced to inform George III that he had left the address in his coach, which had returned home.[64]

Soon thereafter, another Middlesex election was held, but the result was no different. In the Commons two days later, George Onslow, a friend of Wilkes who had become obsessed with maintaining the authority of the House, moved that Henry Lawes Luttrell 'ought to have been returned a member for Middlesex'. After a long debate, with 'the Lobby full of dirty people', and many MPs who owed their seats to the government absent so as not to offend constituents, the motion was carried 197 to 143. Luttrell was seated instead of Wilkes.[65]

The Commons, hitherto the popular safeguard against the Crown's encroachments, seemed to have turned against the people and their champion. Fear that the populace would respond violently was rife. 'The streets were full of soldiers, and people hesitated to go out unless they had footmen to protect them. Luttrell was assaulted as he left St. Stephen's Chapel and began to go about armed', that is, when he dared to leave his house at all.[66]

The implications of the Commons' disturbing action were substantial. If Wilkes's supporters could be disfranchised, what would protect others from similar treatment? This helps explain the passage the following year of George Grenville's act transferring authority to decide disputed elections from the House as a whole to small committee of MPs chosen by lot.[67] More broadly, Wilkes' egregious treatment seemed to confirm claims that the Commons was accountable only to itself, a situation that could only be remedied by profound systemic changes. 'It was from this episode that a revived radical movement began to set its sights on a far more thoroughgoing constitutional reform than had been proposed by the earlier place bills and grumblings from the counties and the cities.'[68]

In 1782, the Commons belatedly recognised its error, formally expunging from its Journal the 17 February 1769 resolution incapacitating Wilkes from being elected to serve in parliament. Such a measure, the House now asserted, was subversive of the rights of electors. Before experiencing this collective epiphany, however, it found itself in another showdown with Wilkes. Again, the issue was one of substantial constitutional significance. And again, most MPs chose sides unwisely.

Wilkes and Liberty III

In keeping with a desire to protect itself from undue public pressure, parliament long had proscribed publication of detailed accounts of its proceedings.[69] By 1771, however, more than a dozen newspapers were printing excerpts of debates without any attempt to disguise who had said what. This prompted George Onslow to demand that the Commons enforce the ban. Printers of several offending publications were summoned. Some not only declined to appear but, apparently suborned by London officials, continued to publish debates. Efforts to bring them to heel met resistance. Wilkes, by now presiding over the London criminal court in his capacity as alderman, ordered the release of a printer arrested by a servant seeking to obtain a reward offered by the king. The Lord Mayor, Brass Crosby, refused to release the Commons' messenger, who had been taken into custody while trying to arrest another printer.[70]

The Commons hardly could tolerate such defiance. Those deemed responsible were summoned to explain themselves. Wilkes replied that he would only attend 'in his place'. Rather than acknowledge him as a duly elected Member, the Commons opted to ignore him. Two other MPs, Crosby and Alderman Richard Oliver, went to parliament on 25 March, accompanied by a 'tumultuous crowd' that 'interrupted Members in their coming into the House'.[71] Undeterred, the Commons sent Oliver to the Tower and ordered Crosby, affected by gout, to return in two days.

Crosby did so on 27 March, accompanied by tens of thousands of supporters who had released his horses so that they could pull his carriage to Westminster Palace. Those deemed unsympathetic to their hero were treated roughly. 'Members, particularly those of the Court party, had the greatest difficulty getting through to the Commons.' The 'two cubs', Stephen and Charles James Fox, had urged the Commons to take a tough line against Oliver and Wilkes. For this, they were splattered with mud, had their clothes torn and their carriages destroyed. Lord North, who had been mistaken for a Fox, had his hat stolen and cut to ribbons, his 'chariot glasses' shattered and his carriage smashed to pieces. Sir William Meredith, an opposition MP, intervened to rescue North from serious injury.

It took five hours, and the efforts of many of the most popular MPs, to get the crowd to disperse. Crosby then was sent to join Oliver in the Tower. (Their release after parliament was prorogued a few weeks later produced widespread celebration, during the course of which, as if to emphasise who would have the final word, a crowd smashed the windows of the Speaker's residence.) However, despite repeated questions about whether Wilkes was above or below the law, the Ministry dared not touch him.[72]

The campaign against the press, like that against Wilkes, was little short of a disaster for parliament. 'The Commons, in spite of their display of authority, suffered a total loss: not only did the defiant printers go unpunished, but the newspapers went on or resumed printing debates, and the House, fearful of stirring up another hornet's nest, had to accept the accomplished fact.'[73] Over the next few decades, parliament's attitude toward the press became much more accommodative. In 1783, journalists were allowed for the first time to take notes during parliamentary proceedings, making more accurate reporting of debates possible. In partisan times, however, neither side trusted the other to do this, so the Treasury subsidised one account of proceedings, 'Parliamentary Debates', while the opposition supported another, John Debrett's 'Parliamentary Register'.[74] And in 1803, parliament formally acknowledged its symbiotic relationship with the press by giving it a designated bench.[75]

Wilkes's triumphs – on general warrants, representation, and press freedom – helped lay the foundation for a more democratic future. But his preferred tactic – 'raising a mob' to put pressure on the government – fast was becoming discredited. 'The Wilkesite disturbances were perhaps the last in which riot was considered legitimate by very large numbers of propertied people.'[76] The Walpolean fear of popular mobilisation would only increase after parliament faced a tumult that made those of the Wilkes era seem tame by comparison.

6

HEYDAY OF THE FIRE EATERS

The decades that followed the victories of 'Wilkes and Liberty' were marked by the intensification of a peculiar snobbery towards violence. Crowd disorder, which previously had been somewhat tolerated and rarely caused serious injury to politicians, became a major concern. On the other hand, violence of a more aristocratic nature, although sometimes fatal to parliamentarians, flourished as never before as official efforts to curb duelling virtually ceased.

Demophobia

Politicians had good reason to fear the mob even after Wilkes, a master mobiliser, finally was able to take his seat in the Commons in 1774. This was amply demonstrated five years later, following an unsuccessful attempt to court martial Admiral of the Fleet Augustus Keppel for a navel defeat at hands of the French. He blamed the setback on the refusal to obey orders of his subordinate, Sir Hugh Palliser, a lord of the admiralty. This might have remained a purely naval matter had not both men been MPs on different sides of the political divide. Instead, a partisan press portrayed the trial as an effort by the administration to turn a naval hero into a scapegoat.

Ministry supporters suffered accordingly. Palliser 'had to escape to Portsmouth while the house he had once occupied in St James's Square was stripped and its contents burned in the street outside'. The house of Lord George Germain was afforded similar treatment. 'Lord North and the Earl of Sandwich (both seasoned enemies of the crowd) had their windows broken.'[1]

The following year saw much worse. In 1778, Sir George Savile's bill for Catholic relief easily had passed parliament. Not only were the restrictions on papists it removed considered embarrassing, but by enabling Catholics to serve in the army, the measure aided the government's efforts to suppress the rebellious American colonies.[2] However, plans to introduce similar legislation in Scotland produced riots. This, in turn, encouraged the formation south of the border of a Protestant Association to push for repeal of the law. Lord George Gordon was chosen to lead the organisation despite having voted for Savile's bill. On 2 June 1780, roughly 60,000 people escorted Gordon to parliament to present the Association's petition.[3]

Things quickly got out of hand. Demonstrators barged into Westminster Hall, forcing adjournment of the Court of King's Bench. Doorkeepers prevented a similar invasion of the Lords. Arriving peers enjoyed no such protection. Those seen as opposing the Association's goals were treated violently. 'Lord Bathurst, the Lord President of the Council, lost his wig and had his legs kicked. The Bishop of Lincoln was seized by the throat and had the wheels removed from his carriage. The Duke of Northumberland was assaulted and relieved of his watch, while Lord Mansfield "narrowly escaped with his life"'.[4] Mansfield, the Chief Justice, also had his coach windows smashed. (He was doubly unpopular: he strongly supported Catholic relief, and in his judicial capacity, he had sent Wilkes to prison a dozen years earlier.) Sir George Sevile's coach was demolished. 'A rush was made at Lord North'; before the prime minister was rescued, 'he lost his hat to a man who opened the carriage door'. Lord Ashburnham 'was dragged into the House over the heads of the crowd'.[5]

Inside the Lords, peers tried to ignore the commotion, even though they could hear the crowd shouting and pounding on the doors. Mansfield, who was presiding due to the absence of the Lord Chancellor, reportedly 'quivered on the Woolsack like an aspen'.[6] News that a colleague was in danger from the mob pushed the Chamber into panic. 'Some of their lordships with their hair about their shoulders; others smutted with dirt; most of them as pale as the ghost in Hamlet, and all of them standing up, in their several places, and speaking at the same instant.' There were calls to send for the guards, the justices or civil magistrates. Many lords called for the House to adjourn, in a scene of 'unprecedented alarm' that lasted for about half an hour.[7]

There was a similar situation in the Commons. 'Members, as they arrived, were subjected to gross outrage and personal violence. Almost all were compelled to put blue cockades in their hats and call out "No Popery!" whilst some were forced to take oaths to vote for the repeal of the obnoxious law.'[8] Gordon presented the Association's petition and moved that it be discussed. As his colleagues debated, he repeatedly left the House to apprise the crowd of the progress of the deliberations. This, combined with his conspicuous refusal to order those assembled to return home, increased the tension.

Clearly, Gordon was using the threat of popular violence to try to intimidate his colleagues. Indeed, he hinted that as long as crowds filled the lobby it would be impossible for the Commons to divide and defeat his motion.[9] Such tactics did not go down well with other MPs, one of whom is said to have threatened, 'My Lord Gordon, do you intend to bring your rascally adherents into the House of Commons? If you do, the first man of them that enters, I will plunge my sword, not into his, but into your body.' Another MP followed Gordon around the House while making similar threats.[10]

Blackstone had argued that the legislature should never submit to popular clamour. To its credit, the Commons did not knuckle under to intimidation on this occasion. As soon as the lobbies were cleared, a division was held, and Gordon's motion was defeated overwhelmingly. The Guards then were summoned, allowing the MPs to return home. Many in the crowd were prepared to do likewise. Others went on to engage in a week-long orgy of rioting forever associated with Gordon's name.

Much of the disorder was not parliamentary; religious minorities were the main targets. But some MPs faced violence, particularly when outside parliament, which was protected by troops. Savile 'had his railings torn down and his house was threatened'.[11] Edmund Burke's residence similarly was imperilled, so much so that 'he began to sort out his most valuable papers in order to effect an escape, but a party of troops arrived and prevented any attack'. When he tried to go to parliament the next day, Burke 'was accosted even before he reached the House, being asked to promise to vote against Catholic relief. So pressing did the crowd become that he was forced to draw his sword to protect himself'.[12] A crowd attacked Sandwich on his way to parliament. The First Lord of the Admiralty received a cut on the head and his coach was damaged and stopped, forcing him to take shelter in a coffee house.[13] Later that day, the contents of Lord Mansfield's house were destroyed, despite intervention by troops that led to the deaths of some rioters. Lord North was luckier: soldiers frustrated an attack on his house by 'a mob brandishing torches and bundles of faggots'.[14]

Many Members opted to be elsewhere on 6 June, but those who turned up at the Commons unanimously supported resolutions condemning the violence. Although Gordon did not oppose this, he continued to wear the Association's blue ribbon, 'which after a threat from the other side of the House his friends removed by force'. Incredibly, Gordon seemed to have learned nothing from the chaos he played such a major role in unleashing. However, his attempt to address again the crowd 'was prevented by his friends "not without a degree of violence"'. A colleague hinted that Gordon's expulsion was warranted. This touched off a spirited debate, but the idea was dropped as too provocative to the rioters. Instead, the House adjourned.[15] Justice Hyde's attempt to disperse the crowd outside parliament by reading the Riot Act had no effect but to prompt the destruction of his house.[16]

The Gordon riots caused immense property damage and claimed at least 285 lives; and 25 of the 450 people arrested for participating were hanged.[17] A less obvious casualty was the notion that respectable politicians could use the threat of mass disorder to their benefit.[18] 'The last vestige of propertied enthusiasm for popular justice as mediated by the mob was dissipated by the Gordon Riots.'[19] Dead too was the idea that rioting served as a fire alarm, alerting parliament to problems that it could solve to prevent revolution.[20] Henceforth, public disturbances themselves would be seen as potentially insurrectionary. As a consequence, the London authorities, which previously had helped mobilise crowds, became cooler toward popular radicalism.[21] In a very real sense, then, 'the English reaction to the French Revolution began well before its outbreak'.[22]

Even if patricians now were disinclined to raise a mob, that hardly meant politicians had nothing to fear from crowds, even those comprised of gentlemen. William Pitt (son of the MP of the same name discussed previously) learned this to his cost soon after becoming prime minister in early 1784.

Pitt had come to power by constitutionally dubious means, after George III engineered the replacement of a Whig administration that included Charles James Fox, whom the sovereign despised. So, it was rather impudent for Pitt's supporters to pull his coach past Brooks's, the Whig club, following a ceremony in which the new prime minister had been given the freedom of the City. The occupants responded violently to the provocation: a shower of missiles rained down from the second floor, and men with bludgeons sallied out to attack Pitt's coach, opening its door and aiming some 'desperate blows' at the premier, who was protected by his brother, Lord Chatham.

Pitt's supporters responded by smashing the club's windows. Pitt was rescued by members and employees of his own club, White's, where he took refuge. His carriage was almost wrecked, and his servants were badly bruised. Pitt's brother recognised among the attackers two friends of the prime minister's great rival, Charles James Fox, but the leader of the opposition disclaimed any involvement in the incident. However, his alibi – that he had been in bed with his mistress at the time – hardly helped Fox's public standing.[23]

The following year, having pushed through a variety of unpopular revenue-raising measures, most notably a tax on retail shops, Pitt repeatedly faced violence of a more plebeian variety. First, there were riots and the prime minister was burned in effigy. Then, in June, a crowd attacked Downing Street, so that 'Pitt did not dare return there'. And, when he went to the City in November, Pitt was afforded 'rough compliments from ye mob', and the windows of his carriage were broken.[24]

A decade later, war with France and deteriorating economic conditions fuelled more attacks on the prime minister. In the summer of 1795, a mob attacked Downing Street, where Pitt's windows were broken.[25] The scene at the state opening of parliament in October was even more shocking, particularly in light of recent events across the English Channel.

The prime minister 'was "surrounded" and cursed by the mob'.[26] George III's arrival was greeted with hisses, and a stone (or possibly a bullet) hit the window of his state coach. Leaving parliament by private coach, the king was pursued by elements of the crowd, one member of which reportedly opened the door of his vehicle and tried to pull the monarch out before the Horse Guards intervened. The empty state coach also was attacked, and its windows broken. The crush outside Westminster Hall was so great that Storey's Gate was locked. Some of the demonstrators got sledgehammers and tried to enter by force.[27]

As with the excise crisis, the government used this violence to its advantage, pushing through parliament two 'Gagging Acts' aimed at curbing the radical movement, which was seen to be behind the tumults.[28] However, this repressive legislation did not prevent further public violence directed at Pitt. The prime minister's unpopularity was such that he often was guarded by soldiers, a highly unusual situation in a much less security-obsessed age. Yet even these extraordinary measures did not shield him from popular threats. On 17 December 1795, while riding through St James's Park, Pitt was pelted with mud by a group of men, one of whom tried to grab his horse's bridle. In June of the following year, his residence was attacked by a mob, which was dispersed by troops. And, when Pitt went to St Paul's in December 1797 for a thanksgiving service following a military victory, he was hissed, pelted with stones and went home escorted by troops.[29]

Parliamentarians in Dublin also were facing increased threats from outsiders in the final decades of the eighteenth century. One source was the Volunteers, local militias raised to allow British troops in Ireland to be sent elsewhere. In late 1779, thousands of Volunteers gathered opposite parliament house to push for lifting mercantilist restrictions and against the importation of English goods. The protesters indicated that MPs faced a choice, implied by a message inscribed upon a cannon situated on College Green, 'FREE TRADE, OR THIS.'[30] But on this occasion, as on those that would follow, parliamentarians seem to have been in little actual danger, even if large assemblies of uniformed men demanding political changes did generate a degree of apprehension.

Other perils were more imminent. Eleven days after the Volunteer demonstration, a crowd of at least 5,000 people invaded parliament house. Arriving MPs were forced to swear to be true to Ireland and to vote for a bill providing less revenue than the government needed. A group attacked the house of Attorney General John Scott, breaking the windows on the ground floor before leaving to search for their quarry at the Four Courts.[31]

There was a similar scene five years later, when a crowd, assembled to protest a paving bill (seen as a parliamentary encroachment on the privileges and liberties of citizens), forced its way into the gallery of the Commons. Sir Boyle Roche was jostled for supporting the legislation, but demonstrators focused their hostility on MPs who had voted down a protectionist measure three days earlier. A motion that Chancellor of the Exchequer John Foster, a staunch foe of tariffs, 'should be hanged' was passed, unsurprisingly given the rioters' presence. Although the government had taken steps to mollify demonstrators in 1779, it remained resolute in 1784. Consequently, the agitation for protection, and the threat of violence, lingered for months. Such was the danger that Attorney General John Fitzgibbon, whose name was on a list of those targeted for tarring and feathering by the mob, during this period felt the necessity of 'always carrying arms'.[32]

Fitzgibbon was targeted again eleven years later. Upon appointment as Ireland's lord lieutenant in late 1794, Earl Fitzwilliam quickly had raised popular expectations of Catholic emancipation, in part by purging the Dublin Castle 'junto', staunch supporters of the Protestant ascendancy. His subsequent dismissal, for exceeding his authority, prompted a Catholic outcry and, on the day his successor took office, violence. The carriages of the Primate and Fitzgibbon, now the Lord Chancellor, 'were showered with stones as they returned from the swearing-in ceremony', one projectile hitting Fitzgibbon above the eye. There followed attacks on the hapless Fitzgibbon's house, and those of Speaker John Foster and Alderman (and MP) Nathaniel Warren. At the Customs House, John Claudius Beresford, an MP and the son of one of the 'junto' members Fitzwilliam dismissed, opened fire on the crowd, killing one and wounding another.[33]

Heyday of the Fire-eaters

At the same time that mob attacks on politicians were arousing considerable attention and apprehension, a looming, and arguably more dangerous, threat to their health and safety was receiving substantially less official action. 'Duels arising out of something said in Parliament were rare but became less so from about 1770.'[34]

Technological change was partly responsible. As pistols replaced swords as the weapon of choice, skill and training mattered less and there were more opportunities for intervention, both of which made it less risky to 'recognize' a slight.[35]

Cultural changes were at work too. While Stuart monarchs frequently condemned duelling (even as they pardoned duellists), Hanoverians sent a different message. George II not only was implicated (albeit rather dubiously) in two affairs of honour himself but also indicated that an officer knocked down by a subordinate should either send a challenge or forfeit his commission.[36] In 1789, Prince Frederick, the second son of George III, was involved in a duel in which his opponent's ball 'grazed his Royal Highness's curl', in the memorable phrase of the seconds.[37] With those at the apex of the social hierarchy setting such an example, how could lesser mortals possibly refuse to fight?

At the same time, other means of restoring a man's good name, such as legal action, had become less effective. Behaving honourably, and showing courage under fire, was an unrivalled means of restoring one's reputation.[38] In an era in which political factions were held together in no small part by personal ties, and reputation and influence were closely intertwined, few parliamentarians could resist a shot at violent redemption.

One politician who found a measure of political salvation on the field of honour was Lord George Germain. As commander of British troops in Germany in 1759, he had earned the sobriquet 'coward of Minden' for his reluctance to follow orders to attack in a battle. As an MP, eleven years later, Germain called for the Speaker to write to those MPs who were the eldest sons of peers requesting that they attend in their places to help carry bills to the Lords. At stake, he claimed, was the honour of the nation. This assertion prompted the contemptuous rejoinder from MP George Johnstone, who said it was strange his colleague was so interested in the honour of the nation when he hitherto had been so regardless of his own. Germain was wounded slightly in the ensuing duel, but his poise on the field, particularly in contrast to Johnstone's visible nervousness, was such that his reputation, allegedly, 'was instantly redeemed'.[39]

That appears something of an overstatement because, eight years later, Germain was involved in similar affair. On 26 May 1778, General John Burgoyne appeared in the Commons to defend his military record in America. Temple Luttrell compared the general to Germain, who, Luttrell asserted, had been promoted for disobedience and timidity. 'Lord George started up in a most violent rage, and, clapping his hand on his sword, said, though he was an old man, he would not hear such an insult from a young man, who was an assassin and of the most wretched character. This produced the highest warmth and clamour.' Luttrell left the House so that he would not be prevented from fighting but was forced to return upon order of the Commons. Eventually, after about two hours of confusion, during which Germain eventually apologised and called Luttrell his noble friend, a sentiment its target rejected with 'great indignation', the latter 'was forced to disclaim any further resentment'.[40]

Burgoyne's defeat at Saratoga nearly was connected to another parliamentary affair of honour a few months earlier. During heated debate on the military setback on 3 December 1777, Edmund Burke was heard to laugh while Solicitor-General Arthur Wedderburn was speaking. The two exchanged 'high words'. Burke left the Commons, evidently intent on sending a challenge. This seems to be the closest the influential political thinker ever came to a parliamentary duel. As it turned out, a letter from Wedderburn, combined with an explanation that he provided via Fox, ultimately dissuaded Burke from pursuing the matter.[41]

Affairs of honour could provide political dividends other than reputational redemption. Provoking a fight with a political opponent could be advantageous. If he rose to the challenge, he could be incapacitated in a duel. If he refused to fight, his reputation could be injured, even if he was not. Political motivations of this sort were suspected in Samuel Martin's successful effort to bait John Wilkes into sending a challenge in 1763. Sixteen years later, William Adam's rencontre with Charles James Fox was viewed in a similar light.

Adam recently had begun to support the North Administration, a move he lamely justified by claiming that the government's ministers were less incompetent than those who opposed them. Fox, the leading light of the Whig opposition, ridiculed this praise by faint damnation. His subsequent assurance to Adam, that 'he meant no personal invective', might have ended the matter, but Adam knew that the insult had become public, the newspapers having provided an account of Fox's speech. He therefore demanded that Fox provide a similar assurance in print. When the Whig declined to do so, a duel ensued in which Fox was wounded slightly.[42]

The encounter was most memorable for Fox's humour under fire. When advised to stand sideways to present the narrowest possible target, the portly MP replied, 'Why? I am as thick one way as the other.' That he could joke at a time like that was much to his credit. On the other hand, the duel did Adam's reputation little good. His rejection of Fox's private explanation and insistence on firing a second shot led to suspicions that, like Samuel Martin, he had sought to eliminate a prominent government critic. In any case, as a Scotsman, Adam was never going to get much sympathy from the English press.

The reaction was similar the following year, when the Earl of Shelburne fought a duel with another Scot, MP William Fullarton. After serving as private secretary to Viscount Stormont, Secretary of State for the Northern Department, Fullarton was gazetted lieutenant-colonel of a newly created regiment. Opposition politicians fiercely criticised the appointment of a man without military experience to such a post. In debate in the Lords, Shelburne referred disparagingly to Fullarton as a 'commis' or clerk, a slight that led to a challenge.[43] Although he was wounded in the groin, Shelburne 'achieved fleeting popularity, since the Scots were even more disliked than he was'.[44]

More generally, the incident prompted concern that parliamentary freedom of speech would suffer if political criticisms were taken as affronts meriting challenges. James Lowther told the Commons on 24 March 1780, 'If free debate were to be interpreted into personal attack, and questions of a public nature which came before either House were to be decided by the sword ... the members would do better to give up all ideas of Parliamentary discussion.' This warning seems to have prompted somewhat greater restraint in debate for a while but no concrete parliamentary action.[45]

In fact, Westminster seemed to be moving in the opposite direction. The Journals of both Houses mention, in the 1760s, four instances in which parliament stopped its business to prevent debate from escalating into duels. One such episode, in the 1770s, was the Germain-Luttrell incident.[46] There were two in the following decade. In 1780, the Lords intervened in a dispute between the Duke of Grafton and the Earl of Pomfret that culminated in the latter being sent to the Tower for sending a challenge.[47] The following year, the Commons ordered writer Theophilus Swift taken into custody for sending a challenge to Sir John Wrottesley, over the MP's conduct on a select committee.[48] The next Journal record of such an intervention does not come until 1813, suggesting a decreased appetite for parliamentary peacemaking.

To be sure, there were times when parliamentary intervention was not recorded in the Journals. On 22 February 1782, for example, Isaac Barre called Lord North the scourge of the country, adding that his conduct in the American War had been 'scandalous, indecent and insulting'. This caused the prime minister, for one of the few times in his life, to lose his temper. North's response that his colleague's language was 'not decent' and 'insolent and brutal' whipped the Commons into an uproar. Called to order by the presiding officer, North asserted that while he was ready to ask the pardon of the House, he would not do so of Barre. A duel looked a distinct possibility. However, 'at the end of a tumult of three hours, he consented to ask pardon even of Barre'.[49]

There also were instances in which the presiding officer was able to soothe ruffled feathers without formal House action. One such episode occurred in May 1788, when Sir James Johnstone, clearly inebriated, entered the Commons while a colleague was speaking and began complaining that someone had taken his place, which he had sought to save with his hat and card. After directing some offensive language at Lord Mornington, the presumed culprit, Johnstone refused to apologise, hinting that he would rather fight. This proved unnecessary, as the Speaker managed to calm Johnstone and end the matter.[50]

In other cases, violence was avoided, but not, apparently, due to parliamentary intervention. In 1790, ardent Whig John Sawbridge claimed in the Commons that the broker of Treasury Secretary George

Rose 'had been involved in malpractices, a charge he was forced publicly to withdraw at the threat of a duel'.[51] The following year, the Earl of Lauderdale criticised the Duke of Richmond in the Lords, for abandoning parliamentary reform. Richmond's angry reply prompted a challenge, although a duel was averted.[52]

Mostly, it was the duels parliament did not prevent that reveal the changing views of its Members. In mid-1792, Lauderdale told the Lords that Richmond was 'the greatest political apostate his Majesty had in his service since General [Benedict] Arnold had left it'. This prompted Arnold to demand an apology. When Lauderdale's response was not deemed sufficient, a challenge followed. On the field, Lauderdale treated his opponent with contempt, receiving his fire but refusing to shoot back, retract his offensive comment, or apologise.[53] Still, that a peer of the realm felt compelled to accept a challenge from a man whose name, in America at least, is synonymous with 'traitor' indicates just how indulgent contemporary notions of honour had become.

An even more shocking demonstration of changing parliamentary attitudes was displayed in early 1798. Faced with the threat of French invasion, Pitt called on 25 May for the Commons to approve, that same day, a measure that would suspend the exemption from naval service of men involved in maritime trades. Two years earlier, following the overwhelming defeat of a motion for parliamentary reform, many opposition MPs had seceded from the Commons as 'a public repudiation of the system of secret influence and repression'.[54] George Tierney, one of the few who remained, criticised Pitt's effort to rush the bill through as a threat to freedom. The prime minister responded that Tierney was seeking to obstruct the country's defence. Attributing this motivation to a Member's conduct was clearly unparliamentary. Speaker Henry Addington called upon Pitt to retract or explain his accusation, but the prime minister refused to do either. Instead, Pitt repeated the charge, which Addington did not compel him to withdraw. To nobody's great surprise, a challenge followed. Informed of this (by Pitt), the Speaker did nothing to prevent the two MPs from fighting. In fact, he did worse than nothing, effectively sanctioning the duel by accompanying his friend Pitt to Putney Heath, where the prime minister and one of his leading parliamentary opponents exchanged two shots, without effect.[55]

The encounter elicited public ridicule.[56] For a prime minister to pursue aggressively a potentially life-threatening affair of honour over a trivial matter, at a time when the nation he led faced an existential threat from the greatest military power of the age, seemed reckless, irresponsible or even insane.[57] Tellingly, however, the official responses were extremely mild. The king sent Pitt an admonitory note, reminding him that public officials needed to consider not only what they owed themselves but also what they owed their country.[58] Parliament's answer was even weaker, perhaps not surprising in view of the Speaker's actions and inactions. After the duel, William Wilberforce told the Commons that he was considering presenting a motion of censure. However, after discussions with 'friends', including Pitt himself, Wilberforce decided not to pursue the matter.[59] As often, the vices of the powerful were of less concern to the crusading evangelical than those of the less exalted.[60]

Irish Emulation

There was a similar surge in duelling across the Irish Sea, where there were over 300 recorded hostile encounters in the 1770s and 1780s.[61] This was partly a response to the example set by prominent figures in Albion – an irony given an English propensity to mock the Irish as inveterate duellists – but also consequence of domestic political developments.[62]

The Octennial Act of 1768 increased political competition by requiring that elections be held every eight years, rather than only upon the death of a monarch, as previously had been the case. This meant greater danger for not only candidates and their friends but also for parliamentarians drawn into bitter electoral disputes.

Many Irish MPs desperately sought to avoid appointment to select committees trying controverted elections, partly out of fear that they could face challenges as a result.[63] The Irish Commons was sufficiently concerned to resolve unanimously in 1778 that provoking, threatening or insulting someone over a petition presented to the House constituted a breach of parliamentary privilege, as did the accepting or sending of a challenge by a Member for the same reason. The Commons threatened to proceed, 'with the utmost severity', against anyone guilty of either of these offences.[64]

Elections hardly were the only danger. As lord lieutenants began to play a more active political role, at the expense of local parliamentary 'undertakers', Irish nationalism grew, particularly calls for greater self-rule. This made the dynamics of conflict in Dublin and Westminster different, in a way seldom acknowledged by English commentators: while many British MPs fought over relatively trivial matters, quite a few of their Irish counterparts took the field of honour over disagreements about the central question of the day, namely the relationship between Ireland and Britain.

The most famous Irish parliamentary confrontation was an obvious exception. Both Henry Grattan and Henry Flood had pushed for greater Irish parliamentary independence, which had been granted in 1782. But the former came to resent that his political star had been eclipsed by the latter's. So in October 1783, Grattan unleashed a bitter harangue against Flood, which a biographer described as 'one of the most deliberate exercises in political character assassination ever attempted in the Irish Parliament'.[65] Grattan summed up his charges most provocatively by directly addressing his target with the accusation, 'You are not an honest man.' Flood responded with some choice words of his own before expressing his willingness to meet Grattan 'anywhere, or on any ground by night or by day'. A duel appeared inevitable, but the men were arrested before they could fight. The Chief Justice bound each to an official recognisance of £2,000 to keep the peace. That the matter ended with a whimper rather than a bang surprised many, who had expected the men to cross the Irish Sea to effectuate their hostile encounter.[66] (The rivalry with Flood almost led to a duel between Grattan and another MP, Lawrence Parsons, six years later.[67])

Similarly, a 1787 duel between Lord Mountnorris and Francis Hely-Hutchinson seems to have been largely personal. The former's criticism of the latter's father in a Lords debate led to a fight in which 'the hat of one of the principals was twisted round by his opponent's ball, and the [other] received a shot which grazed one of his breast-buttons', although other accounts claim the peer was injured somewhat more seriously.[68]

Substantial policy matters were involved in a 1785 affair. During debate on a proposed commercial union between Britain and Ireland, Attorney General John Fitzgibbon had claimed that the Irish were easily angered but also easily appeased. Criticising the proposal Fitzgibbon had supported, John Philpot Curran told the Irish Commons that the Attorney General had formed his opinion of the Irish nation by examining his own character. Fitzgibbon responded with a challenge, resulting in a bloodless duel.[69]

Five years later, Curran found himself involved in a fight with another senior government official, Chief Secretary Robert Hobart. In early 1790, Curran told the Irish House of Commons that the government was so corrupt that a place could be found for 'every bad man'. Curran's anger at what he saw as the misrepresentation of his speeches and those of his allies in the newspaper reports of John Giffard, a man on the government payroll, was well known. Feeling slighted, Giffard shook his walking stick at Curran in a threatening manner, when the two met on the street. Curran then demanded that Hobart dismiss Giffard. When Hobart refused to do so, a challenge followed, as did a bloodless duel.[70]

More fireworks were expected in early 1792, when the Irish Commons debated a petition on easing Catholic disabilities. Solicitor-General John Tolor complained that the proposal had 'the countenance' of James Napper Tandy, a prominent Radical, adding 'it was rather odd they could not contrive to set a better face on the matter'. This was a deliberate and gratuitous insult to Tandy, who possessed a 'strikingly ugly physiognomy'. The Radical demanded an explanation, but Tolor refused to provide one, citing parliamentary privilege. The Solicitor-General acknowledged that the consequences of his response were likely to be 'very disagreeable', implying that he was ready to fight. Tandy's reputation never recovered from his refusal to send the expected challenge.[71]

John Beresford showed no such hesitancy, thereby precipitating a mid-1795 incident that epitomised the contemporary Irish political scene. As the new Lord Lieutenant, Earl Fitzwilliam had signalled his determination to improve conditions for Catholics by dismissing Beresford, First Commissioner of Revenue, and a staunch supporter of the Protestant Ascendancy. After Fitzwilliam's recall, two letters defending his actions in Ireland appeared in newspapers, albeit without the earl's explicit sanction. In one of these letters, he accused Beresford of 'imputed malversation'. Beresford responded with a challenge, but London magistrates managed to prevent violence between the two men, who were personifying reform and reaction.[72]

Fitzwilliam's recall dashed hopes of Catholic relief, leading to increased unrest and ultimately rebellion. As it became clear that the Protestant Ascendancy could not be maintained by force, plans were introduced for a Union with Great Britain, prompting one last spasm of violence by Members of the doomed Irish parliament.

On 18 February 1800, Chancellor of the Exchequer Isaac Corry accused Grattan of 'living in familiarity with rebels and being a conniver at this plan to overthrow the country'.[73] Grattan denied that he had supported the rebellion and implied that Corry was 'a ruffian, a jackanapes, and a coward'. Grattan added that, had Corry made his accusations outside the walls of the House, they would have been answered by 'a blow'. As soon as Grattan finished speaking, Corry left the chamber to write him a letter demanding satisfaction.[74] Grattan increased his public standing considerably by wounding Corry in the ensuing duel, but the political implications of the encounter were meant to be limited: the principals previously had agreed that if one was unable to vote on the Union, the other would abstain.[75]

Central to the government's effort to win approval of the Union Bill was clandestine fiscal munificence: Viscount Castlereagh, the Chief Secretary, offered compensation to the owners of Irish boroughs and bribes to Irish MPs and peers. This nearly precipitated another duel, after Robert Carew threatened to tell the Commons of the scheme. Castlereagh told the MP that he would deny the accusation 'point-blank'. Carew responded that this would force them 'to take a walk to the fifteen acres', that is to fight a duel. Later, however, Carew 'prudently withdrew his challenge on being warned that Castlereagh had been practicing his marksmanship for just such an eventuality'.[76]

The chief secretary may not have been alone. Those of similar political views reportedly had discussed creating a duelling club, the members of which would pledge to challenge MPs who spoke disrespectfully about either Unionist parliamentarians or the merger of Great Britain and Ireland.[77] Although it is not clear that such a club actually was created, that it was even discussed illustrates that at least some politicians considered parliamentary violence an acceptable tactic.

The passage of the Union Bill brought an end to the Irish parliament, but some feared the result would be more fighting in Westminster Palace. *The Times*, for example, sardonically described the extensive institutional changes ostensibly required to accommodate the pugnacious Irish.[78] This was a little rich, coming soon after a British prime minister exchanged shots with a political opponent over words spoken in debate.

7

REFORM OR REVOLUTION?

The first third of the nineteenth century saw three high-profile duels (involving a pair of erstwhile cabinet colleagues, a brace of dukes, and another sitting prime minister), but also signs suggesting a weakening of the code of honour. Yet the ebb of aristocratic violence provided scant comfort to parliamentarians, who faced a growing threat from an increasingly engaged populace. Repeatedly, this seemed to imply a choice between reform and revolution.

Parliamentary Duels

'Members of Parliament were, as a group, the most enthusiastic of duellists.'[1] This ardour helps account for there being no record, in the journals of either House, of efforts to prevent duels in the first decade of the nineteenth century. It also helps explain why Christopher Saville sought court action in 1802, after being challenged repeatedly by fellow MP George Johnstone.

The trouble began in a Commons committee, where Johnstone demanded satisfaction for the improper use of his name in a letter Seville wrote to constituents. In seeking legal remedy, Saville argued that he did not act 'from ill will or malice, but from apprehension of personal danger and bodily harm'.[2] This acknowledgement of fear was the exact opposite of what the code required.

It is unclear whether the committee chair was unaware of the challenges, or simply declined to interfere, but Saville's pusillanimous response seems at least partly due to his rather unusual situation. He sat for a venal borough (Hedon), so did not have to rely on his reputation as an electoral asset. Moreover, he previously had been convicted of perjury, sentenced to pillory and expelled from the Commons. Although he subsequently obtained a royal pardon and zealously pursued other sorts of restitution, Saville may have concluded that his reputation, if not exactly beyond redemption, was at least sufficiently tarnished to be not worth risking his life over.[3]

Parliamentary inaction was more conspicuous in February 1807. While discussing the ministry's finance plan with a colleague, James Brogden was struck by fellow MP Arthur Shakespeare, who reportedly exclaimed, 'You must not mind what Mr B[rogden] says, he is a damned villain.' Brogden subsequently accepted an apology from Shakespeare. However, Brogden's patron the Duke of Northumberland 'expressed surprise that the House had taken no notice of "a Member wishing to charge another with an offense against the independence of Parliament"'.[4]

Perhaps no episode better illustrates parliamentary passivity than that which produced a duel on 21 September 1809. As in the Pitt–Tierney affair a decade before, a policy dispute led to a fight involving leading politicians. Unlike the earlier encounter, however, the principals here were not only on the same side but actually cabinet colleagues. Moreover, while the consequences of the first duel were trivial, the ramifications of the second appear to have been much more significant.

By early 1809, after a number of military setbacks, Foreign Secretary George Canning had lost confidence in the ability of Viscount Castlereagh to carry out his duties as Secretary for War and the Colonies. In meetings with the prime minister, the Duke of Portland, Canning threatened to resign unless Castlereagh was transferred to another post. Although Portland agreed to replace Castlereagh, he did not consider it expedient to do so immediately. Canning's subsequent efforts either to resign or have Castlereagh dismissed were rebuffed. Eventually Castlereagh learned that Canning had 'deceived' him and demanded satisfaction. Although the country was in the middle of a war, there seems to have been no official effort to prevent the ensuing duel, in which Canning was wounded in the thigh and, despite never having fired a pistol, reportedly 'shot a button off the lapel of Castlereagh's coat'.[5]

Unlike most episodes of parliamentary violence, this one had important ramifications. Canning's reputation suffered even though, far from conniving at the deception of his colleague, he had opposed it. Resigning as minister before the duel, the able Canning would not return to the cabinet for seven years. (He became prime minister

in 1827.) By contrast, Castlereagh, seen as in over his head before
the duel, found afterwards that his sins had been at least partially
expiated. He became foreign minister in 1812, and in that capacity
three years later, helped shape the post-Napoleonic European order at
the Congress of Vienna.[6]

At the opposite end of the *gravitas* spectrum was an incident a
few months later. In February 1810, John 'Mad Jack' Fuller, clearly
inebriated, disturbed the Commons while it was in committee by
asking a number of absurd questions. When these were ignored, he
shouted, 'God d—n me Sir, I have as much right to be heard as any
man who is paid for filling the place he holds.' The Speaker, whom
Fuller subsequently characterised as 'the little insignificant fellow in
a wig', was summoned, ordering the MP into custody. The Knight of
the Shire for Sussex did not go quietly. It took the Serjeant-at-Arms
and four assistants to overpower and remove him from the chamber.
Shortly thereafter, Fuller, in the words of his official reprimand,
'forcibly broke from that restraint, and entered these walls with
clamour and outrage unparalleled'.[7]

Not long thereafter, Commons Journals report two interpositions,
suggesting a declining tolerance for another source of disorder.
In early 1813, notice having been taken 'that some words of heat
had passed in the debate' between General Montague Mathew and
William Fitzgerald, the Speaker, 'by direction of the House', required
both MPs to promise not to prosecute the matter further.[8] Two years
later, the Speaker intervened again to broker peace between MPs
Samuel Whitbread and Richard Hart Davis.[9]

Intervention of a different sort helped prevent bloodshed over Irish
policy. In early 1815, Dublin politician John D'Esterre sought to
intimidate Daniel O'Connell by sending a challenge to the advocate
of greater rights for Ireland's Catholic majority. In the ensuing duel,
O'Connell killed D'Esterre, becoming a Catholic hero in the process.[10]
He also became a target for a man whose support for Irish Protestants
had earned him the nickname 'Orange Peel'.

A few months later, Chief Secretary for Ireland Robert Peel delivered
a Commons speech in which he bolstered his criticisms of proposals
for Catholic emancipation with comments O'Connell had made
against similar previous bills. After some public posturing on both
sides, O'Connell goaded Peel into sending a challenge. O'Connell then
was arrested to keep the peace.[11] He tried to go to Belgium to fight,
only to be intercepted by government officials, who informed him that
he could be executed if he killed Peel in a duel. This allowed him to

end the matter with honour intact.[12] Yet, such was the rancour of the affair that the principals' seconds made their own plans to fight a duel, only to be similarly thwarted by the authorities.[13]

Leading politicians did not invariably feel compelled to fight: when Arthur Thistlewood sent Viscount Sidmouth a challenge in 1817, the home secretary responded by having the revolutionary imprisoned. Yet the tyranny of the code of honour remained hard to resist particularly when those of the bluest blood chose to fight.

One of the most aristocratic parliamentary affairs of honour took place in 1822. In April, the Duke of Bedford told a county meeting, held in Bedfordshire to discuss parliamentary reform, that the support of the Duke of Buckingham and Chandos and fellow 'Grenvillites' had been 'purchased' by the administration. There was considerable verisimilitude to this claim: owing to their shameless pursuit of sinecures and rotten boroughs, 'the Grenvillites were seen to represent Old Corruption at its worst'.[14] Buckingham responded with a challenge not only to defend his honour but also as 'a form of damage control, part of an effort to deter further attacks on himself and the Grenvillites'.[15] (That Bedford had fought a duel with Buckingham's father in 1806 probably also mattered.)[16]

The duel on 2 May was bloodless, but the reputations of both dukes suffered. Bedford's conduct was deemed particularly pusillanimous. Despite evidence that the Grenvillites had, in fact, been purchased, Bedford performed a 'delope' on the field by firing into the air. This was interpreted as an expression of contrition. He subsequently stated that he 'meant no personal offence to the Duke of Buckingham, nor to impute to him any bad or corrupt motives whatsoever'.[17] A more snivelling retreat was hard to imagine.

Encounters such as this dishonoured the code. This did not prevent Stanish O'Grady from fighting fellow MP James Grattan two months later 'in consequence of a political dispute'.[18] But the tide was turning.

The Commons Journals record two instances in which the House interrupted its business to mediate quarrels. One came days after the O'Grady duel, when the Speaker interceded to prevent James Abercromby from fighting two men who had published criticisms of the MP's Commons comments. Abercromby's willingness to seek combat over such a trivial matter apparently hurt his reputation.[19]

The second came almost a year later, when the Commons sought to prevent a duel involving George Canning. On 16 April 1823, the foreign secretary had rejected vehemently claims that his policy toward Spain constituted 'truckling to France'. The following evening,

Henry Brougham castigated Canning for compromising his principles in regard to Catholic emancipation in order to obtain a cabinet post, telling the Commons that the secretary had exhibited 'the most incredible specimen of monstrous truckling for the purpose of obtaining office that the whole history of political tergiversation could furnish'. Canning interrupted Brougham's philippic to claim that it was 'false', implying that his colleague was a liar. Brougham's friends prevented him from leaving the chamber to write a challenge. A motion was made to commit both MPs to the custody of the Sergeant-at-Arms in order to prevent a duel. However, after Brougham and Canning each explained his comments to the satisfaction of the other – with the former helpfully indicating that he had used the offensive words 'only in a parliamentary sense' – the matter was allowed to drop.[20]

Revolutionary Violence?

Parliament's increasing indisposition to see its Members fight may have been related to the growth of another, more threatening, sort of violence. In the 1790s, a combination of government repression and growing popular antipathy toward the sorts of policies associated with Revolutionary France pushed British Radicalism underground. Popular violence, at least that of the parliamentary variety, virtually disappeared. Almost a decade into the nineteenth century, it was reborn. As many of the ruling class feared, it was a renaissance that was to have profound implications for the British polity.

The year 1810 witnessed a parliamentary contretemps reminiscent of the Wilkes era. After the Commons sent Radical John Gale Jones to Newgate for printing a handbill criticising efforts to bar the public and the press from a parliamentary inquiry into a disastrous military campaign, Sir Francis Burdett wrote to his Westminster constituents deploring the move. On 6 April, not long after his letter was published, the Commons found Burdett guilty of breach of privilege and ordered him sent to the Tower. Burdett declared the Speaker's warrant illegal and barricaded himself in his Piccadilly house.

Supporters responded with violence directed at Burdett's parliamentary opponents. Sir Thomas Lethbridge, who first directed the attention of the Commons to Burdett's letter, received death threats, was followed by a mob as he left the House, had the windows of his town house broken and fled to the country.[21] The residence of Sir John Anstruther, who spoke in favour of ruling the letter a breach of privilege, suffered not only broken windows but also considerable damage to chandeliers and furniture. At the house of Charles Yorke, who started the controversy by trying to exclude 'strangers' from the Commons, the mob 'broke every pane of glass and some of the window frames and shutters'. Prime Minister Spencer Perceval's Downing Street residence suffered smashed windows and a thorough splattering of mud. Houses receiving similar treatment included those of the Earl of Chatham, the Duke of Montrose, Lord Westmoreland, Sir Robert Peel, Marquess Wellesley, William Wellesley Pole, Lord Dartmouth and Lord Castlereagh.[22] The last of these individuals almost was twice victimised: 'Lord Castlereagh, mingling incognito in the crowd attacking his own house, retired hastily when he was recognised and threatened with a ducking in St James's Square's fountain'.[23]

The ministry, fearing insurrection, brought thousands of troops and artillery into London to secure important locations. A large crowd gathered outside outside Burdett's house, which was protected by London and Middlesex sheriffs. Although he refused to support violent resistance, this seemed a distinct possibility. Instead, after the Serjeant-at-Arms climbed into his house through a window and arrested the MP, while he was listening to his fourteen-year-old son read the Magna Carta, Burdett quietly went to the Tower.[24] Soon thereafter, the troops trying to disperse the large crowd that had gathered outside Burdett's place of confinement killed two people. The government, apprehensive about the reaction should it seek Burdett's expulsion from parliament, opted instead to continue his confinement until the session ended.[25]

Insurrectionary fears grew the following year with the onset of Luddite machine wrecking in response not only to technological change but also to the government's efforts to cut off trade with Napoleonic France and its continental allies.[26] It was in this febrile atmosphere that Perceval was murdered on 11 May 1812 in the Commons lobby.

The man responsible for the only assassination of a British prime minister was John Bellingham, who held the government responsible for his extended imprisonment in Russia. There were serious doubts about Bellingham's sanity (and that of at least two others who attacked parliamentarians over the next dozen years).[27] But while the government sought to dismiss the killing as the work of a deranged gunman, there is at least circumstantial evidence that merchants in his native Liverpool conspired to support the impecunious Bellingham in London, in the hopes that his obsessive and unhinged pursuit of 'justice' might result in the removal of a politician whose economic policies were causing them substantial harm.[28]

They were not alone: the prime minister's policies were so widely associated with the country's economic distress that his killing was seen as an act of political deliverance. 'For a day the country was in turmoil. Popular elation was undisguised.' A crowd cheered Bellingham as he was taken from the Commons after gunning down the prime minister and cried out 'God bless him!' as the assassin was led to the scaffold. 'It was thought inopportune to give Perceval a public funeral. Sheer insurrectionary fury has rarely been more widespread in English history.'[29]

Three years later, another bout of economic illiberalism produced more fury. As prices fell with the end of the Napoleonic War, the government introduced a Corn Bill to help (politically influential) agricultural producers at the expense of consumers. During debate on the third reading of the legislation in early 1815, a large crowd congregated outside the Commons. Members seeking to enter were accosted and asked how they intended to vote. One MP complained to the Speaker that he had been 'grossly insulted by a mob', the members of which demanded his name and his promise to vote against the bill. The 'noble lord' refused to comply with either demand, instead 'with the greatest difficulty, and at the imminent hazard of his life, made his way into the House'.[30] The Speaker then called in troops to disperse the estimated 10,000 to 20,000 people gathered around parliament. Some of the demonstrators responded by attacking the houses of supporters of the bill, including Frederick Robinson, who had moved the measure in parliament, Lord Eldon, the Lord Chancellor, and the ever-unpopular Charles Yorke.[31]

The following day, 7 March, troops again dispersed a crowd outside Westminster Palace. And, as before, the houses of supporters of the bill were attacked. At Robinson's residence, a butler and three soldiers fired on those assembled, killing two. An effigy of Robinson was found hanging from a tree in Islington, with a note reading, 'This is the post of honour for those who support the corn laws.' The next day saw more mob violence directed at the offices of newspapers that supported the bill. The house of George Ponsonby, the (incompetent) leader of the opposition, was 'ransacked'. Foreign Secretary Castlereagh, who had supported the use of military force to protect parliament from intimidation, reportedly watched 'unruffled' as demonstrators smashed the windows of his residence.[32] But neither the violence nor more peaceful demonstrations of opposition – including a petition signed by more than 42,000 people – prevented the bill's passage.[33]

Five years later, the death of George III precipitated another spasm of parliamentary violence. It was a measure of the antipathy toward both the administration and the prince regent that his scandal-plagued, estranged wife, Caroline of Brunswick, became something of a popular heroine.

Caroline returned to England, after many years abroad, on 5 June 1820, after rejecting a ministry offer of a large pension to stay away. In Dover, and London, which she reached the following day, Caroline was greeted by cheering crowds. Passers-by were forced to show their support. At least two senior politicians found themselves in awkward situations as a result. Viscount Sidmouth, the home secretary, 'was unable to get into his own house for a hostile mob'. The Duke of Wellington had the windows of his coach broken before a gang of workers armed with pickaxes demanded he declare his support for Caroline. In response, Wellington declared, 'Well, gentlemen, since you will have it so, God save the Queen – and may all your wives be like her.'[34]

The government subsequently introduced legislation intended to dissolve the marriage and deprive Caroline of her royal title on the basis of infidelity. (Caroline privately conceded that she had committed adultery, but only with 'Mrs. Fitzherbert's husband'; the prince regent, hardly a paragon of marital virtue, had illegally married Catholic widow Maria Ann Fitzherbert a decade before wedding Caroline.) This shabby treatment stirred popular anger. The Lords soon were flooded with petitions and addresses critical of the bill. Deputations poured into Westminster for the second reading of the bill on 17 August. 'So alarmed was the Government, that the artillery were moved up from Woolwich. Two regiments of Life Guards were posed in Palace Yard and another in Westminster Hall, where a train of field-pieces was also stationed.'[35]

Sidmouth and Castlereagh, the foreign secretary, seem to have been the main targets of popular ire. They reportedly 'never appeared in the streets without being hooted and reviled by the mob, and both daily received anonymous letters threatening them with instant death if the bill against her Majesty were not abandoned'. Unfazed, the two aristocrats walked the streets without attendants for protection. In response, 'the people, admiring their spirit, abstained from actual violence'; at least most of the time. On one occasion the pair were surrounded by a 'large mob' and were 'violently hooted'.[36]

The measure narrowly passed the Lords, but its future seemed bleak. 'The prospect of fighting the Bill through the Commons raised not only the spectre of defeat, but also widespread civil commotion in which it was feared that Caroline would be backed by the forces of London radicalism and by the mob.'[37] The government dropped the bill, prompting widespread celebrations and some violence for a peer who had supported it: passing through Watford, the Earl of Bridgewater was 'pelted with animal entrails'.[38]

The Queen Caroline affair was a milestone in at least two respects. First, it was notable less for how much violence it evoked than for how little. 'One of the features which most impressed contemporary opinion was the orderly nature of the demonstrations in support of the Queen and the powers of organisation which they seemed to indicate among the radicals and trade groups.'[39] As the government's willingness and ability to repress had grown, so too had the danger to those involved in public violence.[40] Partly as a result, but also because other 'repertoires of contention' were better suited to middle-class mores, the nature of popular protest was shifting, with spontaneous, violent gatherings giving way to planned, orderly public meetings.[41] Petitions to parliament, often endorsed at such conclaves, exploded as a consequence, from 880 between 1785 and 1789 to 70,369 between 1837 and 1841.[42]

Second, the affair 'helped to discredit the Government as an increasingly self-conscious middle class began to demand greater representation'.[43] The stark demonstration that ministers were out of touch with (respectable) popular opinion added fuel to long-standing demands for parliamentary reform. In the next dozen years, the continued frustration of these demands would test evolving commitments to peaceful protest.

Catholic Emancipation

This happened first in Ireland. After largely ignoring the issue of Catholic emancipation in the two decades that followed the Union, Westminster found this approach increasingly difficult to maintain in the 1820s. Efforts by the (pro-emancipation) lord lieutenant to reduce sectarian tensions incensed Irish Protestants. In late 1822, while attending a theatrical performance, the lord lieutenant was hissed 'and two missiles, a quart bottle and part of a watchman's rattle, were thrown at the viceregal box'. His subsequent unwarranted claim that he was the target of attempted murder, and the government's heavy-handed response to the 'bottle riot', further fuelled Protestant reaction.[44]

The minority's intransigence, in turn, fostered increased assertiveness by the majority, in particular the 1823 formation of the

Catholic Association. By making mass membership affordable, Daniel O'Connell forged a national organisation that proved instrumental in defeating some opponents of emancipation in the 1826 general election.[45] More importantly, two years later, at a by-election for County Clare, it delivered victory to O'Connell, thereby presenting the Duke of Wellington's administration with a dilemma: reform or revolution. That is, either to change the law to allow O'Connell and other Catholics to sit in parliament, or to see the Association mobilise, engulfing Ireland in insurrectionary violence.[46]

The government chose reform: Catholic Emancipation received royal assent in April 1829. Yet, so vehement were the opponents of the change that all three principal actors in the drama found themselves embroiled in parliamentary violence.

Home Secretary Robert Peel had come to believe that reform was necessary but realised that his conversion to this view might displease his University of Oxford constituents. He resigned, hoping to win a new mandate, but instead was defeated. This was unfortunate, for without Peel the government would be hard pressed to push Emancipation through the Commons. He quickly found a seat for the corrupt borough of Westbury, but not before residents, angry at having no-longer-Orange Peel foisted upon them, bombarded the hustings with missiles.[47]

A similar Damascene conversion by Wellington himself brought the prime minister into a confrontation with the Earl of Winchelsea, an ardent Protestant. Upon learning that the duke had decided to support Catholic Emancipation after strongly opposing it in the past, Winchelsea wrote to the secretary of the committee for establishing King's College, London (KCL), asking to withdraw his support for the institution. Explaining that he had been persuaded to support KCL due to its patronage by Wellington, the earl asserted that the prime minister's support for Catholic Emancipation suggested that the duke's 'outward show of zeal of the Protestant religion', as evinced by patronage of KCL, was meant to cloak 'his insidious designs for the infringements of our liberties, and the introduction of Popery into every department of the State'. Winchelsea authorised the publication of this letter, leading Wellington to demand a public retraction of the claim that the duke's motives in supporting KCL were anything but honourable. When the earl refused to provide one, Wellington demanded 'the satisfaction for your conduct which a gentleman has a right to require'.[48]

In hindsight, at least, it is unsurprising that the ensuing duel, fought on 21 March 1829, was bloodless. Lord Falmouth, Winchelsea's second, had agreed to serve in that capacity only on the condition that the earl not fire at the nation's hero. Winchelsea could agree to this condition because, as the challenged party, he was only honour-bound to receive his opponent's fire. He acknowledged that he was in the wrong, but to apologise before an exchange of shots could prompt accusations that his contrition was due to cowardice. By the same token, Wellington had little reason to try to injure Winchelsea. On the contrary, to do so could entail substantial legal difficulties for the leader of the administration. So, once he saw that the earl was not going to fire at him, he followed suit.[49]

Supporters of duelling, who saw the code of honour as a necessary means for curbing incivility, were encouraged by the encounter. *The Times* portrayed the affair as a salutary example, asserting that 'nothing could be more convenient to the fanatics than a licence to revile, and calumniate, and destroy men's reputations with impunity; and it is clear that their choler rises at the untimely check which has been given to this very wholesome privilege'.[50] Yet many mocked the affair, first because it seemed that the prime minister had risked his life over a trivial matter, and then because it became clear that neither he nor his adversary had ever been in real danger.

That Wellington felt compelled to take the field at all is rather remarkable. The courage of the man who defeated Napoleon at Waterloo certainly was beyond question. He presumably could have ignored Winchelsea's provocation without damage to his reputation. All the more so, given that the only other prime minister who fought a duel while in office was castigated by the monarch for a failure to put public duty ahead of private obligations. As a military man, however, Wellington felt he had no choice but to send a challenge, an assessment with which George IV reportedly concurred.[51]

O'Connell felt less compunction to fight. The man, who became known as 'The Liberator' for his role in bringing about Catholic Emancipation, was not an immediate beneficiary of the legislation. His refusal to take the Oath of Supremacy had prevented him from assuming his seat following his election in 1828. The passage of Catholic relief meant the Oath no longer was required, but this provision was not retroactive. Consequently, O'Connell's County Clare seat was declared vacant.

In the ensuing by-election O'Connell was returned unopposed, but not before initiating legal proceedings against a prospective candidate, Talbot Glascock, an Orangeman whom The Liberator suspected of planning a physical attack.[52] And not before William Smith O'Brien's claim in the Commons that O'Connell had no support among the gentlemen of County Clare led to a duel between the former and one of the latter's supporters, and almost another involving his opponent's second, the O'Gorman Mahon, an MP.[53]

Parliamentary Reform: Round One

The passage of Catholic Emancipation was an important precedent, demonstrating that the political system was not immutable. There long had been calls for parliamentary reform.[54] The deficiencies of the system certainly were glaring: some notorious 'rotten boroughs' like Old Sarum, where the only residents were 'twenty-seven rabbits and a badger', returned two MPs.[55] Yet four of the seven largest English towns chose none at all.[56] Parliament's decision to restore political rights to Catholics, a move widely opposed outside of Ireland, only seemed to reinforce claims that the country was poorly represented.

Emancipation also was a model for some reformers, who hoped to emulate O'Connell's Catholic Association in employing peaceful popular mobilisation to force the government to adopt change.[57] Radicals like James Mill, by contrast, adopted a different tactic, deploying a 'language of menace' to try to convince those in power that the populace would respond to a failure to reform with revolution.[58] This was in some ways a tough sell: parliament received only around 2,700 petitions on reform between 1830 and early 1832, compared with roughly 20,000 on Catholic Emancipation, suggesting a rather limited public commitment.[59] On the other hand, a surge in parliamentary violence, almost all of it directed at opponents of reform, made radical warnings of insurrection harder to dismiss.

Parliamentary reform was a prominent issue in the tumultuous 1830 general election, triggered by the death of King George IV. A number of reform opponents lost their seats in larger constituencies, where public opinion was most influential.[60] Although reformers failed to capture a Commons majority, their supporters made their demands clear by attacking a coach mistakenly thought to be carrying Prime Minister Wellington, a staunch conservative, when parliament opened on 2 November. Undeterred, later that day, while Henry Brougham was telling the Commons of his intention to introduce a reform bill within two weeks, the Iron Duke informed the Lords that because he believed that parliament 'answered all the good purposes of legislation', he would resist any efforts to change it.

These remarks proved extremely unpopular. On 8 November, 'government opponents stoned Wellington in Downing Street', while in Carlisle, effigies of the prime minister and home secretary Peel were burned. The government was sufficiently concerned about public disorder to surround the capital with 7,000 troops, while sending 2,000 members of Peel's new police force to Westminster. Wellington stationed armed men at strategic windows in Apsley House, his personal residence overlooking Hyde Park, ordering them not to fire unless the gates were breached or intruders entered the garden from over the fence.[61] Amid threats of assassinations and riots, and warnings from London authorities that they would be unable to maintain order, Wellington felt compelled to advise the king and queen to forgo their traditional attendance at a dinner on Lord Mayor's Day, 9 November, prompting cancellation of the event.[62]

The duke resigned shortly thereafter. Earl Grey replaced him, pledging to bring about parliamentary reform. This proved easier said than done. After the Commons diluted a reform bill supported by the government, Grey sought an election to discern the popular will. The new monarch, William IV, was reluctant to accede to this request but, goaded by Tory assertions that he did not have a prerogative right to dissolve parliament against the wishes of a majority in both houses, eventually consented to go to Westminster Palace to perform the deed in person.[63]

The king's arrival on 22 April was so unexpected that some peers were not wearing the robes required for such a ceremonial occasion. As the sound of cannons indicated that the sovereign was en route to the Lords, violent disorder threatened to break out. According to Hansard, it was 'impossible to describe the confusion, the noise, and impetuosity that prevailed from one end of the House to another .... Some peers were, as it appeared in the confusion, almost scuffling, and as if shaking their hands at each other in anger'.[64] Although most of the tumult died as soon as the king entered the chamber, Charles Vane, 3rd Marquess of Londonderry, an inveterate opponent of change, had 'to be forcibly restrained in his place in the Lords from interrupting William IV's dissolution'.[65]

This unruly and undignified behaviour by some peers of the realm was a profound shock. As *The Times* lamented, 'The violent tones and gestures of noble lords – the excitement, breaking down the conventional usages, not to say civilities of life, astonished the spectators, and affected the few ladies who were present with visible alarm.'[66] If controversy over reform prompted such a display from the Crown's most cultivated and privileged subjects, many presumably shuddered at the thought of a general election animated by the issue.

Events shortly before polling was to begin suggested that such concerns were more than warranted. On 27 April, crowds smashed the windows of the residences of prominent opponents of reform including Wellington, the Bishop of London and the Duke of Newcastle. The latter was not only a staunch enemy of reform but had further transgressed against popular feeling by seeking to evict tenants who had dared resist his demand that they vote as he instructed. When criticised for this, he infamously responded, 'It is presumed then that I am not to do as I will with mine own?'; a comment that epitomised the attitude reform was meant to rectify.[67]

Parliamentary Reform: Round Two

The 1831 general election brought violence to many candidates opposed to reform and a Commons majority to Whigs who supported it. If the people had spoken, it soon became clear that not everyone was listening. The Lords defeated Grey's second reform bill on 7 October. This proved the catalyst for a spate of parliamentary violence that was far more serious than the minor outbreak that had followed the defeat of its predecessor. It soon became clear that 'whatever the Lords had intended to do, their massive rejection of the Bill had brought about a crisis which not only scaremongers and the professionally pessimistic saw as leading rapidly towards revolution'.[68]

A hooting crowd met parliamentarians as they departed Westminster Palace following the Lords' decision. Some demonstrators tried to grab the reins of the horse carrying Lord Dudley Stuart, an Ultra-Tory, but the 'spirited steed' leapt away. The despised, anti-reform Duke of Cumberland 'was pelted with mud which totally covered his body', dragged from his horse and might have suffered great harm had the police not rescued him. The Marquess of Londonderry, another foe of reform, was struck on the arm, and an attempt was made to drag him from his cabriolet, which was foiled when the driver urged on the horses. After this close call, Londonderry resolved to carry arms for his protection. Sir William Horne and Thomas Denman were hooted and pelted; only later did the MPs realise, to their amusement, that their assailants had mistaken them for (anti-reform) bishops.

On 12 October, Radicals in London organised a procession to present the king with an address in support of reform. The Home Office made it clear to the organisers that the monarch would not receive the document, but they carried on regardless, marching past the palace in a show of strength. In the wake of the procession, a large crowd broke many windows at Apsley House before being dispersed by police. The residences of Newcastle, the Marquess of Bristol, Lord Londonderry and Lord Dudley Stuart received similar unwelcome attention. A mob in front of the house of the Home Secretary, Lord Melbourne, was dispersed before any damage could be done.[69]

Outside London there were similar incidents. At Darlington, a carriage in which Lord Tankerville was traveling with his daughter and son-in-law was bombarded with projectiles.[70] On 10 October, a crowd attacked and burned down Nottingham Castle (though unoccupied and largely unfurnished). This prompted its owner, Newcastle, to race to Clumber to fortify his Nottinghamshire family seat in expectation of a mob assault.[71]

Such was the anger in the West Country that Lord Ashley and his wife 'had to choose "an unlikely route" to their house at St Giles, Wimbourne and a secret one to get away'. The Tory MP, a staunch opponent of reform, also kept a pair of pistols handy, something he felt it imprudent to reveal to his new bride. His apprehension was well founded for on 19 October a mob in Sherborne smashed the windows of houses of those who had supported Ashley in a recent Dorset by-election. The angry crowd proceeded to Sherborne Castle, home of the anti-reform Lord Digby, breaking its windows and seeking to force open the great gates.[72]

Such scenes were enough to make a landed gentleman blanch. With the police in its infancy and the military lacking sufficient manpower to protect all the country's isolated estates, vulnerable landowners took steps to safeguard themselves. Sir Robert Peel, whose Drayton Manor was particularly exposed, 'imported carbines and announced that he intended to defend his home as long as he could'. The Tory Duke of Rutland took even more extensive precautions. In January, he had purchased staves with which to arm special constables. Later, the watchmen at Belvoir Castle were provided with flints and gunpowder. Yet, the duke's strongest statement of intent was the deployment of cannons and a 'long gun' on the castle's North East Terrace, which was specially paved in preparation.[73]

Fighting back was less of an option for bishops, twenty-one of twenty-three had voted against reform in the Lords. 'One prelate had the words "Bishop of Worcester Judas Iscariot" scrawled on his cathedral walls; other bishops were said to be confined to their episcopal palaces for fear of outrages.' When the Bishop of Bath and Wells arrived in Bedminster to consecrate a church on 24 October, he 'was greeted outside the building by a noisy group with "marked disapprobation" and, after the service, treated with some earthy epithets and pelted with mud and a few stones as his carriage bore him away'. And, on 5 November, a number of bishops were burned in effigy, a rather ironic twist to a ceremony traditionally reserved on that day for their religious rivals.[74]

There also were disturbances elsewhere, such as reform-related rioting in Derby, but the most serious violence occurred in Bristol. There, as in other parts of the country, economic hardship fuelled popular anger at the defeat of the reform bill. However, the spark that started the blaze was the arrival in Bristol on 29 October of Sir Charles Wetherell, who, as the city's Recorder, was to preside over the assizes. He came despite warnings that his presence could beget violence.

Wetherell had not just opposed the Reform Bill, as might have been expected of the person representing Boroughbridge, where almost all the forty-eight electors were Newcastle's tenants. His obstruction of the measure in the Commons was so successful that on one occasion he managed to force eight divisions and keep the House sitting until half past seven in the morning.[75] Even worse, he had told the Commons repeatedly that Bristol was indifferent to reform.

Wetherell's ceremonial procession into the city therefore presented Bristolians with an opportunity to impress upon him their sentiments regarding parliamentary change. Initially the Ultra-Tory was greeted with nothing more than groans and hisses; then it became ugly. 'At Temple Street, his carriage was showered with stones and rotten eggs; the unfortunate Wetherell was "screwed up in one corner" with an air of complete terror on his face. At the Bristol Bridge, large stones were flung; one policeman was struck and fell to the ground, apparently dead.' Not long after the MP arrived at Mansion House, a large crowd surrounded and then proceeded to sack and burn the building. Wetherell 'only escaped, like some Mozartian character, by dressing as a postillion and fleeing over the roof'.[76]

He was smuggled out of the city quickly, in a bid to end the disturbances, but rioting continued for three days. Although the provocative parliamentarian escaped serious injury, others were not so lucky; by the time troops restored order, at least a hundred were dead or wounded. The property damage was equally severe: rioters burned down three gaols, the Mansion House, the Bishop's Palace, the Excise Office, the Custom House and four tollgate houses. Nearly fifty private houses, warehouses and offices were destroyed or seriously damaged.[77]

These tumultuous events, which many feared were portentous of the sort of revolutionary upheaval that repeatedly had consumed France, most recently in July 1830, cast a shadow upon the third Reform Bill, introduced in December 1831. Although passions ran high, debate in parliament produced little violence. Perhaps tellingly, in the one incident of interest, it was an opponent rather than a supporter of reform who resorted to an *argumentum ad baculum*.

In preparation for debate upon the Reform Bill in the Commons, Lord Ebrington, a prominent supporter, claimed that the delay in considering it had caused great discontent 'out of doors'. Sir Henry Hardinge, a leading opponent of reform, responded that supporters of the bill were being dictated to by the mob, and that Ebrington was the 'organ' of sections of London. Ebrington then stood to 'repel with indignation' Hardinge's claim, to which the latter replied, 'if he [Ebrington] repels what I may address to him, I am ready to meet him in any way and any place he pleases'.[78] Ebrington declined to accept the invitation from the man who had served as Wellington's second in his duel with Winchelsea three years earlier.

Hardinge's apparent attempt to provoke a duel elicited critical commentary. An editorial in *The Times* a few days later claimed that the scene in the Commons had 'excited the disgust of every person who knows what is due from an individual to the deliberative assembly of which he forms part'. Hardinge's demeanour was said to resemble the fire-eaters of the Old Irish parliament, men the government brought forward to put down 'any independent representative of the people, whose propositions, while speaking the language of his constituents, admitted of no answer but from the pistol's mouth'.[79]

This was not the only close call connected with the third bill. Although it quickly passed the Commons, its reception in the Lords was expected to be considerably more hostile. By March 1832, the government was split between those who wanted to put pressure on the king to promise to create enough peers to overcome any resistance in the Lords and those who recoiled from this constitutionally suspect prospect. For Lord Althorp, the tension was almost too much to bear; 'there was a troubling incident when he was found locking away his pistols for fear of having too easy access to them in a moment of madness'. The leader of the Commons confessed to a friend that he was worried he might be tempted to shoot himself to 'make matters easier'.[80]

In May, the legislation was greatly weakened by a Lords' amendment. When the king refused to fulfil a promise to create sufficient pro-reform peers to ensure passage in the Lords, Grey resigned. This triggered an angry, popular mobilisation that seemed to auger further disorder, perhaps even revolution. Although there was no violence on the scale of that which earlier was visited upon Bristol, the Reverend Sydney Smith later recalled the period as marked by a 'hand-shaking, bowel-disturbing passion of fear'.[81] In this atmosphere, the king expected Wellington to support at least minimal reform but, while the duke was ever ready to do his duty, he could not persuade enough of his Tory colleagues to cobble together a cabinet. This forced the king to recall Grey and agree to create a flood of new peers. Faced with this threat, the Lords backed down; the Reform Bill received the royal assent in June.

This did not prevent a few violent indications of lingering bitterness at the stubborn resistance to change. Popular sentiment toward King William, earlier cheered as 'Reform Bill', took a decided turn for the worse. At Ascot, a stone was thrown at the sovereign: 'he was only saved from actual physical harm by the padding in his hat'. On 18 June, Wellington was hissed, 'pelted with every description of missile', pursued by a mob through the streets of London, forced to take refuge in the residence of fellow reform-foe Sir Charles Wetherell, and then compelled to seek a police escort to return home. 'A strange day to choose,' observed the Iron Duke drily – for it was of course the anniversary of the Battle of Waterloo.[82]

8

THE LULL

The Great Reform of 1832 deserves its adjective not just because, by making the parliamentary system a bit more representative, it showed that peaceful institutional change was possible, but also because seats in Westminster became much less dangerous in the half-century that followed. Duels disappeared as the aristocratic code became increasingly at odds with democratisation. So, too, did the threat that Members would be arrested for unauthorised absence from parliament. And even those perils that remained generally diminished.

Parliamentary Duelling's Demise

It has been claimed that 'political duels virtually disappeared' in the 1820s and 1830s.[1] This certainly was not true of affairs of honour arising out of elections. It is an even less accurate description of duels arising from parliamentary activities. These were fairly scarce in the 1820s, although Wellington's sensational encounter with Winchelsea made up in quality what the decade lacked in quantity. The 1830s were even more violent, though this would prove to be the storm before the calm.

House Journals record five instances in which parliament interrupted it business to mediate quarrels in the 1830s (compared to two in the 1820s). In one of these, the Lords intervened in two disputes arising from committee testimony, neither of which involved peers.[2] Similar parliamentary efforts to prevent outsiders (solicitors even!) from fighting, seldom had been recorded since the 1640s, suggesting that critics of the code were gaining ground.

This notion was reinforced by the robust response to a parliamentary quarrel in early 1834. Irish MPs rejected with indignation assertions that some of their number privately had told the government they were glad the Coercion Act had passed even though they publicly had strongly opposed its renewal. One of them, Richard Sheil, pointedly asked whether he was among those who allegedly had expressed pleasure in the Act's passage. When the Chancellor, Lord Althorp, replied in the affirmative, Sheil denied this with such passion that it was feared a duel would take place. The Speaker called upon both MPs to provide assurances that they 'would not prosecute the matter without the walls of the House'. After Sheil declined to give such a pledge, and Althorp providing one that was unsatisfactory, both were taken into custody by the Serjeant-at-Arms, only to be released later after promising not to fight.[3]

The Commons evinced similar resolve two years later after 'a misunderstanding of a personal nature' arose in a committee meeting. Ordered to take his place in the Commons, Sir Frederick Trench assured the House 'that he would not be a party to any hostile proceedings' stemming from his dispute with colleague Rigby Wason. However, the following day the Speaker informed the House that Trench 'considered that he had only given an assurance not to send or accept any challenge within this Kingdom, and that he was not prevented from accepting a challenge sent to him from abroad'. When the Speaker asked Trench to pledge that he would not accept a challenge under any circumstances, he declined to do so. Both he and Wason were taken into custody of the Serjeant-at-Arms. They were released three days later after providing an explanation that satisfied the House that 'no hostile proceedings would take place'.[4]

A few days later, offence was taken at something said in another committee, prompting the House to order that the MPs involved take their places. However, after Colonel Charles Sibthorp assured the House that, following communications with Sir John Hobhouse, he was satisfied that he had meant 'nothing personally offensive' in the Committee, the order for the latter to attend was rescinded.[5]

In April 1837, the Commons once more interrupted its usual proceedings to intervene in a quarrel between MPs. After a newspaper attributed to Sir James Graham 'certain words' about Sir Edward Codrington, the latter called on him to state whether he had used the language in question. Graham declined to make such a statement, which he felt would be contrary to the freedom of debate and parliamentary privilege. After Codrington 'intimated an intention of taking notice of the words out of the House', the Speaker asked him to promise that he would not do so. When Codrington declined to provide such an assurance, a motion was made that he be taken into custody. However, after Graham stated that he 'had not made use of the words attributed to him', the motion was withdrawn.[6]

Despite such efforts, parliament did not always manage to prevent its Members from fighting duels in the decade that followed reform. Many of those involved were Irish, who generated animosity not only for the aim they pursued (repeal of the Union) but especially for the means they employed: violating norms of parliamentary behaviour to cause delays that, occasionally, forced government concessions.[7]

Edward Ruthven, who sat as MP for Dublin City with O'Connell, became notorious in the 1834 parliamentary session for use of obstructive motions. This prompted other MPs to try to prevent him from being heard by loudly coughing and yawning. Eventually Ruthven sought a remedy for this behaviour outside the House, in the form of a duel with Louis Perrin, an Irish opponent of repeal.[8] The encounter apparently contributed to another affair of honour, with Arthur Perrin, the Lord Mayor of Dublin, while Ruthven was running for re-election in 1835.[9]

Given the criticism directed at the Irish for their supposed propensity for duelling, it is ironic that even greater obloquy was aimed at O'Connell for refusing to take the field. After killing his opponent in a duel in 1815, O'Connell made a 'promise to Heaven' to fight no more. That was not objectionable per se. However, advocates of the code argued that the threat of a duel was necessary to curb the excesses to which man's natural passions might lead. A man able to keep his passions in check had no need to fight. O'Connell, however, was not such a man. His refusal both to fight and to curb his vitriolic tongue was thus, in some eyes, the worst of both worlds. As *The Times* complained, 'O'Connell is the first man who has been permitted to emancipate himself from the restraints and penalties of those social laws whose authority has been universally acknowledged as indispensable to the preservation of social harmony and decorum.'[10]

This particular emancipation by The Liberator led those who wanted to hold him to account to seek to do so by other means. In April 1835, Baron Alvanley claimed in the Lords that the Melbourne administration had 'purchased' O'Connell, who had begun supporting the Whigs after bitterly criticising them in the past.[11] O'Connell responded by calling the corpulent Alvanley a 'bloated buffoon'. These were fighting words, but it soon became clear that O'Connell was not willing to accept the peer's challenge. Alvanley did the next best thing by having O'Connell expelled from Brooks's, the Whig club.[12]

The Times portrayed Alvanley's effort as a brave attempt to 'recall Mr. O'Connell to decency'. O'Connell's son, Morgan O'Connell, saw it as a cowardly action by a man who knew his adversary had sworn off duelling. The MP for Meath accordingly accepted Alvanley's challenge on behalf of his father. The two men then fought a bloodless, if rather controversial, duel on 4 May.[13]

The following day, encouraged by the precedent and smarting from his recent electoral defeat for Taunton, Benjamin Disraeli wrote to Morgan O'Connell requesting he again take up the 'vicarious duties of yielding satisfaction for the insults which your father has so long lavished with impunity upon his political opponents'. However, the younger O'Connell declined to fight on behalf of his father with a man he did not know for affronts that were not clearly specified.[14] Even the most stalwart defenders of the code could hardly countenance such an impersonal defence of honour; moxie by proxy did not suit a gentleman.

Daniel O'Connell's sharp tongue almost prompted another affair of honour, and an international incident, a few years later. The hard-won Emancipation Act of 1833 had not, as supporters hoped, led to freedom for slaves in the West Indies. Instead, many were consigned to further bondage as apprentices. By 1838, abolitionist sentiment in England had risen to a level not seen for four years. News that the planters would soon free their apprentices led to plans for a celebration by anti-slavery campaigners. Daniel O'Connell was invited to address the Birmingham meeting.

Pointing to the persistence of slavery in the United States, O'Connell denounced Andrew Stevenson, the American Ambassador to Britain, as 'a slave-breeder ... who trafficks in blood, and who is a disgrace to human nature'. This led Stevenson to send O'Connell a letter requesting that the MP confirm or deny whether he had used a particular phrase in regard to the ambassador. O'Connell denied using the exact phrase Stevenson inquired about, and the latter did not pursue the matter with a challenge. However, Stevenson's letter was enough to prompt former US President John Quincy Adams, a strident opponent of duelling, to call for the ambassador's impeachment on the floor of the House of Representatives.[15]

It is perhaps unsurprising that the anti-slavery campaign did not produce many duels: those who advocated the equality of man were not likely to be enthusiastic for the aristocratic code of honour. In hindsight, it is perhaps less obvious that the accession of a monarch whose reign would become synonymous with sobriety and self-control would elicit a final flurry of parliamentary duels. In the long term, Victorian attitudes effectively put a wet blanket on the embers of the code of honour. More immediately, however, the accession of a young queen was a red flag to a number of chivalrous bulls. Given that such a sovereign could not possibly be expected to defend her own honour, some parliamentary gallants felt compelled to take the lists on her behalf.

The first such episode came in June 1839. After MP Henry Grattan (junior) reportedly claimed that the queen's life would not be safe if the Tories came to power, the Marquess of Londonderry told the Lord's the assertion was 'base and infamous'. Grattan responded by seeking assurances from the peer that the adjectives had not been meant to apply to the MP personally. When these were not forthcoming, he sent a challenge that led to a bloodless duel.[16]

Londonderry's decision to fight received a rebuff from the increasingly emboldened critics of the code. Thirty-one members of the clergy, from the North Yorkshire towns of Ripon and Thirsk, affixed their names to a letter deploring that someone of his high station would give sanction to a practice that 'so grievously violates the law of God and the spirit of Christianity'.[17] While claiming to be flattered by the 'exordium' of the clergy, Londonderry responded that, as a soldier, he was bound to defend his honour.[18]

A few months later Radical James Bradshaw made some remarks to constituents in Canterbury which fellow MP Edward Horsman deemed insulting to the Queen. Perceiving that she was unable to respond to this affront with the challenge it deserved, Horsman took it upon himself to defend her honour. In a speech to his own constituents in Cockermouth, Horsman claimed that Bradshaw, who also was suspected of Chartist sympathies, had 'the tongue of a traitor, but lacks the courage to become a rebel'. This prompted a challenge that led to a bloodless duel in January 1840.[19]

The first of numerous attempts to assassinate Victoria came almost exactly a year after the duel between Londonderry and Grattan. Presumably this did nothing to allay the protective impulses of the defenders of her honour. Craven Fitzhardinge Berkeley certainly sought to demonstrate he was misnamed by demanding that fellow MP Captain Henry Boldero retract some comments deemed disrespectful to the sovereign. The result was a bloodless duel on 15 July 1842.[20]

Death by Ridicule

This was the last non-electoral British parliamentary duel actually fought. Given that the code of honour held sway for almost three centuries, endangering the lives of hundreds of parliamentarians in the process, it seems worth briefly considering why it was abandoned relatively rapidly.

The government, inevitably, sought to claim credit for the demise of duelling. Sir Robert Peel argued in 1844 that his administration's decision to deny a pension to the widow of an officer killed in a duel and the subsequent removal from the Articles of War of provisions that allowed the dismissal of officers who refused to fight to defend their honour contributed to growing disapproval of duelling.[21] Yet the administration hardly sent the sort of firm and consistent message that might have swayed opinion.[22]

Peel's personal conduct actually conveyed a rather different lesson. In addition to his unconsummated affair with O'Connell, Peel challenged two MPs in 1834, although both apologised rather than fight.[23] The following year, as Chancellor, he faced a motion of censure (subsequently withdrawn) for sending MP Joseph Hume a letter demanding an explanation of remarks made in debate, a move seen as a precursor to a challenge.

Cultural change was a factor. Public reputations had come to be seen as less vulnerable to aspersions, and, in any event, less important than private character in determining one's honour.[24] The heavy drinking that often fuelled duels fell out of favour.[25] Martial virtues became less attractive both with the end of the Napoleonic Wars and the safer urban streets that followed Peel's establishment of a London police force in 1829.[26] Perhaps even more importantly, duelling became déclassé.

Originally, fighting in defence of one's honour distinguished a gentleman from the rest. By the nineteenth century, duelling had spread to the bourgeoisie and beyond, making it considerably less attractive to those above them.[27] Meanwhile, elite attitudes changed. Gentlemen, the social group most likely to be accused of murder at the Old Bailey at the start of the eighteenth century, had become the least likely by the end of it.[28] They were now at pains to emphasise their own gentleness.[29] Violence (unless perpetrated against fowl, deer or foxes) was associated with the lower classes.[30] Moreover, at a time when aristocratic privilege was under fire, a code that insisted that murder on the duelling ground be treated differently than that committed elsewhere was a political liability many could do without.

Ridicule perhaps even more than snobbery killed duelling.[31] Defending one's honour was supposed to be deadly serious, but the willingness of some to risk destruction over trivialities brought the code that justified such behaviour into disrepute and mockery. Men died over the pronunciation of a Greek word, 'whether a window should be open or shut', or an insult to a dog.[32]

It was not just the disputes that were risible; the behaviour of duellists often also was a joke. After an exchange of pistol fire failed to resolve their differences (first, do no harm?), two doctors chose medical lancets for further combat.[33] Humphrey Howarth set tongues wagging by turning up at the field for his duel with the Earl of Barrymore either shirtless, or, according to some accounts, in an even more advanced state of undress. There was a method to his madness: having served as a surgeon in India, the MP was aware of the danger of sepsis caused by bits of clothing carried into a wound by the ball.[34] Still, the rotund politician's naked cheek, so to speak, was seen to deprive the situation of the dignity and solemnity the code of honour was meant to foster. No duel was fought.

Perhaps even more injurious to the code than Howarth's immodesty was the sense that he need not have bothered, for the risks associated with duelling seemed to have fallen dramatically.[35] Technological change had reduced not only the danger but the semiotic virility of duelling: 'considered as pure potency, a sort of über-penis, surely the three-foot sword was more satisfying than the nine-inch pistol'.[36] Even worse, toward the end, some of these pistols obviously were firing blanks, as newspapers reported instances of duellists fighting with weapons loaded with powder but no shot. Almost as contemptible were affairs in which the principal was not in any real danger because neither participant made any effort to hit the other. As men fought without risk, and even without balls, they emasculated not only themselves but also an institution supposed to embody manliness.[37]

The Code's Coda

Duelling's days were numbered once adherence to the code came to be seen as an option rather than an obligation. No politician embodied this à-la-carte approach to honour more than John Roebuck.

In March 1835, the Radical MP unsuccessfully sought to have Peel sanctioned for breach of privilege for sending a note requesting, though with an underlying threat of challenge, that Roebuck disavow comments he had made about the Chancellor in debate.[38] A few months later, he fought a bloodless duel with a newspaper editor.[39]

In 1839, he fought Lord Powerscourt, the man to whom he had lost his parliamentary seat two years earlier. Back in parliament in 1841, Roebuck sought to have *The Time*'s printer charged with breach of privilege for publishing an article questioning whether the MP was an honourable man. When this failed, he apparently sought to provoke a challenge by telling the Commons that those responsible for the article should be horsewhipped or cudgelled. *The Times* replied that the MP had forgotten 'his station'.[40]

In 1845, Roebuck sought to bring parliamentary censure upon John Somers, MP for Sligo and a member of O'Connell's Repeal Association, for threatening him with a challenge.

After a prolonged debate, in which most speakers strongly praised Roebuck for his courage in bringing the matter before parliament rather than fighting, the Commons supported his motion that Somers be found guilty of breach of privilege for sending a challenge. However, after Somers apologised and asked to retract his letter to Roebuck, the Commons agreed to proceed no further on the matter.[41]

Treating the affair with the ridicule that had become a common feature of press coverage of such matters, *Punch* published a poem which, when translated from Latin, begins, 'When Sligo's member aims at Roebuck's nose, The frightened Buck to Speaker's bosom goes.'[42] Somers, on the other hand, was castigated for sending a challenge over an incident that did not meet any of the criteria for legitimately doing so.[43]

The combination of ridicule and growing intolerance by the Commons helped ensure the end of the (non-electoral) parliamentary duel. But the conclusion of the code's reign was not immediately apparent to all. Indeed, for some, epiphany did not come until the twentieth century.

There were at least five close calls in 1846, four connected to the bitter split caused by Robert Peel's decision to abandon the agricultural protectionism to which many Conservatives were wedded in favour of a push to repeal the Corn Laws. First, MP Jonathan Peel, the prime minister's brother, 'became involved in a violent argument which almost led to a duel' with Lord George Bentinck, one of the leading opponents of repeal.[44]

Then, on 24 April, a single parliamentary incident almost embroiled Benjamin Disraeli in affairs of honour with both Peels. The precipitant was Disraeli's claim in the Commons that the prime minister, who previously had sought to represent the country gentlemen, had come to support a definition of 'the people' that was limited to those living in towns. This prompted Sir Robert Peel to interject, 'I totally deny it.' Disraeli replied, 'If the hon. Baronet means to say that anything I have said is false, of course I cease – I sit down.'[45]

There followed 'a scene of confusion and excitement', before explanations were exchanged and the possibility of a duel receded. Soon thereafter, however, Jonathan Peel approached Disraeli in the lobby and said that the latter's claim had been 'false'. Disraeli delegated the matter to Bentinck, who demanded Peel retract his comment. Bentinck was referred to Peel's 'friend', Captain Rous. When Disraeli went to bed, it was in the expectation that he would be facing Peel with pistols at Wormwood Scrubs in the morning, but this proved unnecessary.[46]

A little more than a month later, Bentinck almost provoked a challenge from the prime minister after he accused Peel in the Commons of having 'chased and hunted' George Canning to his death in 1827 by refusing to support Catholic Emancipation, even though he had come to believe it necessary. For good measure, Bentinck charged Peel with 'base and dishonest conduct' and 'treason'.[47] After the sitting ended, Peel confided to a close ally that the slur on his honour seemed so great that he felt compelled to challenge Bentinck to a duel. He even asked someone to serve as his second. However, the next day he agreed to answer Bentinck instead in the Commons.[48]

In August 1846, a different parliamentary matter produced another near duel, when John Henry Thomas Manners Sutton took offence at a question posed by William Dougal Christie during a meeting of a committee looking into the Andover workhouse scandal. He called for the room to be cleared before departing in a 'very agitated state'. Fearing that Sutton was about to send a challenge to Christie, Assistant Poor Law Commissioner Henry Parker, who had been testifying, went to court to demand a warrant for the MP's arrest for contemplating a breach of the peace.[49]

Less than two years later, the chairs of a committee considering the Chartist petition told the Commons that the document contained fewer than 2 million signatures, rather than the more than 5.7 million claimed by Feargus O'Connor. This alleged exaggeration and other putative deficiencies in the petition prompted another member of the committee, William Cripps, to assert that he threw 'ridicule and obloquy' upon the Chartist leader and MP for Nottingham, whom he could 'never believe' again. O'Connor replied that Cripps's personal attacks would need to be 'explained elsewhere', and immediately left the House, leading to fears, in the words of the Journal, 'that some personal quarrel might take place'. The Commons then ordered that O'Connor 'attend in his place forthwith'. When he did not do so, the Commons had him taken into the Serjeant's custody. Eventually, after Cripps promised he had meant 'no personal affront' in his comments, O'Connor implied that he was satisfied, ending the matter.[50]

A similar episode in 1850 evoked a more contemptuous response. After Admiral Sir Thomas Hastings's efforts to justify greater military spending were ridiculed by Richard Cobden, an advocate of retrenchment, the Flag Officer sent the MP a challenge. Cobden dismissed it, as he stated in his public reply, as soon as he 'had recovered from the fits of laughter into which' it had thrown him.[51]

To others, the code remained no laughing matter. During debate on Irish matters in early 1862, Chief Secretary Sir Robert Peel, son of the former prime minister of the same name, asserted that only 'a few manikin traitors' and not 'a person of respectability' had been present at a recent Nationalist meeting in Dublin. Daniel O'Donoghue, who had presided at the meeting in question, did not respond in the Commons, but later dispatched a colleague, Major George Gavin, to demand an apology. The Chief Secretary refused to make one for anything said in the House. Gavin then asked Peel to name a 'friend' to handle the dispute. Gavin further indicated that, as he also had been at the Nationalist meeting, Peel should be prepared to give him satisfaction after concluding his affair with O'Donoghue. At the insistence of the prime minister, Peel put the matter before the Commons, where the Speaker compelled O'Donoghue to promise to drop it.[52]

There was a similar intervention in 1877, when Alexander Sullivan complained of an offensive expression addressed to him in the lobby by Dr Edward Kenealy, whom the House ordered to withdraw the remark.[53] And another four years later, when Joseph Biggar objected to comments from a colleague, Frederick Milbank, who was directed to apologise.[54]

The spectre of duelling did not disappear even with the dawning of the twentieth century. In 1904, Winston Churchill was threatened, albeit rather obliquely, with an affair of honour.[55] Eight years later there were attempts to revive duelling, which was advocated as a means of improving manners and discouraging divorce.[56] In the ensuing decade there were at least two instances in which parliamentary debate almost produced something like a duel.[57]

It was only in 1935, apparently, that the last parliamentary challenge was issued. Taking exception to some remarks made in the Commons concerning the dispute between Italy and Abyssinia, the editor of a recently defunct Italian fascist publication demanded satisfaction from the aptly named Clement Attlee. The Deputy Leader of the Labour Party declined the challenge, describing duelling as 'a barbarous and obsolete method of liquidating quarrels'.[58]

Detention Declension

The disappearance of parliamentary duels was not the only reason that MPs had less to fear in the wake of reform. The risk of being arrested for failure to attend also vanished, even though the cost of absenteeism was growing.

Instead of seeking to ensure that all Members occupied their seats daily, an impossible task, the Commons in both Westminster and Dublin had demanded full attendance on designated days, when the House would be 'called over'. Initially, those who 'made default to appear' (or provide a valid excuse) were fined. From the late seventeenth century, they were ordered into the custody of the Serjeant-at-Arms. This detention, though often perfunctory, could be more onerous, adding to the potential danger of a seat.

The Irish parliament became a virtual prison, albeit of the softest variety imaginable. On sixty-five occasions over the course of a little more than a century, an aggregate of 2,732 Irish MPs were ordered into custody for unauthorised absences. (Many Members of the 300-seat Commons were ordered detained multiple times.) The overwhelming majority of these episodes came in the last three decades of the eighteenth century, after parliament began appointing committees to consider controverted elections.

Many MPs were loath to serve on these committees. When too few attended to complete the appointment process, it became standard to call over the House at the beginning of the procedure. This hardly solved the problem. In early 1791, the House spent more than a month struggling to appoint a handful of committees, with most of its time consumed with calling over Members and ordering defaulters (an average of thirty-two per sitting) into custody. In the years that followed, the House frequently ordered the arrest of more than a third of its membership for unauthorised absence during the appointment of an election committee.

Westminster was not nearly so zealous. On seventy-six occasions over the course of almost two centuries a total of 332 MPs were ordered into custody for unauthorised absences. This relative leniency was partly because service on election committees was not nearly so contentious, but also because, as the Irish example demonstrated, the threat of detention was not a very effective deterrent. Yet, even Westminster had its limits as far as unauthorised absenteeism.

In 1846, William Smith O'Brien was appointed to a Scottish railway committee. The Irish Nationalist MP refused to attend, arguing that the body's remit was irrelevant to Ireland, his overriding interest. The House, unimpressed, ordered him to serve on the committee. His refusal to do so led his colleagues to find him guilty of contempt. On 30 April, O'Brien was ordered into the Serjeant's custody. There he remained until discharged on 25 May, although he was allowed to take advantage of the House's previous grant of permission to appear as a witness before a Lords' committee investigating the operation of the Poor Law (Ireland) Act.[59]

This marked one of the last occasions when parliament imprisoned one of its own for failure to attend. The disappearance of calls of the House and detentions for unauthorised absence after 1832 came at a strange time, as Commons was facing an attendance crisis.[60] With parliament unable or unwilling to ensure the attendance of MPs, this task would fall to political parties, and ultimately electors, in the more competitive conditions that developed in the wake of reform.[61]

Other Perils Recede

Seats became less dangerous in the decades following 1832 for other reasons: more effective policing, growing public intolerance of all forms of violence, and the very success of the push for reform encouraged those seeking change to pursue it by peaceful means.[62] The well-organised mass demonstrations of the 'Days of May' in 1832 sent a stronger signal that the alternative to reform was revolution than did earlier scattered episodes of parliamentary violence.[63] The failure, several years later of the Chartists, reformers who sought to follow the same script, would demonstrate that 'intimidatory pressure from without would be found to be insufficient in itself in the short term to coerce an unwilling Parliament to grant further concessions'.[64] The sense that peaceful protest was the only legitimate means of securing change was only reinforced by the obloquy directed at the Chartists' main organisational rival.

The Anti-Corn Law League, formed in 1839, a year after the 'People's Charter' was unveiled, quickly eclipsed the earlier movement, prompting clashes between the two organisations.[65] The League's popularity fell as its rhetoric became more threatening in late 1842, with one supporter ominously predicting that no tears would be shed at Robert Peel's funeral. The prime minister was concerned about his own safety enough, and that of his family, that he made provision for arms and ammunition to be sent to Drayton Manor, his estate.[66] A few months later, a man assassinated Edward Drummond, Peel's Private Secretary, mistaking him for the prime minister.[67] Many saw the killing as the product of the League's menacing rhetoric, with Conservative and Chartist newspapers accusing some of the movement's spokesmen of incitement to murder.[68]

The 1846 repeal of the Corn Laws owed much more to the failure the previous year of the Irish potato crop than to pressure from the largely discredited League. In England, the legislation undermined Radical claims that, without substantial reform, the political system could only serve the interests of the wealthy few at the expense of the less-affluent many.[69] Chartism soon faded, and with it disappeared a latent menace to parliamentarians.

In Ireland, by contrast, the government's response to famine exacerbated divisions within the Nationalist community and, occasionally, produced parliamentary violence. In early 1848, for example, Nationalists who rejected the use of political violence attacked, presumably not ironically, a Limerick meeting of the 'Young Irelanders' movement, which supported a resort to physical force in pursuit of greater Irish autonomy. The leader of the Young Irelanders, MP William Smith O'Brien, received a cut on the head and a suspected broken rib from stones.[70]

Outsiders were not the only threat, as two incidents in 1852 indicate. On 8 June, Sir Benjamin Hall complained to the House that when he stood to call for a division, Feargus O'Connor turned around and struck him in the side. Initially, the MP did not express regret for his behaviour, but when called by name by the Speaker, he apologised. The next day, O'Connor's 'disorderly and offensive conduct' interrupted the Attorney General's address to a committee. Edmund Beckett Denison remonstrated with O'Connor, who 'thrust his half-closed hand into' his colleague's face. The Commons ordered, *nemine contradicente*, that the Serjeant-at-Arms take O'Connor into custody for disorderly conduct and contempt of the House. The MP was released several days later to receive treatment for mental illness.[71]

A more notable incident occurred on 20 December, after William Gladstone stopped for a drink at the Carlton Club. Three nights earlier the Liberal politician had launched a philippic against Benjamin Disraeli, Chancellor of the Exchequer, which contributed to the defeat of the latter's budget and the fall of the Conservative government. The political ramifications of Gladstone's speech, and the fact that he had flouted parliamentary convention by rising to deliver it after the Chancellor had presented the budget but before a division was held, were sufficient causes for Tory peevishness. Yet, what really infuriated many Tories was the personal nature of Gladstone's criticisms of Disraeli. Consequently, when the man who soon would replace Disraeli as Chancellor turned up at the Conservative club for a post-prandial libation, some members were livid.

A group of two dozen Tory MPs, having had a bit to drink themselves, resolved to track Gladstone down. They found him sitting alone in the newspaper room. The mini mob rushed in. 'Hurling furious insults, they moved to throw him out of the window, the better to help him on his way to the (Liberal) Reform Club.' Fearing 'insult or actual ill usage', Gladstone fled the room. He found a friendlier Tory MP, with whom he talked for a little while before departing the club 'with his dignity just about intact'.[72]

Alcohol also was involved, albeit less directly, in an incident three years later. Lord Robert Grosvenor's 1855 bill to ban nearly all Sunday trading in London aroused considerable resentment, particularly given that the previous year had seen restrictions imposed on the Sunday opening hours of pubs but not the clubs favoured by the upper classes. Although he claimed the purpose of the legislation was to enhance the leisure time of the working classes, many suspected the evangelical Christian of seeking to impose Sabbatarianism. A meeting, which had been banned by the authorities, convened in Hyde Park in early July, ostensibly to investigate the extent to which the well-to-do were observing the sabbath, drew a large crowd that soon clashed with police. A group then went to attack Grosvenor's house. The MP was not at home, having fled London the previous day in the wake of personal threats, but the next day, he withdrew the bill, telling the Commons that while nobody 'likes to be mobbed and bullied out of a measure', it was clear that the legislation had little chance of passing.[73]

A somewhat similar scene more than a decade later proved even more momentous. In late July 1866, weeks after William Gladstone's plan for further reform was defeated in the Commons, 20,000 people turned up in Hyde Park to demonstrate in favour of political change. Attempting to enforce the Home Secretary's ban on such a meeting, the police charged with truncheons, leading to a battle that produced one fatality. Conservative politicians, who had opposed Gladstone's bill, feared the worst. One minister wrote to his wife, 'We are expecting to have all our heads broken tonight.' Chancellor Benjamin Disraeli was sufficiently concerned about the safety of his wife to dispatch an aide to his residence overlooking the Park.[74] Soon thereafter the wily politician devised an even better response, winning passage of the Second Reform Act by convincing Conservative colleagues that such a move would pay electoral dividends.[75]

The two statesmen found themselves on different sides of the popular mood a dozen years later. In late January 1878, as parliament was debating the government's plans for war with Russia, Gladstone launched a bitter and personal attack upon his rival in a speech at Oxford. His admission that his opposition to the government's measures was due to his dislike and distrust of the prime minister helped swing public opinion behind Disraeli. The following month, Gladstone was given a demonstration of the dangers of opposing a conflict that would add the word 'jingoism' to the political lexicon, when three groups visited his Harley Street residence: the first cheered him; the second hooted him and broke his windows; and the third was only kept away by a detachment of mounted police lined up in the street on both sides of the house. A week later, another hostile crowd forced the once and future prime minister and his wife to seek refuge in a neighbour's house. When the crowd began to menace that domicile too, the Gladstones were spirited away in a carriage accompanied by a police escort.[76]

Wilkes Redux, ad Absurdum

If the post-reform decades generally saw a decrease in the threats faced by parliamentarians there was one highly ironic exception: some MPs, duly elected in the more democratic conditions that obtained after 1832, faced violence merely for seeking to take their seats. It was as if the Commons had learned nothing from its confrontation with Wilkes a century earlier.

Oaths originally intended to keep Catholics out of parliament continued to exclude, even after they were altered to allow Daniel O'Connell and his coreligionists to take their seats. In 1832, the Commons deliberated for almost a week before deciding that Joseph Pease could affirm the oath, rather than swearing it, an action incompatible with his Quaker beliefs.[77] Fifteen years later, Lionel de Rothschild became the first Jew returned to parliament but was unable to take his seat until eleven years later – despite winning re-election in 1849, 1852, 1854 and 1857 (twice) – when those of his faith were permitted to ignore Christian elements of the oath.[78] Like Pease, Rothschild endured his democratically dubious exclusion without causing a scene. Another Jew, David Salomons, took a different approach.

Returned for Greenwich in 1851, Salomons took the oath but omitted the phrase 'upon the true faith of a Christian'. He then took his seat on the government benches, at least until the Speaker ordered him to withdraw. Three days later, Solomans returned, remaining in his seat even after the Speaker ordered him to leave. The MP's forcible removal was ordered, which the Serjeant-at-Arms accomplished by placing his hands on Solomons' shoulder, thereby threatening stronger measures. A week hence, Solomons was fined after it was learned that he had participated in three divisions.[79]

These minor skirmishes were but a prelude to a test of parliamentary will of almost Wilkesite proportions. In 1880, after three unsuccessful attempts, Charles Bradlaugh was returned for Northampton. The avowed atheist sought to substitute an affirmation for the oath in order to take his seat. When this was rejected, he tried to take the oath, while publicly stating that he would not feel bound by all its words. This, too, was deemed unacceptable.

On 23 June, more than six weeks after he first tried to take his seat, Bradlaugh was permitted to address the House in an effort to persuade his colleagues to allow him to assume his place as a duly elected Member. After he finished speaking, the presiding officer ordered him to withdraw. Bradlaugh refused, arguing that the order preventing him from taking the oath was illegal. 'The Serjeant-at-Arms then removed Mr. Bradlaugh below the bar, but the Member for Northampton immediately returned to the House, declaring that while he would submit to imprisonment, he would not submit to exclusion.' After some discussion, a motion was carried that Bradlaugh be taken into custody for resisting the authority of the House.[80] This marked the last time that the Commons ordered the Serjeant to arrest one of its own. The Commons did not authorise Bradlaugh's release until the following day.[81]

Bradlaugh's seat was declared vacant, but he was returned again in the ensuing by-election. In April 1881, he went to the Commons and sought to take the oath a second time. Ordered to withdraw by the Speaker, Bradlaugh expressed a determination not to retire 'unless force was used to compel him to do so'. Accordingly, the Serjeant, at the direction of the Speaker, 'placed his hand upon Mr Bradlaugh and conducted him below the Bar'.[82]

Twice thwarted by a Commons that seemed to be excluding him because of his progressive views, Bradlaugh vowed to force himself on the House. On 3 August 1881, as many as 5,000 people assembled in the Palace yard in support of petitions favouring his admission. The MP for Northampton sought to enter the House, but the Serjeant, his deputies and some messengers blocked Bradlaugh's way. His demand to be admitted was refused. Bradlaugh then 'made a quick motion forward', coming into 'immediate collision' with one of the messengers. Some police then took hold of Bradlaugh, who 'appeared to offer considerable resistance' as they took him out of the building. 'In the passage leading down to the yard Mr. Bradlaugh's coat was torn down the right side, his waistcoat was also pulled open, and otherwise his toilet was much disarranged.' By the time he reached the Palace Yard, Bradlaugh, 'physically a powerful man, seemed quite exhausted .... The heat and excitement appeared to produce faintness in Mr. Bradlaugh, who gasped out that he wanted a glass of water'.[83]

An editorial in *The Times*, while not defending Bradlaugh's conduct, argued that Parliament's position was untenable. 'This is nothing less than a conflict between the House of Commons and the constituencies of the country; and such a conflict can have but one conclusion, as all history teaches.'[84] *The Guardian* echoed the sentiment, asserting that the Commons had made Bradlaugh 'the representative of a cause which in England at least is sure to be victorious – the cause of freedom of election and of liberty of opinion'.[85]

The ending might have been inevitable, but it was not fast in coming. After the seat again was declared vacant, Bradlaugh was returned for Northampton in 1882 and 1884. In the latter year, he signed the oath and participated in two divisions before the House passed a motion calling for the Serjeant to exclude Bradlaugh from the precincts of the Commons 'until he shall engage not further to disturb the proceedings of the House'.[86] It was only in 1886, following his fifth election for Northampton, that Bradlaugh, finally, was able to take his seat, after the Speaker, overruling opposition, allowed him to take the oath. Two years later, Bradlaugh secured passage of legislation permitting those disinclined to take the oath to make an affirmation instead.[87]

This debacle had a twentieth-century echo, though the source of controversy was, appropriately, class rather than religion. Soon after the death of the 1st Viscount Stansgate in November 1960, parliamentary police were instructed to bar from the Commons his son and heir, Anthony Neil Wedgwood Benn, the Labour MP for Bristol South-East.[88] Benn sought to renounce his peerage so that he could continue to sit in the Commons, but his colleagues eventually declared his seat vacant. After Benn easily won the ensuing by-election, the Commons again banned him from the chamber.[89] It was only after parliament passed legislation in 1963 that allowed peers to renounce their titles and sit in the Commons that Benn was permitted to take his seat once more.[90]

Benn's victory still did not mean that the British people enjoyed complete freedom to elect their representatives. Those convicted of serious crimes continue to be prohibited from sitting in Westminster, a ban that has affected Irish Nationalists in particular.[91] Whether parliament is a more orderly place as a result of this proscription is open to question. What is beyond dispute is that those Irish Nationalists who did get into parliament almost brought the institution to its knees in their pursuit of Home Rule. It is to that epic struggle that we now turn.

9

IRISH HOME RULE

In the nineteenth century, 'more governments were defeated on Irish issues than on any other topic debated in the Commons'.[1] This helps explain why, although calls for the repeal of the 1800 Act of Union were raised almost before the ink on the document was dry, Westminster ignored for decades demands for increased Irish autonomy. By the last quarter of the century, however, this no longer was possible as Irish Nationalists adopted innovative and aggressive tactics that brought the parliamentary system to the brink of collapse and produced the first examples of terrorism. These methods, and Commons' procedures adopted to combat Irish obstructionism, in turn generated passions and violence that once more raised questions about the viability of the parliamentary system.

Animated Suspensions

If the danger of duels between MPs loomed large over the first half of the nineteenth century, the last third was characterised by challenges of a different sort, as Members repeatedly defied the authority of the Speaker and sometimes were forcibly removed from the House. Disorder in the Commons was in sharp contrast to the serenity of the Lords, where the only perturbations came on two occasions when a standing order against asperity of speech was read.[2] Democratisation after 1832 was a major reason for the divergence.

To appeal to an expanding electorate, party leaders began to offer policy programs. Implementing these agendas, which often entailed expanding the state's social welfare role, meant growing government demands on parliamentary time. This threatened backbenchers who, under the more competitive conditions, sought increased visibility with constituents through speaking in debate or proposing bills or amendments.[3] The outcome of this clash of interests was inevitable: parliamentary procedures encouraging backbench participation would be altered to expedite government business.[4] But this might not have happened so quickly had not Irish Nationalists so aggressively exposed the vulnerabilities of the existing rules.

Obstructionism did not begin in the Victorian era. In response to efforts to delay bills in the early seventeenth century, the Speaker had been empowered to bring to order Members who offered superfluous motions or delivered tedious or irrelevant speeches.[5] Until the rules were changed in 1717, a motion was required to bring in candles, sometimes triggering violent resistance from those who hoped to adjourn the sitting.[6]

The Irish were not even involved in the first disorderly episode of the late nineteenth century. On 22 July 1875, the Commons witnessed a 'most painful scene' after the government indicated it would withdraw the Merchant Shipping Bill. Samuel Plimsoll harshly criticised the move, promising to unmask the 'villains' who would send sailors to their deaths. After Plimsoll made it clear that he meant the epithet to apply to MPs, some of whom owned ships that had gone down with loss of life, the prime minister moved that the Member for Derby be reprimanded for 'unparalleled conduct'. Plimsoll responded that this description fit the government's action, shaking his fist at the Speaker, the prime minister 'and indeed all round'.[7] Plimsoll subsequently apologised, avoiding a reprimand, but by then the point was moot: public pressure generated by his outburst forced the government to address his concerns. This instance of 'success through disorder' was seen to have set a dangerous precedent.[8]

Parliamentary order, then, already was under some strain even before the supporters of Irish Home Rule sought to use obstruction to obtain their goal.[9] They had tried a more conventional approach: Isaac Butt, the first leader of the Home Rulers, pursued scrupulously constitutional tactics, introducing numerous bills to address Irish problems, to no avail.[10] Moderation discredited, Home Rulers under Charles Stewart Parnell, adopted a more aggressive approach, speaking frequently and at great length – but rarely on germane matters – repeatedly forcing divisions on motions to adjourn in an effort not only to win support in Ireland but also to demonstrate that Westminster lacked the capacity to rule an empire, and therefore would be better off granting Home Rule.[11]

Irish obstructionism was so crude and blatant that it offended parliamentary sensibilities and discredited their cause. As a sympathetic MP lamented, 'The strongest argument against Home Rule was the Home Rulers.'[12] Other MPs responded not just with changes to parliamentary procedures they might otherwise have been reluctant to pass but also, occasionally, with violence.

In mid-1877, for example, Home Rulers so successfully obstructed passage of the government's South African Confederation Bill that, for the first time, the viability of the parliamentary system was called into question.[13] The Commons debated punishing Parnell for allegedly expressing satisfaction at thwarting the government's intentions on the legislation. The MP for Meath denied making the comments attributed to him but claimed that he had been 'subjected to menaces' by others in the House. The Speaker indicated 'that any Member willfully and persistently obstructing Public Business, without just and reasonable cause [!], is guilty of a contempt of this House' and would be liable to punishment.[14] However, instead of finding Parnell guilty of contempt, the Commons called for an immediate motion of suspension for any Member twice declared out of order by the presiding officer and limits on how often an MP could make motions or speak when the whole House was in committee.[15]

Here were parliament's first tentative steps to tackle Irish obstruction. They were hardly sufficient. In fact, 'one of the most extraordinary sittings ever held by the House of Commons' transpired only three days later. In an attempt to obstruct the South Africa Bill, Home Rulers provoked twenty-two divisions and 'numerous scenes and incidents'. A session that began at 4 p.m. on 31 July did not finish until after 6 p.m. the next day. There had been longer sittings, but this was the first greatly extended by obstruction.[16]

Continued Irish obstruction prompted a stronger institutional response a few years later. On 28 February 1880, the Commons adopted a Standing Order (currently Number 44) authorising the presiding officer to put to a vote immediately a motion for the suspension of a Member named for disregarding the authority of the chair, obstructing the business of the House, or abusing its rules. Although such a provision had not been deemed necessary for the maintenance of order in parliament's previous five centuries of existence, it would be employed almost 200 times in the decades following its adoption. Nearly 40 per cent of the suspensions under this Standing Order came during the 1880s, many in the course of a few days in early 1881.

Deteriorating economic conditions in Ireland earlier had led to agrarian unrest as tenants, no longer able to pay their rents, were evicted. After trying without success to convict of conspiracy Parnell and other leaders of the newly formed Irish National Land League, the government sought to deal with the unrest through repression. On 24 January 1881, it introduced a bill providing for the suspension in Ireland of habeas corpus, essentially authorising unlimited use of arbitrary arrest and preventative detention.[17] The next day, the administration proposed that the bill be given precedence in parliamentary business. This called forth from the Home Rulers all manner of obstructive tactics, from repeated motions for adjournment to time-wasting speeches. Most sailed close to the line of what was permitted by the rules; Joseph Biggar crossed it and was suspended.[18] After a sitting of 22 hours, the government proposal passed.[19]

A few days later, however, continued obstruction of the bill caused not only another marathon sitting but also provoked another procedural innovation.[20] On 2 February, near the end of a 41-hour sitting, the Speaker peremptorily ended debate. This use of '*clôture*', as it initially was called, was not only unprecedented, it was unauthorised by parliamentary rules.[21] The Speaker justified this intervention by referring to the efforts of an 'inconsiderable minority' to block discussion of a bill that had been designated as urgent in the Queen's Speech a month earlier. After a motion to adjourn debate was rejected in a division, discussion of the matter should have continued. Instead, the Speaker called for a vote on the bill. 'The Home Rulers for two minutes shouted "Privilege!" "Privilege!" and then as the Speaker still remained standing, they all left the House in a body, bowing to the Speaker as they did so, the other members cheering their departure.' Later in the day, after an adjournment, there were more 'violent scenes', including one in which an Irish Nationalist shook his fist at Prime Minister William Gladstone, who reportedly had been given a police escort, and his residence police protection, in view of a possible 'Fenian' attack.[22]

The next day's sitting was even more turbulent, with the threat of violence even stronger. The trouble began when the government asserted that Nationalist Michael Davitt had been arrested for activities incompatible with the conditions under which he earlier had been released from prison, but declined to specify what stipulation the Land League leader had violated. When the prime minister sought to speak in favour of a resolution providing for the expeditious consideration of 'urgent' public business, Home Ruler John Dillon rose on a point of order only to be told by the Speaker that Gladstone had the floor. Dillon refused to resume his seat. The Speaker named him, after which a motion for Dillon's suspension for the rest of the day's sitting was passed. The Speaker then asked Dillon to withdraw. Dillon declined to do so. The Serjeant-at-Arms then approached Dillon, putting his hand on the latter's arm. Still, Dillon refused to move. The Sergeant then summoned five messengers to assist him, at which point Dillon rose, said, 'If you use force I will yield' and departed.

As Gladstone tried to speak again, another Home Ruler stood up to call for adjournment. The Speaker insisted that Gladstone had the floor. Parnell then moved 'that the right hon. Gentleman [Gladstone] be no further heard'. The Speaker threatened to name Parnell, but the latter justified his conduct by pointing out that Gladstone himself had made a similar motion, directed at an Irish MP, not long before.[23] This did not prevent Parnell from being named and suspended. Like Dillon, he refused to obey commands to withdraw until the Serjeant had summoned reinforcements. Gladstone then rose again, only for James Finigan to move that the prime minister no longer be heard. Finigan was then named and suspended, but he refused to leave until the Serjeant had mustered assistance.

The Speaker's attention then was called to the fact that two dozen Irish MPs had not left the chamber for a division. All were named and suspended. Each refused to go until the Serjeant assembled sufficient forces to credibly threaten compulsion. When Gladstone rose to speak again, the results were the same. By the time the sitting concluded thirty-six MPs had been suspended.[24] Moreover, something of a Rubicon had been crossed. Irish MPs had resisted the authority of the Speaker in a manner that was both unprecedented and shocking. They had stopped just short of doing so by actual force, but it would not be too long before this final line also was breached.

It has been argued that the 3 February confrontation with the Home Rulers, combined with procedural changes that allowed the Speaker to end debate (closure) and expedite consideration of legislation (urgency), constitute the 'way the House was freed from the obstructionists'.[25] This hardly seems to be the case. It is true that those seeking to waste parliamentary time could no longer rely on the crude techniques that Parnell and friends first had employed, but they simply adopted a somewhat more subtle approach, to such an extent that there were complaints about Irish obstructionism until at least 1902, when, after seven days of debate, parliament had only managed to adopt eleven lines of an education bill.[26]

The immediate impact of the new rules should not be overstated either. These weapons notwithstanding, it took the government a month to pass the Irish Coercion bill.[27] More broadly, even with the procedural innovations, 'the parliamentary breakdown in 1881 was well nigh total'.[28] During that year's session, most of which took place after the supposedly decisive showdown with the obstructionists, 'fourteen Irish members delivered between them 3828 speeches, a daily average of twenty each'. Nor did the Commons return to its previous shorter sittings soon thereafter. 'Up until 1887 the average hour of adjournment was 2.20 a.m.'[29] In late 1882, it was asserted that 'domestic legislation has been practically in abeyance during the last two years of Irish agitation'.[30]

Indeed, between 1880 and 1885, parliament 'was so frequently brought to a standstill that the entire legislative programme was disrupted'.[31]

A clear sign that obstruction remained a problem was the drafting of additional measures to combat it. On 27 November 1882, the Commons adopted another new Standing Order (currently Number 42), which authorises the presiding officer to order to desist from speaking a Member who persists in irrelevance or tedious repetition. The inadequacy of using *clôture* also became apparent fairly quickly, so in 1887 parliament added another weapon to its procedural arsenal: the 'guillotine', a measure that allowed the Speaker to cut off debate at a specified time and put to a vote the bill (and any amendments) then under consideration. (Critics insisted on using foreign words when referring to these procedural innovations to emphasise that they were alien to British parliamentary tradition.[32]) The following year, yet another new Standing Order (Number 43) was put on the books, authorising the presiding officer to order the withdrawal from the House for the remainder of the day's sitting of any Member who engages in grossly disorderly conduct.[33]

The reactions to Irish obstruction were not only procedural. To pass another Irish Coercion Bill in May 1887, ministers were rumoured to 'have ordered to be prepared 60 first-class cells in Milbank Prison for the accommodation of Parnellite Members of Parliament, whose arrest they many deem necessary'.[34] That such (unfounded) claims were taken seriously is indicative of the extraordinary lengths to which both the Home Rulers and the government were thought willing to go in their high-stakes struggle. In such a bitter atmosphere, physical confrontations between MPs, virtually in abeyance for decades, again became a threat.

In late February 1883, William Forster, former Chief Secretary for Ireland, sought to link Parnell with those who had assassinated his successor and the Permanent Under-Secretary for Ireland in Dublin's Phoenix Park the previous year. Parnell responded that this accusation was 'a lie', but the Speaker apparently did not hear him. However, when James O'Kelly repeated Parnell's assertion, the Speaker ordered him to withdraw the expression. After O'Kelly instead reiterated the claim, he was named and a motion for his suspension was carried. Forster, however, evidently deemed this insufficient vindication, for he subsequently challenged O'Kelly to a duel.[35]

Three months later. James McCoun complained that his explanation of his own behaviour on the day of O'Kelly's suspension had prompted the latter to send him a challenge. The Speaker then sought O'Kelly's assurance that he would not pursue the matter further.[36]

During debate on an 1887 crime bill for Ireland, Unionist MP Edward Saunderson told the House that the Irish National League was supported 'mainly by criminals, dynamiters and murderers' in America, adding that the MPs sitting on the opposition benches knowingly associating with murderers. This prompted Timothy Healy to call Saunderson a liar. The Irish MP refused repeated orders from the Speaker to withdraw this unparliamentary expression, arguing that he only would do so if Saunderson retracted his own offensive assertion. After a motion to suspend Healy was carried, the MP 'walked out of the House applauded by all the Parnellites, who stood up waving their hats and raising cheer after cheer'.

When Saunderson sought to resume speaking, another Home Ruler, Thomas Sexton demanded to know whether he would withdraw his accusation. Saunderson's attempt to justify it prompted Sexton to exclaim, 'I say you are a willful, cowardly liar.' This produced another uproar. 'The Parnellites all rose and cheered frantically, waving their hats in the air.' As soon as the noise died down a bit, Sexton continued, 'If I only met you outside the door of this house, I would thrash you within an inch of your life.' The Speaker rose to address the House but 'his voice was inaudible above the din'. Eventually, the Speaker was able to coax Saunderson into withdrawing his claim that Sexton associated with murderers. This allowed Sexton to withdraw his charges as well.

However, when Saunderson resumed his remarks, he asserted that Sexton had been present at a meeting of Clan na Gael, 'a murder society of America'. The Speaker advised the MP to withdraw his expression. 'Another scene of confusion ensued.' Instead of withdrawing his words, Saunderson repeated them. Sexton stood and exclaimed, 'The honorable gentlemen is again a liar.' The Speaker called upon both men to withdraw their remarks, which they did.[37]

Following several close calls, actual violence erupted in early 1889. After Healy, an attorney, defended parishioners accused of fatally attacking a police inspector who had tried to arrest their priest for preaching anti-landlord sermons, Liberal Unionist Thomas Russell asserted in the Commons, as he looked at the Nationalists across the chamber, 'You paid for the defence of the murderers.' John Dillon rose 'excitedly' to respond, 'That is a foul lie.' As a result of the Speaker's intervention, Russell withdrew his comment, but only with regard to Dillon. This prompted Nationalist Thomas O'Hanlon to shout, 'Who do you intend it for?' Soon thereafter, O'Hanlon took a seat directly behind Russell. There ensued a 'considerable disturbance'. O'Hanlon explained that he wanted Russell to apologise, adding, 'I will just give him a minute to think, and if he does not apologize I will ...' The Speaker cut him off with a demand for order. Another MP stated that he had seen Sir Henry Havelock-Allan 'personally assault' O'Hanlon. The Speaker, indicating that he also had witnessed 'the hon. and gallant Gentleman's throwing himself on the hon. Member', insisted that Havelock-Allan apologise, which he eventually did.[38]

Around the same time, Havelock-Allan 'dogged another [MP] to the Library and back making threats such as: "I'll do you in on your doorstep, where I will be at 2 a.m. and cut your liver out."' Called upon by the Speaker to apologise, Havelock-Allen, a recipient of the Victoria Cross who had been wounded several times in combat, brought laughter to the House by seeking to excuse his behaviour on the grounds that he was in great pain, having shut his finger in a window the previous day.[39]

There was yet another incident in late 1889. During debate on the Irish estimates, Arthur Balfour, Chief Secretary for Ireland, caused an 'uproar' by claiming that Timothy Harrington 'had denounced the police as cowards, liars, and uniformed bloodhounds'. Harrington demanded to know on what authority Balfour made this accusation. Balfour replied that 'he spoke on the best of authority'. Harrington 'started across the floor apparently with the intention of assaulting Mr. Balfour', only to be pulled back by fellow Irish Nationalist Pierce Mahony. 'A tremendous uproar followed. The Chairman's calls for order were drowned in Irish yells.' Healy accused Balfour of using an insulting gesture toward Harrington 'and told Mr. Balfour to keep quiet or else they would make him. The tumult continued a quarter of an hour, the Chairman warning the Parnellites to control their feelings'. Eventually, order was restored. Balfour denied using an insulting gesture and Harrington apologised for his actions.[40]

Fenian Terrorism

At the same time that Irish MPs were moving to the brink of physical resistance within parliament, some of their compatriots were pioneering equally innovative but far more violent means to the same end outside of it. The Irish Republican Brotherhood, or Fenians, formed in 1858, initially sought to foment insurrection. When this proved impossible despite the substantial agrarian distress in the late 1870s, they switched to spectacular acts of violence (typically in England) to sow panic and sap the government's will to continue to rule Ireland, becoming in the process the progenitors of modern terrorism.[41]

The Fenian threat prompted extraordinary security arrangements for debate on the Irish Coercion Bill in early 1881, with 400 additional police stationed around parliament and another 50 constables posted within the Palace of Westminster. 'The members' lobby was cleared from an early hour, and strangers were not allowed to enter for several hours.'[42] In the wake of the suspension of three dozen Home Rule MPs, Prime Minister Gladstone reportedly was 'inundated' with correspondence threatening his life and a number of bombs were sent to him through the post.[43]

A year later, Lord Frederick Cavendish, the newly appointed Chief Secretary for Ireland, and Thomas Burke, the Permanent Under-Secretary, were assassinated in Dublin's Phoenix Park. The leader of the Home Rulers, who days earlier had struck a deal with the government to use his influence to reduce disorder in Ireland in return for public money to wipe out arrears in rent owed by Irish tenants, worried he could be next. 'At Westminster Parnell habitually carried a revolver in his overcoat.'[44] Moreover, acutely embarrassed by the killings, Parnell felt compelled to embrace moderation even more strongly.[45] As a consequence, the 'threats of the ultras of the knife became so violent' that the government gave him police protection.[46]

Although Fenians were not responsible for the Phoenix Park murders, they bore responsibility for numerous bombings in England and Scotland in the early 1880s.[47] Two of their attacks were parliamentary. In mid-1884, John Daly was sentenced to life imprisonment for his part in a plot to throw bombs from the Strangers' Gallery into the House of Commons. Early the following year, Fenian dynamiters planted two explosives in Westminster Palace (and another in the

Tower of London's White Tower). One of these detonated as police were carrying it up the stairs from the Chapel of St Mary Undercroft. The second bomb tore through the House of Commons itself. It was a Saturday, so the Commons was not sitting. However, had the many visitors not vacated the chamber following the earlier explosion, the number of casualties could have been considerable.[48]

If the Fenians expected their handiwork to further the Irish cause, they soon were given reason to reconsider. Yes, the bombings generated terror, but they also evoked outrage. Politicians in the United States, who hitherto had shown little inclination to curb the activities of the Fenians, immediately announced measures to do so.[49] In Britain, fairly or not, the Fenian campaign weakened growing political momentum for greater Irish autonomy, a bill for which was defeated in the Commons in 1886. 'To concede home rule to Parnell seemed like handing over Ireland to a king of the ogres.'[50] This sentiment helps explain why *The Times* subsequently saw fit to publish the pseudonym under which Parnell resided in London, a move even his critics thought likely to expose him to 'molestation'.[51]

Nor was it apparently only Irish politicians who suffered. When Gladstone, whose embrace of Home Rule split the Liberal party, arrived in Dover in December 1887, his entourage was greeted with a hail of snowballs, one of which struck the ex-premier on the shoulder. A crowd at the railway station also subjected the 77-year-old leader of the opposition to 'considerable inconvenience by jostling from behind'.[52]

Attitudes in Ireland were, perhaps not surprisingly, somewhat different. Jeremiah O'Donovan Rossa, a leading Fenian known to critics as 'O'Dynamite', was returned in an 1869 County Tipperary by-election while imprisoned but was denied his seat as an unpardoned felon. Fifteen years later, John Daly was elected MP for Limerick while in prison for conspiring to throw bombs into the Commons. He, too, was disqualified but, another fifteen years on, was elected Mayor of that city.[53]

Even in London, site of a number of Fenian incidents, there was some support for the Irish cause. An 1887 demonstration in Trafalgar Square, ostensibly in support of William O'Brien, an Irish MP imprisoned under the Coercion Act for organising a rent strike, sparked 'the most considerable émeute in London during the latter half of the nineteenth century'.[54] It culminated in Radical MP Robert Cunninghame Graham leading a charge on police lines by a few thousand men armed with sticks and stones.[55]

Chaos on the Floor

Similar scenes soon would visit the Commons. When Gladstone's support of Home Rule divided the Liberals, both of Westminster's main parties became more cohesive. Government leaders now had less need to compromise to win opposition support in order to compensate for defections from their benches.[56] The procedural changes adopted in response to Irish obstruction further weakened the ability of parliamentary minorities to extract concessions from the government. Repeatedly in the 1890s and 1900s, MPs responded violently to their marginalisation.

This first happened in 1893, as the Gladstone government sought to pass a second Home Rule Bill. Unionists, who previously had deplored the Home Rulers' obstructionist tactics, now proved quite happy to employ them in opposition. The government's first use of closure, after six hours of debate, prompted Unionist cries of 'shame', and Nationalist replies of 'remember what you did in 1887'.[57] Its second use, a little more than a week later, 'incensed' the opposition. 'Great disorder prevailed, angry cries and countercries being heard in distant parts of the house. Chairman John Mellor repeatedly appealed for order, but his appeals were unheard.'[58] When the legislation remained bogged down, the government resorted to another procedural expedient, the guillotine, triggering violence in the Commons on a scale not seen for centuries.

On 27 July 1893, as the time at which debate would be cut off drew near, Unionist Joseph Chamberlain launched an impassioned denunciation of the government's use of the guillotine, during the course of which he compared Prime Minister Gladstone to Herod. This prompted Nationalist Timothy O'Connor to leap to his feet and call Chamberlain 'Judas', a name other Irish Members quickly began shouting. The Unionists soon responded with their own exclamations, creating such a din, that when the witching hour arrived and Chairman Mellor sought to end debate, he was inaudible. A division then was called, but the Unionists refused to participate unless Mellor disciplined O'Connor. The chair responded that he did not know what the latter had said. Vicary Gibbs attempted to go enlighten him, 'but in the general jostling and shouting he was pushed about and was so confused that he gave up his purpose and Mr. Mellor remained uninformed'.

The situation rapidly deteriorated. In response to Gibbs's abortive effort, some Unionists climbed onto benches and began yelling, 'Gag! Gag!' The air was full of 'curses, yells of pain, and gross insults'.

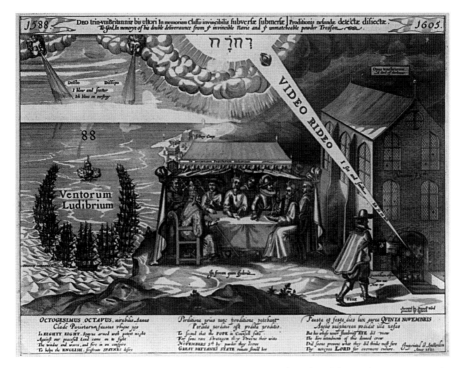

The role of Providence in the 'Double Deliverance' of England from the twin 'Popish' threats of the 1588 Spanish Armada and the 1605 Gunpowder Plot formed the subject of one of the first examples of English graphic satire. (Courtesy of the Library of Congress)

Oliver Cromwell's 1653 dissolution of the Long Parliament marked one of the many times in the mid-seventeenth century when MPs were threatened by soldiers. (This and all subsequent images courtesy of The Lewis Walpole Library, Yale University)

The Rump was so unpopular that news of its 1653 dissolution sparked celebrations in which MPs were hanged and burned in effigy.

A CONSEQUENCE OF THE MOTION

Above: The 1731 duel between MPs William Pulteney and Lord Hervey was seen as fight by proxy between Prime Minister Robert Walpole (right) and his most prominent critic, Viscount Bolingbroke.

Left: Robert Walpole's 1733 Excise Bill was portrayed as unconstitutional and, enforced by the army, a harbinger of tyranny, as denoted by the English 'Lyon' wearing the wooden shoes associated with slavery.

Such was the animus generated by Robert Walpole's premiership that it sparked a duel between his brother, Horatio, and fellow MP Richard Chetwynd, two years after it ended.

The Earl of Bute, the first Scot to serve as prime minister since the Union, was so unpopular that he hired 'bruisers' to protect him on the streets of London.

THE BAGSHOT FROLICK or the POT-LID & INKHORN.

Above left: Ridicule of the equestrian skills displayed by the Lord High Steward at George III's coronation on the pages of *North Briton* led to a 1762 duel between MP John Wilkes and Earl Talbot.

Below left: The continued imprisonment of MP John Wilkes after parliament opened in 1768 led to unrest and the Massacre at St George's Fields.

Below: The 1780 Gordon Riots discredited the practice of 'raising a mob' to intimidate parliament.

The Mob destroying & Setting Fire to the KINGS BENCH PRISON & HOUSE of CORRECTION in St Georges Fields.

Henry Grattan's 1783 philippic against rival Henry Flood (right) on the floor of the Irish House of Commons surprisingly did not culminate in a duel.

William Pitt repeatedly faced violence on the streets of London soon after becoming, at twenty-four, Britain's youngest prime minister.

After an inebriated Sir James Johnstone (right) picked a quarrel with Lord Mornington in the Commons, the Speaker reconciled the MPs.

The MEETING of PARTIES, or, HUMPHREYS & MENDOZA fighting for a CROWN.

The REPUBLICAN-ATTACK.

Above: Prime Minister William Pitt (left) and his great rival Charles James Fox were portrayed as 'fighting for a crown', during the Regency Crisis.

Above left: Fox, a supporter of the French Revolution, was depicted as 'Guy Vaux', whose attempt to destroy parliament was thwarted by a watchman, in the person of Edmund Burke.

Below left: Fox and his allies are pictured as leading the mob attack on George III's carriage (and Prime Minister Pitt, portrayed as the coachman), on the way to the 1795 state opening of parliament.

Pitt's unpopularity as a result of the 'Gagging Acts' he pushed through parliament in the wake of the attack on the King's carriage led to another mob attack on the prime minister two months later.

Many mocked Prime Minister William Pitt's decision to fight a 1798 duel with MP George Tierney while Britain was at war.

An invasion by Revolutionary France was seen to portend an orgy of parliamentary violence, with members manacled and the Speaker gagged.

When the Duke of Wellington and Robert Peel began to support Catholic Emancipation in 1829, they faced both parliamentary violence and calls to 'remember the 5th of November'.

Liberal John Logan ran to the opposition front bench and started 'upbraiding' Edward Carson, the former Solicitor-General for Ireland. 'As he shook his fist under Carson's nose, two Unionists seized Mr. Logan by the neck, threw him to the floor head first, and then bundled him under a bench.' Timothy Healy's high hat was smashed down over his eyes. He tore it off and 'sprang into the aisle in full fighting posture', only to collide with Robert William Hanbury, who had been shouting for the Chairman to name O'Connor. 'Mr. Hanbury was knocked over a bench by the force of the collision before Mr. Healy got in a blow. A free fight then broke out at the top of the gangway.'

William Redmond took 'advantage of the general license to push over Colonel Saunderson', the Unionist leader, who then led an attack on the Parnellites. 'Blows were struck right and left. Members fell and were picked up by their friends to fight again. The whole space between the front benches was filled with a struggling, cursing mass of members, striking, clawing, and upsetting each other.' Eventually, the Serjeants-at-Arms, aided by appeals for calm from Gladstone and the pacific efforts of his 'sturdy' co-partisan, Edward Marjoribanks, managed to restore order. Saunderson emerged first from the combatants, holding keys over his black eye. 'Others followed in more of less damaged condition .... Not a few of them showed the effects of rough handling. Timothy Healy had received a hard blow in the face, and one cheek was badly swollen. William Redmond also had a bad spot on his face.' At the prompting of the Speaker, who had taken the chair, O'Connor apologised if his words had contributed to a 'most regrettable' affair. Although accusations were traded about who struck the first blow, the Speaker urged the House to drop the matter.[59]

This most unparliamentary scene was deplored universally, but there was considerable disagreement about how blame should be apportioned.[60] *The Times*, which previously had railed against obstruction by Home Rulers, maintained a sort of consistency by excoriating the Irish for having, through 'an insolent passion for trampling and silencing all opponents ... goaded the minority, deprived of the right to discuss the measure involving vast constitutional changes, into an outburst of angry indignation'. The disgraceful scene in the Commons therefore should be seen as a warning for 'what would occur in the Irish Legislature should Mr. Gladstone succeed in establishing that preposterous body'.[61]

The New York Times, eager to portray the incident as a riposte to British claims that republican institutions failed to foster the dignity necessary for public respect for law, blamed the (often blue-blood) Unionists and the press that propounded their virulent views, while asserting sanctimoniously (if not entirely accurately) that the US House of Representatives 'has never in its whole history presented anything like such a spectacle'.[62]

Even worse was to come. By early 1901, a Unionist ministry had come to power intent on killing Home Rule with kindness, introducing important land reforms and more democratic local government in an effort to dampen support for the creation of a parliament in Dublin. Instead, these measures fostered increased agrarian agitation that put pressure on Irish Nationalist MPs to heal their divisions and stay politically relevant. They responded by using obstructive tactics to hold up government business for a week, in an effort to win more parliamentary time for the discussion of Irish matters. In early March, the government responded by applying closure to debate, precipitating another unprecedented scene of parliamentary violence.[63]

Nationalist MPs refused to leave the House for a division, protesting 'against the manner in which all the Irish votes have been closured without a single Irish voice having been heard'. The Speaker named a dozen Irish MPs for disorder. A motion for their suspension was carried without division after nobody was willing to serve as teller for the Noes.[64] The suspended MPs were ordered to withdraw from the chamber. They refused.

The Speaker then called upon one of their number, Eugene Crean, to leave the House. The Irish MP respectfully declined to do so. The Speaker bade the Deputy Serjeant-at-Arms to see that Crean left the House. The parliamentary officer asked the MP to leave, but again he refused to budge. 'Never before had such a scene occurred in the House as then followed.' The Deputy Serjeant called for assistance, but Crean 'struggled fiercely with the attendants, who summoned the police, a dozen constables entering the House'. Amid Nationalist jeers, 'Four or five stalwart policemen proceeded to seize' the MP, 'who stuck his legs under the seat and could not be moved for some minutes'. As some Irish sought to prevent the police from reaching Crean's seat, others shouted, 'Don't kill him! Don't kill the man!' Despite a frantic struggle by the Nationalists, 'at length a superior force of police succeeded in dragging Sir [sic] Eugene out by the legs and arms and carrying him down the floor of the House, the Irishmen standing and wildly shouting "Shame!" "Murderers!" "South African brutality!"'

The Speaker than asked another suspended Irish MP, Patrick McHugh, to withdraw. He refused, producing a similar scene.

'A strong body of twenty policemen again stormed the Irish benches.' McHugh 'fought, struggled with, and impeded them in every way. Angry shouts rent the air. The benches below the gangway on the opposition side were a mass of mad, struggling humanity. Several policemen were struck with fists. Free fights between the police and the members were fairly general'. As McHugh, 'his outer garments torn away in the struggle', was being carried out, Nationalist Michael Flavin shouted, 'Nineteen policemen to remove one Irishman!'

Next John Cullinan was removed 'after struggling violently'. In response to an entreaty from an Irish Member to stop 'this most distressing scene', the Speaker asked the remaining named Members if they would withdraw 'peaceably and decently'. When they refused, he ordered their removal. 'Amid renewed howls of execration, the police grappled with them and carried them by arms and legs over the benches and out of the House.' After other Irish Members indicated that they would not leave for a division, the presiding officer called for a voice vote, declared the 'ayes' the victor and adjourned the House.[65]

When the Commons met the following day, 'in view of possible disturbances the whole police force on duty at St. Stephen's had been mobilised and reinforced by reserves'.[66] A motion providing for the suspension for the remainder of the session of those who forcibly resist the Speaker's demand to withdraw passed, after an amendment, authorising their imprisonment, was rejected unanimously.[67]

A year later, a different highly emotive issue, the Boer War, sparked another challenge to parliamentary norms. During debate, Liberal leader Sir Henry Campbell-Bannerman accused Colonial Secretary Joseph Chamberlain of 'malignant slanders' for referring to him as 'pro-Boer'. The Speaker ruled the former expression to be unparliamentary. Chamberlain then praised Boers who were supporting the British war effort, prompting John Dillon to interject that they were 'Traitors!' Chamberlain responded that Dillon 'was a good judge of traitors'. Dillon called Chamberlain 'a damned liar' and was named and suspended for refusing to withdraw this remark.[68] The Nationalists later took the highly unusual step of proposing to censure the Speaker for allowing Chamberlain's comments. Although this motion was defeated overwhelmingly, it clearly reflected the frustrations felt by many Irish MPs at what they perceived was unfair treatment by the presiding officer.[69]

Complaints that the Irish unfairly were being denied parliamentary time again seemed to portend violence on 17 October 1902. Shortly after parliament reopened, Prime Minister Arthur Balfour moved that the rest of the session be devoted entirely to government business, including bills on education, supply and water, as well as the Indian budget, the Uganda railway, and the Transvaal. Patrick O'Brien asked if at least one day could be devoted to the 'serious state of affairs' in Ireland. 'Mr. Balfour replied that if the request for such an opportunity came from the Liberal leaders the Government would grant it, but they could not notice it from the Irish Party.' Other Irish Members echoed O'Brien's call for discussion of affairs in their homeland, which was said to be on the verge of revolt. Timothy Healy took a different approach: speaking 'as a native of Uganda', he sarcastically thanked the premier for devoting time to the discussion of matters in that African land rather than 'that distant and distressful country, Ireland'.

At length, Balfour moved for closure, provoking 'uproar'. F. Hugh O'Donnell stood up and refused to obey the Speaker, despite repeated warnings that he was out of order. Balfour moved for O'Donnell's suspension. O'Donnell then 'crossed the floor, stood in front of the Premier, shouted defiance and shook his fist in Mr. Balfour's face'. The prime minister 'smiled quietly as the Irish Member shouted and gesticulated, and other members of the Cabinet, fearing that Mr. O'Donnell would actually assault the Premier, moved toward him, but Mr. O'Donnell, having concluded what he had to say, returned to his seat'. The Speaker's request that O'Donnell withdraw 'drew forth derisive cries of "Call the police!" "Muster the Horse Guards"', but O'Donnell departed without incident.[70]

Incidents such as these fostered the impression that the Commons was becoming almost ungovernable.[71] In December 1902, a new Standing Order (currently Number 46) was introduced authorising the Speaker to suspend a sitting in the face of 'grave disorder'. This made the presiding officer's life easier in one respect: Speaker Gully had been harshly criticised for bringing police onto the floor of the Commons to remove unruly members in 1901; henceforth his successors could leave the chair and adjourn the sitting rather than being required to take more active steps to restore order.[72] But the new rule hardly discouraged disorderly behaviour, so even before it was enacted, it had become customary for leading members of the two main parties to negotiate over the smooth transaction of Commons' business, an informal mechanism nicknamed 'the usual channels'.

Others preferred conflict resolution methods from an earlier era. In early 1904, Liberal Unionist MP James Wanklyn sent a letter to Liberal Winston Churchill complaining of his conduct the previous day. Churchill's 'friend', Liberal Duncan Pirie, had interrupted Chief Secretary for Ireland George Wyndham, only to be told by the Speaker to sit down. At this point, Wanklyn had interjected, 'Order, order'. Churchill then 'had the impertinence' to turn and rebuke Wanklyn for 'shouting people down'. Wanklyn's letter continued ominously, 'Permit me to warn you that if I have any more impertinence from a young man like yourself, I shall know how to deal with it.'[73] Such a menacing missive would not have been out of place a century earlier, when the code of honour still held sway.

A few months later, there was an incident that showed just how much had changed in a hundred years. On 6 July 1904, the government used closure to push through the first part of its Licensing Bill. As in the past, this procedural device generated quite a bit of animus on the other side of the chamber. Balfour sought to speak towards the end of the debate, only to be 'drowned out by loud cries of "Gag!"' Eventually, 'after hopelessly facing the tumult', Balfour sat down. This was thought to be the first time in modern parliamentary history that the prime minister had been unable to obtain a hearing on the floor of the Commons.[74]

Perhaps ironically, it was Balfour's reluctance to speak a year later that resulted in the first official episode of grave disorder. On 22 May 1905, the prime minister told the Commons that while he had promised not to seek a change in colonial preferences in parliament without going to voters first, this did not prevent him from proposing such alterations in trade relations at an upcoming colonial conference. Liberal leader Sir Henry Campbell-Bannerman, accusing Balfour of violating his pledge, moved adjournment of the House to discuss the matter. A number of Members then sought to speak, only to be howled down by those across the aisle. After more than an hour, in which he 'had been unable to secure even a semblance of order', the Speaker, citing rules pertaining to grave disorder, adjourned the sitting.[75]

The limitations of these rules quickly became apparent. So great was the sense that Balfour must address concerns that he was guilty of a breach of faith, that more disorder was expected should someone other than the prime minister seek to speak when the Commons resumed. He precluded this by agreeing to allow discussion of a vote of censure relating to the government's fiscal policy and the proposed conference.[76]

For all the sound and fury evoked by the use of debate-curbing procedures, their impact should not be overstated, partly because initially they were employed sparingly.[77] In 1909, despite the Liberal government's large majority and repeated use of such restrictive measures, the passage of Chancellor David Lloyd George's controversial 'Peoples' Budget' occupied 70 parliamentary days and produced 554 divisions.[78] Then the Lords rejected the budget, the first time it had done so since the seventeenth century. This triggered a two-year constitutional crisis that culminated in a measure stripping the Upper House of its legislative veto, but not, as promised, that body's reconstitution on more democratic grounds.[79] Perhaps not surprisingly, a number of incidents of parliamentary violence were generated along the way.

Although some peers hinted darkly that they might fight to the last ditch, employing force to protect their veto, this proved nothing more than bluster. The closest the Lords came disorder was when two aristocrats of different political persuasions stood at the same time and neither was willing to give way to the other. A vote was taken to determine who would speak first.[80]

In the Commons, by contrast, 'the temper of the times showed itself in what was called "the new style" – an unaccustomed violence of language, a furious disregard for polite forms, and insistent pursuit of partisan advantage'.[81] In this atmosphere, physical confrontations threatened on a number of occasions.

In mid-April 1910, after the Commons had passed overwhelmingly three resolutions calling for the abolition of the power of the House of Lords to veto legislation, Prime Minister H. H. Asquith indicated that, should the Upper House refuse to pass these measures, he would advise the king on the steps that should be taken to ensure that the government's policy, endorsed in a recent election, would be implemented. Opposition leader Arthur Balfour then criticised Asquith for compromising the dignity of his office by anticipating his advice to the Crown and for making budgetary concessions to Irish Parliamentary Party leader John Redmond in order to buy his support for the resolutions. (The January 1910 general election had left the Liberals without a parliamentary majority and therefore dependent on the support of the Irish nationalists.) The adjournment that immediately followed Balfour's remarks witnessed loud cheers and counter cheers from both sides of the House, during which Conservative Arthur Wilson nearly precipitated a fight by shouting, 'Why don't you cheer John Redmond, your master. He has won.' William Redmond, John's brother, 'rose and excitedly stepped down the gangway' toward Wilson, 'but was intercepted by several gentlemen, who were apparently endeavouring to restrain him'.[82]

Less than a year later an 'open riot' almost broke out in the Commons during a 19-hour sitting devoted to the budget. Tempers flared, as insults and taunts were exchanged. In response to 'an excited demonstration' by Irish MPs, Unionist James Craig indicated to the presiding officer, that if the latter gave the word, 'the Opposition would gladly throw the whole Nationalist Party out of the House. This remark drew a hurricane of angry shouts from the Irish benches, and it was some time before the Chair was able to restore order.' Home Secretary Winston Churchill, leading the government's efforts in the absence of the prime minister, was called to order by the chair several times.[83]

Weeks later, William Clough was 'mobbed' by Unionist MPs near the division lobby, following a vote on an amendment to the Parliament Bill. 'There was great confusion and pushing and shouting. A Member's hat was lifted from his head and tossed into the air.'[84] Churchill informed the Speaker that, for perhaps the second time that evening, Clough had been subjected to 'a gross and organised insult', as he left the 'Aye' lobby. The Speaker responded MPs were entitled to pass from the lobbies without molestation. Another Member then suggested that a new door be created to prevent the 'unseemly contacts between the two parties' that had resulted in this 'brawl'. The Speaker agreed this option should be examined.[85]

A more serious incident occurred a few months later. On 24 July 1911, Prime Minister Asquith's attempts to address the House during debate on the Lords' amendments to the Parliament Bill were interrupted by repeated points of order and drowned out by persistent shouting, including repeated cries of 'Traitor!' and 'Divide!' from the opposition benches. Tempers ran very high. 'The wonder was that the crowded house did not come to blows, but the belligerent members were often pulled down by their neighbors.' The Speaker appealed for order to no avail. After trying to make himself heard for at least half an hour, Asquith finally gave up and sat down. Foreign Secretary Sir Edward Grey subsequently moved that, if the prime minister could not be heard, then the sitting should be adjourned. When Conservative F. E. Smith jumped to his feet to reply, 'pandemonium' again broke loose. 'So violent were the Opposition members, and so indignant were the Ministerialists, that the Speaker, after two hours, decided to suspend the sitting in order to obviate graver disorder.'[86]

Three days later, the Commons witnessed 'an exchange of insults, which, had it occurred anywhere else, would certainly have led to a personal encounter'. The protagonists were members of different Irish Nationalist factions. William O'Brien complained to the Speaker after

Thomas Lundon claimed that he was a descendant of Pierce Nagle, a man a colleague characterised as 'the most blackguardly informer that ever appeared in Ireland'. When Lundon refused to retract his words, O'Brien called him 'an infamous liar and scoundrel'.[87] Lundon 'made a dive' for O'Brien, 'but friends seized his coattails and the incident was closed'.[88]

Unpopular Targets

Increased rambunctiousness in the Commons was not the only danger of the period. Improved policing and changing attitudes were creating greater public order, but crowd violence remained something of a threat to politicians.

In 1890, for example, Sir Henry Havelock-Allen had to be rescued from Temperance activists in Hyde Park. When the MP encountered a demonstration against legislation compensating publicans who lost out when the number of licences to serve alcohol was reduced, some in the crowd 'poured ridicule and insult upon' him and then, when he responded in kind, 'attacked him with such violence that the police were, for a short time, compelled to make brisk use of their truncheons'.[89]

A decade later, those deemed insufficiently patriotic during the Boer War faced popular retribution. On 6 March 1900, for example, a 'stormy' meeting was held in Glasgow under the auspices of MPs David Lloyd George and Henry Wilson. Despite a hostile crowd struggling to force its way into the hall, participants backed resolutions condemning the war and supporting independence for the two Boer republics. The real danger, however, came as the speakers sought to leave the hall after the meeting. Despite efforts to organise for their protection, Lloyd George, former (and soon-to-be) MP Keir Hardie 'and three ladies of his family were roughly handled and had to be rescued by the police'. Lloyd George escaped in a cab, the windows of which were broken.[90] The next day there was another disorderly meeting, in Edinburgh, where Hardie failed to gain a hearing, the platform was rushed, and those who previously had occupied it 'were rather roughly treated on appearing outside'.[91]

A month later, there were similar scenes as Lloyd George spoke at a meeting in Bangor, in his constituency. Securing the use of Penrhyn Hall required, rather unusually, the provision of a guarantee against damage. Prior to leaving London for the meeting, Lloyd George's agent delivered 'the comforting news that nothing worse was to be expected than the throwing of missiles at the audience as they arrived and left'.

Far from shying away from such violence, however, the Welsh Wizard almost embraced it by choosing to enter the hall via the front door, outside of which an 'unfriendly' crowd had gathered. Despite smiling and bowing to the crowd, Lloyd George was greeted with howls, shouts of 'Pro Boer' and a clod of earth, flung in his direction. 'He spoke for an hour, to the accompaniment of cheers, interruptions, and the smashing of windows at the back and front of the hall.'

Afterwards, disdaining the advice of friends to leave by cab, Lloyd George insisted on walking home. As he entered the High Street, 'some zealous patriot struck him a heavy blow on the head with a bludgeon. His hat was crushed, and for a few moments he was stunned, but he managed to make his way into a café close by, where he remained for some time under police protection'. The building was besieged, but after several hours the future prime minister was able to slip out a back door.[92]

He had a similar, if more celebrated, escape in December 1901, after touching off a riot, when he attempted to speak in Birmingham Town Hall. His criticism of both the Boer War and one of its most strident champions, local hero Joseph Chamberlain, had earned Lloyd George many enemies in the city. So, it was not entirely surprising that the assembled audience was rather hostile. 'All attempts at speechmaking were futile, owing to the continuous din of hissing, hooting, and singing.' Then, the large crowd gathered outside the hall began throwing stones through its windows, hitting members of the audience. There also was an attempt to force the (barricaded) doors. Inside the hall, men, some of them armed with sticks, hammers and knives, tried to rush the platform only to be barely beaten off by police, with considerable bloodshed. Meanwhile, those on the platform were assailed with stones, bottles, cans and bricks wrapped in barbed wire. The MP and his friends were forced to seek refuge in a nearby room. The overwhelmed police prevailed upon Lloyd George to exit the building in disguise. Although some recognised the diminutive man dressed in a constable's coat surrounded by a gaggle of police, Lloyd George escaped unscathed. The rioting, however, claimed one life.[93]

Public tolerance for disorder of this sort, whether on the streets or in the Commons, was falling.[94] Among the many objections was the fear that violence discouraged (limited) political participation by women, on whom parties increasingly were reliant at the grassroots. So, it is not a little ironic that a small group of militant females seeking expanded electoral rights would soon unleash the most extensive campaign of parliamentary mayhem in British history.

10

SECTARIANS, SOLDIERS AND SUFFRAGETTES

The introduction of a third Home Rule bill in 1912 stirred sectarian passions. The outbreak of the Great War, two years later, generated patriotic fervour. Both sentiments proved perilous for MPs in the second decade of the twentieth century, but neither threatened them on the scale of the militant supporters of female enfranchisement. The Suffragettes not only unleashed the most prolific campaign of parliamentary violence in British history, one in which the disorder was primarily distaff in character, but they also were harbingers of an era in which attacks on politicians became a form of propaganda.

A Worm for Churchill

The Suffragettes were not the first women to employ unorthodox tactics. In 1743, some women spectators in the Strangers' Gallery urinated on Members below, one of whom was 'almost blinded'. A few decades later, a party led by the Duchess of Devonshire refused to leave the Strangers' Gallery when ordered to do so, clinging to their seats 'assisted by sympathetic members'. Following the two-hour disturbance, women were excluded from the gallery, banished instead to a room behind a grille far above the chamber.[1]

It also may be that as a result of more conventional methods, 'the case for women getting the vote had been made and largely accepted by the 1890s, and the opponents of women's suffrage were fighting a losing battle'.[2] But winning the intellectual argument mattered little if the public was apathetic, and it was here that the innovative methods employed by the Women's Social and Political Union (WSPU) and other militant groups were most effective.[3]

If the Home Rulers employed industrial-scale disruption on floor of the Commons in pursuit of their objectives, the Suffragettes did the same through a decade-long campaign waged (mostly) outside the walls of Westminster Palace. The first phase, from 1905 to 1909, saw considerable violence as militants from the WSPU or the Women's Freedom League (WFL), a rival, caused several commotions inside parliament and repeatedly sought to 'rush' either Westminster Palace or 10 Downing Street by breaking through police cordons in an effort to present appeals to lawmakers. Dozens were arrested as a result, generating considerable publicity for the militant cause.[4] These incidents posed a danger primarily to the militants involved, and to a lesser extent to those responsible for parliamentary security, but not to MPs, so are not of interest here.

Frustration at police success in keeping them out of parliament led some militants to adopt more aggressive tactics. In mid-1908, as Suffragettes again were prevented from reaching the lobby of the Commons, an effort that resulted in the arrest of twenty-nine women, two militants took a cab to Downing Street, where they threw stones that broke the windows of the premier's residence.[5] One of the perpetrators, Mary Leigh, subsequently told a court that sentenced her to two months at hard labour for the deed, 'The next time we come out you can expect bombs.'[6]

This remained hyperbole for several years, but parliament's repeated failure to pass a women's suffrage bill encouraged more aggressive tactics.[7] Opinion in the Commons appeared less of an obstacle to change than the attitudes of some on the government front benches. Accordingly, in late 1909, militants began targeting senior politicians with violence, typically doing so far away from Westminster's security bubble.

On 20 August, Suffragettes threw bricks at the windows of the Liverpool hall in which Secretary of State for War Richard Haldane was speaking. Two weeks later, Prime Minister Asquith was struck repeatedly by one of three Suffragettes, who approached him as he was leaving Lympne Church. Later that day, a group of WSPU members approached Asquith's party on the golf course. Herbert Gladstone interceded and had his cap knocked off. That evening, two stones were thrown through a window of the house in which Asquith was dining.

The prime minister was targeted again on 17 September, during a visit to Birmingham. Although women were barred from the hall in which Asquith was to speak, two WSPU members cut slates from the roof of a neighbouring house and threw them at the hall's windows and Asquith's car. Later that day, as Asquith returned to London by train, Suffragettes threw a metal object at the train, breaking a window of a compartment in which passengers were sitting. And that evening, others, armed with axes, did extensive damage to the windows of the Birmingham Liberal Club.[8]

Ominously, Mary Edwards, one of the perpetrators, later told a Birmingham magistrate that she regretted her restraint when she found herself near the prime minister while in possession of an axe and a penknife. 'I had the opportunity, had I chosen to take it, of seriously injuring Mr. Asquith. I am now sorry I did not do it. As he will not listen to words I think it is time that blows should be struck.'[9] She apparently was not alone in such views. At around the same time a government informant in the WLF reported that two militants had been practising at a shooting range in preparation for an attempt to assassinate Asquith.[10]

Militants did not just target inveterate opponents of female suffrage such as Asquith. Winston Churchill supported giving women the vote in principle, but also publicly refused to be 'henpecked' by militant pressure.[11]

The first attack on Churchill came on 13 November 1909. As the President of the Board of Trade and his wife were leaving Bristol railway station, a 'smartly gowned' Suffragette, Therese Gurnett, suddenly darted out from the crowd and began to 'belabor' him with a dog whip, while shouting 'Take that you brute!' Churchill's hat 'broke the force of the blow, and the lash curled about his face and left a red mark'. As police led her away, Gurnett pointed at Churchill's dented hat and cried, 'That's what you've got and you'll get more of the same from British women.'[12]

Such unladylike behaviour provoked antipathy towards the Suffragettes. When WSPU leader, Christabel Pankhurst, sought to speak in Bristol ten days later, she was shouted down and 'struck in the face by two flour balls', before protesters seeking to storm the platform forced police to clear the hall.[13] More broadly (and ironically), the political participation of women was further restricted as they increasingly were excluded from meetings for fear they would cause disruptions.[14]

The militants were undeterred. On 16 December, a Suffragette assaulted Lloyd George, as he arrived to address an election rally in London. As his car approached Queen's Hall, one Suffragette climbed inside while another locked the door and stood on the floorboard. 'The woman within upbraided and shook the Chancellor, who merely smiled. The crowd resented this action and roughly handled the two suffragettes.'[15] Four days later, two women were arrested after throwing a ginger beer bottle into Asquith's car moments after the prime minister left it.[16]

The WSPU suspended its campaign of violence in early 1910, while parliament considered a bill providing for the enfranchisement of some (wealthier) women. The legislation passed its second reading in the Commons with a large (299 to 190) majority, but subsequently died when the government refused to allocate further time for its discussion.[17] When parliament reopened in November 1910, Asquith dashed hopes that another bill would be on the agenda, provoking a Suffragette attempt to rush parliament that resulted in over 100 arrests.[18]

Militant attacks on leading politicians soon resumed. As Asquith was leaving the Commons on 22 November, 'he was surrounded by frenzied, breathless suffragettes'. Henrietta Williams struck the prime minister, shouting, 'You tax women as heavily as men, yet women are not represented in parliament.' Police quickly bundled Asquith into a taxi, 'as the women struggled frantically among themselves for the privilege of getting at him'. As the vehicle departed, Williams made another attempt to reach Asquith 'and in doing so put her militant fist through the glass of the cab window. She was pulled away, still crying "Traitor!" and "Coward!"'

Some of the women subsequently accorded similar treatment to Augustine Birrell, Chief Cabinet Secretary for Ireland, who was discovered walking through St James's Park on his way to the Athenaeum Club. The Suffragettes 'swooped down on the aged statesman, knocking his hat over his eyes and kicking him about the legs. When help came and the women were driven off, Mr. Birrell limped to his motor car, on the arms of policemen'. Later, women armed with bamboo poles fought pitched battles with police at Downing Street. The houses of Foreign Secretary Sir Edward Grey, Home Secretary Winston Churchill, and Secretary of State for Colonies Lewis Harcourt were stoned, with Grey's bearing 'the brunt of the assault'. Roughly 150 women, and a few men, were taken to jail as a result.[19]

Less than a week later, a male advocate of women's suffrage attacked Churchill with a whip as the Home Secretary was returning to London by train. Police accompanying the minister parried the blow and overpowered the assailant. However, when the train reached London, 'three women tried to assault the Home Secretary, but the detectives drove them off'.[20]

The militant campaign again was suspended to pave the way for the introduction of another bill providing for (partial) female suffrage in early 1911. It easily passed its second reading (255 to 88) only to stall thereafter.[21] Although Asquith sought to encourage hope that enfranchisement might come in the next parliamentary session, his abandonment of this second bill caused the most militant Suffragettes to alter their entire approach. 'For some members of the WSPU after 1911, resistance was no longer about convincing the government or the public that women ought to have the vote; rather, women's goal became to make political life so difficult that the government would be compelled to give women the vote.'[22]

If something like terrorism was the intention, the execution was rather lacking. The violence that followed tended to be vexatious rather than terrifying, with minor acts of vandalism and arson predominating. Most of the targets were not parliamentary. And when politicians were attacked, the reaction suggested that the militants were doing their cause no good.

In February 1912, for example, a Suffragette, shouting 'take that you cur!', hit Churchill in the face with a flag bearing the words 'No Referendum for the Suffragettes', an allusion to his suggestion that a plebiscite on female suffrage might be held. In response, she was 'rather roughly hustled by the crowd', but the First Lord of the Admiralty reportedly ensured that she was not harmed.[23]

The following month, while 150 women were smashing windows on the Strand and Oxford and Regent Streets, three Suffragettes took a cab to 10 Downing Street, where they managed to break four windows before being arrested. Days later, a large phalanx of police surrounding Westminster Palace thwarted an effort to 'rush' parliament, but individual militants managed to break windows at the House of Lords, the residences of at least two ministers, and a number of government buildings and commercial properties. Many in the crowd reportedly were hostile toward the activities of the militants, jeering and threatening suspected Suffragettes and cheering when police detained the window breakers. A group of 200 'well-dressed young men' responded to the militants' efforts by breaking windows in buildings occupied by (non-militant) suffragist organisations, to the apparent delight of spectators.[24]

It was not just some members of the general public who appeared upset with the militants' handiwork. In late March 1912, another suffrage bill failed at the second reading. A number of MPs who had supported similar legislation in the past indicated that they had voted against this bill as a direct result of militancy. To do otherwise, they argued, would have created the appearance either of condoning Suffragette violence or succumbing to intimidation.[25]

This might have given some militants pause for thought, but, if so, the hiatus was brief. On 14 June, Asquith was assaulted three times at a reception he hosted at the India Office in honour of the king's birthday. As he was greeting guests, a well-dressed woman of around 30, instead of shaking his hand, placed both her hands on his shoulder and 'began tugging violently at the epaulettes of the Premier's official coat. Mr. Asquith showed considerable sang-froid and managed to shake off the women, but she returned to the attack and tried with all her might to wrench off the epaulette from his right shoulder'. After she had been 'dragged away, resisting stubbornly', a 'pale-faced youth' of 20 approached Asquith, 'took hold of him rudely by the arms and shouted something inaudible'. This assailant was also removed unceremoniously. Shortly thereafter, 'another well-dressed young woman seized the Premier's arm, and in the ensuing struggle beat him on the head with her fan with considerable violence'.[26]

On 26 June, a Suffragette attacked Home Secretary Reginald McKenna, who was accompanying the king and queen on a visit to Llandaff Cathedral. With the royal couple only feet away, Helen Cragg rushed from the crowd and seized McKenna's arm, holding it until a detective led her away.[27]

Asquith again was assaulted two days later, at a reception given by Lady Glenconner. A woman 'caught him by the lapels of his coat and shook him vigorously until the Premier was breathless'. Two male guests grabbed the assailant and 'hurled her down the stairs. The struggle was so violent that a sleeve was torn out of the suffragette's dress, her combs fell out of her hair, her gold watch was broken, and she lost her diamond brooch'.[28] That Suffragettes could infiltrate even a gathering hosted by a peeress was deeply unsettling, which helps account for the woman's ungentlemanly treatment.

In mid-July, Mary Leigh, who less than two years earlier had expressed regret for not injuring the prime minister when she had a chance, threw a hatchet into the carriage in which Asquith, his wife and others were riding on their way to a Dublin hotel. It cut the ear of John Redmond, leader of the Irish Parliamentary Party. Later that evening, Leigh, who had been arrested nine times and served more than 15 months in prison, joined other women in attempting to burn down the theatre in which Asquith was scheduled to speak.[29] The next day, as Asquith 'was motoring from Chester station to the Dublin Town Hall, a woman broke through the police cordon and threw a bag of flour in the direction of the Premier'. She missed.[30] Around the same time, at a public ceremony in Monmouthshire, a woman emerged from the crowd, seized Home Secretary Reginald McKenna by the shoulders 'and shook him vigorously'.[31]

More of the same was to follow in the ensuing months. In mid-September, McKenna and Asquith had a 'lively encounter' with two Suffragettes on a golf course.[32] Soon thereafter, while Churchill 'was golfing in the vicinity of Balmoral an unknown woman suddenly appeared and threw a large worm in his face'.[33] In early November, a Suffragette 'uproar' prevented McKenna from delivering a speech at Holborn Town Hall. 'The Home Secretary escaped a mauling by fleeing with his wife through a side door.'[34] At the end of that month, a Suffragette mistook a Baptist minister for Chancellor Lloyd George in Aberdeen and, 'after accusing him of trying to disguise himself, assaulted the astonished victim with a dog whip. She was arrested, but indignantly refused to admit that she was mistaken'.[35]

It was not just the persons of ministers that were threatened. In January, Lewis Harcourt had been told that British women 'would do all in their power to make his life miserable', after he told a delegation that he opposed female suffrage.[36] Six months later, the Colonial Secretary learned what this meant, after two 'respectably dressed women' were discovered preparing to burn down Nuneham House, his residence.[37] The houses of two other Cabinet members were attacked subsequently.[38]

The cumulative effect of this onslaught was to prompt security measures not seen since the Fenian campaign of the 1880s. Political meetings were cancelled or restricted to men only. Police were mobilised to protect ministers, whose travel arrangements were altered on short notice. Despite these precautions, the attacks continued, leaving senior politicians concerned for their safety and that of their families.[39]

Ironically, while the militants largely abided by their pledge not to cause serious injury, their tactics were so provocative that opponents did not always exercise similar restraint. On 23 September, for example, three Suffragettes tried to disrupt a meeting addressed by Lloyd George in Wales. Such behaviour, while appropriate at an election rally, was unacceptable at an address by a senior politician, adding to the sense that the women were violating political norms.[40]

Police managed to escort two of the women away from the 'infuriated crowd', but a third barely escaped with her life. 'She had scarcely uttered the cry, "Votes for women!" when the man nearest to her struck her in the face with his fist, and men and women seized her ... In an instant she was stripped to the waist and then pummeled and beaten with fists and sticks. Her hair was torn out, and she was dragged through the crowd and flung, bruised and bleeding over a hedge, literally into the arms of a policeman.' The police then successfully fought members of the crowd to take the woman to safety.[41]

Angry Birds: Level Three

The demise of another suffrage bill in early 1913 elicited increasingly millenarian, deranged and misanthropic rhetoric from WSPU leaders, which led some militants to quit the group but incited others to escalate their offensive.[42] The government responded with increased repression, prompting a further ratcheting up of Suffragette violence.

On 29 January 1913, a package addressed to Chancellor Lloyd George burst into flames, when opened in a post office.[43] Although the incendiary device did not cause any injuries, the attempted attack on the Chancellor suggested to some that a Rubicon had been crossed.

This impression was reinforced a few weeks later when Suffragettes bombed a country house being constructed for the Chancellor, causing heavy damage. WSPU leader Emmeline Pankhurst later accepted full responsibility for what she termed 'a fine affair successfully carried out', one that was intended to 'wake up' the minister to the need for women's suffrage. That message may have been somewhat vitiated by reports that Lloyd George did not yet own the structure, meaning that the costs of the damage might be covered by local ratepayers.[44]

Pankhurst's subsequently imprisonment for inciting the destruction of the house prompted followers to unleash what one of them called a 'reign of terror'. Previous militant violence would be, she asserted, 'the merest pin pricks' compared to what would follow. Another Suffragette vowed that her comrades no longer would respect human life. Although this was mostly bluster, over the next year, Suffragettes engaged in an orgy of violence that virtually every day produced new incidents of arson, bombing, window breaking, telegraph-cable cutting, mail destruction, artwork slashing and a variety of other forms of vandalism.[45]

The first parliamentary victim was Arthur Phillip Du Cros, a Unionist who had been warned that his opposition to women's suffrage would bring retaliation. On 15 April, his (recently vacated) house at St Leonards-on-Sea was completely destroyed by fire. Suffragette literature was found nearby.[46] A few weeks later, a bomb was placed in the office of Home Secretary McKenna.[47]

The government, under pressure to stem the militant attacks, banned Suffragette meetings in London, arguing that such gathering tended to produce disorder. In late April 1913, it pushed through parliament what came to be called the Cat and Mouse Act. Hitherto, militants had won release from prison (and, effectively, an abolition of their sentence) by going on hunger strike. Now, the police were authorised to re-arrest them once their health had improved. Many saw this as unfair. Consequently, the state's treatment of Suffragette prisoners became the object of parliamentary protest.

In June 1913, a professed member of the Men's Political Union for Women Suffrage threw a bundle, 'about the size of a child's football', from the Strangers' Gallery on to the floor close to where Prime Minister Asquith was standing. The missile burst open, scattering white powder, which proved to be harmless. He also flung down 'a militant pamphlet on forcible feeding entitled "Grace before Meat"'. As the protester was being ejected, he shouted, 'Remember Miss Davison', a reference to Suffragette Emily Davison, who had died a few days earlier of injuries sustained after being knocked down by the king's horse, to which she apparently had been trying to attach Suffragette colours during the running of the Epsom Derby.[48]

A month later, two male supporters of female suffrage interrupted discussion in the Commons of the Plural Voting Bill. In the first instance, a man fired a toy pistol from the Strangers' Gallery, shouted 'Justice for women!' and threw onto the floor of the House a toy mouse in a cage. Shortly after that man had been forcibly ejected, another rose in the Strangers' Gallery and called out 'in a rather faint voice, "When are you going to give women the vote?"' He, too, was quickly ejected.[49]

In late August, Asquith was attacked while playing golf with his daughter Violet in Scotland. On the seventeenth green, 'two women suddenly appeared, rushed at him, knocked his hat off, struck him with a book, and then proceeded to drag him about. Miss Asquith grappled with the women, and a struggle was waged, the militants shouting wildly about "justice for women"'. The two women were taken to a police station, where a large crowd 'hissed them, and threatened to throw them into the sea'.[50]

A few days later, Asquith was targeted again in what was dubbed 'a suffragette battle of Bannockburn'. As the prime minister was 'motoring from Stirling', his car was forced to stop by four women standing in the road. 'One of them then threw pepper on the occupants of the vehicle while another attempted to strike the Premier with a dog whip.' Police following in another car quickly arrested the women.[51]

On 14 November, while speaking in Bristol, Chief Secretary for Ireland Augustine Birrell was hit in the chest by a dead cat, thrown by a male suffragist. 'The hall was in an uproar immediately. Blows were exchanged and there was much struggling.' Meanwhile, as John Redmond and his wife were travelling by train to Newcastle, 'a woman passenger came to the door of their compartment and threw flour over them, giving expression at the same time to the usual suffragette cry'.[52] Scottish Secretary Thomas McKinnon Wood suffered a similar fate, being made to look 'like a miller', after an 'irate suffragette' threw a bag of flour at him while he was addressing a meeting in Edinburgh.[53]

By 1914, police efforts effectively had driven the WSPU underground. The destructiveness of the militant campaign did not reach a crescendo until February of that year, when damage was estimated at a minimum of £62,000.[54] But improved security often forced Suffragettes to attack softer targets, ones that had less direct relevance to their cause.

On 12 February, an incendiary device was discovered on the windowsill of the house of Arthur Chamberlain, the late brother of MP Joseph Chamberlain. Nearby was some Suffragette literature and a postcard addressed to Home Secretary McKenna reading, 'Militancy is not dead, but if you are not, you soon will be.'[55]

A week later, a Suffragette attacked Lord Weardale at Euston Station. While the peer was walking with his wife along the platform, 'he was approached from behind by the militant, who struck a severe blow at him with a powerful dog whip, as a result of which he fell to the ground'. Weardale speculated that he was attacked because he was co-President of the Anti-Suffragist Society. However, his assailant apparently mistook him for Asquith, an embarrassing mistake given that Weardale was considerably older than the prime minister and bore 'but a slight resemblance to him'.[56]

On 5 March, Suffragettes used chairs as weapons as they tried to break up a meeting of the Independent Labour Party. The focus of their ire was Ramsay MacDonald, who was called a 'traitor' for his complicity in the Liberal government's 'torture' of women. The MP's attempt to address the gathering triggered about an hour of 'pandemonium' that saw 'free fights' between the men and 'the women tearing one another's clothes, scratching each other's faces until they bled, and rolling about on the floor in a confused and frantic mess'. In the end, between fifty and sixty people were ejected from the hall.[57]

Ten days later, six Suffragettes attacked the residence of Home Secretary McKenna with hatchets and hammers. Surprising the policemen who kept continual guard over the house, the women managed to smash 'every pane of glass on the ground floor', before being arrested. In court, the women, most of who provided false names, were sentenced to two months' hard labour. 'One of the prisoners, who gave the name of Boardicea [sic], said in court: "I wouldn't have given much for him – Mr. McKenna – if we had got inside."'[58] A few months earlier, militants had burned down the Hampshire mansion of McKenna's brother, Theodore.[59]

The Suffragette campaign ended not with victory but with the outbreak of the First World War. Much of the recent discussion of their legacy concerns whether they were 'terrorists', a label some militants applied to themselves.[60] Yet their final years, when the description was most applicable, seem to have been their least effective politically, largely because their actions were sufficiently damaging to vex and anger but not destructive enough to force concessions.[61] This, combined with their increasingly unhinged rhetoric, made even politicians who supported female suffrage wary of doing so publicly.[62]

For present purposes, the earlier activities of the Suffragettes were far more significant. At first, they used violence and disruption as propaganda, a means to draw attention to their cause. Crucially, the publicity was positive only to the extent that others were not injured in their stunts, a lesson some of the more extreme Suffragettes failed to learn. In the second half of the twentieth century, it would become common for activists to employ almost non-violent violence to draw attention to their cause. But well before that, others had begun following the path blazed by the Suffragettes. In May 1915, for example, Frederick Charrington, 'wearing evening dress, an overcoat, and a silk hat', rushed into the Commons and seized the mace. The Christian activist and Temperance crusader, heir to a brewery fortune, was upset that alcohol was served at a bar in the Members' lobby. [63]

Home Rule, Act Three
Even before the Suffragette campaign drew to a close another source of parliamentary violence was looming.

In 1912, the Asquith Government, dependent on Irish parliamentary support, introduced a third Home Rule bill. Ulster Protestants began arming to resist a change expected to result in their political domination by Ireland's Catholic majority. Unionist leader Andrew Bonar Law, hoping to force an election, openly supported these preparations, stating, 'I can imagine no length of resistance to which Ulster can go in which I should not be prepared to support them.' Civil war appeared a distinct possibility.[64]

In this atmosphere, Winston Churchill went to Belfast to speak in favour of Irish self-government. The trip did not begin well: on the boat over, Suffragettes kept the Churchills up all night by shouting 'Votes for Women!' outside their cabin. Police reports that large quantities of bolts and rivets were being abstracted from the (mainly Protestant) shipyards suggested that their reception in Belfast could be even worse. In the event, they faced little actual violence. Fists were shaken at them in the lobby of the Grand Central Hotel, which was besieged by a hostile crowd, said to number 10,000. As the Churchills left for the meeting, the car in which they were riding 'was hustled and for a moment was in some danger of being overturned'. The actual speech, held in a Catholic area of the city, saw little disorder, but Churchill's cousin, Freddie Guest, had armed himself with a revolver, just in case.[65]

The Liberal politician's foray into the Unionist lion's den won him plaudits for pluck. 'Mr. Churchill behaved as a brave man would. He shirked no danger; he adopted no ruse; he went out openly and boldly, and scorned undoubted risks.'[66] Whether this provocative action, which nearly precipitated a riot, was responsible is another matter entirely.

Churchill was involved in another incident several months later, this time on the floor of the House of Commons. On 11 November 1912, the government's hopes of passing a Home Rule bill were greatly damaged, when the opposition won a snap vote on a resolution that cut, by more than half, the funds a future Irish government would receive. Rather than accede to calls to resign as a result, however, the Asquith administration sought to rescind the decision two days later. The Speaker ruled that such a move was in order, although he admitted that no precedent could be found. This decision turned the Commons into a tumultuous 'beer garden'.

Opposition leader Law called the prime minister's attempt to force a re-vote 'a blow worthy of old Cromwell himself' and moved for adjournment. Asquith rose to reply, only to take his seat again in the face of cries of 'Adjourn!' After a motion to do just that was rejected, the Speaker ordered Sir William Bull to withdraw for repeatedly calling Asquith a traitor. The House then refused to hear a number of speakers, prompting a suspension of the sitting. When it resumed, the disorder continued, with Members hurling insults at each other and 'paper pellets' at the prime minister. The Speaker summarily adjourned the House.[67]

The 'grave disorder' did not abate immediately. 'When the Mace had been removed it seemed doubtful for several anxious moments whether the two parties would leave the House peaceably.' Members stood in the middle of the floor shouting insults at each other. Churchill waved his handkerchief to encourage cheers for the prime minister, as the latter left the Commons. He then waved it mockingly in the direction of the opposition. In response, Unionist Ronald McNeill threw a copy of the House Standing Orders at Churchill, hitting him in the face. 'Mr. Churchill turned, but was restrained from taking notice of the insult by two Ministers standing by, who persuaded him to leave the Chamber.'[68]

A few days later, a Conservative MP argued in *The Times* that 'it is not only the right but the duty of the minority' to resist by disorder any majority attempt to undermine parliamentary precedent and procedure, a claim historically more attractive to Parnellites than to the 'party of order'.[69] Others pointed out that rules pertaining to 'grave disorder' actually encouraged misbehaviour by those who opposed whatever parliament happened to be doing at the time, an assertion that would find ample support in the coming decades.[70]

Conservatives justified their extraordinary resistance partly by asserting that the Liberal administration was spectacularly corrupt. Exhibit A was the Marconi scandal, in which several ministers acquired shares of an American company shortly before their government awarded a lucrative contract to its British sister organisation. This sordid episode briefly threatened to produce an affair of honour in early 1913, on April Fool's Day as fate would have it.

Conservative John Kebty-Fletcher caused an 'uproar' by asking Chancellor David Lloyd George whether the latter's salary was not sufficient 'without wrongfully and improperly gambling'. Lloyd George, 'pale and trembling with anger, retorted: "Let the honorable member say what he has to say about me in a place where he can be examined."' Rather than do so, at the possible risk of violence, Kebty-Fletcher dismissed the Chancellor's demand as 'mock heroics'.[71]

Less than a year later, however, MPs came even closer to fighting. On 19 March 1914, heated discussions of the Third Home Rule Bill and the status of Ulster led to 'a very extraordinary incident'. When Nationalist John Dillon argued that the English should make an effort to conciliate the Irish in America, Unionist Martin Archer-Shee interjected, 'They are foreigners and cowards!' Nationalist Michael Flavin shouted back, 'You are a coward to call them so!' Archer-Shee left the chamber to write a challenge to Flavin. The latter went out into the lobby, where he offered Archer-Shee 'satisfaction in any form of combat he desired'. Amid 'intense excitement', Nationalist Joseph Devlin 'played the peacemaker, and brought them to moderation, but only with great difficulty'.[72]

By late May, the Commons was on the verge of passing the Home Rule Bill. When Asquith announced that amendments to the legislation would be introduced in the Lords but refused Law's request to provide details of the specific changes, the result was a disorderly sitting, deemed 'more characteristic of the Austrian than of the English Parliament'. Unionist back-benchers then began shouting 'Adjourn!', preventing any further business. At length, the Speaker rose and asked Law if the demonstrations were taking place with the latter's assent and approval. To this very unusual question, which might have forced him to choose between his responsibilities to the House and his obligations to his supporters, Law replied, 'I do not presume, Mr. Speaker, to criticize what you consider your duty, but I know mine. It is not to answer such a question.' After the leader of His Majesty's opposition sat down, the disorder continued, causing the Speaker to suspend the sitting.[73]

Unionist obstruction failed to prevent passage of Home Rule legislation, but the outbreak of the Great War led to the suspension of its provisions. As a result, the ructions in Westminster caused by Irish matters continued.

One obstreperous Irish MP single-handedly managed to bring Commons proceedings to a standstill twice in the space of a year, by forcibly resisting the authority of the Speaker. Laurence Ginnell had form in this regard.[74] In July 1916, he was named and suspended after repeatedly defying the Speaker by seeking to ask questions about government actions during the Easter Rising. Ginnell then refused to withdraw even after the Serjeant-at-Arms had been summoned, prompting the Speaker to suspend the sitting.[75]

A year later, amidst rumours that Sinn Féin members intended to throw bombs or fire revolvers from the Strangers' Gallery to mark

Ginnell's expected announcement that he would quit parliament to join the radical Irish Republican party, the Speaker informed the Commons that he had requested the presence of 'Secret Service men'.[76] The following day, Ginnell denounced their summoning and declared his own life to be in danger, reading a number of threatening and insulting letters that he had received to substantiate the claim. Ordered to resume his seat, Ginnell refused. He was named and suspended. When he did not depart the chamber as instructed, the sitting was adjourned under the provisions for grave disorder, 'while the attendants hustled Mr. Ginnell from the chamber'.[77]

Ginnell's determination to remain in the Commons, by force if necessary, was a tad ironic given his sympathy for Sinn Féin, which he joined soon after this episode. The party long had been committed to a policy of abstentionism: those elected to parliament under its banner were to seek to form an independent assembly in Dublin rather than take their seats in Westminster. Following triumphs in a few by-elections, Sinn Féin virtually destroyed its Nationalist rival, the Irish Parliamentary Party, in the 1918 general election. In January 1919, Sinn Féin MPs met in Dublin to form an Irish parliament, the Dáil *Éireann*.[78] (A few years later, Ginnell would be expelled from the Dáil for persistently questioning its constitutionality.[79])

Seats in the Dáil were dangerous, particularly early on, but that story is beyond the scope of the current study.[80] For present purposes, the last incident of parliamentary violence in the twenty-six counties of what would become an independent Ireland came in late 1919, when three months after the government ordered the suppression of the Dáil, the Irish Republican Army came very close to assassinating Viscount French, the Lord Lieutenant.[81] Yet, even as the British government was forced to concede substantial autonomy to Southern Ireland, events there still were causing problems in Westminster.

On 1 November 1920, for example, controversial Irish security measures almost produced a physical altercation between Lord Henry Cavendish-Bentinck and the Chief Secretary for Ireland. As Sir Hamar Greenwood sought to defend the government's arrest and deportation to Dublin of Violet Bryce, the elderly wife of a former MP, enough Members walked out to deprive the House of a quorum. Cavendish-Bentinck suggested that the Chief Secretary ought to 'face the music', prompting an exchange in which Greenwood reportedly called his colleague a coward. Cavendish-Bentinck replied, 'You called me a coward. Either you withdraw, or I fight you.' Violence was avoided after both men eventually agreed to rescind their objectionable expressions.[82]

Three weeks later, the events of 'Bloody Sunday' were mirrored by a significantly less sanguinary encounter in the Commons on the following day. After Greenwood informed the House that fourteen men, twelve of them British officers, had been murdered – many in their beds – in Dublin, Joseph Devlin inquired why the government had not mentioned that later that same day British forces had opened fire on spectators at a sporting event at Croke Park, killing fourteen. Devlin's intervention provoked an uproar, but he refused to sit down, as some MPs loudly demanded. In an attempt to compel the Irish Nationalist to comply, Conservative Major John Molson, who was sitting in front of Devlin, 'put his arm around Mr. Devlin's shoulders, which were bent forward, and pulled him down head first over the back of the bench'. As Devlin struggled to free himself, there was a shout of 'Kill him'. Having escaped, Devlin turned on Molson, who fought back. 'All blows missed their aim, but an innocent neutral was hit across the mouth.' Other Members joined the fray, either to make peace or fight. The Speaker suspended the session for ten minutes and left the chair.[83] After the session resumed, both Molson and Devlin apologised. The Speaker, evidently hoping to put the matter behind him, did not punish Molson and also claimed not to hear Sir Edward Carson call Nationalist Jeremiah MacVeagh a 'liar', for asserting that it was the Unionists who began using rifles in Ireland.[84]

Jingo Jangles

The eruption of the Great War not only postponed Home Rule but also generated patriotic fervour dangerous to parliamentarians reminiscent of conflict in South Africa more than a decade earlier. Ramsay MacDonald's claim that secret treaties were at least partially responsible for the war and his call for reasonable peace terms to forestall future conflict may have been vindicated subsequently, but publicly expressing such opinions made the future prime minister one of the most vilified men in the country. 'MacDonald was barred from his [Lossiemouth] golf club, which complained that "we are tainted as with leprosy"; he was later beaten up and narrowly escaped being thrown in a canal.' His allies did not fare much better: 'Liberal MP Charles Trevelyan's local council passed a resolution calling for him to be "taken out and shot"'.[85]

Glasgow was one of the few places where enough people shared his views to allow MacDonald to speak freely. However, his plans to address a meeting of the Independent Labour Party (ILP) in the summer of 1915 were threatened when it became clear that the Scottish Patriotic League was seeking to disrupt the event. MacDonald's apprehension was eased by the arrival of two future Labour MPs, Manny Shinwell and John McGovern, the latter armed with a lead pipe. McGovern declared himself 'a pacifist', prompting MacDonald to reply, 'That's the sort of pacifist I like!' Later, 'when one of the Patriotic League speakers hammered on the stage door at the head of a mob, Shinwell went down and knocked him out'.[86]

More frequently, however, MacDonald and other critics of the war faced violence more than a little reminiscent of the conservative 'Church and King' riots of an earlier time. In November 1915, a meeting of the London branch of the Union of Democratic Control was broken up by soldiers and medical students, some of whom had gained entrance to the hall with fake tickets. The scheduled speakers, including Trevelyan, 'were unceremoniously thrown from the platform. Those who clung to their chairs were bundled off chair and all, and they were followed by some of the platform furniture itself'.[87]

A year later, 'aggressive patriots' broke up a conference of the National Council for Civil Liberties in Cardiff before Macdonald and fellow MP James Thomas were able to speak. A large crowd tried to force its way into the hall, meeting 'stout resistance' but eventually breaking down the doors. 'Fist fighting followed in which it is reported that the women delegates fought like tigers.' Thomas 'attempted to rally his supporters but was dragged from the platform and narrowly escaped serious injury'. Most of the other speakers and delegates quickly departed through a side door.[88]

Two months later, a 'whirlwind rush by soldiers in khaki' terminated a 'peace meeting' in Walthamstow. One of the soldiers advised MacDonald to leave the speakers' platform. '"I won't do it!" shouted MacDonald, "This is a meeting of free Britons, and we won't let any one interrupt us."' The soldier threatened to 'put out' MacDonald and the others on the platform, but the MP called on his comrades to stand firm. A line of soldiers advanced. 'MacDonald tried to cling to the edge of the table, but it was swept away and he was pushed rapidly off the platform.'[89]

The next day, as MacDonald and ILP President Frederick Jowett prepared to sail to Petrograd to attend a socialist conference, they were 'seized and imprisoned' by members of National Seamen's and Firemen's Union, upset that the MPs planned to meet with comrades from countries with which Britain was at war.[90] Several months later, the same issue produced another fracas at a Labour conference.

MacDonald's support for a resolution calling for the party to send a delegation to another meeting in Stockholm produced 'an uproar', during which he 'came to blows' with Will Thorne, a fellow Labour MP and founder and General Secretary of the National Union of General Workers.[91]

There was more violence in September 1918, when MacDonald sought to address a meeting in London organised by the ILP and the Woolwich Trades and Labour Council. A rival gathering arranged by a branch of the National Federation of Discharged and Demobilized Sailors and Soldiers sought to storm the platform from which MacDonald was seeking to speak. 'Free fights, stone-throwing, combats with sticks and riotous proceedings' ensued, leading to numerous injuries, but MacDonald was well defended. Order was restored after he left the platform, but when he returned, chaos erupted, and stones again filled the air. 'For a minute or two Mr. MacDonald faced the fusillade, and endeavoured to speak, but what he said could not be heard. Then came a rush for the platform, and Mr. MacDonald again disappeared.'[92]

Not all the excitement took place outside Westminster. Noel Pemberton Billing was perhaps the most controversial MP of his time.[93] So it is perhaps not surprising that he found himself in not one but two violent scrapes.

After Billing made comments critical of certain military officers in mid-July 1917, Martin Archer-Shee called him a 'cad'. Billing asked if Archer-Shee would repeat that epithet outside the House, to which the latter replied, 'Certainly'. The two then 'had a set-to on the greensward outside of the House of Commons, when after a brief spar both fell to the ground. Then the police arrived and parted the gasping and dishevelled tribunes'. Billing subsequently challenged his foe to a twenty-round boxing contest. Archer-Shee declined, instead proposing a twenty-round bout with 'single-sticks, without body or head protection'.[94] (Both MPs seem to have taken a few too many blows to the noggin.)

A year later, Billing's advocacy of the internment of enemy aliens brought him into conflict with the Speaker, resulting in another violent parliamentary scene. When the MP called for adjournment in order to discuss the matter, the Speaker informed him that a 'blocking order' prevented such a motion. Billing persisted even as the Speaker tried to move on to other business. At one point, when colleagues yelled for him to be seated, he replied, 'I'm not going to sit down when there are a lot of damned Germans running around this country.' After repeated warnings, the Speaker finally named the recalcitrant MP. A vote for his suspension was carried without division.[95] He refused to leave. The Speaker instructed the Serjeant-at-Arms to remove Billing, who walked to the table to inform the Speaker that he disputed the latter's ruling. The Speaker suspended the sitting amidst this 'grave disorder' and left the Chamber.[96] 'Then, at a signal from the Serjeant-at-Arms, four of the attendants came in and, seizing Mr. Billing by the arms and legs, lifted him out of his seat and carried him, struggling, out of the House.'[97]

Some argue that the Great War fatally split the Liberal Party.[98] Others contend that the Asquith administration's illiberal response to demands for women's suffrage not only goaded militants into escalating levels of violence but also alienated local activists, many of them female, allowing the party's eclipse by a new progressive champion, Labour.[99] Whatever the cause, the demise of the Liberal party would coincide with an increase in class-based politics that would transform parliamentary violence in the wake of the First World War.

11

THE CLYDESIDERS

Early in the interwar period, German political theorist Carl Schmitt asserted that actual practice had become sufficiently divergent from liberal ideals to constitute a 'crisis of parliamentary democracy'.[1] The subsequent collapse of democracies in Europe and Japan made this claim appear prescient. Some argue Britain avoided this fate, because Westminster continued to function.[2] Yet the 1920s and 1930s were sufficiently turbulent to call into question the survival of the British political system.[3] A key reason was the activities in Westminster of a small group of parliamentary class warriors called the Clydesiders.

Labour Pains

Parliamentary disorder became considerably more prevalent in the 1920s: compared to the previous decade, the number of MPs suspended rose almost six-fold (from five to thirty-three), while the frequency of 'grave disorder' grew by 50 per cent (from six to nine). This increased turmoil reflected a division in the ascendant Labour Party.

Leader Ramsay MacDonald believed that the party could best serve its constituents and expand its electoral appeal by pursuing moderate aims by scrupulously parliamentary means. This approach had helped Labour increase its parliamentary strength from 42 MPs, following the December 1910 general election, to 142, in the wake of that of 1922.[4]

From the beginning, not everyone agreed with this strategy. For more than a decade after its founding in 1906, the Labour Party allowed individuals to join only indirectly, through membership in an affiliated organisation. Many, including MacDonald himself, entered Labour's ranks by signing on to the Independent Labour

Party (ILP). Despite this connection, there was considerable friction between the two groups: those in the ILP generally preferred a less accommodating, more confrontational approach than that pursued by the trades-union dominated Labour Party.[5]

One of the first public manifestations of this discord came in October 1908, when ILP member Victor Grayson's disorderly attempts to force a Commons discussion on unemployment led the Speaker first to order the Serjeant to remove the MP and then, the next day, to name him, prompting his suspension for the remainder of the session.[6] MacDonald subsequently disavowed 'those who would degrade the House of Commons by an exhibition of conduct ... like what marked the life of the London vestries', but much more was to follow.[7]

Prior to the 1922 general election, Lenin urged English Communists to stand, so that they could make violent scenes on the floor of the Commons that would bring parliament into disrepute and improve the prospects for revolution.[8] The members of the group of Glaswegian Labour MPs known as the Clydesiders were not Communists, but like many ILP members, their impatience to address the grievances of the working class led them to take something of the Bolshevik leader's approach. For them, agitation and propaganda were central to the role of the MP. 'Parliament was a soap-box writ large; suggestions that the techniques of the soap-box might be out of place in it were signs of timidity, if not of treachery. Debates in the House of Commons were skirmishes in the class war', a struggle that had to be waged both inside and outside the chamber.[9] By making 'scenes' in parliament, the Clydesiders would not only undermine MacDonald's efforts to portray Labour as a constitutionally minded party that could be trusted with the reins of government but also call into question the very viability of the parliamentary system.[10]

The first incident of note came in February 1923, when John Walton Newbold called Clydesider Neil Maclean an 'opportunist'. Newbold, the first MP elected as a Communist, claimed that his colleague had once strongly supported 'the Commune' but had lately gone 'well to the Right'. In response to Newbold's jibe, Maclean 'jumped up from his seat on the front of the opposition bench and turned towards Mr. Newbold, who was standing immediately to his right on the bench behind him'. Maclean 'assumed a threatening attitude' towards Newbold, 'pointed excitedly towards the door' and made some remarks inaudible to those in the Press Gallery. However, Maclean was 'restrained by two of his Labour colleagues', who persuaded him to resume his seat.[11]

Two months later, procedural irregularities led to a sitting described, not entirely accurately, as witnessing the 'worst scenes since Parnell days'.[12] After suffering defeat in a division, the government sought to move on to another matter rather than establishing a committee of inquiry, as precedent suggested. When the Speaker called a vote, the opposition refused to participate, its Members first shouting 'Adjourn!' and then breaking into 'a fortissimo rendering' of the 'Red Flag'. The Speaker then announced that the government's motion was carried. 'Pandemonium followed.'

A Member rose to begin debate on another matter only to be drowned out by 'a kind of Labour antiphonal chorus of "Sit down" and "Speak up"'. Eventually, the Speaker decided to adjourn the sitting for an hour. Labour Members immediately 'surged' toward the ministerial bench. One of them, Robert Murray, demanded of Conservative William Ormsby-Gore, 'Take that grin off your face!' This led a nearby Conservative MP, evidently thinking that Ormsby-Gore was about to be assaulted, to 'flick' Murray with an order paper. Murray responded with a blow, which landed on the nose of a bystander, Walter Guinness. The Under-Secretary for War 'seized Murray in his arms and several Conservatives came hurrying up to join in the scrap'. Stanley Baldwin, the ranking Tory, and MacDonald 'thrust themselves into the struggling group, imploring their supporters to remember the dignity of the House'. Although some MPs spoke of moving the fight outside, after they arrived in the lobby, 'shouting and shoving', they dispersed.[13] When the Speaker returned, he decided that passions had not cooled sufficiently and therefore adjourned the House.[14]

There was another, more minor, physical confrontation in mid-May after Newbold repeatedly interrupted Sir Philip Lloyd Graeme's efforts to speak on Soviet propaganda. When the Communist MP was heard to accuse his colleague of telling a falsehood, the Chair called him to order. Newbold replied, 'Do you allow charges to be made against me and not give me a chance of answering, like the bourgeois that you are.' The Chair ordered Newbold to withdraw. When the Deputy Serjeant sought to approach the MP, 'his way was barred' by Clydesider James Maxton. Newbold eventually was suspended, but no action was taken against Maxton.[15]

A month later, Maxton and three colleagues did not escape punishment as a result of another febrile episode. While Maxton was criticising the Scottish Board of Health for withdrawal of a milk grant, Sir Frederick Banbury interjected 'Hear, hear' to a mention that the board also, for reasons of economy, had refused isolation treatment of children with measles. Maxton was acutely sensitive to this issue: only months earlier his wife had died, after spending a year nursing their seriously ill young son back to health.[16] He turned to the government benches and declared, 'I call that murder.' There were cries of 'Order' and attempts to get Maxton to agree that he had not meant the term to apply to any individual MP, but not only did he refuse to back down, but John Wheatley endorsed the wording used by his fellow Clydesider. The chair ordered both Maxton and Wheatley to withdraw. They refused. The Speaker was sent for. He named the pair, whose suspensions then were voted.

Immediately after the division, another Clydesider, the Reverend Campbell Stephen, rose and uttered the word 'murderer', leading to his suspension. After this division, a fourth Clydesider, Manny Shinwell, sought to continue the debate, only to be interrupted by the shout of 'Jew' by Sir George Hamilton. This brought some of Shinwell's allies to their feet, loudly protesting the epithet. Clydesider George Buchanan called Deputy Speaker James Hope a 'disgrace', for not being impartial. When Buchanan refused to obey the chair's order that he resume his seat, the Speaker was summoned. Buchanan was then named, and a motion for his suspension was carried.[17] After the division, Hope informed the House that he had not heard Hamilton's expression. He demanded that the latter withdraw it, and Hamilton did so.[18]

MacDonald was furious with Maxton, who apparently was not offered a place in the Labour government formed a few months later because of the episode.[19] The Labour leader publicly had sought to persuade the Glaswegian MP to withdraw his most provocative assertions in order to avoid suspension, but Maxton had refused, thereby challenging MacDonald's authority. Indeed, *The New York Times* began an article on this incident with, 'Members of the Scottish contingent of the Labor Party broke loose from disciplinary control in the House of Commons this evening.'[20] More infuriating still, Maxton's parliamentary contretemps made him a Labour hero. This helps explain a rather puerile incident between the two men at the party conference on the following day.

After MacDonald asked the delegates to allow the party executive time to decide what steps should be taken in response to the suspension of the four MPs, Maxton tried to address the conference. The chair sought to proceed to other business, despite growing cries of 'Maxton, Maxton'. Failing to obtain the chair's recognition, Maxton approached the rostrum, only to find his path blocked by MacDonald. An eyewitness later recounted what happened next, 'Remembering his dignity, Mr MacDonald could not forcibly push him back and so he contented himself by jabbing his elbows into Mr Maxton's ribs' just as a schoolboy might do in order to escape the notice of a teacher.'[21]

This rebuff did not induce Maxton or the other suspended MPs to display much contrition or respect for parliamentary norms. On the contrary, the four Clydesiders sought to turn their suspension into a confrontation with parliament of almost Wilkesite dimensions. According to the rules then in place, they would be suspended until the end of the parliamentary session unless they apologised. This they refused to do, embarking instead upon a campaign to publicise the dreadful social conditions in Glasgow. After several weeks, pressure was growing to allow them to return to their seats.

Parliament would soon adjourn, meaning that their suspension would carry into autumn. A decade earlier, Conservative William Moore had been suspended for three weeks for accusing a colleague of 'disgraceful trickery'. If the Clydesiders were excluded from the Commons for much longer than this, it would lend credence to their claim that they were being treated more severely due to their political views. Consequently, three weeks into the showdown, Prime Minister Stanley Baldwin and MacDonald came to an agreement that the Clydesiders should be readmitted without being required to apologise.

Having learned of this concord, the four stirred the pot by sending the Speaker a letter, complaining that they were being treated more harshly because of their party affiliation. They reminded the Speaker that not only had Baldwin voted against Moore's suspension in 1913, but that the Speaker himself (though not then in that office) had supported publicly Prime Minister Asquith's assertion that three weeks was long enough to deprive a constituency of its representative. The Clydesiders concluded by pledging to go to parliament on 30 July to claim their seats.[22]

What happened on that fateful day is not entirely clear. Gordon Brown, Maxton's biographer, asserts that the suspended MPs 'attempted to force their way into Parliament but were prevented by the police'.[23] *The Times*, however, paints a less confrontational picture, in which Maxton, Wheatley and Stephen, as 'for some reason Mr. Buchanan did not put in an appearance', arrived at Westminster, only to depart soon after they had 'argued mildly with the police, who denied them admittance'. Whether violent or not, this *coup de théâtre* was followed shortly by Baldwin's announcement that he would present a motion for lifting the suspensions the following day. *The Times* was quick to reassure its readers that, as Baldwin had decided on this course a week earlier, 'the motion is in no way a submission to clamour'.[24]

Despite, or perhaps because of, such antics, Labour managed to increase its parliamentary strength by almost fifty seats in the general election of December 1923. Teaming up with the Liberals, Labour created a minority government with Ramsay MacDonald as prime minister. The formation of this first Labour administration did not result in any violence, but it did produce a moment of exquisite awkwardness. Shinwell was appointed Parliamentary Under-Secretary for Mines. Lacking a ministerial vehicle, the former trade union organiser opted to walk to Buckingham Palace. A policeman at the gate inquired who he was. Shinwell told him, adding that he had come 'to kiss hands with the Sovereign'. The bobby's response was dismissive and succinct, 'Fuck you.'[25]

The behaviour of the Clydesiders did not improve noticeably once they were sitting on the government benches. On 9 April 1924, during debate on evictions at Woolwich, Leo Amery denigrated the 'sob-stuff used by Labour' to support their claims. In response, George Buchanan shouted across the floor, 'You are a swine and a guttersnipe.' After the Speaker had left the chair, Buchanan and Maxton crossed the floor, approaching Amery 'in an aggressive manner'. (According to Gordon Brown, Maxton 'appeared to take a swipe' at his colleague.[26]) Amery, a former First Lord of the Admiralty, punched Buchanan in the jaw. 'There was for a few moments a rough-and-tumble.' Labour Member Will Thorne restrained Buchanan, while others surrounded Maxton. Neil Maclean, 'who was very excited', tried to reach Amery, but was held back. 'After considerable excitement the incident closed.'[27]

The day after this 'fistic combat', the Speaker promised to put a stop to the growing 'habit of flinging unparliamentary expressions across the floor during debates'.[28] Maxton's attitude was somewhat different. In an article, entitled 'Should MPs Fight?', he conceded that he had been wrong to do so 'but did not rule out any form of protest to ensure advanced socialist measures'.[29]

There was concern that the chair's ear was more sensitive to potentially unparliamentary expressions launched from Labour lips than those tripping off Tory tongues. The presiding officer's actions during debate on George Buchanan's private Member bill on Scottish Home Rule in May 1924 did nothing to allay such fears of partiality.

When Liberal Sir Robert Horne sought to speak, he was denied a hearing, partly because he had not followed the debate from the beginning. Another MP then attempted to talk the measure out, to kill it by using up the time allocated for its consideration. This prompted several Clydesiders to try to force a vote by moving closure. However, 'each time the Unionists rose in serried columns to continue the debate', leading the Speaker to decline to accept the motions. When the time allocated for debate was up, and the Speaker sought to move to other matters, there was 'great perturbation in the ranks of the Scottish members'. Clydesider Neil Maclean asked the Speaker whether he had not previously indicated that he would accept a motion for closure. The Speaker acknowledged that he had intended to do so, but implied that he had changed his mind when Horne had been denied a hearing. 'Pandemonium followed.' Amid persistent efforts to challenge his ruling on closure, the Speaker declared the House adjourned, 'grave disorder' having arisen.[30]

An even more significant confrontation with the presiding officer took place in March 1925. In advocating that Germany should be included in a security treaty, Foreign Secretary Austen Chamberlain referred to a secret document that he had received from that country. This prompted Clydesider David Kirkwood to interject, 'What about the Red Letter now?' A missive purportedly from Communist International head Grigory Zinoviev had proved acutely embarrassing to the Labour government, when it was published on the eve of the 1924 general election. It was later acknowledged to be a forgery. Kirkwood's insinuation that Chamberlain's document might be similarly unreliable may have been apt, but the Chair ordered him not to interrupt again. In response, Kirkwood rose, but before he could speak, the Chair called upon him to leave the House, threatening to name him if he did not withdraw. After Kirkwood indicated that he had no intention of leaving, the Speaker was called.

The latter named Kirkwood, but, before a vote on suspension could be taken, MacDonald sought to inform the Speaker about what had transpired. The Speaker refused to listen, indicating that the rules required an immediate vote. After the motion of suspension was carried, MacDonald led his party out of the House.[31] Although most Members departed in silence, Jack Jones shouted across the benches, 'Come outside and we'll settle it!'[32]

For a party leader to take his followers out of the House over a dispute about the authority of the Chair was seen to be unprecedented.

Many in the Labour Party felt that Kirkwood's behaviour had fallen far short of the persistent and wilful obstruction of business that is grounds for suspension. Accordingly, in a highly unusual move, MacDonald gave notice of his intention to seek a resolution of censure against the chair, James Hope, for his treatment of Kirkwood.[33] A few days later, MacDonald consented to drop his resolution and Prime Minister Baldwin agreed to a motion to end Kirkwood's suspension.[34]

Kirkwood's reputation may have preceded him. The previous month he had proposed reducing appropriations for a tour of South Africa and South America by the Prince of Wales, telling the Commons that the heir to the throne would be better served visiting his own country to learn about the conditions of the working classes. The motion was heavily defeated, and Kirkwood and his allies reportedly received not a few threatening letters.[35]

Class War in the Commons

Deteriorating economic conditions, combined with the apparently meagre returns from Labour's brief spell in government in 1924, fuelled working-class scepticism about the efficacy of parliamentary politics and contributed to the 1926 General Strike, 'the clearest display of class war in British history'.[36] In the wake of the strike's collapse, Ramsay MacDonald found it even more difficult to keep in line the more militant Labour MPs.[37]

During a highly contentious June 1926 debate about whether Soviet funds had contributed to the strike, for example, Labour Members became upset when the Deputy Speaker recognised Conservative Sir Reginald Banks instead of Thomas Jones, a miner. Jones's claim, on point of privilege, that since the discussion concerned aid to miners, one of their number should be allowed to address the House, was rejected by the Deputy Speaker. However, when Banks sought to speak, he was unable to make himself heard, prompting the presiding officer to suspend the sitting under provisions for grave disorder.[38]

Soon thereafter, a bill postponing (for five years) the enactment of earlier legislation that had reduced the working day of miners from eight to seven hours passed its first reading in the Commons, according to the often-hyperbolic *The New York Times* amid 'scenes of rowdyism', 'which must have made the urbane statesmen of the courtly British of yesterday turn in their graves'.[39] A few days later, during the bill's third reading in the Commons, one Labour MP, Jack Jones, was ordered to withdraw after calling the First Lord of the Admiralty a murderer. A colleague was 'pulled into his seat', by other

Labour MPs, to spare him punishment by the Speaker. The Secretary of Mines was called a 'dastardly coward', and some speakers were shouted down. Such was the ill temper that the paper predicted, 'There will be a free fight in the House of Commons one of these days if things keep on as they are going just now.'[40] This prognostication became reality only a few days later.

On 8 July 1926, the Miners' Bill passed its third reading in the Lords, but only after the unprecedented application of closure in the face of alleged obstruction by a Labour peer. Before the vote, Labour MPs who had been making 'disorderly interjections' were commanded to leave the bar of the Lords. When Black Rod arrived at the Commons to summon its Members to hear the bill receive the Royal Assent, Labour MP Tom Williams, moved that the attendant 'be not entertained here this evening'. The Speaker ignored the motion and soon left the chair.[41]

Gathered in the Lords for the reading of the letters patent, some Labour MPs 'set up a chorus of hisses and coughs. These strengthened into shouts of "A murder bill!"' As MPs walked back to the Commons, Roy Bird reportedly cried, 'It's a damned scandal to make a row in the House of Lords', while swinging his fist at George Buchanan, whom he evidently deemed responsible. Bird's punch landed instead on James Gardner, a Socialist. 'A melee followed, but the police, mingling with the irate members, succeeded in soothing them.' The conciliation was completed at the House bar, not the bar of the House.[42] Bird's actions not only won him a measure of 'fame' but also, reportedly, a pugilistic challenge from a Socialist MP to 'a bout for a stake of £10 to be donated to a fund in aid of the striking coal miners'.[43]

Such scenes brought the House of Commons into disrepute. *The New York Times* crowed, 'The Mother of Parliaments is in disgrace. Instead of setting an example to her children the world over she has lately been unable to keep the peace even in her own household.' Many Tories believed the Clydesiders deliberately were using disorder to bring parliament into contempt. As a result, 'only the tact of the party leaders prevented the younger Conservatives from organising concerted physical assault on Labor members who heckled their leaders or made unpleasant remarks concerning their characters or careers during a recent debate'.[44]

This danger again was evident in late 1927, after MacDonald moved a resolution censuring the government for deficiencies in its policy toward the coal mining industry and neglect of unemployment.

When Sir Philip Cunliffe-Lister, President of the Board of Trade, rose to reply for the government, he was shouted down. Many Labour MPs demanded a response from Prime Minister Baldwin himself. As it became clear that Members would not heed the Speaker's assertion that they had no right to refuse a hearing to the spokesman nominated by the government, he suspended the sitting for an hour. When it resumed, the commotion continued. Seeing that there was no hope of orderly debate, the Speaker adjourned the House under the provisions for grave disorder.[45] Amid cries of 'coward' directed at Baldwin, there was danger that violence might break out. 'A Conservative called to his colleagues, "Let's clear them out."' Labour Members responded with their own challenges. As often happens, however, the tension was defused with humour, as a Labour MP held a mock vote on the motion of censure.[46]

MacDonald argued that the use of disorder to make principled points was an established parliamentary convention, one that Conservatives had availed themselves of not long before.[47] However, he was considerably less willing actually to employ such tactics than the Clydesiders, whose desire to provoke did not ebb even after Labour formed its second government in 1929. Yet even the most radical Clydesiders, such as Maxton, could not abide by the disrespect for parliamentary norms displayed by some junior Labour Members.[48]

The most egregious violation in this regard transpired in mid-1930, when there occurred what was described, with considerable overstatement, as 'the worst scene witnessed in Parliament in 300 years'.[49] After Archibald Fenner Brockway refused to desist from persistently demanding debate on Indian affairs, the Speaker named the Labour MP, and a vote on his suspension was held.[50] Before the results could be announced, John Beckett, one of the tellers against the motion, 'struck a truculent attitude, failed to bow to the Speaker, and exclaimed, "I don't know what you think, Mr. Speaker, but it's a damned disgrace."' The Labour MP then picked up the mace and carried it toward the door. The House cannot sit without the mace on (or, when in committee, under) the table, so Beckett's action threatened adjournment.[51] 'A storm of indignation burst like a tornado from both sides of the House as soon as Members recovered from the shock. Prime Minister MacDonald stood white and shaking. Several Members sprang from their seats with arms raised as if to attack Mr. Beckett. The Serjeant-at-Arms, Admiral Sir Colin Keppel, reached him first and wrested the mace from his grasp.' As the mace was being put back on the table, Beckett 'lounged in one of the aisles with his hands in his pockets, shouting insults at the protesting members – many of the most bitter of whom belonged to his own party. Then he disappeared through a doorway'.[52]

Beckett was suspended from the Commons and censured by his party for what *The Times* memorably called 'The Rape of the Mace'.[53] This did not deter other MPs from treating the symbol of parliamentary authority with similar, or even greater, disrespect.

Before this happened, parliamentarians resumed treating each other poorly. During a November 1930 debate on a motion of censure of the MacDonald government for alleged shortcomings in the recent Imperial Conference, Earl Winterton reportedly referred to the chancellor as an 'insolent dog'. Although neither the chancellor nor the Speaker took notice of the remark, Charles Simmons did. When a division was called, the Labour MP 'crossed the floor of the House and hit' Winterton 'in the face with a folded order paper'.[54] Apparently, one of Simmons's colleagues sought satisfaction of an older sort, as Winterton subsequently claimed that he had been challenged to a duel.[55]

Perhaps not coincidentally, Winterton had displayed a desire for similar extra-parliamentary retribution the previous day. When John Bromley raised the possibility that some companies were holding work back 'to create unemployment', Winterton asked whether the Labour MP 'would repeat his allegation outside the House'. This led Bromley to ask the Speaker 'for protection against the insinuations' made by the Irish peer.[56]

A few months later, there was an incident that arguably posed a much more serious challenge to parliamentary authority and Labour's reputation than Beckett's violation of the mace. After importunately demanding the release of four men arrested for preaching on Glasgow Green without a permit, Clydesider John McGovern was named and suspended.[57] The Speaker then ordered McGovern to withdraw. He refused. The Serjeant-at-Arms, directed to remove the MP, asked McGovern to leave. Again, he refused. The Serjeant, 68-year-old Admiral Sir Colin Keppel, summoned 'six elderly assistants in full evening dress', who laid hold of McGovern. He shouted, 'Be Men!' This prompted fellow Clydesiders to begin 'struggling violently to rescue their colleague, who inch by inch was pulled along the benches toward the door'.[58] Amidst this 'grave disorder', the Speaker suspended the sitting.[59] Yet, even after he did so and left the chamber, 'the panting, tugging, shirt-tearing, tie-mussing, hair-tousling tussle went on'. Eventually, the attendants managed to drag McGovern 'to a point within the Parliament Building where they could conscientiously say, "We have removed the Honorable Member from the House."[60]

McGovern was suspended for the remainder of the session.[61] His would-be rescuers escaped punishment after apologising to the House, although some colleagues wanted them expelled from the Labour party.[62]

The government's decision soon thereafter to reduce unemployment benefits in order to balance the budget split the ruling Labour party and polarised politics. 'The trenches of class war ran along the floor of the House of Commons.'[63] Something like the apotheosis of this conflict came in September 1931, when Lady Astor and Leah Manning 'created a minor sensation ... by engaging in an altercation' following the former's remarks on the National Economy Bill, which provided for cuts in government spending. The Labourite Manning confronted the Conservative Astor as the House emptied, leading to an argument. 'The other members cheered and jeered, but when it appeared that there might be a closer encounter the two women were led out by their friends.'[64]

There was another close call at the opening of parliament in late 1933. Shortly after King George V finished the Throne Speech, John McGovern shouted out, 'What about the means test and cuts in unemployment insurance?' Then, gesturing to the House of Lords as a whole, he continued, 'It's a shame to have all this rubbish and show while people are starving outside. You're a gang of lazy, idle parasites living on wealth created by the people.' The sovereign affected not to hear this outburst.

McGovern subsequently compounded his offence by indicating that he did not regret his eruption. 'It was not premeditated. I simply couldn't help expressing my disgust and resentment for all that medieval pomp and all it costs the State. When I saw those robes and crowns and diamonds in the House of Lords, I could see at the same time the rags of starving men and women on the banks of the Clyde in my own Glasgow constituency.'[65] He had little reason to fear parliamentary sanction. The Lord Chancellor, who presides over the Peers, is unable to punish Members of the Commons, while the Speaker lacks jurisdiction in the Lords. Yet, such was the anger at his comments that extra-parliamentary punishment evidently was a real threat: police subsequently were alerted that Fascists intended to tar and feather McGovern for his effrontery.[66]

One of McGovern's colleagues responded to a disturbance in a similarly violent fashion. When a heckler yelled 'You haven't got the pluck', as James Maxton was addressing an ILP rally, the MP beckoned the man to come up to the platform. 'His appearance there was brief. When he rushed into the wings Maxton followed him, returning in a few minutes to say that "it was rather unfair to leave an audience of 1,000 people to attend to one man."' Leaving little doubt about what had just transpired, Maxton assured his audience that while he had fought the Labour Party with his brain, he was more than willing to fight other enemies of the working class with his fists.[67]

The Clydesiders were not alone in their aggressive response to the economic distress of the 1930s. One of the more obscure organisations to emerge from the period was the Greenshirts, a paramilitary movement advocating an economic ideology called Social Credit. For present purposes, its primary claim to fame rests on a single violent act: in June 1934, an unemployed man threw a brick, painted green, wrapped in paper and emblazoned with the words 'All power to the Greenshirts', through the window of 11 Downing Street while the Cabinet was meeting next door. Questioned by the police, the vandal admitted that he had made a mistake: the brick had been intended for the prime minister's residence.[68] This misdirected brickbat seems a fitting epitome of the movement itself.

Not all the dangers politicians faced in this era were directly tied to the country's economic travails. When Walter Elliot visited the University of Glasgow in 1934, tensions were high because a rectorial election was imminent and the Tory Club, the sponsor of the meeting he had arrived to address, was backing an unpopular candidate. As the Agriculture Minister took the stage he was met with 'a barrage of eggs and tomatoes from all parts of the hall'. He was unfazed; his wife, less so, especially after being hit by a tomato. 'A student in the gallery took aim with a water pistol and emptied the contents over the Minister's clothing.' Elliot later lamented, 'It is a pity some of the students forgot there were ladies present.'[69]

After keeping a somewhat lower profile in Westminster for a few years, the Clydesiders caused another scene in the Commons in mid-1936, outraged both that the unemployment assistance measures proposed by the government were inadequate and that their hometown was being insulted.

Minister of Health Sir Kingsley Wood sought to defend the government's bill by telling the Commons that it would provide more generous help to those out of work than that currently available from the city of Glasgow. George Buchanan interjected that Wood had 'challenged Glasgow with being mean'. When Home Secretary Sir John

Simon averred that this had not been the point of Wood's remark, Buchanan then accused Simon of lying. After Buchanan repeatedly refused to withdraw that expression, he was named, and Simon moved his suspension. This prompted another Clydesider, Campbell Stephan to ask, 'Are we going to have robbers and murderers of the working class and of the unemployed carrying on like this?' Stephan went on to describe the Minister of Labour as a 'dirty, contemptible little rat' and to repeat Buchanan's claim that Simon was a liar. In reply to shouts for him to resume his seat, Stephen flung back, 'I am not going to sit down till I have said a few more things.' At this point the Deputy Speaker, who had been standing (and thus demanding the floor) throughout Stephen's remarks, left the chair, suspending the sitting.

When it resumed, a motion for Buchanan's suspension was carried. Aneurin Bevan then asked whether the ten additional policemen in the lobby were there in anticipation that a Member would not withdraw from the House voluntarily after being named. The Speaker did not respond directly, observing only, 'The authorities of the House have to keep order in the House.' Stephen then was named and suspended. After he withdrew, Simon sought to continue his speech, prompting Seymour Cocks to point to the Home Secretary and declare, 'We all know he is a liar.' The Speaker told the Labour MP that this was unparliamentary language. Cocks replied, 'I am aware of that, Mr. Speaker.'

When the Speaker took no further action regarding Cocks's remarks, McGovern asked (with some justification) whether there were different rules for different Members of the House. To emphasise the point, he reiterated, 'I say that the Home Secretary is a damned liar. Put that under your wig!' The Speaker asked McGovern to withdraw the remark. His refusal resulted in him being named and suspended. After twice ignoring the Speaker's order to withdraw from the House, McGovern 'allowed himself to be escorted out of the Chamber' by the Serjeant-at-Arms.[70] Taking place during the course of a 28-hour sitting, this episode prompted the wry comment that, like a child, the Commons 'cannot sit up all night without losing its temper'.[71]

Another slight prompted the final instance of Clydesider parliamentary violence two years later. Asked in early 1938 whether Franco's 'agent' in London had been given the diplomatic privileges normally accorded to ambassadors and whether this constituted effective recognition of the nationalist government in Spain, a foreign ministry spokesman gave an evasive reply, which Manny Shinwell characterised as 'humbug'. Conservative Robert Bower responded by shouting, 'Go back to Poland'. The Labour MP rose from his place, crossed the floor to the government benches, and, using the open palm of his right hand, struck Bower with 'a resounding blow on the left cheek'. Bower, a '6-foot heavyweight boxer', remained seated despite Shinwell yelling 'Come on' and gesturing to follow him out of the House. The Speaker considered both Bower's comment and Shinwell's behaviour 'thoroughly disorderly' but proposed to ignore the matter beyond encouraging the two to apologise. This they quickly did.[72]

The class politics championed by the Clydesiders faded with the eruption of the Second World War, just as the gender conflict espoused by the more militant Suffragettes largely was abandoned in the wake of the outbreak of the First. Partly as a result, the middle decades of the twentieth century, like those of the nineteenth, would see a marked diminution of parliamentary violence, at least at first.

12

FADING POST-WAR COMITY

In the four decades following the start of the Second World War, parliamentary violence fell in both quantitative and qualitative terms with one major exception: Northern Ireland, the subject of the next chapter. The continued growth of public intolerance of violence – a trend presumably accelerated by the greatest conflict in human history – combined with reduced class antagonism, partisan ideological convergence and unprecedented economic growth mitigated the peril faced by parliamentarians.[1] Yet if politicians, like many Britons, had 'never had it so good', the threat of parliamentary violence did not disappear completely. Nor was the respite more than temporary; by the early 1970s, the danger was growing again.

Order in Commons

The sustained economic boom following the War contributed to ideological convergence – as both main parties adopted 'hubristic Keynesianism', a substantial increase in public spending. It also fostered support (albeit temporary) from even the most militant Labour MPs for the basic rules of the parliamentary game.[2] The result was period of remarkable tranquility in the Commons: between 1940 and 1979, the frequency with which sittings were adjourned due to 'grave disorder', or politicians were suspended or ordered to withdrawal for inappropriate behaviour, declined compared to the preceding and following decades.[3]

Disorder is somewhat subjective, so it is possible to quibble with these numbers.[4] Yet the trend was similar with parliamentary violence, a related phenomenon: the post-war era saw a dip, but not

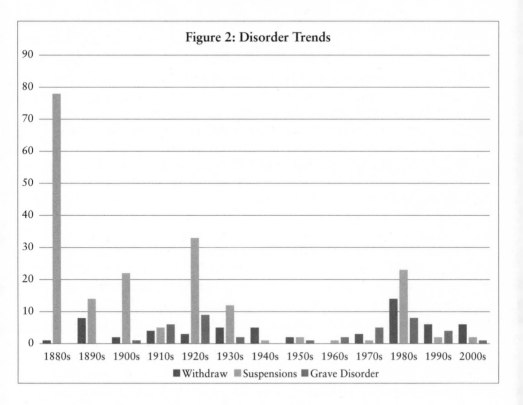

Figure 2: Disorder Trends

■ Withdraw ■ Suspensions ■ Grave Disorder

a disappearance. Indeed, MPs resumed tussling with each other, even before the War ended.

On 28 July 1943, there was a 'peculiar outburst of fisticuffs' between Oliver Locker-Lampson and Alec Cunningham-Reid, in the corridor connecting the Lords and the Commons. In response to the government's decision to move Prince Paul of Yugoslavia from Kenya to South Africa for health reasons, Cunningham-Reid asked Foreign Secretary Anthony Eden, 'Why has such favored treatment been given to this foreign royal Quisling?' In response, Locker-Lampson interjected, 'What medical disability was Captain Cunningham-Reid suffering from when he left England in the Blitz?' This reference to Cunningham-Reid's trip to Honolulu to visit heiress Doris Duke Cromwell, ostensibly in connection with a plan for her to provide sanctuary for 500 British children, provoked laughter in the House. An irritated Cunningham-Reid asked the House, 'Is it not a fact that a characteristic of the cuckoo is that it makes a nuisance of itself in other people's nests, and is not Commander Locker-Lampson a cuckoo?'[5]

Later, in the corridor, Cunningham-Reid 'blockaded' Locker-Lampson against the wall and demanded to know whether he intended to continue his 'personal attacks'. When the 61-year old Locker-Lampson answered evasively, Cunningham-Reid, fifteen years his junior, threatened to employ the same tactics. Locker-Lampson protested that this was 'blackmail'. Cunningham-Reid replied, 'You can call it what you damned well like, you nasty old man.' Locker-Lampson demanded, 'Take that back or I'll hit you.' 'Well, hit me', replied Cunningham-Reid. This Locker-Lampson did, and Cunningham-Reid responded in kind, before other MPs separated the two Conservatives.[6] Later, both polyonymous parliamentarians apologised for the unhappy incident 'in the purlieus of the House'.[7]

A few years later, in April 1949, 'angry scenes' prevented Minister of Food John Strachey from completing his remarks on meat supplies. The problem began when the Labour MP 'accused the Opposition of allowing political prejudice to emerge stronger than patriotism'. This prompted Conservative Martin Lindsay to ask whether it was in order for 'an ex-member of the Fascist party' to cast aspersions. When the Deputy Speaker took no action in response, another Labour MP asked whether it was in order for a Member to make a 'lying accusation' against a minister. Conservatives reacted with fury when the Chair deemed this unparliamentary, shouting 'withdraw', so that Strachey was unable to continue speaking. According to *The Times*, when a division was called, a few MPs 'engaged in heated controversy on the floor of the Chamber', and 'something very much like a scuffle below the Bar' erupted.[8]

One of the MPs present recorded a rather more violent situation. 'After the question was put, there were nearly some free fights.' Labour MP Leah Manning 'wanted to hit' a Conservative. 'The Government Chief Whip had to push Lindsay out of the way of enraged comrades.' Tory Beverley Baxter expressed displeasure at this apparent manhandling of her colleague, 'whereupon a Socialist hit Baxter in the face'. Sir Waldron Smithers, 'who was well away, tried to push into the middle of the scrum', shoving Lady Davidson in the process. This provoked a verbal exchange between the two Conservatives.[9]

One of the stranger incidents of post-war parliamentary violence took place during debate on the Anglo–Iranian Oil Company in June 1951. Secretary of State for Foreign Affairs Herbert Morrison accused popular Tory newspapers of making militaristic and imperialistic declarations, demanding the starting of wars in Egypt and Persia.

This produced an 'uproar' in the Commons, during which a coin was heard to drop onto the table. Conservative Henry Legge-Bourke subsequently admitted to the Speaker that he had thrown a penny at Morrison, indicating that it was his way of suggesting that the secretary 'put on another record'. Legge-Bourke was then ordered to leave the Commons.[10]

Around the same time, another violent incident entered Westminster legend. The 1950 election had reduced Labour's majority from 146 (in 1945) to just 6. The Conservatives responded with a sustained effort to prolong sittings in the hopes that sufficient Labour MPs would go home to bed to allow the opposition to inflict an embarrassing defeat on the government. Such tactics put a great strain on all MPs, but particularly those on the government benches. Roy Jenkins called the period the worst in his thirty-four years in the Commons. 'The chamber was frequently a bear garden, and the lobbies, corridors and public rooms of the building were overcrowded with irritable and not notably sober MPs of both sides milling around like members of conscript armies who did their duty but had doubtful faith in their commanders.'[11] In such circumstances, it perhaps is surprising that the violence that transpired was not of an inter-party nature.

With the parties almost evenly matched, the attendance of a handful of MPs could determine the result of a division. The whips therefore were assiduous in seeking to ensure that all their charges were in their places at the proper time, to the extent that on at least one occasion an ailing MP was carried into the House on a stretcher to vote.[12] Thus it was that Sir Walter Bromley-Davenport was posted at the doors to see that his Tory colleagues did not quit the Commons without permission. Spying a well-dressed man departing along a dimly lit corridor, the recently appointed whip sprang into pursuit. He remonstrated with and, for emphasis, applied his knee to the posterior of, the retreating figure. The Belgian Ambassador to the Court of St James, Bromley-Davenport's victim, was not amused.[13] Quite a few others were.

The first post-war instance of grave disorder came in the context of the Suez Crisis. During discussion of the military situation in Egypt on 1 November 1956, the opposition pressed the government for basic information, such as whether Britain legally was at war. When the government's response was deemed inadequate, attempts were made to induce the Speaker to give a ruling on the constitutional situation. He refused, arguing that debate on this matter was appropriate for an upcoming motion of censure of the government. Repeatedly challenged and his pleas for order ignored, the Speaker eventually suspended the sitting for half an hour.[14]

This did not prevent MPs from coming to blows. After Tory Leslie Thomas called opposition leader Hugh Gaitskell 'a bloody traitor', Labour MP George Wigg retorted 'he'd rather be led by a bloody traitor than a fucking murderer'. Thomas then invited his interlocutor to take their disagreement outside. When he did, Thomas hit him. Wigg responded in kind, as a result of which, according to the Labour MP, Thomas 'went down like a felled ox'. Wigg then scurried off to the Speaker to apologise.[15]

Five years later, there was more grave disorder. As so often in the past, it was sparked by a dispute with the Chair. On 9 February 1961, the Commons, meeting in committee, considered a technical resolution relating to the Conservative Government's plan to raise contributions and charges for the National Health Service (NHS). Labour adamantly opposed the introduction of NHS fees. Moreover, when the Chair, Deputy Speaker Sir Gordon Touche, recognised Financial Secretary Sir Edward Boyle, many suspected a trick. Fearing that Touche had arranged to allow the government Chief Whip to move closure after he finished speaking, the opposition refused to give Boyle a hearing. Labour efforts to get Touche to disavow such an intention were frustrated. After Boyle rose repeatedly, only to be shouted down, the Chief Whip did indeed move that the question be put, provoking 'a storm of shouting from the packed Opposition benches'.

While government supporters headed for the division lobby, Labour MP James Callaghan moved that Touche leave the chair. Opposition Members began to boo the Deputy Speaker and shout, 'Leave the Chair.' 'In all the confusion and noise, reinforced by the drumming of feet, it became apparent that, in the absence of Opposition tellers, the chairman had declared the closure carried.' After the mace was put on the table and Touche assumed the Speaker's chair, Labour MP George Brown moved that Touche leave the chair after sending for the Speaker. Touche's reply that the House was then considering a motion for adjournment led to renewed opposition disorder and shouts of 'send for the Speaker'. Touche then declared the Commons adjourned.[16]

Later that year, the unfortunate Touche again was at the centre of controversy. Meeting in committee on 6 December to discuss a bill that would limit immigration from Commonwealth countries, Labour Members were 'incensed by the abrupt closure moved by the Government on nine opposition amendments which were being considered together'. The refusal of ministers to address opposition claims that, since 1952, more people had left Britain than had immigrated to it did not calm tempers. Nor did it help that the chair, Touche, had to reverse himself, after mistakenly stating that the opposition amendments had passed. Amid Labour complaints that the opposition was being steamrolled, Touche suspended the sitting.[17]

In February 1965, a few days after a sitting marked by 'venomous and mindless barracking', the leader of the House, Herbert Bowden, and a number of newspapers suggested that televising Commons proceedings might deter such misbehaviour.[18] Four newly elected Liberal Members introduced a motion deploring 'the persistent rowdyism and barracking during the debate'. In reply, four Conservative Members introduced a motion regretting the 'smug comments' of the Liberals.[19] At issue was the sitting of 2 February, in which the Labour Government survived a vote of confidence in Commons. 'Fists were shaken, insults shouted, speakers drowned beneath a solid torrent of noise.' Towards the end, the Speaker felt compelled to ask the House to be mindful of its reputation. 'Over-enthusiasm in the matter of gestures had already come close to causing a free fight on the Labour benches.' *The Times* remarked, 'The House looked less like a debating chamber than a Rugby clubhouse at the climax of a victory celebration by the extra B XV.'[20]

The simile was apposite, for partisan scrums became more frequent in the 1970s. Part of the problem was that both major parties were less cohesive than they had been in the past, with backbenchers increasingly willing to vote against their leaders. Labour in particular faced a militant, coherent and organised left wing that repeatedly voted against the rest of the party.[21] As a result, disorder sometimes seemed to become less the result of an outburst of anger than a calculated political tactic. As before, however, the catalyst frequently was a sense that parliamentary procedures were being abused to deprive the minority of its rights.[22]

On 25 January 1971, for example, large numbers of Labour left-wingers, upset at the government's motion to use the guillotine on the Industrial Relations Bill, stood in the gangway facing the Speaker in an effort to halt proceedings. Eric Heffer, one of the leaders of the demonstration, later conceded that this was not a spontaneous expression of indignation. Rather, forewarned of the government's intentions, members of Labour's Tribune Group previously had met to discuss how to respond in a way that would demonstrate to the workers who had made sacrifices to protest against the legislation that the MPs were 'just as serious' in their commitment to oppose it. Accordingly, it was decided to 'cause a Parliamentary rumpus', in the expectation that those who participated would be suspended, one after another, a process that would both manifest their solidarity with the workers and long delay consideration of the bill.[23]

Things did not go exactly according to plan. In response to the demonstrators' efforts to shout down Minister of Labour Robert Carr, Selwyn Lloyd, who had been Speaker for less than two weeks, suspended the sitting and left the chamber. Expecting the protests to continue when the sitting resumed, the Speaker rejected the option of employing repeated adjournments until the demonstrators gave up. He also declined to seek to suspend the protesters, either individually or en masse, convinced the House would not support such a move. Instead, the Speaker called for the suspension of the '10 o'clock rule', thereby allowing debate to continue after that time. Now, empowered to seek to obstruct the bill by more licit means, the protesters returned to their seats.[24]

The planned disorder, by the champions of 'bilious often xenophobic proletarianism', may not have been very effective, but it did anger quite a few MPs outside the Tribune Group.[25] Some of Heffer's Labour colleagues subsequently called for him to be removed from the opposition front bench.[26] The six Liberal MPs subsequently announced that, as a result of the 'anti-parliamentary demonstration', they would no longer vote with Labour against the guillotine motion but would abstain instead.[27] The ill will generated by the 'rumpus' also helps explain the violence that transpired a few days later.

Continued debate on the Industrial Relations Bill on 28 January led to at least three incidents of note. After a division on an amendment to one clause of the legislation, some Labour MPs claimed they had been unable to leave the chamber to vote before the doors were locked because a number of Tories were blocking the way. The government Whip (unintentionally) exacerbated the situation by putting his arm across the exit from the lobby to prevent anyone from leaving the chamber by this route. Edward Short claimed to have been left with a 'bleeding arm', from his efforts to get through the door, an assertion discredited somewhat by the Deputy Chair's observation that she had seen the Labour MP seeking to depart through a different portal. Nevertheless, she acceded to Labour requests to call the division again.[28]

Quite a few clauses, and hours, later another division produced a somewhat similar incident. After the Chair ordered that the doors be locked for the vote, 'a number of Conservative MPs dashed for one of the doors and pushed passed the uniformed doorkeeper on duty'. Labour MPs claimed that this resort to force nullified the division. The Chair did call for another division, but on the basis that Members previously had been afforded insufficient time to get to the lobbies. At the insistence of a Labour MP, the incident subsequently was referred to the Committee of Privilege, which ruled that, while the actions of the Tories may well constitute a contempt, no further action should be taken, because there had been no deliberate assault on the doorkeeper and (more dubiously) there had been no attempt to prevent him from carrying out his duties.[29]

All told, the opposition forced twenty-two divisions during the sitting to protest both the bill and the use of the guillotine to expedite its passage. The deliberative marathon finally came to an end just before 5.30 a.m. When it did, there was a final spasm of violence: Labour MPs departed the Chamber 'singing a rousing chorus from *The Red Flag* and ducking under coins hurled at them by jeering Conservatives'.[30]

A year later, a miners' strike had, the Speaker later recalled, 'created in the House not just criticism and resentment but an undertone of bitterness and almost hatred'. The atmosphere 'was most unpleasant, and explosions threatened almost every day'.[31]

Such certainly was the case on 20 January 1972. Prime Minister Edward Heath's entry into the chamber, on a day it was reported that the number of people unemployed had reached one million, caused many Labour MPs to stand and shout 'Heath out' and 'Resign'. Lord Balniel, Minister of State for Defence, was repeatedly interrupted as he attempted to respond to a question about the cost of transferring polo ponies from Malta to Britain. When Heath stood for Prime Minister's Questions, Thomas Swain 'left his position on the Labour benches, walked over to the Government front bench, and slapped a folded copy of a London evening newspaper [presumably containing the unemployment figures] on the dispatch box in front of the Prime Minister. Mr. Heath swept it aside with his hand. The uproar continued'.[32] After repeatedly and fruitlessly asking the House to give the prime minister a hearing, the Speaker suspended the sitting for ten minutes.[33]

The following month, the second reading of a bill enabling the UK to join the European Economic Community led to similar scenes. The vote was expected to be so close that 'excited MPs were scuffling and at times almost fighting as they attempted to gain better vantage points from which to view the announcement of the division figures'. Despite fifteen Tories voting against it, the Heath government emerged from the division lobbies with a majority of eight, a slender victory provided by the support of five Liberals. This prompted angry Labour MPs to vent their fury at Liberal Leader Jeremy Thorpe. 'At one point they seemed to be bent on attacking him physically,' until Labour Chief Whip Bob Mellish came to Thorpe's aid.[34] The Speaker could not tell whether an MP actually had assaulted Thorpe but later suggested that investigating the incident would have been more trouble that it was worth. 'The noise was so great that I would have had to suspend the sitting had I wanted to pursue the matter that night.'[35]

A month later, an incident occurred that illustrated the challenge that bitter partisanship posed to the authority of the Chair. During a debate on civil aviation on 13 March 1972, Charles Loughlin complained that Minister for Trade Michael Noble was being allowed to speak even though he had already addressed the House. Deputy Speaker Sir Robert Grant-Ferris replied that it was perfectly acceptable for the Member in charge of a substantive motion to speak twice. As Loughlin questioned whether Noble would be able to speak for the whole of the rest of the time allotted to debate the issue, he was interrupted by Kenneth Lewis, to whom he said, 'Shut up, you fool.' When Grant-Ferris told Loughlin that he should confine his remarks to the Chair, the latter replied that the former had a duty to restrain Lewis. Upset at this criticism, the Deputy Speaker ordered Loughlin to resume his seat. Instead, Loughlin repeatedly tried to make a point of order despite warnings to desist. As Grant-Ferris reiterated that he would take no more points of order, Loughlin interjected, 'I do not give a damn whether you will or will not.' The Deputy Speaker then named Loughlin.

This was disorder of the most run-of-the-mill, banal, variety. It is what happened next that made the incident interesting. A motion for Loughlin's suspension was carried 299 to 220.[36] Typically a vote for the suspension of a disorderly MP is not contentious, with a few dozen colleagues at most opposing such a motion. Here, by contrast, more than 42 per cent of those MPs voting effectively opted to reject the authority of the presiding officer. Indeed, in what was considered a particularly 'bad omen', this reportedly marked the first time that 'the two front benches had not joined unanimously in supporting the Chair in a ruling about conduct in the House'.[37] Not all Labour Members followed their leaders into the 'noes' lobby, with one of the most prominent dissidents being the party's Deputy Chief Whip.[38] Still, it was a sad commentary on the decline in respect for the authority of the chair.

This was not only a problem on the floor of the House. Normally, standing committees and their chairs do not have the authority to discipline MPs. Thus when a number of MPs staged a sit-in to protest their exclusion from the committee considering a Scottish Local Government Bill in January 1973, the House felt compelled to pass a privilege motion enabling the committee chairman to order those not on the committee to withdraw and the Serjeant-at-Arms to enforce such orders. However, the protesting MPs, claiming to have made their point, promised not to repeat their demonstration.[39]

Two years later, perceptions of procedural irregularities produced not only grave disorder but a physical confrontation between MPs. On 3 March 1975, the Labour Government announced that it would employ the guillotine to facilitate passage of the Finance Bill. This provoked outrage from Conservatives, who strongly objected to provisions for a capital transfer tax. The leader of the House, Edward Short, justified this unusual expedient by claiming that the chairman of Norton Villiers Triumph (NVT) had told the government that the motorcycle firm would soon announce redundancies unless money was provided. Accelerated consideration of the Finance Bill would allow the Commons to debate aid to NVT.

However, on 4 March, Shadow Industrial Secretary Michael Heseltine told the House that he had been informed by the chairman of NVT that the latter had not recently spoken to the government, implying that Short had misled the Commons. 'As noise in the chamber reached volcanic proportions, with MPs ignoring pleas for order from the Chair', the Speaker suspended the sitting for twenty minutes. This did not immediately end the excitement. 'As MPs milled round the table' Tory Nigel Lawson hit Clinton Davis, Parliamentary Under Secretary of State for Trade, 'across the face with his order paper. Whips intervened and the two were separated'. Later, Lawson denied striking Davis deliberately, asserting, 'I had been haranguing another Labour member when Mr Davis started hurling abuse at me and I attempted to brush him aside.'[40]

Three weeks later, Elaine Kellett-Bowman punctuated a bitter debate in the Commons by throwing coins at the government front bench. A number of local councils had declined to increase the rents on council housing, as mandated by the 1972 Housing Finance Act. As Shadow Attorney General, Sam Silkin had spoken against proposals to provide retrospective indemnity to councillors who had broken the law. When he supported just such a measure as Attorney General, Kellett-Bowman sought to reward this tergiversation by flinging a metaphorical thirty pieces of silver in his direction. Unfortunately, the Conservative MP's symbolism was more potent than her aim: the coins missed Silkin, but one struck his parliamentary secretary, Arthur Davidson, in the face.[41]

An even more dramatic scene the following year had similar causes. On 27 May 1976, the House debated a government proposal to suspend certain standing orders to expedite consideration of the Aircraft and Shipbuilding Industries Bill, which provided for nationalisation of those sectors. The Tories found both the bill and the proposal objectionable, but what really made them angry was the apparently unsporting manner in which the latter was passed. Earlier, a division on a wrecking amendment, proposed by Conservative leader Margaret Thatcher, had produced a tie. Following precedent, the Speaker broke the tie by voting against the matter. This gave the Tories good reason to expect that the proposal to suspend the standing orders also would be defeated.

As it turned out, however, the proposal was carried 304 to 303. Even more exasperating for the Conservatives, the decisive vote was cast by Tom Pendry, a Labour whip. This was seen to violate an informal arrangement known as 'pairing', whereby an MP from one party agrees with a colleague from another party not to vote in one or more divisions. This allows parliamentarians to absent themselves (typically due to illness, travel or other commitments) without greatly affecting the partisan balance of the House. Conservatives claimed that Pendry had been paired with Peter Fry, a Tory MP who, apparently defying repeated warnings from his party, had left for a holiday in Corfu. That the decisive vote had been cast by someone who, according to Conservatives, should not have been participating in the division at all, helps explain the scene that followed the announcement that the proposal to suspend the standing orders had passed.[42]

Labour backbenchers began to sing the 'Red Flag'. In response, Shadow Industry Secretary Michael Heseltine grabbed the mace and 'brandished it defiantly' at the Labour benches. There was some 'scuffling', and at least one Member claimed to have been punched in the stomach. The Speaker suspended the sitting for 20 minutes, 'after the Serjeant at Arms had separated MPs who seemed to be threatening to come to blows'. The Conservative chief whip subsequently announced that he was closing the 'usual channels' of informal inter-party consultation and refusing to pair with the government, even for ministers, for the remainder of the session.[43]

Stranger Danger

The public threat to parliamentarians also waned and then waxed over the course of the four decades following the beginning of World War Two. Much, but not all, of the danger came from 'strangers' visiting Westminster Palace.

The first such incident came in 1947, when Philip Piratin twice scuffled with journalist Thomas Lucy within the precincts of parliament. The row began after Lucy ceded a place in the cafeteria queue for tea to the Communist MP, who subsequently complained of having been pushed in the back. This led to an exchange of offensive words. Piratin then told Lucy, 'Shut your mouth.' Lucy responded by grabbing Piratin's arm and shouting, 'And shut yours.' Piratin then struck Lucy with a 'violent blow'. Ninety minutes later, Lucy accosted Piratin in a corridor, demanding that he 'face up to me now for the dirty blow you struck'. This led to a second physical encounter, in which Piratin kicked Lucy, who punched him in the face. An inquiry by the Committee of Privileges subsequently adjudged Piratin guilty of 'gross contempt' of the House but Lucy guilty only of 'contempt', reflecting a belief that the former bore more responsibility for the violence. The only opponent of a motion calling for acceptance of the Committee's resolution censuring the two men was Communist William Gallacher, who denounced it as 'outrageous'.[44]

To many, it was the behaviour of Piratin and Lucy that merited this description. However, with public interest in politics declining, those seeking to win attention for a cause often felt they had to do something a bit outrageous to get noticed.

Thus a May 1949 sitting of the Commons was disrupted by two men in the public gallery shouting and attempting to throw pamphlets into the chamber in protest of the government's detention of Gerhart Eisler, a Communist agent who had fled the US by stowing away on a ship bound for England.[45] Incidents of this sort, while rare before the war – with the notable exception of the media-savvy Suffragettes – would become more common after it.

Other episodes were clearly anachronistic, as was the case when, a century after Conservatives sought to defenestrate William Gladstone, parliamentary violence returned to a gentleman's club.

In January 1951, not long after he had denigrated Tories as 'lower than vermin', Minister of Labour Aneurin Bevan went to White's club, as a guest of Marshal of the RAF Sir John Slessor, Chief of Air Staff. Informed of Bevan's presence, the Hon. John Fox-Strangways, second son of the Earl of Ilchester, left Brooks's club, at which he was dining, traveled to White's and kicked the minister in the buttocks as he was leaving the establishment. Following publication of the details of the incident, White's announced that Fox-Strangways had resigned his membership.[46]

There was a similar expression of contrition for exposing another parliamentarian to danger, in the heated atmosphere of the Suez Crisis. On 22 November 1956, during Prime Minister's Questions, Arthur Lewis asked the government to transfer some of the money allocated for humanitarian relief in Hungary to Egypt, where, he asserted, thousands 'have been rendered homeless and destitute by British shelling'. Three days later, a newspaper printed the Labour MP's home telephone number, suggesting readers ring Lewis to express their disapprobation at his proposal. He subsequently complained to the Commons of having been subjected to 'threatening, abusive and intimidating' phone calls, beginning at two in the morning and continuing throughout the day. This campaign, Lewis asserted, not only had rendered his phone effectively inoperable but also frightened his wife. The newspaper's editor was deemed guilty of a breach of parliamentary privilege, but, following his apology, no further action was taken.[47]

An early 1958 ceremony, to install R. A. Butler as Rector of Glasgow University, 'degenerated into utter chaos', due to 'unbridled hooliganism' by students. The home secretary and other distinguished guests occupying the platform 'were pelted mercilessly with fruit, eggs, flour, soot, and toilet rolls' for almost the entire 35-minute ceremony, which was conducted 'against a background cacophony of ringing bells, whistles, bugles, and fireworks'. The festivities were brought to a close, ten minutes ahead of schedule, soon after a flour bag 'exploded on Mr. Butler's forehead'. The victim later appeared unfazed. '"It did not worry me", he claimed gallantly. "After all, I am used to trouble in the House of Commons."'[48]

A few days later, another Tory politician, Housing Minister Henry Brooke, was given a 'rough reception', when he went to discuss his Rent Act at a public meeting in Holborn Hall. Although the conclave had been convened by the local Conservative Association, Brooke's arrival on the platform 'was greeted by a solid block of booing and stamping from the back half of the hall'. After eight minutes of largely inaudible remarks, the minister gave up and left the platform, prompting a brawl as members of Communist and Fascist organisations fought to take his place. Brooke soon left by a side door, escorted by half a dozen police.[49]

Much better behaved were demonstrators several months later, when leaflets containing an appeal from caravan dwellers were thrown from the public gallery into the Commons. The incident was intended to draw attention to the plight of residents of a Surrey caravan site, which was being closed without the local council helping to relocate those affected. By order of the Serjeant-at-Arms, twelve men, four women and a 14-year-old boy were detained. 'After about three hours the women and the boy were released but the 12 men were kept in custody until midnight. During their period of detention, the men were given ham sandwiches and tea.'[50]

A few years later, a similar display of hospitality helped prevent a political disaster. In April 1964, Sir Alec Douglas-Home attended a Scottish Unionist conference in Aberdeen. He was approached by a group of left-wing university students, 'who asked him to sign a forfeit for charity in return for not kidnapping him'. The Conservative prime minister 'signed, gave them £1, and assumed it was all in good fun'. It wasn't. Afterwards, Sir Alec drove to the home of some friends with whom he would be staying. Unbeknownst to him, the students were following him. They had planned to cause an accident and kidnap the prime minister for a few hours but could not summon the courage to carry out the scheme. Instead, they trailed him to the house, walked to the front door, and rang the bell. Sir Alec appeared. What is more, he was alone. His hosts were out, and there was no room in the house for the prime minister's bodyguard. The students announced that they intended to kidnap the prime minister. He joked that if they did so, the Tories would definitely win the upcoming election. This did not deter the students, but the man who had until recently been the 14th Earl of Home posed for pictures, plied them with beer and otherwise stalled until his hosts returned and the plot fizzled. Sir Alec's bodyguard, rightly concerned about his job following one of the worst security breaches of recent times, swore the prime minister to secrecy.[51]

What might have seemed almost like a quaint prank at the time, became considerably more foreboding in hindsight. The paucity of public disorder in Britain in the 1960s, in marked contrast to the situation in the United States or on the Continent, appeared to substantiate claims that 'The Conquest of Violence' was a major theme in British history.[52] Less than a decade later, an analysis of contemporary affairs was entitled 'Britain in Agony: The Growth of Political Violence'.[53] The eruption of the Troubles in Northern Ireland was a major reason for these starkly different assessments. Yet, the more pessimistic outlook also reflected generational change, in particular the rise of 'student power', which saw the advent of less deferential and more aggressive political activism.[54] Parliamentarians often were the targets.

In October 1967, for example, a large group of students tried to attack Prime Minister Harold Wilson and his wife, when they arrived at Cambridge Guildhall for a Labour Party rally. His car was punched and kicked, its roof was dented and its aerial damaged. Police surrounded Wilson and escorted him to the back door of the Guildhall, as protesters, some of whom evidently were upset about government policy toward Vietnam, tried to hit him over the heads of his protectors.[55]

The following year, a visit to Leeds University by Patrick Wall, a Tory notorious for his support of the white minority regimes in southern Africa, prompted disorder. The MP was 'spat at and insulted', while his wife 'was kicked to the ground and trampled on' before they were escorted to safety. Mrs Wall characterised the incident, with some understatement, as 'damn bad manners'.[56] Six months later, Wall's efforts to address Conservative supporters at York University were hindered when students stormed the platform and wretched the microphone from the MP. He grabbed another, only to find that the students had cut the power. The meeting eventually had to be abandoned.[57]

In May 1969, red paint was squirted in the face of Harold Gurden, while the MP was speaking at a meeting organised by the Conservative Society of the University of Manchester Institute of Science and Technology.[58] The following year, a disgruntled Labour supported splashed the same substance on Edward Heath as the new prime minister arrived at 10 Downing Street.[59] The hapless premier was the victim of another 'dye-hard' assault two years later, as he arrived in Brussels' Palais d'Egmont to sign a treaty that would make Britain part of the European Common Market. A protester, upset not with the controversial decision to join the Market but with the government's handling of a London urban renewal project, hit Heath in the face with black printing ink.[60]

Some of the violence of the era was considerably more serious, and not just that involving Northern Ireland. In November 1972, police intercepted a letter bomb addressed to Maurice Edelman, the Jewish MP for Coventry North. Dozens of similar devices were sent to Jewish targets in London and around Europe, apparently by the Palestinian terrorist organisation Black September.[61]

Somewhat less menacing was the Angry Brigade, 'Britain's only home-grown urban terrorist group', which was responsible for more than two-dozen bombings in 1970 to 1971. The Angries, whose peeves included the Vietnam War, internment in Northern Ireland, and the government's confrontation with Clydeside shipyard workers, targeted government and corporate offices as well as the homes of Conservative MPs such as Employment Secretary Robert Carr, Attorney-General Sir Peter Rawlinson and Secretary of State for Trade and Industry John Davies. Like the Suffragettes, their attacks seemed aimed more at humiliating the government than causing serious injury; in all the bombings, only one person was hurt, and not seriously. Indeed, a former Angry later lamented that the revolutionary commitment of his comrades was so tepid that they should have called themselves the Slightly Cross Brigade.[62]

Even in the more politically charged 1970s, however, most of the violence directed at MPs by members of the public was considerably less dangerous. Indeed, on occasion it seemed benign enough to pose something of a moral dilemma. In an effort to discourage publicity-seeking behaviour, MPs typically pretend to ignore attempts by those in the Strangers' Gallery to disrupt Commons proceedings. This convention, however, may be in tension with an MP's desire to represent constituents or support a cause. The result can be a more ambivalent reaction to popular protests in the Commons.

Such was the case on 5 November 1976, when protesters shouting in Welsh and throwing leaflets into the chamber, repeatedly interrupted a Commons debate on Welsh affairs. The disturbances lasted more than half an hour, because as soon as one demonstrator was ejected another stood up to continue the commotion. Jeffery Thomas, Labour Member for Abertillery, who was trying to speak during the disruptions, asked Plaid Cymru spokesman Dafydd Wigley to condemn the 'astonishing scenes', but the latter refused to do so.[63]

The following year saw another sustained campaign of disruptions in support of a different cause. In July 1977, Commons debate on a bill to reduce the time limit for abortions was interrupted twice in twenty-four hours, as people in the public gallery shouted pro-abortion slogans and threw into the chamber leaflets of the same character.[64]

This act of harmless parliamentary violence provides a fitting end to the early post-war era. Margaret Thatcher's premiership saw a polarisation of the country that was reflected in increased and less benign parliamentary violence. Yet, her advent to power exacerbated rather than precipitated the surge in disorder. As we have seen, it began at least a decade before she entered 10 Downing Street in 1979. Nowhere was this more evident than in Northern Ireland.

13

ULSTER'S TROUBLES

Almost none of the parliamentary violence discussed so far has been lethal by intention. Crowds typically sought to humiliate, castigate, and perhaps injure, but not to murder. Even duellists usually were not purposefully homicidal, if for no other reason than because 'killing one's man' brought unwelcome legal complications. The violence connected with post-partition Ireland is a sad and significant exception to this tale of relative mercifulness.

$32 - 6 = 2$: *Trouble before the Troubles*
The 1920 Government of Ireland Act provided for the (ostensibly temporary) creation of a 'Home Rule' parliament in southern Ireland and another (Stormont) in the six counties of Ulster that were to become Northern Ireland.[1] The implications for parliamentary violence were profound.

By creating twice as many parliaments as Parnell, and others, had demanded, Westminster Palace became more tranquil. Irish matters, that long had provoked discord and disorder in the Commons, disappeared from the political agenda. Problems in Northern Ireland largely were ignored, both because the Unionists typically returned to Westminster had little interest in bringing up contentious matters that might result in unwelcome British intervention in the province, and because a 'Speaker's Convention' emerged by which discussion of matters in the purview of the Ulster administration were deemed to be out of order.[2] As a result, it would be almost half a century before events in Ulster prompted the sorts of 'scenes' in Westminster that had been frequent prior to partition.

Outside the Commons, however, turmoil in Northern Ireland proved dangerous to parliamentarians. Indeed, two murders had profound consequences on each side of the newly created partition.

On 22 May 1922, as part of an effort to destabilise the north and make unification with the south more likely, the Irish Republican Army (IRA) assassinated William Twaddell, a prominent Unionist Member of the Ulster Parliament. Sir James Craig, the Prime Minister of Northern Ireland, pledged 'just retribution'.[3] The IRA and other extreme nationalist groups were proscribed. The lord lieutenant, who previously had resisted internment of those suspected of 'endeavouring to subvert our parliament', capitulated. Within weeks, authorities had arrested over 500 IRA suspects and sympathisers, a setback that doomed the planned republican Northern Offensive and contributed greatly to the diminution of violence in the province.[4]

Farther afield, IRA schemes to assassinate Prime Minister Lloyd George, to truck-bomb the House of Commons or to poison Buckingham Palace's horses came to naught.[5] An attack on a somewhat softer target, however, proved within their competence, though the consequences again were greatly unwelcome.

On 22 June 1922, two republican gunmen shot to death Field Marshal Sir Henry Wilson, as he returned to his London home after unveiling a war memorial. The MP for North Down was a (hardline) security advisor to the government of Northern Ireland. Wilson's killing, like Twaddell's, was a major strategic blunder. The British Government threatened to use its troops in Dublin unless the Free State took strong action against those responsible. Republicans who supported the Anglo–Irish Treaty were compelled to crack down on republicans who opposed it. 'The Irish civil war was thus begun on British orders. All Irishmen resented this, even when they were fighting against each other.'[6]

In Ulster, Unionist politicians quickly changed the electoral system to encourage sectarian appeals, thereby decreasing competition and entrenching the power of the Protestant majority.[7] The Unionists' political stranglehold, their limited ambitions, and the proclivity of nationalist MPs to abstain from parliamentary business all militated against disorder in Stormont.[8] There were, however, some notable exceptions.

In November 1928, the police were called three times to the Belfast Commons to remove Members named by the Speaker. The government had proposed that the House sit on Mondays in order to expedite debate on a bill expanding the franchise to women of at least 21 years of age. The opposition objected both because of the 'rush' tactics employed by the government and because a Monday sitting would conflict with a meeting of the nationalist party. When nationalist leader Cahir Healy protested against this change, he was ordered to take his seat. He refused, and was ordered to withdraw. After he declined to do that, the Serjeant-at-Arms was summoned. Healy's rejection of the Serjeant's request that he depart lead the Deputy-Speaker to order that 'sufficient force' be brought into the House to remove him. Healy left quietly after the police arrived. Then, one by one, his nationalist colleagues rose in protest and were ordered to withdraw. Some left without a fuss; others waited until the police had been called. In the end, only two Members remained on the opposition benches.[9]

A few years later, the shadow of Beckett (unfortunately John not Samuel) was cast upon Stormont. On 30 September 1932, upset that his motion on unemployment had not made it onto the Order Paper, Labour MP Jack Beattie asked the Speaker for an explanation. Unsatisfied with what was proffered from the chair, Beattie 'seized the Mace and, throwing it under the table, exclaimed: "Out of the road with this. It is only the emblem of hypocrisy. I will not stand here and allow it to continue."' The prime minister stooped to pick up the mace, only for Beattie to snatch it away. Eventually the Serjeant-at-Arms replaced the mace in its stand, 'holding it in position with his two hands'. Beattie returned to his seat but, as business was about to resume, he again halted proceedings by removing the mace. 'This time he hurled it up the carpeted floor in the direction of the Speaker's chair.' Only then did Beattie accede to the Speaker's order to withdraw, albeit 'with a strong protest'.[10]

The Troubles Begin

Fast forward more than three decades. Not long after becoming Prime Minister of Northern Ireland in 1963, Terence O'Neill, under pressure from Westminster, sought to reduce the discrimination faced by Ulster's Catholics.[11] His reforms were the catalyst for 'the Troubles', decades of sectarian conflict that would claim over 3,500 lives. Parliamentary violence was a small, but significant, part of the sad saga.

O'Neill's limited reforms went too far for some hardline Protestants, who made their displeasure known through violence. On 12 July 1967, George Forrest, a Unionist MP, was treated in hospital for injuries suffered at an Orange demonstration in Co. Tyrone. A resolution of support for both O'Neill and his policies produced first heckling and then 'a scuffle with a section of the audience' that resulted in Forrest being knocked unconscious.[12]

Less than a year later, the premier himself was 'mobbed' at a Unionist hall in Belfast. The police escorted O'Neill into the building after a crowd of more than hundred, urged on by the Reverend Ian Paisley, 'surrounded his car, thumped the windows with their fists and shouted at him'. After the meeting, 'stones, eggs and bags of flour' were thrown at the prime minister, who was surrounded by police. The police car in which he departed 'was stuck by missiles and placards as it drove off amid shouts and jeers'.[13]

If some Protestants saw O'Neill's reforms as excessive, many Catholics viewed them as inadequate, a view reinforced by violence involving sympathetic MPs. Austin Currie's eviction, on 20 June 1968, from a council house he had illegally occupied to draw attention to discrimination in the allocation of housing, generated extensive press coverage, prompting additional efforts to publicise Catholic grievances.[14] Four months later televised images of police beating demonstrators in Derry, and, in particular, of MP Garry Fitt with blood streaming down his face, shocked viewers, spurred riots, and made events in Northern Ireland much harder for Britain to ignore.[15] In August 1969, the Stormont MP (and future Nobel Peace Prize laureate) John Hume was shot 'in the chest with a gas cartridge at point-blank range' by a police officer, as he sought to mediate between Catholics in Derry seeking to defend their neighbourhood and Protestant marchers seeking to enter. This helped demonstrate the manifest inability of the Royal Ulster Constabulary (RUC) to restore order, partly due to Catholic anger at the complicity of some of its members in loyalist violence. British troops were introduced two days later.[16] And in June 1970, riots erupted in Derry when Bernadette Devlin, recently re-elected as MP, was jailed after the rejection of her appeal of a conviction for taking part in the town's disturbances the previous August.[17]

The first whiff of the Troubles came to Westminster in late July 1970, not long after the British Army imposed the 'Falls Road Curfew', a house-to-house search for weapons in a Catholic area of Belfast that saw heavy use of tear gas. Two CS gas canisters were thrown from the Strangers' Gallery into the Commons, leading to 'grave disorder' and the suspension of the sitting.[18] One MP, Thomas Swain, was taken to the hospital suffering from the effects of the irritant, which had been lobbed into the chamber by an Irish labourer, accompanied by the shout, 'How do you like that, you bastards? Now you know what it's like in Belfast.'[19] The attack led to calls for improved security measures, including a proposal to protect the Commons with bulletproof glass. An MP and a former MP were given police protection following death threats.[20]

A little more than a year later, another ill-conceived initiative further fanned the flames. British authorisation for the Northern Ireland administration to detain indefinitely without trial suspected terrorists resulted in the arrests of Catholics but not loyalist paramilitaries. The result was a two-fold challenge to the regime.

First, two Stormont MPs, John Hume and Ivan Cooper, appealed their fine for taking part in a peaceful protest, leading to a court ruling that the British Army's actions in Northern Ireland since 1970 had been illegal. This awkward decision was relatively easy to overcome through hastily passed legislation.[21]

The second consequence of internment proved much less amenable to quick fixes. Violence exploded: in the two years prior to its introduction in August 1971, 66 people were killed in the Troubles; in the following 17 months, the toll reached 610.[22] Moreover, what changed was not merely the quantity of violence but also its nature. Specifically, the IRA launched the 'fourth wave' of its campaign, targeting for the first time public officials.

The first parliamentarian to die was Stormont Senator John Barnhill; on 12 December, three IRA gunmen went to his home in Stabane, shot the Ulster Unionist Party (UUP) legislator, 'ordered Barnhill's wife out, placed a bomb near the body and blew up the house'.[23]

The danger came not only from republicans; deepening divisions with the unionist community also posed a threat to parliamentarians. This was demonstrated most clearly when Protestant militants targeted with bombs the homes and offices of moderate unionist politicians and organisations, including Stormont MPs Richard Ferguson and Sheelagh Murnaghan.[24]

In response, the Government of Northern Ireland stepped up security arrangements for Members of the Stormont Cabinet, who were assigned armed plain-clothes police bodyguards.[25] That such a basic precaution had not previously been considered necessary is a testament to the extent to which parliamentary violence previously had been considered 'out of bounds'. In any event, these rudimentary protections were inadequate against a paramilitary organisation that was both resourceful and determined. Before this was demonstrated in Ulster, the Troubles were again brought home to Westminster.

In late January 1972, an illegal but peaceful demonstration against internment turned into 'Bloody Sunday', when the British Army opened fire, killing thirteen, and further inflaming Catholic enmities. The following day, this violence was replicated, albeit in much attenuated form, on the floor of the Commons. Home Secretary Reginald Maudling's claim that the soldiers had fired only in self-defence aroused furious indignation from Bernadette Devlin, 'the diminutive, mini-skirted MP for Mid-Ulster', who had witnessed the sanguinary episode at first hand. After repeatedly interrupting to call him a liar and a 'murdering hypocrite', and being denied a chance to present her own version of the events, Devlin's frustration boiled over. She 'swooped down from her back bench like an avenging fury', pulled Maudling's hair with one hand and 'struck him several times with the other'.[26]

As the Speaker later recalled, Frank McManus, who represented the constituency next to Devlin's, followed Devlin across the floor, 'apparently ready to engage in fisticuffs with anyone. In seconds it might have become a free for all'. The opposition Chief Whip and a government whip averted the danger by 'hustling' Devlin from the Chamber. The Speaker opted to take no action against Devlin, arguing that, where strong feelings are aroused, 'there are times when the Chair can appropriately be deaf or indeed blind'.[27]

His restraint was much criticised. Although ministers had no wish to turn Devlin into a 'martyr', many considered it 'intolerable that the Treasury bench should be in a situation where, apparently, it was liable to assault from any quarter without disciplinary action being taken against the MP'. Devlin's subsequent comments hardly helped. She expressed contrition, but only that she had not been more violent. 'My only regret is that I didn't seize Mr Maudling by the throat while I had the chance. I was not allowed to have my say on the brutal murder of the 13 people yesterday. I walked up to Mr Maudling and hit him across the face as hard as I could with my fist. I was cold and calm and the blow was a calculated one. I did not lose my temper.'[28]

Less than a month later, there was another, more serious, incident of parliamentary violence, this time in Ulster. John Taylor, Northern Ireland's Minister of Home Affairs, was shot four times by two IRA gunmen while getting into his car in Armagh. Taylor was seriously wounded but survived. A staunch critic of the IRA, he had been considered one of its top targets, and was under the protection of armed police at the time of the shooting. This attack reportedly followed four unsuccessful attempts to kill Ulster Prime Minister Brian Faulkner in the previous year.[29]

Rising disorder prompted the British government to prorogue Stormont and resume direct rule over Northern Ireland in March 1972. Although there had been some hope that this would result in a more even-handed approach toward political violence, almost a year passed before the first loyalists faced internment. When this finally transpired in February 1973, it provoked an upsurge in loyalist attacks.

By now, some politicians in Northern Ireland had begun to carry guns for protection. Paddy Wilson, a popular Social Democratic and Labour Party member of the Northern Ireland Senate, refused to do so, unwilling to bear responsibility for shooting anyone even in self-defence. His conscience may have been his downfall: in late June 1973, members of the Ulster Freedom Fighters stabbed to death the nationalist legislator and his Protestant secretary. The same day as Wilson's murder, a bullet was fired through the window of the home of a Unionist candidate for the Northern Ireland Assembly.[30]

The parliamentary violence of the early Troubles was not confined to the United Kingdom. In March 1974, it spilled across the border, as Senator Billy Fox became the first Member of Republic of Ireland's parliament to be assassinated since 1927. Although the Ulster Defence Association claimed responsibility for killing one of the few Protestant Members of the Oireachtas, five suspected Provisional IRA members were convicted of the crime.[31]

Three months later a 20lb gelignite bomb exploded in a corner of Westminster Hall, fracturing a gas main and sparking serious fires. Casualties probably would have been much worse than the eleven who suffered mostly minor injuries as a result of the blast, had not a coded IRA warning given the police six minutes to begin evacuating the area. Although one peer subsequently condemned parliamentary security as 'little better than a joke', it was deemed impossible simultaneously to protect MPs absolutely and to preserve their democratically vital accessibility to constituents.[32]

It presumably was scant consolation to those in Westminster that they operated in a veritable oasis of tranquillity compared to the atmosphere endured by their cousins in Belfast. Elections were held for a new body, the Northern Ireland Assembly, a year after the imposition of direct rule. As before, Unionists held a majority, but they now were divided bitterly by proposals contained in a recent government White Paper that Dublin be allowed to play a role in Ulster affairs.[33]

The Assembly's first meeting on 31 July 1973 grimly foretold the institution's fate. Members of Reverend Ian Paisley's anti-White Paper, hardline Democratic Unionist Party (DUP) 'turned what should have been a solemn, historic occasion into a farce'. Making good on their pledge to make the assembly unmanageable, the 'loyalists' shouted and caused such commotion that business was impossible. When a member of a more moderate party had the temerity to stand amidst the DUP seats and talk to one of the Paisleyites, John McQuade took exception and 'roughly' pushed the offender into the aisle. Eventually, after two hours, the Assembly was able to elect a Speaker, but further progress proved impossible and the sitting was adjourned. Paisley, however, was not finished. Despite the lights in the chamber being turned off, the DUP Members occupied the presiding officer's chair and cheered wildly as Paisley denounced both the British government and the assembly's officials. The loyalists claimed that their meeting constituted the legitimate Assembly, vowing to challenge the authority of the other one in the courts.[34]

Four months later, representatives of the Governments of Northern Ireland, the Irish Republic and Britain met at Sunningdale to negotiate details of the Council of Ireland, which would give Dublin a role in the administration of Ulster. The Unionists opposed to such a scheme had not been invited to the talks largely because of their disruptive behaviour in the Northern Ireland Assembly.[35] They demonstrated the wisdom of this decision by sparking a brawl in the Assembly, on the day the Sunningdale conference began.

In the wake of the defeat of their motion that the Assembly should sit the following day to hold a debate on the conference, Members of the DUP and the Vanguard Party, an offshoot of UUP, sought to eject from the chamber Unionists who supported the Faulkner-led executive. In the course of 'a three-minute struggle unparalleled in Northern Ireland politics', Minister of Education Basil McIvor 'was pulled and struck'. A colleague was 'knocked to the floor and kicked by a Vanguard member'. Herbert Kirk, a Unionist former finance minister, 'exchanged blows' with loyalist Hugh Smyth. Those not involved in the intra-Unionist fracas watched, 'as assembly men were pulled by their ties or reeled and swayed on the jammed benches'. John McQuade, 'a former boxing trainer, ran along the rear of the Unionist benches throwing punches'. The police were summoned (but did not enter the chamber), as the Speaker adjourned the sitting.[36]

Less than two months later, large numbers of police, supported by military police and armoured cars, were on duty outside Stormont in anticipation of a violent public reaction to the formation of a power-sharing executive. As it turned out, however, the only disturbances took place on the floor of the assembly. The trouble began right away as the Speaker asked the hardcore loyalists who had rushed to occupy the front bench to vacate it, so that the members of the executive could sit there, as was customary. This prompted shouts of 'No!' from the loyalists. Professor Kennedy Lindsey of the Vanguard Party responded by trying to climb onto the Speaker's table. On his first try he succeeded only in knocking a glass of water onto the floor. Redoubling his efforts, he kicked the dispatch box before managing to clamber up and seize a microphone. He managed to shout 'the temples have been cleansed', before being pulled down.

The Reverend Ian Paisley, meanwhile, began building a barricade of chairs. As the moderates sought to escape the chaos by moving to the back of the chamber, Paisleyite James Craig grabbed the mace from the Speaker's table. 'Pursued by one of the doormen, he handed it off to Mr William Beattie, another DUP man, who was chased down an aisle by another doorman.' When a member of the security staff finally succeeded in recapturing the mace, Beattie complained, 'That's not your bloody job.'

At some point the Speaker adjourned the sitting. Then the police arrived. Paisley was 'carried from the Chamber, red-faced and breathing heavily, by eight policemen'. He later accused them of nearly breaking his arm. John McQuade 'was taken out shouting: "I'll fix you, you're murdering me, you're killing me", while Professor Lindsey was heard to murmur 'Please let go', as he too was taken horizontally from the Chamber'. Craig, on the other hand, 'departed in more valiant style, struggling furiously, pushing a policeman against the Speaker's chair and shouting: "Go ahead if you want – use brute force"'. Paisley's wife, Eileen, also a Member of the Assembly, 'walked out on her own after insisting on her right to a frontbench seat by sitting briefly on the knee of Mr Robert Cooper, Minister for Manpower'. In the course of removing eighteen loyalists, seven by force, five policemen were injured.[37]

Although Paisley had vowed to employ the same violent tactics when the assembly met the next day, in the end the loyalists opted to stage a walkout, ostensibly to protest a proposal to change the standing orders to allow the Speaker to suspend for fourteen sittings Members who create a disturbance.[38] As it turned out, a general strike outside of the assembly, rather than loyalist violence inside it, led to collapse of the power-sharing executive negotiated at Sunningdale. However, the disruptive reputation of extreme unionists helped ensure that they were not invited to negotiations of 1985 Anglo–Irish Agreement.[39]

The Troubles Worsen

Quite a bit of blood was spilled, before the hard men (and one notably adamantine woman) were ready for such talks. Politicians, hardly immune to attacks hitherto, would be targeted more frequently and with more lethal intent, in the wake of the abortive plan to share power. Even when they were not injured, their vulnerability to terrorist violence was at times amply demonstrated.

In July 1974, for example, a telephoned warning led a Belfast-bound aircraft to make an emergency landing in Manchester. A bomb, subsequently revealed to have an inoperable timing device, was found hidden on board. Among the plane's eighty-five passengers was MP James Molyneaux, Chief Whip of the UUP and Deputy Grand Master of the Orange Order.[40]

A year later, a bomb destroyed Hugh Fraser's car, which was parked outside the Conservative MP's London home. The explosion killed Professor Gordon Hamilton Fairley, a leading cancer specialist, who had been out walking his dogs, and injured seven others. Police blamed the IRA for the attack on Fraser, who recently had received a number of death threats.[41]

Much of the violence that followed the demise of the Sunningdale Agreement was sectarian in character, but the accord also opened a nasty rift in loyalist ranks. One of the MPs who almost paid dearly for his suspect devotion to the cause was Enoch Powell.

Having declined to stand as a Conservative in the first 1974 general election, Powell won a seat for South Down in the second, as a candidate for the UUP. Perceptions that he was an outsider were reinforced when he broke with many in his new party to abstain in a March 1977 vote of confidence, thereby helping the minority Labour Government retain power. The following month, Powell, accompanied by UUP leader Molyneaux, opened a fair at the Orange Hall at Lisburn. The next day, a man claiming to represent a banned loyalist organisation called a local newspaper to report that a bomb had previously been placed in the Hall but had failed to detonate. The caller asserted that Powell had been the target of the explosive device, subsequently discovered hidden on a disused staircase leading to the stage, because the erstwhile Tory 'is just here to take advantage of our people'.[42]

There were more signs of discord in the Unionist ranks the following month, as Harold McCusker 'was kicked, punched and abused', when he went to court to present evidence in defence of Loyalists accused of operating illegal road checkpoints. The UUP MP's condemnation of violent strike tactics and intimidation apparently earned him the enmity of the supporters of the Reverend Ian Paisley, who set upon the parliamentarian as he left the courthouse. McCusker was mobbed, until two police constables 'linked arms behind the slightly built MP and half hustled, half carried him through the mob to safety'.[43]

Loyalist divisions were only one consequence of the failure of power sharing. The British Government sought to 'normalize' its direct rule in Northern Ireland by abandoning internment and treating republican prisoners as common criminals. They responded to the denial of what they saw as their rightful status as political prisoners by embarking in early 1978 on a 'dirty protest': refusing to shave or bathe and smearing the walls of their cells with excrement.[44]

Soon thereafter, the dirty protest came to Westminster as protesters, upset about the treatment of republican prisoners, threw three bags of horse manure from the Strangers' Gallery into the Commons. Although no MPs were injured, the sitting was suspended in 'grave disorder', and several trips to the dry cleaner reportedly were required.[45]

Much worse was to come. On 30 March 1979, an Irish National Liberation Army bomb killed Airey Neave, the Conservative Northern Ireland spokesman, as he drove out of the House of Commons car park. The assassination of a staunch unionist may have been an attempt to influence the upcoming general election.[46] Or, it may have aimed at preventing a vocal opponent of republican violence from assuming responsibility for Northern Ireland, following the expected Conservative victory. Either way, it spawned tit-for-tat attacks on leaders on both sides of the sectarian divide. Among the casualties were three former parliamentarians: Bernadette Devlin McAliskey was seriously wounded; Sir Norman Stronge, erstwhile Speaker of the Northern Ireland House of Commons, and his son James, an ex-Member of that assembly, were killed.[47]

When dirty protests and a variety of other tactics did not win them the political status they craved, republican prisoners turned to hunger strikes. This won some of them a different political status.

On 9 April 1981, Bobby Sands was elected MP by voters who had been urged to save the hunger striker's life. Although this victory did not rescue Sands, who died on 5 May, it did alarm the government sufficiently to prompt an amendment to the Representation of the People Act, prohibiting prisoners standing for parliament. In June, two other republican prisoners, Kieran Doherty and Paddy Agnew, were elected to the Dáil, thereby putting Ireland's Fianna Fáil party out of power. These victories at the polls, combined with the public support demonstrated for the hunger strikers, helped convince Sinn Féin to enter electoral politics, a move that would eventually pave the way for a political solution to the Troubles.[48]

Sinn Féin's pursuit of votes did not entail an end to republican violence. Indeed, as an activist explained, the party aimed to take power with a ballot paper in one hand and Armalite (explosives) in the other. Seeking elective office was not seen to be incompatible with murdering elected officials. On 14 November 1981, a little more than a month after the end of the hunger strikes, Provisional IRA gunmen killed Unionist MP Robert Bradford in the community centre in which he was holding a constituent surgery. The militants subsequently released a statement indicating that Bradford had been targeted because his rhetoric was seen to have motivated loyalist violence.[49]

Two days later, this incident twice provoked grave disorder in the Commons. During discussion of the security situation in Ulster, Secretary of State for Northern Ireland James Prior asserted that the proper response to recent violence was to work calmly but firmly under the law. The Reverend Ian Paisley, now also a Westminster MP, derided this assessment as 'nonsense'. Peter Robinson interrupted Prior's subsequent remarks to assert, 'The blood of Ulster is on your hands.' As the Speaker repeatedly demanded order, John McQuade exclaimed, 'The Secretary of State is the guilty man.' This prompted the Speaker to order McQuade to leave the chamber. Paisley prompted even greater commotion by pointing at Prime Minister Thatcher and shouting, 'There is the guilty woman!' After his repeated attempts to maintain order were ignored, the Speaker suspended the sitting for ten minutes.

When it resumed, the Speaker named McQuade, Robinson and Paisley for 'grossly disorderly conduct and ignoring the authority of the Chair'. A motion for the suspension of the three DUP MPs was carried, when no tellers were appointed for the Noes. The Speaker ordered them to withdraw. Paisley refused. The Speaker ordered the Serjeant-at-Arms to 'ensure that the hon. Members leave the precincts of the House'. He also warned the three that 'if they have so much as a touch on their arms [that is, show any resistance to the Serjeant], they will be suspended for the rest of the Session'. Despite this warning, the three apparently did not leave. The Speaker again suspended the sitting for ten minutes to allow for their removal. Later, Paisley told reporters that, having concluded that there was nothing he could do in parliament to protect his people, he would return to Northern Ireland to make the province ungovernable and thereby force the Thatcher administration to address the security concerns of Protestants.[50]

As a force for institutional chaos, Paisley quite possibly was unrivalled. He managed to bring to a standstill three parliaments, at three levels, over three decades. Indeed, perhaps even more impressive than his disruptions of Stormont or Westminster was his ability to foment disorder in Strasbourg, the home of a body that often seems the antithesis of commotion. On 11 October 1988, Paisley was ejected from the European Parliament after interrupting an address by Pope John Paul II. All he did was to hold up a sign equating the pontiff with the Anti-Christ. For some reason, this did not go down well. On the contrary, the action of the minister of the fundamentalist Free Presbyterian Church of Ulster precipitated 'several minutes of shouting, pushing and shoving', during which some of his parliamentary colleagues sought to divest the placard from his grasp. 'During the brief melee, some of Mr Paisley's fellow MEPs threw the odd wildly aimed punch at him. He was finally hustled from the chamber by a dozen security men after ignoring the pleas of Lord Henry Plumb, the British President of the Parliament, to "respect the dignity of this place".'[51]

Institutional indignities were not the exclusive preserve of the hardline Protestants. In 1982, Owen Carron, his election agent, and seven others were charged with assault and disorderly behaviour, after fighting broke out in Belfast Magistrates' Court following a decision to try nine alleged IRA members without the usual preliminary hearing. Carron had been Sands' election agent and succeeded him as MP for Fermanagh and South Tyrone.[52]

Deadly violence against politicians resumed the following year, with the IRA claiming responsibility for the assassination of UUP Assembly Member Edgar Graham. Three months later, Sinn Féin leader Gerry Adams was shot in the neck, shoulder and arm as he was leaving Belfast Magistrates' Court. The MP for West Belfast subsequently complained that, despite repeated death threats, the police had refused to give him a permit to carry a gun for protection.[53] The Ulster Freedom Fighters carried out the attack – which seriously injured some of Adams's colleagues – but there have been suggestions that the operation was planned with help from British intelligence.[54]

Ironically, it may have been the IRA Armalite rather than Sinn Féin's support at the ballot box that provided crucial impetus to the peace process. It certainly produced the most spectacular episode of parliamentary violence during the Troubles. On 12 October 1984, seven months after the attempt to kill Adams, the Provisional IRA sought to assassinate Prime Minister Thatcher and her Cabinet with a large bomb at Brighton's Grand Hotel, then hosting the Conservative Party Conference. Although Thatcher was not hurt, two of her Ministers – Industry Secretary Norman Tebbit and Parliamentary Secretary to the Treasury John Wakeham – sustained serious injuries. Among the five killed by the blast was Sir Anthony Berry, Conservative MP for Enfield South. It was thought that the republican group felt a spectacular attack was needed to restore its credibility after a series of setbacks at the hands of law-enforcement officials.[55]

Whatever the intention, the bombing was what one minister described as a Tet-Offensive moment, a point at which it became clear that the enemy could not be defeated militarily.[56] Pressure to find a peaceful way forward led to the 1985 Anglo–Irish Agreement (AIA), which provided for enhanced security cooperation between London and Dublin and also gave the government of the Republic some role in affairs in Ulster.[57] Inevitably, this provoked violence.

A few days after the AIA was signed, Secretary of State for Northern Ireland Tom King visited Belfast. As he arrived at city hall, a group of men who had been part of a protest attacked his entourage. The minister was 'hit by an egg, severely jostled and grabbed in a headlock .... At least one punch was thrown, but it apparently missed King as his aides threw up their briefcases to fend off attackers'. Finding the front doors of the building locked, King was forced to seek refuge in his car, which drove him to a side entrance. Among King's assailants were several local politicians, including Belfast City Councillor George Seawright, who was seen jumping on the trunk of King's car.[58]

It was not just the details of the agreement that angered Unionists. They also were upset that their politicians had not been consulted, an omission presumably at least partially attributable to the disruptive reputation of Paisley and others. Ostensibly to give their constituents a chance to show their opposition to the AIA, Unionist MPs in both Westminster and Stormont resigned. The chaos caused by the plethora of by-elections contributed to the British government's decision to dissolve the Northern Ireland Assembly on 23 June 1986. Unionist politicians responded by refusing to leave the chamber. 'The RUC provided their final service to the Anglo-Irish Agreement by carrying protesting assembly members from the building.'[59]

The next spate of parliamentary violence did not occur until mid-1990, the result of an IRA campaign on the British mainland. The first incident was somewhat reminiscent of a botched Suffragette attack. On 12 June, an IRA bomb severely damaged West Green House, a Queen Anne mansion in Hampshire, in an apparent attempt to assassinate Lord McAlpine, a member of Prime Minister Thatcher's inner circle and until recently Conservative Party treasurer. His name had been on a list found in a 'bomb factory' two years previously. However, republican intelligence was outdated, for McAlpine had moved out of the house three weeks earlier, having sold it to the National Trust. He subsequently described the violence as 'an act of complete stupidity. It is a tragedy to go around ruining very beautiful houses like that'.[60]

Considerably less farcical was the IRA bombing of the Carlton Club, on 25 June. The attack on the Tory club, a popular dining spot for MPs, left six injured, including Lord Kaberry of Adel, Conservative Party Vice-Chairman from 1955 to 1961.[61]

The following month, another IRA bomb killed Ian Gow, of the Conservative Party's committee on Northern Ireland, as the MP was starting his car in his driveway.[62] Described by Thatcher as an 'unflinching enemy' of the IRA, Gow, a few years earlier, had become one of the few MPs to resign from her government on a point of principle when he quit as Treasury Minister to protest the AIA.[63]

In February 1991, the IRA carried out perhaps its most audacious attack ever, launching three mortars at 10 Downing Street from a van parked in Whitehall. Two landed behind the Foreign Office without exploding. A third detonated in the garden behind the prime minister's residence, breaking windows. There were no injuries, but a session of the war cabinet was adjourned hastily. 'As one official put it: "The meeting was interrupted for ten minutes to resume in a room with less draught."'[64]

The Troubles often are said to have ended with the 1998 signing of the Good Friday Agreement. But exposure to extremist bloodshed in Ulster was so widespread and prolonged that some argued it had created a culture, unique in advanced industrial societies, in which a substantial minority of the population, both Protestant and Catholic, came to condone paramilitary violence as a means of achieving communal goals.[65] So it is perhaps not surprising that parliamentary violence in Northern Ireland did not end with the Troubles.

The sight of Paisley sharing power with Sinn Féin's Martin McGuinness, and doing so with such joviality that the whilom enemies would be dubbed 'The Chuckle Brothers', was very difficult for some to accept. In late 2006, Michael Stone was wrestled to the ground inside the front door of Stormont. The former Ulster Defence Force Member was found in possession of a gun, a knife and a number of nail-bombs. Bystanders heard him shout, 'No surrender, no sell-out, Paisley.'[66] Stone subsequently was sentenced to sixteen years imprisonment, after the court rejected defence claims that his armed incursion into Stormont while the Assembly was meeting and his earlier letters to journalists promising to kill Adams and McGuinness, were simply elements of 'performance art'.[67]

In late 2012, East Belfast MP Naomi Long received a death threat amid loyalist disturbances, after members of her Alliance Party voted in the City Council to limit the days on which Union Jack is flown on City Hall.[68]

A year later, a letter bomb was sent to Theresa Villiers, Secretary of State for Northern Ireland, forcing the evacuation of Stormont Castle. This marked the fourth time in a week that such explosives (none of which detonated) had been sent to senior political figures in the province, apparently the result of a dissident republican campaign to disrupt the peace process.[69]

The early-2017 collapse of Ulster's power-sharing government thankfully has not, two years on, led to the return of the Troubles, the most lethal spate of parliamentary violence in British history.[70] Incredibly, it could have been much worse: paramilitaries generally refrained from attacking the other side's political leaders, knowing that otherwise their own would become targets.[71]

14

CUSTARD'S FIRST STAND

Northern Ireland has not been the only source of parliamentary violence in the last few decades. British politics had become quite a bit feistier even before Margaret Thatcher became prime minister in 1979, but partisan divisions, and parliamentary violence, grew on her watch. Yet her departure did not greatly reduce the danger. Indeed, recently MPs have faced a panoply of threats, from the deadly serious to the intentionally innocuous, even delicious.

Parliamentarians Behaving Badly

Since the 1960s, MPs increasingly have been career politicians rather than amateurs for whom entry into the Commons followed success in other fields.[1] At the same time, government business has dominated the parliamentary agenda as never before, limiting the opportunities for backbencher involvement and, since the mid-1970s, leading to greater use of the guillotine and other procedures for limiting debate.[2] The growing gap between backbencher ambitions and their scope for effective action, exacerbated by rising ideological polarisation during the Thatcher era, fuelled an increase in both dissent and government defeats in divisions.[3] This, in turn, seems, particularly for Labour, to have spurred new approaches to party discipline, as Jack Straw discovered soon after entering the Commons in 1979.

As the former minister recounts in his memoirs, 'I was getting a bit cocky, until Labour's deputy chief whip, Walter Harrison, took me in hand.' The stocky former electrician 'was not a man to pick an argument with. Unwisely, I did'. Accosting the junior MP in a corridor, Harrison told Straw to change his tactics on a finance bill. The latter demurred. The disagreement continued until the whip adopted a different mode of persuasion:

> He fixed both eyes upon me and as he did so, I felt a pain between my legs I'd not experienced since the school rugby field. His grip tightened. I rose on tiptoes as he pushed up as well. My mouth came open; only a little screech came out. 'Now, lad. Have you got the point, or do you want some more?' 'Yes', I whimpered in reply. Walter released his grip. I did as I'd been told.[4]

It was not just within parties that order became more difficult to maintain. There was 'a sustained assault on the procedure of the House by some of its members' in the wake of the 1979 general election. Standing orders aimed at disorder were used more frequently. 'Procedural vandalism', such as shouting down speakers, rose.[5] The bounds of parliamentary speech were tested, and not infrequently, breached.[6] As in the 1920s, the miscreants often were few in number, but their attempts to use disorder to leverage their influence raised questions about the stability of the parliamentary system.[7] It did not help that, in an atmosphere of partisan distrust, the government sometimes appeared to engage in sharp practices.

On 13 November 1980, for example, Secretary of State for the Environment Michael Heseltine indicated that the government had begun a consultation process expected to result in a substantial increase in council housing rents. Opposition Environment spokesman Roy Hattersley accused Heseltine of 'a scandalous denial of the rights of this House' for revealing this on the day the parliamentary session was due to end, making it impossible for Members to ask questions. The debate was cut short by the announcement of Black Rod's arrival. 'Infuriated Labour MPs formed a phalanx across the bar of the Chamber' to prevent him from entering the Commons to invite members to the proroguing ceremony. The Speaker asked the 'honourable members' to make way for Black Rod, only to be answered by shouts of 'No, No, No'. After another request of this sort was ignored, the Speaker suspended the sitting for ten minutes. When the Speaker returned, he once more asked Members to make way for Black Rod. Again, they refused. Opposition leader Michael Foot argued that 'the rights of the House of Commons had been grossly interfered with' by

Heseltine's behaviour. Following a recommendation by the Leader of the House, the Speaker again suspended the sitting, this time for fifteen minutes.

When it resumed, Heseltine announced that he was willing to withdraw the consultative document and reintroduce it in the next session in order 'to uphold the Speaker's authority'. This did not fully soothe tempers: Nicholas Fairbairn, Solicitor-General for Scotland, later accused Labour MPs of assaulting him and preventing him from leaving the Chamber; some opposition lawmakers, by contrast, said he and other Tories had been pushing and shoving.[8]

Procedural irregularities were not always necessary to provoke violence, for the Left's antipathy toward the government could be almost deranged, as was demonstrated in late 1982, when Ron Brown was arrested in Glasgow after a 'lunge' at the prime minister. Thatcher was outside a hotel, when the Scottish MP, nicknamed 'Red Ron', ran to her, 'shouting and gesticulating wildly and waving his hands only inches from her face. Before he could touch her', Brown 'was thrown against the wall of the Holiday Inn hotel by five policemen and then, still yelling and fighting, dragged to a van near by'. Brown was charged with breach of the peace, although Thatcher subsequently stated that he had not touched her, and she had not felt she was being attacked.[9]

By early 1984, a veteran Labour MP complained that rowdiness and catcalls had created 'the worse Parliament I can recall for 20 years'.[10] And that was before the miners' strike poisoned the atmosphere still further. In November, Secretary of State for Social Services Norman Fowler's attempt to explain why the government had decided to deduct an additional pound from the supplementary benefit paid to the dependants of miners provoked what Thatcher later called, with considerable hyperbole, 'the rowdiest scenes this House has ever seen'.[11] Amidst 'constant angry barracking from the Labour benches', a group of left-wing MPs, in planned protest, left their seats and went to stand beside the mace. Despite the Speaker's appeals for order, around thirty MPs were soon gathered by the symbol of parliamentary authority. Faced with these disturbances, Fowler gave up and sat down. One of the protesting MPs, David Nellist, 'seized and tore up the Secretary of State's papers and hurled them at him, shouting'. Unable to obtain order, the Speaker suspended the sitting for ten minutes. When it resumed, and MPs continued to defy the Speaker by standing, he declared the House adjourned.[12]

Two months later, left-wing Labour MPs again implemented a planned disruption of parliament. On this occasion, the grievance was that in the following week's schedule no time had been allocated to discussion of the miners' strike. The Leader of the House refused calls to schedule a debate on the topic but indicated that there would be opportunities to discuss the matter in the future. Labour MPs then repeatedly sought, under points of order, to induce the Speaker to provide time to debate the strike. The Speaker responded that not only was it outside his power to allocate such time, but the many points of order were cutting into the period allotted to the discussion of other matters. This did nothing to dissuade a handful of MPs from their efforts to make strike-related points of order. Faced with fifteen MPs standing, despite his repeated entreaties for them to resume their seats, the Speaker suspended the sitting for twenty minutes.[13]

The plight of the miners was at the heart of another parliamentary scene in 1987. After Conservative Andrew Mackay characterised as 'gutless' the behaviour of Frank Cook on an earlier vote to help mining communities, the left-wing Labour MP announced, 'If the honourable member wants to find out how gutless I am, I'll see him outside.' Cook then 'walked to the bar of the House and stood close to Mr MacKay, beckoning him to step outside the chamber. Although MacKay declined the offer, the Speaker nevertheless opined, with some understatement, "This does not show us in a very good light."'[14]

The same sentiment could have been expressed regarding a variety of disruptive incidents in the Commons the following year. First, John Hughes was named and suspended for interrupting a chaplain saying the customary prayers at the start of a session.[15]

Two months later, Alex Salmond suffered the same fate for disrupting the chancellor's Budget Statement with the claim 'This is an obscenity'. Others soon picked up where Salmond had left off, leading to the suspension of the sitting, reportedly the first time 'in living memory' that this had happened during a Budget Speech.[16]

Perhaps the defining moment of the 'loony Left' of the Labour Party took place a month later, when Ron Brown, apparently upset that he had not been called upon in debate on the poll tax, threw papers at Social Services Minister Michael Portillo and then dropped the mace on the floor, damaging it. Two days later, Labour whips drafted a brief apology in agreement with the Speaker. Brown refused to read it in the Commons, describing it as a 'grovelling statement' and 'rubbish'. After trying unsuccessfully almost a dozen times to get Brown simply to read the statement rather than preface it with an explanation, the Speaker ordered the Labour Member to leave the chamber. A motion that Brown be both suspended and held responsible for the damage to the mace subsequently was approved 463 to 27.[17]

Yet, assertions made during the debate on Brown's suspension, that parliamentary disorder had become a Labour monopoly, were not completely accurate, as would be demonstrated seven months later.[18] As Members waited to vote following a boisterous debate on the Transport (Scotland) Bill in December 1988, George Galloway and Barry Porter 'appeared to square up to each other'. Other MPs intervened to separate the two men. Jim Sillars subsequently claimed that the Conservative had 'taken a swing at' his Labour colleague. Despite Sillars's suggestion that this constituted unparliamentary conduct, the Deputy Speaker declined to take action because Galloway had not reported the incident to him.[19]

There were two instances of 'grave disorder' in 1990, both caused by a combination of procedural disagreements and the ideologically charged issue of healthcare. In March, Labour efforts to obstruct a government attempt to adjourn debate on the National Health Service and Community Care Bill prompted the Speaker to suspend the 23-hour sitting.[20]

Four months later, Secretary of State for Health Kenneth Clarke's decision to answer questions about proposed NHS reforms collectively (rather than individually, as was customary) led to Labour protests that resulted in the suspension of the sitting. Although a compromise was reached through the 'usual channels', this did not preclude further excitement for, later that day, Left-winger David Nellist 'was ushered from the chamber ... after he had crossed the floor to berate' (or, by some accounts, to physically intimidate) the education minister, Angela Rumbold, who, he claimed, had not answered his question in a debate on schools.[21]

Thatcher's late-1990 replacement by John Major helped lower the parliamentary temperature. Disorder on the floor, which surged under her tenure, largely disappeared, although 'tolerated' rowdiness – such as heckling and barracking – since has grown.[22] Yet the contentious issue of healthcare in 1992 did provoke one final (Member-generated) incidence of 'grave disorder'.

Upset that the minister responsible for the decision to allow Scottish hospitals to opt out of health board control did not come to the Commons to answer questions, a group of Scottish Labour MPs forced the suspension of the sitting by standing in front of the mace. When the sitting resumed, there were more disruptions, leading to a second suspension.[23]

Food Fighting

The public targeting of politicians, which resumed in the 1960s after a hiatus of several decades, also picked up steam in the 1980s and beyond. Bitter divisions within Labour left its parliamentarians vulnerable. In Brighton, the venue for the party's 1981 conference, Neil Kinnock, who two years later would become the Labour leader, 'was involved in several scuffles and finally, when attacked by a man in a public toilet, "beat the shit out of him ... apparently there was blood and vomit all over the floor"'.[24]

Most public attacks, however, were on the Tories, the party in power. In early 1981, Conservative MP Robert Hicks 'was pelted with rotten potatoes', when he appeared on a platform to debate nuclear arms with Yorkshire miners' leader Arthur Scargill.[25] The following year, Environmental Secretary Michael Heseltine was bombarded with eggs and rotten fruit while visiting Liverpool.[26]

University campuses proved particularly parlous. In early 1983, Norman Tebbit was 'jostled' by over 100 student demonstrators as he went to speak to Young Conservatives at Bristol Polytechnic. The employment secretary emerged from the scrum looking 'pale and shaken'. Forced to leave via a fire escape after delivering his remarks, Tebbit 'was pursued to his car' by protesters.[27]

Less than a month afterward, Heseltine, by now the Secretary of State for Defence, 'was punched and pushed by about one hundred women peace protesters', as he sought to enter a Conservative meeting in Berkshire. One woman managed to drag the minister to his knees even though he was protected by a large number of police.[28]

Later that year, Heseltine was given another unwelcome welcome by Manchester University students angry at the government's policies on nuclear weapons. As the defence secretary approached the student union building surrounded by police, he was hit in the face with red paint. The minister managed to address the meeting, wearing a shirt borrowed from a police inspector, despite constant heckling and being forced to duck to avoid incoming eggs. Afterwards, a phalanx of police escorted him to a car, which was showered with eggs before driving away with its shaken passenger.[29]

Heseltine was targeted twice more, in February 1985. First 200 student demonstrators prevented the defence secretary from speaking at Strathclyde University. Then, later that day, he 'faced a barrage of flour, eggs and stink bombs', when he arrived at Glasgow University.[30]

The following month 500 chanting protesters tried to keep Leon Brittan from speaking at Manchester University's student union. A hundred police eventually cleared a path for the Home Secretary to enter the building, but not before eggs and other missiles were thrown.[31] Several months later, at the same institution of higher learning, the Home Office minister responsible for immigration was assaulted as he sought to deliver a speech to the Conservative Association. 'Minutes into his speech, a crowd of about 50 students surged forward, knocking over furniture and the microphone. One stepped forward and hit Mr [David] Waddington in the face.'[32]

In February 1986, John Carlisle was subjected to a violent assault that prevented him from addressing the Federation of Conservative Students at Bradford University. As the Tory MP entered a hall to speak about the right of sportsmen to play in South Africa, he was 'punched and kicked and broke his finger as he tried to break free'. These incidents evoked government concern that politicians were being prevented from speaking on university campuses, but this worry did not lead to the passage of a backbench bill to strengthen the safeguards for free speech, which Carlisle, among others, advocated.[33]

In February 1988, debate in the Lords on Section 28 of the Local Government Bill, prohibiting the 'promotion' of homosexuality in schools, was interrupted when three women tried to abseil into the chamber. One reached the floor, where she 'was immediately tackled by Black Rod and his ex-servicemen doorkeepers'. Two others 'hung indecisively above the chamber', until other doorkeepers pulled them up into the public gallery. Lord Monkswell subsequently apologised to peers for providing the protesters with passes to a side gallery that facilitated their invasion. Yet, his refusal to condemn the demonstration and his assertion that the legislation was similar to what the Nazis did to the Jews both elicited cries of 'shame' from the assembled peers.[34]

Five years, and a prime minister, later demonstrators returned to attacking a more habitual victim: Michael Heseltine, by now the President of the Board of Trade. 'Bricks, eggs and flour were thrown at Mr Heseltine from a crowd protesting about pit closures as he arrived to open a new steelworks in Doncaster, South Yorkshire.'[35]

The following year a large demonstration against the Criminal Justice Bill erupted in violence, as mounted police twice charged protesters seeking to pull down the iron gates leading to Downing Street. Prime Minister Major avoided any danger or inconvenience by spending the afternoon watching cricket at Lord's.[36]

Days after condemning classroom strikes and vowing to dismiss incompetent teachers and close failing schools, David Blunkett was forced to flee from angry educators at the April 1995 National Union of Teachers conference in Blackpool. As the blind MP entered the hall accompanied by his guide dog, about thirty demonstrators accosted him, shouting, 'Sack the Tories, not the teachers!' Conference stewards managed to lead Blunkett and his dog to a side room, where he was besieged by about two dozen demonstrators, many wearing Socialist Workers' Party badges. They chanted and banged on the door and glass partition, trying to get at Labour's education spokesman. Union General Secretary Doug McAvoy had to leave the platform to persuade the militants to return to their seats and release Blunkett.[37]

Several months later, at the State Opening of parliament, supporters of the anti-racism group, Movement for Justice, splashed orange paint on Conservative Party Chairman Brian Mawhinney to protest the government's Asylum and Immigration bill.[38]

This was followed, a few months hence, by a rather curious incident in which Commons' debate on a proposal that Britain re-join UNESCO was interrupted when protesters threw lottery tickets into the Chamber.[39] Considerably more effective, apparently, was the demonstration by two women in the public gallery in December 1996. After they unfurled a banner protesting arms sales to Indonesia and began to shout, some Scottish and Welsh nationalist MPs, disdaining the parliamentary convention dictating that such interruptions should be ignored, started applauding the demonstrators so enthusiastically that one, Plaid Cymru's Cynog Dafis, was warned by the Speaker.[40]

New Labour in Old Battles?

The Labour leadership that entered government after the 1997 general election was praised for pushing the party sufficiently toward the centre to end two decades of Conservative rule. Such was the tension this created that many of the tiffs between politicians over the next thirteen years were intra-party in nature. Yet, conflicts during this period were not simply a case of 'New Labour' fighting old internal battles. Perhaps the Blair administration's most interesting achievement, at least from the present perspective, was to provoke at least a modicum of disorder in the previously placid House of Lords.

The tranquillity of the Upper House has been explained by its political impotence (even before the Lords lost their veto in 1911), by the collective mechanism for maintaining order (peer pressure, if you will), and by the existence of an institutionally sanctioned means of protest.[41] In the second half of the twentieth century, however, the increasing complexity of legislation and a growing desire by peers for involvement led to an increase the Lords' political role.[42] This came at a cost: the chamber's standing orders aimed at disorder, which were not employed at all in the first half of the century, were called upon a number of times in the second.

The prohibition of asperity of speech was read in 1950.[43] Sixteen years later it was requested, but not actually read, because a peer withdrew the 'way' he had spoken, if not the comment he had made.[44] It was invoked again in 1980.[45] Moreover, twice during the turbulent 1980s, peers took the highly unusual steps of motioning that a colleague be no longer heard. And once, in 1985, there was an attempt to employ a parliamentary device of even greater rarity in the Lords: closure, although in this case the deputy chairman refused to put the motion.[46] More alarming still, in 1998, for the first time ever, the call for a reading of the ban prompted a division.[47]

An institutional pessimist, trying really, really hard, might read these incidents – particularly the last one – as indicating that the Lords was sliding inexorably toward the sort of disorder regularly observed in the Commons. Such a view received spectacular support in late October 1999, when the Lords debated a government bill to restrict the number of hereditary peers sitting in the Upper House.

As heir to the Duke of St Albans, the Earl of Burford by right could sit on the steps of the throne and listen to, but not participate in, proceedings. On this occasion, however, he rose, pushed past the Deputy Speaker, jumped onto the Woolsack, and began shouting about the 'abolition of Britain'. Ushers quickly pulled him down. Then Black Rod ejected the man memorably described in the press as a 'lord a-leaping'.[48] A few days later, Burford again was ejected from the Palace of Westminster, after trying to hold a press conference to announce that he was standing (ironically, but ultimately unsuccessfully) as a Democratic Party candidate in an upcoming by-election.[49]

These unseemly scenes notwithstanding, however, most of the parliamentary excitement during the Labour era concerned the

Commons, where the 1997 general election had left the party with a huge majority. Although Thatcher's departure and the advent of a more centrist 'New Labour' reduced partisan tension, the Tories occasionally proved just as willing as their rivals to test the bounds of parliamentary propriety in defence of what they perceived as the institutional prerogatives of the opposition.

Thus, in early 2001 Ann Widdecombe, the Shadow Home Secretary, and three other senior Conservatives brought proceedings of a standing committee considering the Criminal Justice and Police Bill to a halt by sitting in seats reserved for members of that body, which they were not. When the four refused to withdraw, the committee ordered their behaviour to be reported to the House. After they again declined to leave, the chair adjourned the committee under the provisions for grave disorder.[50]

It is perhaps indicative of the cooler political temperature that this potentially explosive and constitutionally significant dispute produced no violence. Indeed, the only physical encounter between MPs from different parties during the Blair era apparently occurred over a matter of infinitely less import. Appearing on the Talksport radio program in October 2005, Labour MP Stephen Pound read out an email from a staffer of Philip Davies encouraging local Tories to call in to support the Conservative MP. According to Pound, Davies 'completely lost the plot' after the program, injuring the Labour MP as he tried to wrestle a printout of the email from his grasp. The Tory denied that any violence had taken place.[51]

This disputed incident aside, almost all altercations between MPs since 1997 have been intra-Labour affairs, as a leadership acutely focused on party discipline faced occasional rebellions. The response could be the sorts of persuasive techniques Jack Straw encountered as a junior MP, decades earlier.

In December 2001, for example, Paul Marsden publicly complained of being attacked by 'thugs' from his own party. Earlier, the Labour MP had criticised provisions of the Blair administration's Anti-Terrorism Bill in debate. He had then compounded the offence to partisan sensibilities by openly conferring on the floor with Liberal Democrats. Leaving the chamber, Marsden allegedly was jeered and jostled by a group of whips and former whips. He accused senior whip Gerry Sutcliffe of seeking to intimidate him by stating that, if Marsden did not stop criticising the government, the whips would not be able to prevent angry Labour backbenchers from physically attacking him. Instead, the dissident MP responded in a manner that left few bridges unburned: he wrote Tony Blair a letter urging the prime minister to rein in his 'attack dogs' and issued a press release denouncing the 'Stalinist tendencies and desperate methods' of New Labour. A few months later, Marsden joined the Liberal Democrats.[52]

Another serial rebel, Bob Marshall-Andrews, was involved in two violent incidents with Labour colleagues in little more than three months. In November 2005, as the government vainly struggled to win parliamentary approval for a bill that would allow terrorist suspects to be held for ninety days without charges, he was seen talking to several Tory MPs in the Members' lobby, during a break following a division. A few Labour MPs, possibly under the influence, reproached their colleague for contributing to what would be the Blair Government's first Commons defeat. The practising barrister and part-time judge reportedly responded by calling one of them, former whip Jim Dowd, a 'faggot'. (Marshall-Andrews insists the word he used was *'faccio'*, or menial assistant.) Dowd responded by seizing his Labour comrade by the lapels, pushing him across the lobby, and pinning him against the wall before being pulled away by a junior Labour whip.[53]

A few months later, Marshall-Andrews was involved in another spat, this time at the Commons bar. The Labour MP apparently asked whip John Heppell to take time off from the Commons. Heppell not only refused to grant permission but asserted to his rebellious colleague that 'there's others who are a bloody sight more deserving than you'. As the two apparently squared off to fight, Heppell, nicknamed 'Knuckles' for the tattoos that once resided thereon, shocked onlookers by biting his antagonist.[54]

The highly contentious politics surrounding plans to expand Heathrow Airport threatened more intra-Labour violence in 2009. When it appeared that the government intended to build a third runway without putting the matter to a Commons vote, John McDonnell, whose constituency includes Heathrow, left his seat and marched down the gangway. For a second, it seemed his intention was to assault Transport Secretary Geoff Hoon, who was defending the plan. Instead, after walking up to Hoon, pointing at him and calling him 'a disgrace', the left-wing Labour MP merely picked up the mace and placed it upon a green bench, earning a five-day suspension for his troubles.[55]

Some expected the violent aspects of party discipline to disappear once the Conservatives returned to power in 2010. After all, the new prime minister, David Cameron, was said to come 'from a world where displays of anger are unacceptable, even boorish'.[56] Yet, the commitment of the upper classes to social proprieties and self-control is rather contingent, as the 'antics' of the Bullingdon Club at Oxford University attest. In any case, the challenge of holding together a coalition government meant that he and other Tories at times reacted to dissent in a manner reminiscent of previous Labour administrations.

One target of Conservative intimidation was Jesse Norman, who helped organise a revolt against government plans for reforming the House of Lords in July 2012. Prior to the vote, he felt Cameron's wrath as the prime minister accused his fellow old Etonian of 'dishonourable' behaviour and jabbed his finger at him. Displaying considerably semantic flexibility, Cameron's spokesman subsequently insisted that the prime minister had been 'irritated', not 'angry'. Still, when four Tory whips found Norman and another rebel drinking on the Terrace, they 'suggested that it might be better if he left the parliamentary estate, given the ill feelings toward them from members of the Government'.[57]

The potentially dangerous mix of alcohol and tribal feeling had been demonstrated several months earlier, when Labour MP Eric Joyce was arrested and charged with three counts of assault after attacking several Tories in a Commons bar. The incident apparently started when a Conservative MP politely asked to have his seat back. Joyce, a former Army major and Scottish Judo champion, reportedly replied, 'No you f***ing can't.' He then 'flipped' and began assaulting some Tory MPs at the back of the bar. A Conservative councillor and two researchers for MP Jackie Doyle-Price allegedly were hit as they tried to intervene. This prompted Doyle-Price to step in, saying, 'Punch me before you punch my staff.' As Joyce reportedly complained there were 'too many f***ing Tories in here', drinks were thrown over some in the bar, nicknamed the Kremlin for its popularity with Labour MPs. Two such parliamentarians apparently were caught up in the fracas as they sought to calm things down. Arriving at the bar, police initially restrained Joyce but released him after he protested that he was an MP. Joyce then reportedly ran straight at Conservative MP Stuart Andrew, whom he head-butted in the face, drawing blood. As he was led away by police, Joyce allegedly broke a window on a door near the bar. The Labour Party suspended the Falkirk MP pending the results of the police investigation.[58] A little more than a year later, Joyce, now an Independent MP, having been expelled from the Labour Party, was arrested again after a fight in another Commons bar.[59]

Mostly Trivial, Occasionally Tragic

These well-publicised incidents notwithstanding, the frequency of physical confrontations between MPs in the two decades since Labour came to power in 1997 has been little different than during the previous twenty years. What has changed has been the number of attacks on politicians by members of the public. These have increased substantially of late, although many of these incidents were publicity stunts rather than attempts to cause injury. Indeed, given that the weapon of choice often was edible, it was hard to take some assaults very seriously at all. There were, however, important exceptions.

The increased constituency services that MPs have provided over the course of the last century have been the source of both electoral support and aggravation. While some voters are grateful for MPs' help, others overestimate the extent to which their parliamentary representatives can solve their problems. Greater and more intimate contact with potentially irate or disturbed constituents occasionally has meant increased jeopardy to the health of parliamentarians.

In early 1982, for example, a man attending Michael O'Halloran's weekly constituency surgery in North London leapt at the MP and slashed his hand with a butcher's knife before being restrained by others. O'Halloran, who had left Labour to join the Social Democratic Party the previous year, was not wounded seriously.[60]

The outcome of a similar confrontation, almost two decades later, was less fortuitous. In early 2000, a deranged constituent armed with a samurai sword gravely injured Nigel Jones and killed his assistant, Andrew Pennington, a local councillor, in the Liberal Democrat MP's Cheltenham surgery. The assailant had visited the office repeatedly for assistance on a variety of matters, most recently the repossession of his home.[61]

An aide to a different MP subsequently lamented, 'The nature of the MPs' job makes them sitting ducks for the more dangerous and delusional of their constituents.'[62] Three years later, another lawmaker had a close call when a man, subsequently detained under the Mental Health Act, threatened Roger Godsiff with a knife in the Labour MP's Birmingham surgery.[63]

Rather than risk facing importunate and possibly violent voters, some MPs, typically those with secure seats, have abandoned constituency surgeries altogether. Others have sought to limit their public interactions in them. Even MPs who continue to meet with voters no longer feel compelled to ignore obnoxious or hurtful behaviour that previously would have been overlooked in an effort to avoid alienating electors.

In March 2005, for example, Chris Bryant secured a court order prohibiting a constituent from coming within 100 metres of the MP. The man repeatedly had shouted homophobic abuse at the openly gay parliamentarian, at public meetings in South Wales, and threatened him in the MP's Rhondda constituency surgery.[64]

Eight years later, another MP sought to do much the same thing by less legalistic means. In March 2013, Tim Loughton announced that he was 'sacking' a constituent who had made his life hell by constant complaining and abuse, including calling the former children's minister a 'Nazi'. The Conservative MP indicated that he would no longer respond to any communication from the constituent, who had contacted the police to accuse Loughton of sending a racist email.[65]

The unhinged are not the only danger. This became apparent in May 2010, when Labour MP Stephen Timms, returned with one of the highest majorities in the country, was stabbed twice while holding a constituency surgery in East London. His assailant told police she had been inspired to act by extremist Islamist websites. She was jailed for life for attempted murder, but her attack raised fears in Scotland Yard that other lone Muslim 'self-radicalisers' might be prompted to target politicians too. Indeed, several months later one of the websites she had visited called on Muslims to 'raise the knife of jihad' against British MPs who had voted in favour of the Iraq war.[66]

Similar sentiments apparently led to an incident in March 2017, in which parliament was 'placed on lockdown for hours' and Prime Minister Theresa May was evacuated to Downing Street after a man drove a vehicle into pedestrians on Westminster Bridge and fatally stabbed a police officer guarding Westminster Palace, before being shot to death. The Islamic State claimed the attacker, a recent Muslim convert with a history of violent crime, as one of its 'soldiers', but his exact relationship to the extremist organisation was unclear.[67]

These disturbing incidents notwithstanding, claims that the danger posed by Islamic extremism 'dwarfs altogether any previous terrorism directed against the British state, including the campaign waged by the IRA', so far, have proved wildly inaccurate, both in general and from the standpoint of parliamentary violence.[68] For politicians at least, the typical threat in recent decades has been about as far from terrorism as possible. That is, what violence there has been has aimed to humiliate rather than injure, and the motivation typically has been considerably more parochial than a clash of civilisations.

Characteristic of this genre were the actions of Danbert Nobacon, guitarist for the band Chumbawamba, who sought to demonstrate his feeling of betrayal by 'New Labour' by pouring ice water on Deputy Prime Minister John Prescott at the 1998 Brit Awards.

A few days after the attack on Nigel Jones, there was another incident of this sort when a protester shoved a chocolate éclair into the face of the agriculture minister at the National Farmers' Union conference. Nick Brown dismissed the incident as a 'silly stunt' unconnected with agriculture, which was then in the midst of the BSE crisis. Showing commendable sangfroid, he observed, 'It was not a samurai sword. It was a chocolate éclair. Although I am not a particularly brave person, I am not frightened of chocolate éclairs.'[69]

An opposition frontbencher was subjected to a similarly sapid savaging two months later, when Shadow Home Secretary Ann Widdecombe was hit in the face by a custard pie while signing copies of her book in Oxford. Her alleged assailant, identified by protesters as 'Agent Orange' of the Campsfield High Command of the Biotic Baking Brigade, reportedly was upset about the Conservative policy on asylum seekers, which was seen to stir up racial hatred against refugees.[70]

In January 2001, the food flingers scored their most impressive success, when Tony Blair was hit in the back by a tomato thrown by a woman protesting against sanctions on Iraq. She subsequently explained to a Bristol court that, having seen a youth throwing tomatoes ineffectually, she impulsively took one because she believed (rightly as it turned out) that she was a better shot. Her flatmate also was found guilty of harassment for throwing a 'mouldy tangerine' at the prime minister.[71]

Soon thereafter, three pie-wielding women set upon International Development Secretary Clare Short as she prepared to address a public meeting at Bangor University. 'She was unhurt in the incident, but the pies, planted firmly on her head and face, left a thick trail of yellow custard on the left shoulder of her red jacket.'[72] Police apprehended one of the assailants, who was fined £100, after Short told a court that she had been humiliated by the attack, which had been carried out to draw attention to globalisation and the power of multi-national companies.[73]

In 2004, activists from a group called Fathers4Justice began a campaign of minor parliamentary violence. Their tactics harked back to the Suffragettes, even their cause was almost the exact opposite: where the militant women sought to be treated equally in the political sphere, the men were pushing for greater parity at home, where family law was seen to discriminate against their sex.

In May, they provoked the suspension of a Commons sitting, by throwing flour-filled condoms into the chamber. Prime Minister Tony Blair was hit by one of the projectiles, which left the back of his suit mottled with purple powder. Another missile landed at his feet, splattering nearby cabinet members. Embarrassingly for the government, the attack came weeks after the installation of glass in the main public gallery aimed at preventing just such an incident (or worse). The protesters avoided this impediment by purchasing tickets at a charity auction that allowed them to view Prime Minister's Questions from the special visitors' gallery, which was not behind the glass.[74]

In September, those responsible for security at Westminster Palace suffered more embarrassment, when five individuals protesting against a proposed ban of fox hunting invaded the Commons chamber and forced the suspension of the sitting. One invader 'harangued' Rural Affairs Minister Alun Michael, who championed the ban. 'Commons officials, including Mark Harvey, the Assistant Serjeant at Arms, in tail coat, ceremonial sword, silk stockings and knee breeches, rushed forward to tackle the T-shirted intruders.' After a 20-minute suspension, the government managed to ram the bill through, as armed police stood guard at all entrances to the chamber.[75]

In the wake of these incidents, more stringent security measures were introduced for visitors to Westminster Palace. This has resulted in the confiscation of hundreds of weapons. Between January 2009 and September 2011, a combination of airport-style x-ray machines and frisk searches uncovered not only 371 knives and 127 sprays (mostly for self-defence) but also knuckledusters, a cosh, a truncheon, a bullet, a meat cleaver and a catapult.[76]

Politicians are less well protected when they leave Westminster Palace, as Fathers4Justice demonstrated in November 2004 when two of its activists crashed a conference on family law in Manchester in an attempt to make what they characterised as a citizen's arrest of the minister for children. One demonstrator managed to handcuff himself to Margaret Hodge, but conference participants tackled his accomplice before he could do likewise.[77]

Members of the group subsequently were involved in two attacks on Education Secretary Ruth Kelly. In April 2005, the Bolton West MP turned up at a constituency election debate only to have an activist attempt to put handcuffs on her. An egg also was thrown (inaccurately) at the minister. The following February, another fathers' rights campaigner smashed an egg on the back of Kelly's head as she left the court escorted by police. She later observed dejectedly, 'This is just one of those things that comes with being a politician.'[78]

Not all of her colleagues shared this nonchalant attitude. Several months later, a man rushed into a shop on Highbury Corner to get some eggs, telling the owner he would pay for them shortly. He went outside where he proceeded to throw them at Boris Johnson, the Shadow Minister for Higher Education. The MP reportedly 'started effing and blinding and tried to push the man away in a rather girly way with his knees'. A cab came. Johnson got in, then got back out in order to continue upbraiding his assailant. 'In all the excitement, he fell over.'[79]

Immigration Minister Phil Woolas was hit in the face by a custard pie, as he took part in an environmental debate at the University of Manchester in late 2008. The campaign group Manchester No Borders claimed responsibility for the attack, which was in response to the minister's indication that the government was planning to cap immigration.[80]

The following year, Lord Mandelson, the Business Secretary, won plaudits for imperturbability after being covered in green custard, thrown by an environmental protester upset about plans for a third Heathrow runway. Security for the senior minister was so lax that his assailant not only was able to walk away without being arrested but spent thirty minutes explaining her action to journalists.[81] Bookmaker William Hill subsequently began 'inviting bets on which pudding will next be thrown over any British government minister'.[82]

It was at this point that popular violence directed at politicians became rather less risible. In late 2009, Baroness Warsi, the Shadow Minister for community cohesion and social action and the most senior Muslim politician in Britain, was pelted with eggs by a group of male co-religionists during a visit to Luton. The men, who screamed at Warsi for backing the war in Afghanistan and claimed she was not a 'proper Muslim', declined her offer to debate the issues publicly.[83] This rejection of a forum to air their views, more than the minor violence, sets this incident apart from those immediately preceding it.

The advent of a coalition government in 2010 brought the return of mob violence of the sort that had not threatened MPs for quite some time. In early November, about 200 people broke off from a demonstration in central London against government plans to increase university tuition fees and cut spending to attack Conservative Party headquarters.[84] Two weeks later, another large protest against the same matter prompted the deployment of 800 police to protect parliament and the headquarters of the Liberal Democrats, whose leader, Nick Clegg, had aroused particular animus by supporting coalition plans for tuition fee increases, despite having pledged prior to the election to abolish such fees altogether. The next day 40 demonstrators occupied the London office of Simon Hughes, the party's deputy leader.[85] Meanwhile Clegg, whom students were burning in effigy, was advised by police not to cycle to work due to threats against his life.[86]

A third demonstration in early December produced even more disorder. Five protesters managed to force their way into the Commons, where debate was underway on the tuition fee bill. Outside, there was some violence, as police sought to keep protestors away from parliament. And a group of protestors broke away from the main demonstration to attack a car containing the Prince of Wales and the Duchess of Cornwall.[87]

Education was not the only policy to provoke parliamentary violence: a coalition plan, quickly abandoned, to sell off some national forests also prompted an outcry. When Mark Harper appeared at meeting of his Forest of Dean constituents to discuss the issue in early 2011, the Tory MP 'faced a barrage of abuse', before leaving 'in a police van that was pelted with eggs by an angry crowd'.[88]

A few months later, a protester forced the suspension of a parliamentary inquiry into phone hacking by attempting to throw a plate of shaving foam at News Corporation Chairman Rupert Murdoch, whom he characterised as a 'naughty billionaire'. Murdoch's wife played a prominent role in fending off the attack on her husband, displaying in the process what an MP subsequently described as 'a very good left hook'.[89]

It was Nick Clegg, however, who remained the main target of violent protestors. Fears that students might try to kidnap or attack the deputy prime minister reportedly forced Sheffield police to spend £1 million on security for a Liberal Democrat conference in March 2011. That he had pushed for the conclave to be held in his constituency, and now required tight security to protect him from those who sent him to parliament, was more than a little embarrassing.[90] Although Clegg avoided violence on this occasion, a few months later he was not so lucky, when a disgruntled former Liberal threw an egg filled with blue paint at him. Willie Rennie, the party leader in the Scottish parliament, bore the brunt of the attack, but paint also splashed onto Clegg's face.[91]

The recent development of social media has added another dimension to parliamentary violence. In the past, threatening messages occasionally had been sent to politicians, but such incidents rarely were publicised, in part to deny attention to those responsible. New technology has enabled people to make threats both publicly and anonymously. Moreover, it allows them to more easily collect intimate information about the target. As a result, politicians may feel a heightened sense of vulnerability and violation, even if those who send threats by new means are no more likely try to carry them out than those who convey them in a more traditional manner.

It is hard to say how much anonymous threats to politicians have increased of late, precisely because missives of this sort rarely have been discussed publicly in the past. Neither parliament nor the Metropolitan Police collect statistics of this sort. What is clear is that recently both MPs and the police have begun to take such threats quite seriously. In late 2011, a man was arrested for sending email and Twitter messages threatening Louise Mensch and her children, after the Conservative MP called for social networking sites to be shut down during riots.[92]

In early 2013, David Burrowes, a Tory MP leading the campaign against gay marriage, contacted police after receiving death threats and political opponents posted his travel arrangements online. The father of six also claimed that classmates had bullied his children at school, calling him 'homophobic'.[93] A few months later, police advised Tory MP Pauline Latham to install extensive security systems at her home and constituency office, after her support for a proposed badger cull led to the publication of her address and contact details on the website of animal rights activists.[94]

After Stella Creasy made comments supporting a woman threatened with rape for campaigning to have a female honoured on the redesigned £10 note, the Labour MP herself was the subject of threats of death and sexual assault on Twitter. The individual responsible made similar menacing comments regarding Tory MP Claire Perry, who has sought to restrict access to online pornography.[95]

The situation has deteriorated ever further since then. In early 2019, Parliamentary Security Director Eric Hepburn testified that the volume of online abuse directed at MPs has been 'absolutely skyrocketing' in the last few years, with women and members of the Black, Asian and Minority Ethnic communities receiving the 'lion's share'.[96]

Not all recent threats have involved new technology. Amidst police reports of growing far-right violence, members of the Islamic community in Britain, including at least five MPs, received letters in March 2018 calling for a 'Punish a Muslim Day', in which assailants would be awarded points based on the level of damage inflicted. Parcels accompanying some of the letters contained noxious, though apparently harmless, substances that prompted the evacuation of some parliamentary offices and the precautionary hospitalisation of some politicians' staff.[97]

Similar sentiments evidently were behind another recent attack. In 2014, days after declaring that Bradford, the city that sent him to parliament, should be an 'Israel-free zone', George Galloway was hospitalised after being assaulted on the streets of London. His suspected assailant, whom the MP's spokesman accused of shouting the words 'Holocaust' and 'Hitler' during the attack, was charged with religiously aggravated assault. Galloway, a fierce critic of Israeli military activity in Gaza, was under police investigation for saying, 'We don't want any Israeli goods; we don't want any Israeli services; we don't want any Israeli academics coming to the university or college; we don't even want any Israeli tourists to come to Bradford.'[98]

Two years later, the lead up to a referendum on whether Britain should leave the European Union was a stark rejoinder to those who, not long before, had bemoaned the public's political apathy.[99] Yet, the passions unleashed, particularly in the 'Leave' campaign, often were far from salutary, with xenophobia and racism at times only barely concealed. It was in this atmosphere that there occurred, a week before the referendum, one of the most serious acts of parliamentary violence in decades.

Arriving at a library in Birstall, where she was scheduled to hold a constituency surgery on 16 June, Jo Cox was fatally attacked by a man who reportedly shouted 'Britain First' as he stabbed the pro-EU Labour MP fifteen times and shot her with a sawn-off hunting rifle.[100]

Any hopes that Cox's murder would reduce political tensions soon were dashed. The unexpected, narrow referendum support for leaving the EU, 'Brexit', proved polarising. Labour leader Jeremy Corbyn, criticised for supporting continued EU membership too tepidly, saw more than two dozen members of his shadow cabinet resign. Then over three-quarters of the party's MPs backed a motion of no confidence in his leadership. Yet his support among the party's base remained passionate: when Angela Eagle, one of those who had resigned from the shadow cabinet, announced that she would seek to replace Corbyn as Labour leader, a brick was thrown through the window of her constituency office and she received hundreds of 'abusive, homophobic and frightening messages'.[101]

There was more disruption as the date for Britain's departure from the EU loomed. In December 2018, Labour MP Lloyd Russell-Moyle seized the mace and sought to remove it from the Commons in the middle of a sitting to protest the government's decision to postpone a vote on the exit agreement negotiated by Prime Minister Theresa May.[102]

When parliament finally voted on May's agreement the following month, it was rejected by a huge margin. Alarmed by the prospect of Brexit without a deal in place, two moderate MPs pledged to present to parliament an amendment that would delay Britain's departure until an acceptable agreement could be negotiated. As a consequence, one of them, Nick Boles, 'had received a string of threats from unhappy Brexiteers', including one who threatened to burn his house down. As he lamented to the BBC, 'I feel like I'm bound to get one of those vile treatments from one of the particularly unpleasant characters in "Game of Thrones".'[103]

And when, after extended resistance, Corbyn agreed to back a second referendum on Brexit, retribution was not long in coming. In early March 2019, while Corbyn was visiting a mosque in London, a man smashed an egg into the back of the Labour leader's head while screaming, 'When you vote, you get what you vote for.'[104]

Deplorable though such incidents have been, they are not all that surprising given that Britain's relationship with Europe has riven both main parties and the country in general. What is altogether astonishing is that Brexit also managed to bring violent division to the organisation most closely associated with the push to separate from Europe, the UK Independence Party (UKIP).

With the success of passage of the Brexit referendum, Nigel Farage resigned as UKIP leader, though not, strangely, as a Member of the European Parliament. His successor lasted all of eighteen days. Steven Woolfe hoped to become the second post-Farage leader, but his admission that he had considered abandoning UKIP for the Tories raised questions about his suitability for the post. It also appears to have provoked a confrontation with (appropriately named) Mike Hookem, the party's defence spokesman. The two MEPs left an early October 2016 UKIP meeting in the European Parliament building in Strasbourg ostensibly to compose their differences, but shortly thereafter television cameras showed Woolfe 'sprawled on the floor outside the debating chamber'. He subsequently was hospitalised, claiming to have been punched by Hookem, who denied striking his colleague.[105]

Coming exactly seven hundred years after Hugh le Despenser struck John of Roos in a 1316 parliament in Lincoln, the Woolfe–Hookem contretemps brings an examination of the danger of a seat almost back to where it began. Yet it is hardly the case that parliamentary violence has changed little over the centuries, as a concluding analysis of historical trends makes clear.

W(H)ITHER PARLIAMENTARY VIOLENCE?

Like the state under socialism, parliamentary violence might have been expected to wither away with the advent of liberal democracy. After all, British society has become both less violent and less tolerant of violence over the centuries.[1] A people for whom physicality previously had been seen as remarkably pervasive came to be identified with a particular aversion to violence.[2] At the same time, the polity grew increasingly representative, meaning that those who held seats (in the Commons at least) faced greater pressure to act in ways that reflected the values and interests of their electors. Fear of retribution at the polls should have discouraged MPs both from fighting each other and from ignoring constituents in a manner that previously might have prompted parliamentary violence. Have historical trends in the United Kingdom conformed to this progressive (or Whig) expectation? And what does this suggest about the future?

Parliamentary Violence Withers?

There were at least 27 documented incidents of parliamentary violence in the 1500s, 159 in the 1600s, 200 in the 1700s, 138 in the 1800s, and 222 in the 1900s. The trend in the first three centuries seems easy to understand: as parliament's power grew, so too did the danger of a seat. The nineteenth century also seems to conform to expectations: as Britain became more democratic, parliamentary violence fell substantially. In the twentieth century, however, as political representativeness and social disdain of physicality were reaching their peak, so too was violence involving parliamentarians. What was going on?

The raw numbers do not lie, but they may exaggerate. For one thing, given the unprecedented scrutiny of politicians today, violent incidents involving them are more likely to find their way onto the public record precisely because such activity is now socially reprobated. For another, even if the frequency of parliamentary violence has changed over time, so too has its nature, and the latter has evolved in a manner that is quite consistent with the bigger picture.

To understand why, it is useful to distinguish between three types of parliamentary violence. Insider violence features threats between parliamentarians. Outsider violence occurs when those who do not have seats menace those who do. And disciplinary violence is that involving the enforcement of parliamentary norms and procedures. (Disciplinary and insider violence often overlap, as when a peer is sent to the Tower for sending a challenge to a colleague or a physical confrontation between MPs leads the Speaker to adjourn a sitting under provisions for 'grave disorder'. If both occur together, the incident is considered 'insider' violence, arguably the more interesting and subversive of the two.) All three types have varied over the centuries, both in absolute terms and in proportion to each other. Their dynamics also have changed over time.

Consider first insider violence. Fights between parliamentarians, threatened or actual, peaked in the seventeenth and eighteenth centuries, as the code of honour impelled those who were insulted, or thought others might think them to be so, to respond with a challenge. The catalyst typically was the use of 'fighting words', personal aspersions that a gentleman could only answer properly with violence. Duels were supposed to be a means of redeeming individual honour, not methods of gaining political advantage, which is why encounters in which the latter motivation was suspected, such as Wilkes's fight with Martin, were so controversial.[3]

Things began to change in the nineteenth century, at least in the Commons. (Peers effectively abandoned duelling, and insider parliamentary violence, in the eighteenth century.) The growing influence of the middle class exerted powerful political pressure on MPs to renounce the aristocratic code, indeed, to eschew violence in general. This helps explain why the number of incidents of insider violence fell by around a third in the 1800s and 1900s compared to the two previous centuries.

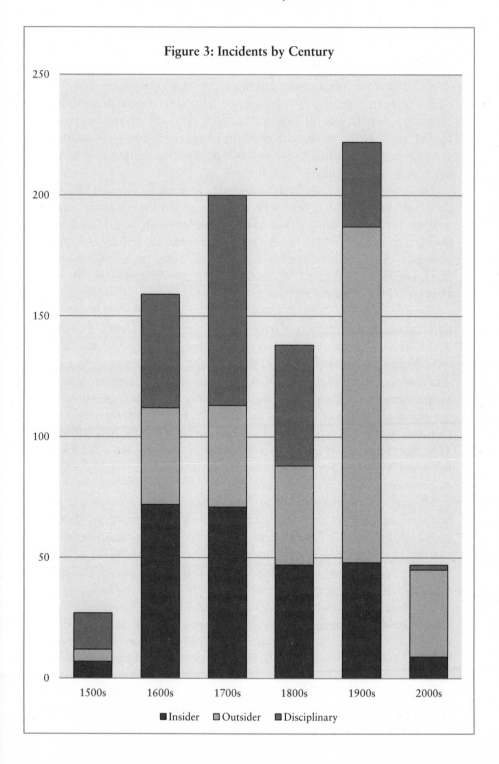

Figure 3: Incidents by Century

What is more, when MPs did fight, the encounters tended to be politics writ small. Not only were the combatants typically on different sides politically but the precipitant often was a procedural irregularity that disadvantaged those on the opposition benches. Violence here was less a response to personal insults than to the seemingly unfair use of political power. And as parliamentarians fought each other on behalf of short-changed electors rather than out of wounded pride, insider violence became more in tune with the more democratic times.

The story with disciplinary violence is broadly similar. In the sixteenth and early seventeenth centuries, parliamentarians were punished (typically with a stint in the Tower) by, and for displeasing, the monarch. Two MPs died in captivity for their parliamentary actions. As parliament asserted its rights, such royal punishment increasingly was resented. Indeed, one trigger for civil war was the king's attempt to arrest the 'Five Members'.

Once parliament began locking up its own Members in the mid-seventeenth century, the nature of disciplinary violence changed. Yes, MPs still were sent to the Tower occasionally for incautious words, or for refusing not to fight each other, but the main danger came from unauthorised absence. Such violence peaked in the eighteenth century as parliament, particularly that in Dublin, repeatedly resorted to the mass detention of MPs, in an effort to bolster attendance. Still, this was a sign of progress: where monarchs typically had arrested MPs for seeking to expand parliamentary rights, the Commons punished Members for ignoring their responsibilities, thereby seeking to encourage better representation.

The most interesting change in disciplinary violence has come in the last 150 years. Representation has been defined as 'the making present of something that is nevertheless absent'.[4] Since the mid-nineteenth century, a greater variety of interests and voices clearly have been made present in parliament. But increased diversity is not the only mark of improved representation. Some politicians, most notably Home Rulers, Clydesiders and members of Labour's Tribune Group, sought to make representation more intensive. That is, instead of merely supporting their electors rhetorically and in the division lobby, these politicians tried to 'make present' social conflict within Westminster Palace.

By creating disorderly 'scenes' in parliament, they intended not only to demonstrate emotional fidelity to their constituents – angry voters represented by equally angry MPs – but also to discourage violence in the streets.[5] Physical resistance to the authority of the presiding officer, once all but unthinkable, became simply the continuation of politics by other means. Where once MPs were punished for failing to make present their constituents by attending in their places, now they often are sanctioned for seeking to represent them overly enthusiastically. Like its insider cousin, disciplinary violence has become less frequent and more overtly political of late, both trends consistent with the evolution of a more representative and pacific polity.

The logic of outsider violence, unlike the other two, has been consistent over time. This is by definition; incidents in which outsiders attack parliamentarians for reasons other than the political activities associated with a seat are excluded from this study. Until recently, the frequency of outsider violence also was remarkably stable: there were 40 instances in the 1600s; 42 in the 1700s; and 41 in the 1800s. This is puzzling. One might have expected that attacks on politicians would have risen with parliament's growing public role, as people sought to influence the ascendant institution, and then fallen as more democratic elections provided them with less dangerous ways to hold their representatives accountable.[6]

Even stranger is what happened next. Public violence in general fell, as the government became more responsive to public opinion and increasingly assertive in addressing the causes of popular discontent.[7] But outsider attacks on parliamentarians increased more than threefold in the 1900s, to 136 episodes. In a society that overwhelmingly was spurning violence, why were people making an exception for parliamentarians? Again, the answer lies in the changing nature of outsider violence.

In days of yore, outsiders typically posed two sorts of threats to parliamentarians: duels and 'mobbings', that is crowd attacks. Both entailed the risk of substantial injury, even death. Today, neither is much of a danger. To be sure, politicians do occasionally face hostile crowds. But where once demonstrators threw rocks, now they are more likely to wield eggs or even less harmful projectiles. Crowd danger has moderated (except, perhaps, on university campuses), in a way that reflects increasing public distaste for violence.

In recent decades, the predominant outsider threat to parliamentarians has come not from crowds but from individuals or very small groups. Improved policing is one reason, but more representative politics is another.

Crowd violence often was a way for those without the vote to punish politicians for ignoring popular, but not necessarily majoritarian, sentiment. It seems no accident that those in the Commons have faced this menace far more often than those in the Lords. As the franchise expanded, citizens increasingly had another, non-violent, mechanism by which to hold politicians accountable. Crowd violence diminished at least partly because politicians sought to avoid angering large segments of voters.

So, why has outsider violence burgeoned in the last century or so? Largely because its role has changed. Democratisation has resulted in increased competition for political influence. Interests or causes that have substantial popular support, or backers with deep pockets, have a distinct advantage over those that do not. They tend not to be ignored politically. However, as the Suffragettes discovered, violence gets attention, precisely because it has become taboo. This makes it an attractive option for those seeking to promote obscure or unpopular causes. Since this method is cheap and easy, compared to traditional lobbying efforts, its use has proliferated. Where once outsider violence could be seen as a rough reflection of public opinion, in recent times it frequently has become a means to influence it.

This has happened in two very different ways. The first could be called activism, though it is really a refinement of the violent propaganda pioneered by the Suffragettes. Here, those seeking publicity attack a politician to get it. Crucially, however, to avoid overly offending public sensibilities and thereby discrediting the cause they are seeking to promote, perpetrators need to keep violence to a minimum. It must be sufficiently disorderly and humiliating to command attention, but not so vicious as to pose much risk of physical injury, since this could undermine support for the cause. A bit of custard or a chocolate éclair applied to the face of a prominent parliamentarian in a public setting works wonderfully, according to this political calculation.

At the other end of the spectrum is terrorism. If activists employ almost innocuous violence, terrorists threaten the most lethal action imaginable. Where activists are optimistic, convinced that the public will embrace their cause if it only is brought to people's attention, terrorists are pessimistic, believing that their goals will never become widely supported simply on their merits. Terrorists therefore seek less to persuade than to compel, to make a failure to concede their demands unacceptably costly, politically and otherwise. In pursuit of this aim, terrorists killed more parliamentarians in the twentieth century than died from outsider violence in the preceding five hundred years. When it comes to politicians, then, democratisation has made attackers both much less and much more violent.

Whither Parliamentary Violence?

If parliamentary violence has not faded away with the advent of greater democracy, then, it has evolved in ways broadly consistent with British social and political developments. Might the danger of a seat diminish in the future? After all, some of the greatest perils of the twentieth century seem unlikely to recur, precisely because Britain has become more democratic. Female enfranchisement, an issue tied to almost half of the outsider violence in the last century (66 of 136 incidents), surely will not pose the same threat in the years ahead. Similarly, greater representation of Catholics in Northern Ireland, as a result of the 1998 Good Friday Agreement, appears to have reduced, if not eliminated, a grievance linked to 22 per cent of the parliamentary violence (and 100 per cent of the fatalities) in the twentieth century. Absent such issues, the twenty-first century may be less dangerous for politicians.

Then again, other contentious matters are sure to arise. Indeed, Britain's relationship with the European Union already has become particularly polarising. The Metropolitan Police commander responsible for parliamentary security testified in early 2019 that his work had been growing 'exponentially', both because politicians had become much more willing to report threats in the wake of the murder of Jo Cox and because the danger was escalating at least partly due to frustration with Brexit. The political atmosphere has become so rancorous that politicians can feel menaced even absent explicit threats. An MP told the same inquiry that she faced such abuse walking across Westminster Bridge on the night of the pro-Brexit Leave Means Leave protest that 'I was the most frightened I have ever been in my life'.[8] The toxicity appears to have permeated even the local level: at least three candidates in 2019 council elections were physically assaulted; others were spat at, had their vehicles forced off the road or received death threats.[9]

The ructions over Brexit seem at least as much a symptom as a cause of the body politic's current dyspepsia. As Magnus Linklater argues,

'We live in a society that has thrown off many of the constraints that once governed public life, and where personal abuse has become a routine part not just of politics but of sport, entertainment and journalism.'[10] Although complaints about declining manners and civility seem almost as old as civilisation itself, there is abundant anecdotal evidence of a recent decline of the deference and respect that once provided a measure protection to politicians and others serving the public.

Teachers have faced increased attacks from pupils and parents.[11] Patients have posed a growing threat to doctors, nurses and midwives.[12] Family judges in England recently called for greater security to protect them from attacks from emotional parents.[13] Similar measures were taken to safeguard library staff, traffic wardens and binmen.[14] Posted warnings that 'assaults on staff' will not be tolerated have become ubiquitous, not only in public buildings but also in places like petrol stations. And, in what may be the most compelling indication that those previously inviolable now increasingly are at risk of violence, parents upset that a Dorset holiday theme park provided attractions far inferior to those advertised, 'reportedly attacked two elves and a Father Christmas'.[15]

It is not just members of the public who seem to be losing their tempers with greater frequency and effect. Parliament, perhaps reflecting voters, also seems to have witnessed a coarsening of debate, even from senior politicians. In the Commons in early 2008, one minister called a colleague an 'arsehole'. Another dismissed opposition assertions as 'absolute bollocks'.[16] Two years later, a third minister referred to Speaker John Bercow as a 'stupid, sanctimonious dwarf'. Around the same time, John McDonnell, then a candidate for the Labour leadership, earned a standing ovation at the GMB Union's conference by 'joking' that he wished he could go back in time and assassinate Margaret Thatcher.[17]

The danger is not just that crude insults or offensive remarks will invite a violent riposte. To many MPs and those who work for them, parliament has become a hostile environment, in which bullying and sexual harassment are rife.[18] Such an atmosphere not only discourages capable people, particularly women, from participating in politics but it also adds to the unprecedented stress that comes with a parliamentary seat.[19]

Where once parliament was seen as the best club in town, today it is more like a sweatshop. In many ways, MPs have never had it so bad. They are under more pressure than ever before to provide increasingly extensive and complicated constituent services.[20] This, coupled with the need for media visibility and the lack of clear boundaries between work and leisure has a 'devastating' effect on the personal lives of MPs, many of whom have found that a seat comes with a pay cut. [21] Stress, and the copious quantities of alcohol that long have been part of parliamentary culture, tend to pose a greater threat to the health and safety of Members than violence, to which they also contribute.[22]

All this is to suggest, albeit tentatively, that parliamentary violence, whether by insiders or outsiders, is unlikely to disappear any time soon. On the contrary, it very well could get worse, both qualitatively and quantitively. Splenetic voters (or colleagues) are less likely to worry about causing at least minor injury than are those who use disorder mainly to get attention. And the frequency of parliamentary violence is on pace to make seats more dangerous in the twenty-first century than ever before.[23] Is that so terrible?

The preceding pages hardly have been a paean to parliamentary pandemonium. Violence typically is institutionally subversive, which is precisely why it is of interest here. Sometimes it is profoundly so. The parliamentary regime in interwar Yugoslavia, for example, did not long survive an episode in which a Serbian deputy gunned down four of his (Croatian) colleagues on the floor of the chamber. Legislative violence also has proved destabilising in settings as varied as the antebellum U.S, *fin de siècle* France, Weimar Germany and post-war Japan.[24] And, as we have seen, parliamentary disorder has been linked to occasional wobbles in the political system in the United Kingdom. Violence that seriously injures either individual politicians or the polity in general certainly does seem terrible.

It does not necessarily follow that a political system without any parliamentary violence would be optimal. One need look no further than Stalinist Russia or present-day North Korea and China, environments in which parliamentary violence is all but inconceivable, to see the phenomenon as a somewhat perverse indicator of political vitality. Like a teapot's whistle, limited parliamentary violence often serves both as a signal that politics is aboil and, perhaps, as a means of letting off some steam and preventing an explosion.

Parliamentary violence in the UK long has followed this pattern, waxing and waning along with political passions. The formal inclusion of greater and greater shares of the population into the political system has not made the problem go away. Quite the opposite; under democratic conditions, politicians have faced more and graver threats than ever before. But the alternative to occasionally excessive political participation is apathy and disengagement, which seems even worse. Indeed, to the extent that a healthy democracy sometimes requires that an indifferent majority bow to the wishes of a passionate minority, evidence that some care strongly about particular issues is welcome. If this means that politicians infrequently are reminded – with a custard pie, egg, or even a fist – that seats, even those that are electorally 'safe', can be a little physically dangerous, that might not be such a bad thing.

BIBLIOGRAPHY

[anon], *The Life and Noble Character of Richard Thornhill, Esq.; Who Had the Misfortune to Kill Sir Cholmley Deering, Bart. Knight of the Shire for the County of Kent, in a Duel in Tuttle-Fields, on Wednesday the 9th of May, 1711* (London Richard Newcomb, 1711).

——, *A True Account of What Passed at the Old-Bailey, May the 18th, 1711. Relating to the Tryal of Richard Thornhill, Esq; Indicted for the Murder of Sir Cholmley Deering, Bart.* Second Edition Corrected edn (London: John Morphew, 1711).

Aldous, Richard, *The Lion and the Unicorn: Gladstone Vs Disraeli* (London: Pimlico, 2006).

Amey, Geoffrey, *City under Fire: The Bristol Riots and Aftermath* (Guildford: Lutterworth Press, 1979).

Armitage, Faith, 'Peace and Quiet in the British House of Commons, 1990–2010', *Democratization,* 20 (2013), 456–77.

Arthur, Paul, 'Northern Ireland, 1972–84', in *A New History of Ireland,* ed. by J. R. Hill (Oxford: Oxford University Press, 2003).

Atherton, Herbert M., *Political Prints in the Age of Hogarth* (London: Oxford University Press, 1974).

Baldick, Robert, *The Duel: A History of Duelling* (London: Chapman & Hall, 1965).

Banks, Stephen, 'Killing with Courtesy: The English Duelist, 1785–1845', *Journal of British Studies,* 47 (2008), 528–58.

Bardon, Jonathan, and Dermot Keogh, 'Ireland, 1921–84', in *A New History of Ireland,* ed. by J. R. Hill (Oxford: Oxford University Press, 2003).

Barton, Brian, 'Northern Irleand, 1920–25', in *A New History of Ireland,* ed. by J. R. Hill (Oxford: Oxford University Press, 2003).

——, 'Northern Irleand, 1925–39', in *A New History of Ireland,* ed. by J. R. Hill (Oxford: Oxford University Press, 2003).

Bawcutt, N. W., ed., *The Control and Censorship of Caroline Drama: The Records of Sir Henry Herbert, Master of the Revels 1623–73* (Oxford: Oxford University Press, 1996).

Bearman, C. J., 'Confronting the Suffragette Mythology', *BBC History* 2007, pp. 14–8.

——, 'An Examination of Suffragette Violence', *English Historical Review,* 120 (2005), 365–97.

Beckett, J. V., 'Aristocrats and Electoral Control in the East Midlands, 1660–1914', *Midland History,* 18 (1993), 65–86.

Beckett, John, 'The Nottingham Reform Bill Riots of 1831', *Parliamentary History,* 24 (2005), 114–38.

Beer, Samuel H., *Britain against Itself* (London: Faber and Faber, 1982).

——, *Modern British Politics.* 3rd edn (London: Faber and Faber, 1982).

Bendix, Reinhard, *Kings or People: Power and the Mandate to Rule* (Berkeley: University of California Press, 1978).

Berrington, Hugh, 'Partisanship and Dissidence in the Nineteenth-Century House of Commons', *Parliamentary Affairs,* 21 (1968), 338–74.

Blackburn, R. W., 'Unparliamentary Language', *The Political Quarterly,* 56 (1985), 396–402.

Bolingbroke, 'A Dissertation Upon Parties', in *Works* (Philadelphia: Carey & Hart, 1841).

Bowie, Karin, *Scottish Public Opinion and the Anglo–Scottish Union, 1699–1707* (Woodbridge: Boydell Press, 2007).

Braddick, Michael, *God's Fury, England's Fire: A New History of the English Civil Wars* (London: Penguin, 2008).

Brazier, Rodney, *Constitutional Practice: The Foundations of British Government.* 3rd edn (Oxford: Oxford University Press, 1999).

Brown, A. L., 'Parliament, C. 1377–1422', in *The English Parliament in the Middle Ages,* ed. by R. G. Davies and J. H. Denton (Manchester: Manchester University Press, 1981).

Brown, Gordon, *Maxton* (Glasgow: Collins/Fontana, 1986).

Brown, Keith M., 'Gentlemen & Thugs in 17th-Century Britain', *History Today,* 40 (1990).

——, 'Party Politics and Parliament: Scotland's Last Election and Its Aftermath, 1702–3', in *The History of the Scottish Parliament,* ed. by Keith M. Brown and Alastair J. Mann (Edinburgh: Edinburgh University Press, 2005).

——, 'The Reformation Parliament', in *The History of the Scottish Parliament,* ed. by Keith M. Brown and Roland J. Tanner (Edinburgh: Edinburgh University Press, 2004).

Brown, Keith M., and Alastair J. Mann, 'Introduction: Parliament and Politics in Scotland, 1567–1707', in *The History of the Scottish Parliament,* ed. by Keith M. Brown and Alastair J. Mann (Edinburgh: Edinburgh University Press, 2005).

Brown, Keith M., and Roland J. Tanner, 'Introduction: Parliament and Politics in Scotland, 1253–1560', in *The History of the Scottish Parliament,* ed. by Keith M. Brown and Roland J. Tanner (Edinburgh: Edinburgh University Press, 2004).

Bibliography

Brown, Michael, 'Public Authority and Factional Conflict: Crown, Parliament and Polity, 1424–1455', in *The History of the Scottish Parliament*, ed. by Keith M. Brown and Roland J. Tanner (Edinburgh: Edinburgh University Press, 2004).

Burleigh, Michael, *Blood and Rage: A Cultural History of Terrorism* (London: Harper, 2009).

Cam, H. M., 'The Legislators of Medieval England', in *Historical Studies of the English Parliament*, ed. by E. B. Fryde and Edward Miller (London: Cambridge University Press, 1970).

Campbell, John, *Pistols at Dawn: Two Hundred Years of Political Rivalry, from Pitt and Fox to Blair and Brown* (London: Jonathan Cape, 2009).

Campion, Lord, and T. G. B. Cocks, eds., *Sir Thomas Erskine May's Treatise on the Law, Privileges, Proceedings and Usage of Parliament*. 15th edn (London: Butterworth, 1950).

Cannon, John, *Parliamentary Reform, 1640–1832* (Cambridge: Cambridge U. Press, 1972).

Cash, Arthur H., *John Wilkes: The Scandalous Father of Civil Liberties* (New Haven: Yale University Press, 2006).

Cavill, P. R., 'Debate and Dissent in Henry VII's Parliaments', *Parliamentary History*, 25 (2006), 160–75.

Chafetz, Josh, *Democracy's Privileged Few: Legislative Privilege and Democratic Norms in the British and American Constitutions* (new Haven: Yale University Press, 2007).

Clarke, Aidan, *The Old English in Ireland 1625–42* (Ithaca: Cornell University Press, 1966).

Clarke, Aiden, 'The Breakdown of Authority, 1640–41', in *A New History of Ireland*, ed. by T. W. Moody, F. X. Martin and F. J. Byrne (New York: Oxford University Press, 1993).

——, 'The Government of Wentworth, 1632–40', in *A New History of Ireland*, ed. by T. W. Moody, F. X. Martin and F. J. Byrne (New York: Oxford University Press, 1993).

Clarke, Aiden, with R. Dudley Edwards, 'Pacification, Plantation, and the Catholic Question, 1603–23', in *A New History of Ireland*, ed. by T. W. Moody, F. X. Martin and F. J. Byrne (New York: Oxford University Press, 1993).

Clarke, Peter, *Hope and Glory: Britain 1900–2000*. ed. by David Cannadine. Second edn, *The Penguin History of Britain* (London: Penguin, 2004).

Clutterbuck, Richard, *Britain in Agony: The Growth of Political Violence* (London: Faber and Faber, 1978).

Coates, Willson Havelock, ed., *The Journal of Sir Simonds D'Ewes* (New Haven: Yale University Press, 1942).

Comerford, R. V., 'Gladstone's First Irish Enterprise, 1864–70', in *A New History of Ireland*, ed. by W. E. Vaughan (Oxford: Oxford University Press, 1989).

——, 'Isaac Butt and the Home Rule Party, 1870–77', in *A New History of Ireland*, ed. by W. E. Vaughan (Oxford: Oxford University Press, 1989).

————, 'The Land War and the Politics of Distress, 1877–82', in *A New History of Ireland*, ed. by W. E. Vaughan (Oxford: Oxford University Press, 1989).

Connolly, S. J., 'Mass Politics and Sectarian Conflict, 1823–30', in *A New History of Ireland*, ed. by W. E. Vaughan (Oxford: Oxford University Press, 1989).

————, 'Union Government, 1812–23', in *A New History of Ireland*, ed. by W. E. Vaughan (Oxford: Oxford University Press, 1989).

Coogan, Tim Pat, *The Troubles: Ireland's Ordeal 1966–1995 and the Search for Peace* (London: Hutchinson, 1995).

Corish, Patrick J., 'The Cromwellian Regime, 1650–60', in *A New History of Ireland*, ed. by T. W. Moody, F. X. Martin and F. J. Byrne (New York: Oxford University Press, 1993).

Cottrell, Peter, *The Irish Civil War 1922–23* (Oxford: Osprey, 2008).

Cox, Gary W., *The Efficient Secret* (New York: Cambridge U. Press, 1987).

Crewe, Emma, *Lords of Parliament: Manners, Rituals and Politics* (Manchester: Manchester University Press, 2005).

Critchley, T. A., *The Conquest of Violence: Order and Liberty in Britain* (London: Constable, 1970).

Cruickshanks, Eveline, Stuart Handley, and D. W. Hayton, *The House of Commons 1690–1715*. vol. 6, *The History of Parliament* (London: Cambridge University Press, 2002).

————, *The House of Commons 1690–1715*. vol. 5, *The History of Parliament* (London: Cambridge University Press, 2002).

————, *The House of Commons 1690–1715*. vol. 4, *The History of Parliament* (London: Cambridge University Press, 2002).

————, *The House of Commons 1690–1715*. vol. 3, *The History of Parliament* (London: Cambridge University Press, 2002).

Cunningham, Hugh, *The Challenge of Democracy* (Harlow: Longman, 2001).

Cust, Richard, 'Honour and Politics in Early Stuart England: The Case of Beaumont V. Hastings', *Past and Present,* 149 (1995), 57–94.

Dabhoiwala, Faramerz, 'The Construction of Honour, Reputation and Status in Late Seventeenth- and Early Eighteenth-Century England', *Transactions of the Royal Historical Society*, 6 (1996), 2001–13.

Dawson, Jane E. A., *Scotland Re-Formed 1488–1587*. ed. by Roger Mason, *The New Edinburgh History of Scotland* (Edinburgh: Edinburgh University Press, 2007).

Dennis, Alfred L. P., 'The Parliament Act of 1911', *American Political Science Review,* 6 (1912), 194–215.

Denton, J. H., 'The Clergy and Parliament in the Thirteenth and Fourteenth Centuries', in *The English Parliament in the Middle Ages*, ed. by R. G. Davies and J. H. Denton (Manchester: Manchester University Press, 1981).

Dion, Douglas, *Turning the Legislative Thumbscrews: Minority Rights and Procedural Change in Legislative Politics* (Ann Arbor: University of Michigan Press, 1997).

Dixon, Paul, *Northern Ireland: The Politics of War and Peace*. Second Edition edn (Basingstoke: Palgrave Macmillan, 2008).

Bibliography

Dorey, Peter, 'The House of Lords since 1949', in *A Short History of Parliament*, ed. by Clyve Jones (Woodbridge: Boydell Press, 2009).

du Parcq, Herbert, *Life of David Lloyd George*. vol. II (London: Caxton, 1912).

Eagles, Robin, 'The House of Lords, 1660–1707', in *A Short History of Parliament*, ed. by Clyve Jones (Woodbridge: Boydell Press, 2009).

Edwards, Gonronwy, 'The Emergence of Majority Rule in the Procedure of the House of Commons', *Transactions of the Royal Historical Society*, 15 (1965).

Edwards, J. G., '"Justice" in Early English Parliaments', in *Historical Studies of the English Parliament*, ed. by E. B. Fryde and Edward Miller (London: Cambridge University Press, 1970).

——, 'The *Plena Potestas* of English Parliamentary Representatives', in *Historical Studies of the English Parliament*, ed. by E. B. Fryde and Edward Miller (London: Cambridge University Press, 1970).

Egloff, Carol S., 'The Search for a Cromwellian Settlement. Exclusions from the Second Protectorate Parliament. Part 1: The Process and Its Architects', *Parliamentary History*, 17 (1998), 178–97.

——, 'The Search for a Cromwellian Settlement. Exclusions from the Second Protectorate Parliament. Part 2: The Excluded Members and the Reactions to the Exclusion', *Parliamentary History*, 17 (1998), 301–21.

Emsley, Clive, *Hard Men: The English and Violence since 1750* (London: Hambledon Continuum, 2005).

Ensor, R. C. K., *England, 1870–1914*. ed. by Sir George Clark, *Oxford History of England* (Oxford: Clarendon Press, 1936).

Evans, Eric J., *Political Parties in Britain: 1783–1867* (London: Methuen, 1985).

Falkiner, Caesar Litton, 'The Parliament of Ireland under the Tudor Sovereigns: Supplementary Paper', *Proceedings of the Royal Irish Academy*, 25 (1904/1905), 553–66.

Farrell, Brian, 'The First Dáil and After', in *The Irish Parliamentary Tradition*, ed. by Brian Farrell (Dublin: Gill and Macmillan, 1973).

——, 'The Paradox of Irish Politics', in *The Irish Parliamentary Tradition*, ed. by Brian Farrell (Dublin: Gill and Macmillan, 1973).

Ferguson, Naill, *Empire: How Britain Made the Modern World* (London: Penguin, 2003).

Field, John, *The Story of Parliament in the Palace of Westminster* (London: James & James, 2002).

Fisher, D. R., *The House of Commons 1820–1832*. Vol. 3, *The History of Parliament* (Cambridge: Cambridge University Press, 2009).

——, *The House of Commons 1820–1832*. Vol. 6, *The History of Parliament* (Cambridge: Cambridge University Press, 2009).

——, *The House of Commons 1820–1832*. Vol. 7, *The History of Parliament* (Cambridge: Cambridge University Press, 2009).

——, *The House of Commons 1820–1832*. Vol. 2, *The History of Parliament* (Cambridge: Cambridge University Press, 2009).

——, *The House of Commons 1820–1832*. Vol. 4, *The History of Parliament* (Cambridge: Cambridge University Press, 2009).

———, *The House of Commons 1820–1832*. Vol. 5, *The History of Parliament* (Cambridge: Cambridge University Press, 2009).

Foord, Archibald S., *His Majesty's Opposition* (Oxford University Press, 1964).

———, 'The Waning of "the Influence of the Crown"', *English Historical Review*, 62 (1947), 484–507.

Fraser, Antonia, *The Gunpowder Plot: Terror and Faith in 1605* (London: Phoenix, 1996).

———, *Perilous Question: The Drama of the Great Reform Bill 1832* (London: Weidenfeld & Nicolson, 2013).

Fraser, Ian H. C., 'The Agitation in the Commons, 2 March 1629, and the Interrogation of the Leaders of the Anti-Court Group', *Bulletin of the Institute of Historical Research*, 30 (1957), 86–95.

Freeman, Joanne B., *Affairs of Honor: National Politics in the New Republic* (New Haven: Yale University Press, 2001).

———, 'Dueling as Politics: Reinterpreting the Burr–Hamilton Duel', *William and Mary Quarterly*, 53 (1996), 289–318.

Fryde, E. B., 'Introduction', in *Historical Studies of the English Parliament*, ed. by E. B. Fryde and Edward Miller (London: Cambridge University Press, 1970).

Garnett, Mark, *From Anger to Apathy: The Study of Politics, Society and Popular Culture in Britain since 1975* (London: Vintage, 2007).

Gatrell, Vic, *City of Laughter: Sex and Satire in Eighteenth Century London* (London: Atlantic Books, 2006).

Gaunt, Peter, 'Cromwell's First Purge? Exclusions and the First Protectorate Parliament', *Parliamentary History*, 6 (1987), 1–22.

Gaunt, Richard, 'The Fourth Duke of Newcastle, the "Mob" and Election Contests in Nottinghamshire, 1818–1832', *Midland History*, 33 (2008), 196–217.

George, M. Dorothy, *English Political Caricature*. Vol. 2 (London: Oxford University Press, 1959).

Gilmour, Ian, *Riot, Risings and Revolution: Governance and Violence in Eighteenth-Century England* (London: Pimlico, 1992).

Godfrey, Mark A., 'Parliamentary and the Law', in *The History of the Scottish Parliament*, ed. by Keith M. Brown and Alan R. MacDonald (Edinburgh: Edinburgh University Press, 2010).

Goodare, Julian, 'The Parliament of Scotland to 1707', in *A Short History of Parliament*, ed. by Clyve Jones (Woodbridge: Boydell Press, 2009).

Graves, M. A. R., 'The Management of the Elizabethan House of Commons: The Council's "Men-of-Business"', *Parliamentary History*, 2 (1983), 11–38.

Grey, Anchitell, ed., *Grey's Debates of the House of Commons* (London: T. Becket and P. A. de Hondt, 1769).

Griffith, M. C., 'The Talbot–Ormond Struggle for Control of the Anglo–Irish Government, 1414–47', *Irish Historical Studies*, 2 (1941), 376–97.

Gurr, Andrew, *Playgoing in Shakespeare's London* (Cambridge: Cambridge University Press, 1987).

Hague, William, *William Pitt the Younger* (London: Harper Perennial, 2004).

Hamburger, Joseph, *James Mill and the Art of Revolution*. ed. by David Horne. Vol. 8, *Yale Studies in Political Science* (New Haven: Yale University Press, 1963).

Hanham, H. J., 'Opposition Techniques in British Politics (1867–1914)', *Government and Opposition*, 2 (1966), 35–48.

Harris, Bob, 'The House of Commons, 1701–1800', in *A Short History of Parliament*, ed. by Clyve Jones (Woodbridge: Boydell Press, 2009).

Harris, Tim, *London Crowds in the Reign of Charles Ii*. ed. by Anthony Fletcher, John Guy and John Morrill, *Cambridge Studies in Early Modern British History* (Cambridge: Cambridge University Press, 1987).

———, *Restoration: Charles Ii and His Kingdoms, 1660–85* (London: Penguin, 2005).

———, *Revolution: The Great Crisis of the British Monarchy, 1685–1720* (London: Penguin, 2006).

Harrison, Brian, 'The Sunday Trading Riots of 1855', *The Historical Journal*, 8 (1965), 219–45.

Hasler, P. W., *The House of Commons 1558–1603*. Vol. 2, *The History of Parliament* (London: Her Majesty's Stationary Office, 1981).

Hawkins, Angus, *British Party Politics, 1852–1886* (London: Macmillan, 1998).

Hayes, Burnadette C, and Ian McAllister, 'Sowing Dragon's Teeth: Public Support for Political Violence and Paramilitarism in Northern Ireland', *Political Studies*, 49 (2001), 901–22.

Hayes-McCoy, G. A., 'The Royal Supremacy and the Ecclesiastical Revolution, 1534–47', in *A New History of Ireland*, ed. by T. W. Moody, F. X. Martin and F. J. Byrne (New York: Oxford University Press, 1993).

Hayton, D. W., 'Voters, Patrons and Parties: Parliamentary Elections in Ireland, C. 1692–1727', *Parliamentary History*, 24 (2005), 43–70.

Heffer, Eric S., *The Class Struggle in Parliament* (London: Victor Gollancz, 1973).

Henning, B. D., *The House of Commons, 1660–1690*. Vol. 2 (London: Secker and Warburg, 1983).

———, *The House of Commons, 1660–1690*. Vol. 3 (London: Secker and Warburg, 1983).

———, *The House of Commons, 1660–1690*. Vol. 1 (London: Secker and Warburg, 1983).

Higley, John, and Michael Burton, 'Elite Settlements and the Taming of Politics', *Government and Opposition*, 33 (1998), 98–115.

Hilton, Boyd, *A Mad, Bad, and Dangerous People?* ed. by J. M. Roberts, *The New Oxford History of England* (Oxford: Oxford University Press, 2006).

Hindley, Geoffrey, *A Brief History of the Magna Carta* (London: Robinson, 2008).

Hinton, R. W. K., 'The Decline of Parliamentary Government under Elizabeth I and the Early Stuarts', *Cambridge Historical Journal*, 13 (1957), 116–32.

Holland, Barbara, *Gentlemen's Blood: A History of Dueling from Swords at Dawn to Pistols at Dusk* (New York: Bloomsbury, 2003).

Hopkinson, Michael, 'Civil War and Aftermath, 1922–4', in *A New History of Ireland*, ed. by J. R. Hill (Oxford: Oxford University Press, 2003).

——, 'From Treaty to Civil War, 1921–2', in *A New History of Ireland*, ed. by J. R. Hill (Oxford: Oxford University Press, 2003).

Hopton, Richard, *Pistols at Dawn: A History of Duelling* (London: Piatkus Books, 2007).

Hosking, Geoffrey, and Anthony King, 'Radicals and Whigs in the British Liberal Party, 1906–1914', in *The History of Parliamentary Behavior*, ed. by William O. Aydelotte (Princeton: Princeton University Press, 1977).

Houfe, Simon R., 'Buckingham Versus Bedford: The Kensington Duel', *Bedfordshire Magazine*, 9 (1964), 223–6.

Hughes, Edward, 'The Changes in Parliamentary Procedure, 1880–1882', in *Essays Presented to Sir Lewis Namier*, ed. by Richard Pares and A. J. P. Taylor (London: Macmillan, 1956), pp. 287–319.

Hulme, Harold, 'The Winning of Freedom of Speech by the House of Commons', *American Historical Review*, 61 (1956), 625–53.

Hunneyball, Paul M., 'The House of Commons, 1603–29', in *A Short History of Parliament*, ed. by Clyve Jones (Woodbridge: Boydell Press, 2009).

Hunt, Giles, *The Duel: Castlereagh, Canning and Deadly Cabinet Rivalry* (London: I.B. Tauris, 2008).

Hurd, Douglas, *Robert Peel* (London: Phoenix, 2007).

Ilie, Cornelia, 'Gendering Confrontational Rhetoric: Discursive Disorder in the British and Swedish Parliaments', *Democratization*, 20 (2013), 501–21.

Innes, Thomas, 'The Scottish Parliament: Its Symbolism and Its Ceremonial', *Juridical Review*, 44 (1932), 87–124.

Jellinek, Georg, 'Parliamentary Obstruction', *Political Science Quarterly*, 19 (1904), 579–88.

Jenkins, Roy, *Churchill* (London: Pan Macmillan, 2001).

——, *Mr Balfour's Poodle* (London: William Collins, 1968).

Jennings, George Henry, *An Anecdotal History of the British Parliament* (London: Horace Cox, 1899).

Jennings, Ivor, *Parliament*. 2nd edn (Cambridge: Cambridge University Press, 1957 [1939]).

Jones, Clyve, 'Dissent and Protest in the House of Lords, 1641–1998: An Attempt to Reconstruct the Procedures Involved in Entering a Protest into the Journals of the House of Lords', *Parliamentary History*, 27 (2008), 309–29.

Judge, David, 'Disorder in the "Frustration" Parliaments of Thatcherite Britain', *Political Studies*, 40 (1992), 532–53.

——, 'Disorder in the House of Commons', *Public Law* (1985), 368–76.

Jupp, Peter, *The Governing of Britain, 1688–1848* (London: Routledge, 2006).

Kearney, Hugh 'The Irish Parliament in the Early Seventeenth Century', in *The Irish Parliamentary Tradition*, ed. by Brian Farrell (Dublin: Gill and Macmillan, 1973).

Kearney, Hugh F., *Strafford in Ireland, 1633–41: A Study in Absolutism* (Manchester: Manchester University Press, 1956).

Keeler, Mary Frear, 'The Emergence of Standing Committees for Privileges and Returns', *Parliamentary History*, 1 (1982), 25–46.

Bibliography

Kelly, James, *'That Damn'd Thing Called Honour': Duelling in Ireland 1570–1860* (Cork: Cork University Press, 1995).

Kemp, Betty, *King and Commons 1660–1832* (Greenwood Press, 1957).

Kiernan, V. G., *The Duel in European History* (Oxford: Oxford University Press, 1989).

Kishlansky, Mark, 'The Emergence of Adversary Politics in the Long Parliament', *The Journal of Modern History*, 49 (1977), 617–40.

Kleineke, Hannes, ed., *Parliamentarians at Law: Select Legal Proceedings of the Long Fifteenth Century Relating to Parliament*. ed. by Elaine Chalus. Vol. 2, *Parliamentary History: Texts & Studies* (Chichester: Wiley-Blackwell, 2008).

Kramnick, Isaac, *Bolingbroke and His Circle* (Harvard University Press, 1968).

Landale, James, *Duel: A True Story of Death and Honour* (Edinburgh: Canongate, 2005).

Lander, J. R., 'Attainder and Forfeiture, 1454–1509', in *Historical Studies of the English Parliament*, ed. by E. B. Fryde and Edward Miller (London: Cambridge University Press, 1970).

Langford, Paul, 'The Eighteenth Century (1688–1789)', in *The Oxford History of Britain* (Oxford U. Press, 1992).

———, *Englishness Identified: Manners and Character, 1650–1850* (Oxford: Oxford University Press, 2000).

———, *A Polite and Commercial People: England 1727–1783*. ed. by J. M. Roberts, *The New Oxford History of England* (London: Guild Publishing, 1989).

Lassiter, John C., 'Defamation of Peers: The Rise and Decline of the Action for Scandalum Magnatum, 1497–1773', *The American Journal of Legal History*, 22 (1978), 216–36.

LaVaque-Manty, Mika, 'Dueling for Equality: Masculine Honor and the Modern Politics of Dignity', *Political Theory*, 34 (2006), 715–40.

Lawrence, Jon, *Electing Our Masters: The Hustings in British Politics from Hogarth to Blair* (Oxford: Oxford University Press, 2009).

Lindley, Keith, *Popular Politics and Religion in Civil War London* (Aldershot: Scolar Press, 1997).

Linklater, Andro, *Why Spencer Perceval Had to Die* (New York: Walker & Co., 2012).

Lloyd, Selwyn, *Mr Speaker, Sir* (Exeter: A. Wheaton & Co., 1976).

Loewenberg, Gerhard, 'The Influence of Parliamentary Behavior on Regime Stability', *Comparative Politics*, 3 (1971), 177–200.

Lydon, James, 'The Impact of the Bruce Invasion, 1315–27', in *A New History of Ireland*, ed. by Art Cosgrove (New York: Oxford University Press, 1993).

———, 'The Years of Crisis, 1254–1315', in *A New History of Ireland*, ed. by Art Cosgrove (New York: Oxford University Press, 1993).

Lyons, F. S. L., *The Irish Parliamentary Party, 1890–1910*. ed. by T. W. Moody, R. Dudley Edwards and David R. Quinn, *Studies in Irish History* (Westport, Connecticut: Greenwood Press, 1974).

———, 'The New Nationalism, 1916–18', in *A New History of Ireland*, ed. by W. E. Vaughan (Oxford: Oxford University Press, 1989).

———, 'The War of Independence, 1919–21', in *A New History of Ireland*, ed. by W. E. Vaughan (Oxford: Oxford University Press, 1989).

Macdonagh, Michael, *The Speaker of the House* (London: Methuen, 1914).

MacDonagh, Oliver, 'Politics, 1830–45', in *A New History of Ireland*, ed. by W. E. Vaughan (Oxford: Oxford University Press, 1989).

MacDonald, Alan R., *The Burghs and Parliament in Scotland, C. 1550–1651* (Aldershot: Ashgate, 2007).

———, 'The Parliament of 1592: A Crisis Averted?', in *The History of the Scottish Parliament*, ed. by Keith M. Brown and Alastair J. Mann (Edinburgh: Edinburgh University Press, 2005).

———, 'The Third Estate: Parliament and the Burghs', in *The History of the Scottish Parliament*, ed. by Keith M. Brown and Alan R. MacDonald (Edinburgh: Edinburgh University Press, 2010).

MacIntosh, Gillian H., 'Arise King John: Commisioner Lauderdale and Parliament in the Restoration Era', in *The History of the Scottish Parliament*, ed. by Keith M. Brown and Alastair J. Mann (Edinburgh: Edinburgh University Press, 2005).

MacIntosh, Gillian H., and Roland J. Tanner, 'Balancing Acts: The Crown and Parliament', in *The History of the Scottish Parliament*, ed. by Keith M. Brown and Alan R. MacDonald (Edinburgh: Edinburgh University Press, 2010).

Mackay, Charles, *Extraordinary Popular Delusions and the Madness of Crowds* (New York: Barnes & Noble, 1989 [1841]).

Mackenzie, Kenneth, *The English Parliament* (Harmondsworth: Penguin, 1950).

Maddicott, J. R., 'Parliament and the Constituencies, 1272–1377', in *The English Parliament in the Middle Ages*, ed. by R. G. Davies and J. H. Denton (Manchester: Manchester University Press, 1981).

Maddicott, John, 'Origins and Beginnings to 1215', in *A Short History of Parliament*, ed. by Clyve Jones (Woodbridge: Boydell Press, 2009).

Manchester, William, *A World Lit Only by Fire* (Boston: Little, Brown, 1992).

Mann, Alastair J., 'House Rules: Parliamentary Procedure', in *The History of the Scottish Parliament*, ed. by Keith M. Brown and Alan R. MacDonald (Edinburgh: Edinburgh University Press, 2010).

———, '"James VII, King of the Articles": Political Management and Parliamentary Failure', in *The History of the Scottish Parliament*, ed. by Keith M. Brown and Alastair J. Mann (Edinburgh: Edinburgh University Press, 2005).

Manning, Brian, *The English People and the English Revolution* (Harmondsworth: Penguin, 1976).

Marquand, David, *Britain since 1918* (London: Phoenix, 2008).

———, *Ramsay Macdonald*. ed. by Ruth Winstone (London: Richard Cohen Books, 1997).

Marr, Andrew, *A History of Modern Britain* (London: Pan Macmillan, 2007).

———, *The Making of Modern Britain* (London: Pan, 2009).

Martin, F. X., 'The Coming of Parliament', in *The Irish Parliamentary Tradition*, ed. by Brian Farrell (Dublin: Gill and Macmillan, 1973).

Mayhall, Laura E. Nym, *The Militant Suffrage Movement: Citizenship and Resistance in Britain, 1860–1930* (New York: Oxford University Press, 2003).

McAlister, Kirsty F., and Roland J. Tanner, 'The First Estate: Parliament and the Church', in *The History of the Scottish Parliament*, ed. by Keith M. Brown and Alan R. MacDonald (Edinburgh: Edinburgh University Press, 2010).

McCafferty, John, *The Reconstruction of the Church of Ireland: Bishop Bramhall and the Laudian Reforms, 1633–1641* (Cambridge University Press).

McCavitt, John, *The Flight of the Earls* (Dublin: Gill & Macmillan, 2005).

McCord, James N., Jr., 'Politics and Honor in Early-Nineteenth-Century England: The Duke's Duel', *Huntington Library Quarterly*, 62 (2000), 88–114.

McCracken, J. L., 'Protestant Ascendancy and the Rise of Colonial Nationalism, 1714–60', in *A New History of Ireland*, ed. by T. W. Moody and W. E. Vaughan (New York: Oxford University Press, 1986).

McDowell, R. B., 'The Age of the United Irishmen: Reform and Reaction, 1789–94', in *A New History of Ireland*, ed. by T. W. Moody and W. E. Vaughan (New York: Oxford University Press, 1986).

——, 'The Age of the United Irishmen: Revolution and the Union, 1794–1800', in *A New History of Ireland*, ed. by T. W. Moody and W. E. Vaughan (New York: Oxford University Press, 1986).

——, 'Colonial Nationalism and the Winning of Parliamentary Independence, 1760–82', in *A New History of Ireland*, ed. by T. W. Moody and W. E. Vaughan (New York: Oxford University Press, 1986).

McGrath, Charles Ivar, 'The Parliament of Ireland to 1800', in *A Short History of Parliament*, ed. by Clyve Jones (Woodbridge: Boydell Press, 2009).

McQueen, Alison A. B., 'Parliament, the Guardians and John Balliol, 1284–1298', in *The History of the Scottish Parliament*, ed. by Keith M. Brown and Roland J. Tanner (Edinburgh: Edinburgh University Press, 2004).

Middlemas, Robert Keith, *The Clydesiders* (London: Hutchinson, 1965).

Miller, Edward, 'Introduction', in *Historical Studies of the English Parliament*, ed. by E. B. Fryde and Edward Miller (London: Cambridge University Press, 1970).

Monypenny, William Flaville, *The Life of Benjamin Disraeli*. Vol. II (London: John Murray, 1912).

Moody, T. W., 'Introduction: Early Modern Ireland', in *A New History of Ireland*, ed. by T. W. Moody, F. X. Martin and F. J. Byrne (New York: Oxford University Press, 1993).

——, 'The Irish Parliament under Elizabeth and James I: A General Survey', *Proceedings of the Royal Irish Academy*, 45 (1939), 41–81.

Morgan, Austen, *J. Ramsay Macdonald*. ed. by David Howell, *Lives of the Left* (Manchester: Manchester University Press, 1987).

Mortimer, Ian, *The Greatest Traitor: The Life of Sir Roger Mortimer, Ruler of England, 1327–1330* (London: Pimlico, 2004).

Murphy, Sean, 'Charles Lucas and the Dublin Election of 1748–9', *Parliamentary History*, 2 (1983).

———, 'The Dublin Anti-Union Riot of 3 December 1759', in *Parliament, Politics and People: Essays in Eighteenth-Century Irish History*, ed. by Gerard O'Brien (Blackrock: Irish Academic Press, 1989).

Namier, Lewis, *England in the Age of the American Revolution* (Macmillan, 1961).

Namier, Sir Lewis, and John Brooke, *The House of Commons 1754–1790*. Vol. 2, *The History of Parliament* (London: Her Majesty's Stationary Office, 1964).

———, *The House of Commons 1754–1790*. Vol. 3, *The History of Parliament* (London: Her Majesty's Stationary Office, 1964).

Neale, J. E., 'The Commons' Privilege of Free Speech in Parliament', in *Historical Studies of the English Parliament*, ed. by E. B. Fryde and Edward Miller (London: Cambridge University Press, 1970).

———, *Elizabeth I and Her Parliaments, 1559–1581* (New York: St. Martin's Press, 1958).

———, *Elizabeth I and Her Parliaments, 1584–1601* (New York: St. Martin's Press, 1958).

———, *The Elizabethan House of Commons* (London: Jonathan Cape, 1949).

———, 'Peter Wentworth: Part I', in *Historical Studies of the English Parliament*, ed. by E. B. Fryde and Edward Miller (London: Cambridge University Press, 1970).

———, 'Peter Wentworth: Part II', in *Historical Studies of the English Parliament*, ed. by E. B. Fryde and Edward Miller (London: Cambridge University Press, 1970).

Norton, Philip, 'The Changing Face of the British House of Commons in the 1980s', *Legislative Studies Quarterly*, 5 (1980), 333–57.

———, *Dissension in the House of Commons, 1974–1979* (Oxford: Oxford University Press, 1980).

O'Donnell, F. Hugh, *A History of the Irish Parliamentary Party*. Vol. 1 (London: Longmans, Green, and Co., 1910).

———, *A History of the Irish Parliamentary Party*. Vol. 2 (London: Longmans, Green, and Co., 1910).

O'Farrell, John, *An Utterly Impartial History of Britian: Or 2000 Years of Upper-Class Idiots in Charge* (London: Doubleday, 2007).

O'Gorman, Frank, *The Emergence of the British Two-Party System 1760–1832*, *Foundations of Modern History* (London: Edward Arnold, 1982).

———, *Voters, Patrons, and Parties: The Unreformed Electoral System of Hanoverian England 1734–1832* (Oxford: Oxford University Press, 1989).

Paxman, Jeremy, *The English: A Portrait of a People* (London: Penguin, 1998).

Payling, Simon, 'The House of Commons, 1307–1529', in *A Short History of Parliament*, ed. by Clyve Jones (Woodbridge: Boydell Press, 2009).

Pearce, Edward, *The Great Man: Sir Robert Walpole: Scoundrel, Genius and Britain's First Prime Minister* (London: Pimlico, 2007).

Pearl, Valerie, *London and the Outbreak of the Puritan Revolution* (London: Oxford University Press, 1961).

Peltonen, Markku, *The Duel in Early Modern England: Civility, Politeness and Honour* (Cambridge: Cambridge University Press, 2003).

Bibliography

Penman, Michael, 'Parliament Lost – Parliament Regained?: The Three Estates in the Reign of David II, 1329–1371', in *The History of the Scottish Parliament*, ed. by Keith M. Brown and Roland J. Tanner (Edinburgh: Edinburgh University Press, 2004).

Pennington, D. H., 'A Seventeenth-Century Perspective', in *The English Parliament in the Middle Ages*, ed. by R. G. Davies and J. H. Denton (Manchester: Manchester University Press, 1981).

Phillips, Melanie, *Londonistan* (New York: Encounter, 2006).

Pincus, Steve, *1688: The First Modern Revolution* (New Haven: Yale University Press, 2009).

——, '"Coffee Politicians Does Create": Coffeehouses and Restoration Political Culture', *The Journal of Modern History*, 67 (1995), 807–34.

Pitkin, Hanna Fenichel, *The Concept of Representation* (Berkeley: University of California Press, 1976).

Plucknett, Theodore F. T., 'Parliament', in *Historical Studies of the English Parliament*, ed. by E. B. Fryde and Edward Miller (London: Cambridge University Press, 1970).

Plumb, J. H., *The Growth of Political Stability in England 1675–1725* (Macmillan, 1967).

——, 'The Growth of the Electorate in England from 1600 to 1715', *Past and Present*, 45 (1969), 90–116.

Pole, J. R., *The Gift of Government* (Athens, Georgia: University of Georgia Press, 1983).

——, *Political Representation in England and the Origin of the American Revolution* (St. Martin's Press, 1966).

Popofsky, Linda S., 'The Crisis over Tonnage and Poundage in Parliament in 1629', *Past and Present*, 126 (1990), 44–75.

Porritt, Edward, 'Amendments in House of Commons Procedure since 1880: The Aims and Tendencies of the Newer Standing Orders', *American Political Science Review*, 2 (1908), 515–31.

Porritt, Edward, and Annie G. Porritt, *The Unreformed House of Commons*. Vol. 1 (Cambridge: Cambridge University Press, 1903).

——, *The Unreformed House of Commons*. Vol. 2 (Cambridge: Cambridge University Press, 1903).

Pugh, Martin, *The Making of Modern British Politics 1867–1939* (Oxford: Blackwell, 1982).

Purkiss, Diane, *The English Civil War: A People's History* (London: Harper, 2006).

Quinn, D. B., 'The Hegemony of the Earls of Kildare, 1494–1520', in *A New History of Ireland*, ed. by Art Cosgrove (New York: Oxford University Press, 1993).

Rait, Robert S., *The Parliaments of Scotland* (Glasgow: Maclehose, Jackson and Co., 1924).

Redlich, Josef, *The Procedure of the House of Commons: A Study of Its History and Present Form, Volume I*. trans. A. Ernest Steinthal (London: Archibald Constable, 1908).

Richardson, H. G., and G. O. Sayles, *The Irish Parliament in the Middle Ages* (Philadelphia: University of Pennsylvania Press, 1952).

Richter, Donald C., *Riotous Victorians* (Athens, Ohio: Ohio University Press, 1981).

Riddell, Peter, *Honest Opportunism* (London: Indigo, 1996).

Robbins, Caroline, *The Eighteenth-Century Commonwealthman* (Harvard U. Press, 1959).

Roberts, Stephen K., 'The House of Commons, 1640–60', in *A Short History of Parliament*, ed. by Clyve Jones (Woodbridge: Boydell Press, 2009).

Robinton, Madeline R., 'Parliamentary Privilege and Political Morality in Britain, 1939–1957', *Political Science Quarterly*, 73 (1958), 179–205.

Rogers, Nicholas, *Whigs and Cities: Popular Politics in the Age of Walpole and Pitt* (Oxford: Oxford University Press, 1989).

Rogers, Robert, *Order! Order!: A Parliamentary Miscellany* (London: JR Books, 2009).

Rogers, Robert, and Rhodri Walters, *How Parliament Works*. 6th edn (Harlow: Pearson, 2006).

Rosen, Andrew, *Rise up, Women: The Militant Campaign of the Women's Social and Political Union, 1903–1914* (London: Routledge & Kegan Paul, 1974).

Roskell, J.S., 'Perspectives on English Parliamentary History', in *Historical Studies of the English Parliament*, ed. by E. B. Fryde and Edward Miller (London: Cambridge University Press, 1970).

Royle, Trevor, *Lancaster against York: The Wars of the Roses and the Foundation of Modern Britain* (Basingstoke: Palgrave Macmillan, 2008).

Rudé, George, *The Crowd in History, 1730–1848*. ed. by Norman F. Cantor, *New Dimensions in History* (New York: John Wiley & Sons, 1964).

——, *Hanoverian London, 1714–1808*. ed. by Francis Sheppard, *The History of London* (Berkeley: University of California Press, 1971).

——, *Wilkes and Liberty* (London: Oxford University Press, 1962).

Ruff, Julius R., *Violence in Early Modern Europe*. ed. by William Beik and T. C. W. Blanning, *New Approaches to European History* (Cambridge: Cambridge University Press, 2001).

Rush, Michael, *Parliament Today*. ed. by Bill Jones, *Politics Today* (Manchester: Manchester University Press, 2005).

——, *The Role of the Member of Parliament since 1868: From Gentlemen to Players* (Oxford: Oxford University Press, 2001).

Russell, Conrad, *The Crisis of Parliaments: English History 1509–1660* (London: Oxford University Press, 1971).

Sabine, Lorenzo, *Notes on Duels and Duelling* (Boston: Crosby, Nichols & Co., 1855).

Sachise, William L., 'The Mob and the Revolution of 1688', *Journal of British Studies*, IV (1964), 23–40.

Sainsbury, John, '"Cool Courage Should Always Mark Me": John Wilkes and Duelling', *Journal of the Canadian Historical Society*, 7 (1996), 19–33.

Salmon, Philip, 'The House of Commons, 1801–1911', in *A Short History of Parliament*, ed. by Clyve Jones (Woodbridge: Boydell Press, 2009).

Scally, John J., 'The Rise and Fall of the Covenanter Parliaments, 1639–51', in *The History of the Scottish Parliament*, ed. by Keith M. Brown and Alastair J. Mann (Edinburgh: Edinburgh University Press, 2005).

Schmitt, Carl, *The Crisis of Parliamentary Democracy*. trans. Ellen Kennedy (Cambridge: MIT Press, 1985 [1923]).

Searing, Donald D., 'Rules of the Game in Britain: Can Politicians Be Trusted?', *American Political Science Review*, 76 (1982), 239–58.

Searle, G. R., *A New England?: Peace and War 1886–1918*. ed. by J. M. Roberts, *The New Oxford History of England* (Oxford: Oxford University Press, 2004).

Seaward, Paul, 'The House of Commons since 1949', in *A Short History of Parliament*, ed. by Clyve Jones (Woodbridge: Boydell Press, 2009).

——, 'The House of Commons, 1660–1707', in *A Short History of Parliament*, ed. by Clyve Jones (Woodbridge: Boydell Press, 2009).

Sedgwick, Romney, *The House of Commons 1715–1754*. Vol. 2, *The History of Parliament* (London: Her Majesty's Stationary Office, 1970).

Seitz, Don C., *Famous American Duels* (Freeport, NY: Books for Libraries, 1966 [1929]).

Shoemaker, Robert, *The London Mob: Violence and Disorder in Eighteenth-Century England* (London: Hambledon Continuum, 2004).

Shoemaker, Robert B., 'The Taming of the Duel: Masculinity, Honour and Ritual Violence in London, 1660–1800', *The Historical Journal*, 45 (2002), 525–45.

Sieveking, A. Forbes, 'Duelling and Militarism', *Transactions of the Royal Historical Society*, 11 (1917).

Simms, J. G., 'The Case of Ireland Stated', in *The Irish Parliamentary Tradition*, ed. by Brian Farrell (Dublin: Gill and Macmillan, 1973).

——, 'The Establishment of Protestant Ascendancy, 1691–1714', in *A New History of Ireland*, ed. by T. W. Moody and W. E. Vaughan (New York: Oxford University Press, 1986).

——, 'The Restoration, 1660–85', in *A New History of Ireland*, ed. by T. W. Moody, F. X. Martin and F. J. Byrne (New York: Oxford University Press, 1993).

Simpson, Antony E., 'Dandelions on the Field of Honor: Dueling, the Middle Classes, and the Law in Nineteenth-Century England', *Criminal Justice History*, 9 (1988).

Smith, Jeremy, 'Bluff, Bluster and Brinkmanship: Andrew Bonar Law and the Third Home Rule Bill', *The Historical Journal*, 36 (1993), 161–78.

Smyth, James, 'Dublin's Political Underground in the 1790s', in *Parliament, Politics and People: Essays in Eighteenth-Century Irish History*, ed. by Gerard O'Brien (Blackrock: Irish Academic Press, 1989).

Smyth, Jim, *The Men of No Property: Irish Radicals and Popular Politics in the Late Eighteenth Century* (New York: St. Martin's Press, 1992).

Somerset Fry, Peter and Fiona, *A History of Ireland* (New York: Barnes & Noble, 1993).

Spufford, Peter, *Origins of the English Parliament* (London: Longmans, 1967).

Stater, Victor, *High Life, Low Morals* (London: Pimlico, 1999).

Steinmetz, Andrew, *The Romance of Duelling*. Vol. I (London: Chapman and Hall, 1868).

Stevenson, David, *Revolution and Counter-Revolution in Scotland, 1644–1651* (Edinburgh: John Donald, 2003).

——, *The Scottish Revolution, 1637–1644: The Triumph of the Covenanters* (New York: St. Martin's Press, 1973).

Stevenson, John, *Popular Disturbances in England, 1700–1832*. 2nd edn (London: Longman, 1992).

——, 'The Queen Caroline Affair', in *London in the Age of Reform*, ed. by John Stevenson (Oxford: Blackwell, 1977), p. 11748.

Stevenson, John, and Chris Cook, *The Slump: Society and Politics During the Depression* (London: Quartet Books, 1977).

Stone, Lawrence, *The Crisis of the Aristocracy, 1558–1641*. Abridged edn (New York: Oxford University Press, 1967).

——, 'Interpersonal Violence in English Society 1300–1980', *Past and Present*, 101 (1983), 22–33.

Straw, Jack, *Last Man Standing* (London: Macmillan, 2012).

Tanner, Roland, '"I Arest You, Sir, in the Name of the Three Astattes in Perlement": The Scottish Parliament and Resistance to the Crown in the Fifteenth Century', in *Social Attitudes and Political Structures in the Fifteenth Century*, ed. by Tim Thornton (Phoenix Mill: Sutton, 2000).

——, *The Late Medieval Scottish Parliament: Politics and the Three Estates, 1424–1488* (East Linton: Tuckwell Press, 2001).

Taylor, A. J. P., *English History 1914–1945* (London: Book Club Associates, 1965).

Temperly, Howard, 'The O'connell–Stevenson Contretemps: A Reflection of the Anglo–American Slavery Issue', *The Journal of Negro History*, 47 (1962), 217–33.

Thatcher, Margaret, *The Downing Street Years* (London: HarperCollins, 1993).

Thomas, P.D.G., *The House of Commons in the Eighteenth Century* (Oxford: Oxford University Press, 1971).

Thompson, E. P., *Customs in Common: Studies in Traditional Popular Culture* (The New Press, 1993).

——, *The Making of the English Working Class* (New York: Random House, 1963).

Thompson, Faith, *A Short History of Parliament, 1295–1642* (Minneapolis: University of Minnesota Press, 1953).

Thorne, R. G., *The House of Commons 1790–1820*. Vol. 3, *The History of Parliament* (London: Secker & Warburg, 1986).

——, *The House of Commons 1790–1820*. Vol. 4, *The History of Parliament* (London: Secker & Warburg, 1986).

——, *The House of Commons 1790–1820*. Vol. 5, *The History of Parliament* (London: Secker & Warburg, 1986).

Thornley, David, 'The Irish Home Rule Party and Parliamentary Obstruction, 1874–87', *Irish Historical Studies*, 12 (1960), 38–57.

Thrush, Andrew, and John P. Ferris, eds., *The House of Commons 1604–1629*. Vol. 6, *The History of Parliament* (Cambridge: Cambridge University Press, 2010).

———, eds., *The House of Commons 1604–1629*. Vol. 4, *The History of Parliament* (Cambridge: Cambridge University Press, 2010).

———, eds., *The House of Commons 1604–1629*. Vol. 5, *The History of Parliament* (Cambridge: Cambridge University Press, 2010).

Tilly, Charles, 'Contentious Repertoires in Great Britain, 1758–1834', *Social Science History*, 17 (1993), 253–80.

———, 'Parliamentarization of Popular Contention in Great Britain, 1758–1834', *Theory and Society*, 26 (1997), 245–73.

———, *Popular Contention in Great Britain, 1758–1834* (Cambridge: Harvard University Press, 1995).

Toland, John, *The Danger of Mercenary Parliaments* (London: 1698).

Towson, Kris, '"Hearts Warped by Passion": The Percy–Gaunt Dispute of 1381', in *Fourteenth Century England*, ed. by W. M. Ormrod (Woodbridge: Boydell Press, 2004).

Toye, Richard, '"Perfectly Parliamentary"? The Labour Party and the House of Commons in the Inter-War Years', *Twentieth Century British History*, 25 (2014), 1–29.

Treadwell, V., 'The Irish Parliament of 1569–71', *Proceedings of the Royal Irish Academy*, 65 (1966/1967), 55–89.

Treharne, R. F., 'The Nature of Parliament in the Reign of Henry III', in *Historical Studies of the English Parliament*, ed. by E. B. Fryde and Edward Miller (London: Cambridge University Press, 1970).

Underdown, David, *Pride's Purge: Politics in the Puritan Revolution* (London: George Allen & Unwin, 1985).

———, *Revel, Riot and Rebellion: Popular Politics and Culture in England 1603–1660* (Oxford: Oxford University Press, 1985).

Veitch, George S., *The Genesis of Parliamentary Reform* (Archon Books, 1965).

Walker, Graham, 'The Northern Ireland Parliament and Assembly at Stormont', in *A Short History of Parliament*, ed. by Clyve Jones (Woodbridge: Boydell Press, 2009).

Watt, J. A., 'The Anglo–Irish Colony under Strain, 1327–99', in *A New History of Ireland*, ed. by Art Cosgrove (New York: Oxford University Press, 1993).

Webb, R. K., *Modern England* (New York: Harper & Row, 1968).

Webster, C. K., H. Temperly, and E. Cooke, 'The Duel between Castlereagh and Canning in 1809', *Cambridge Historical Journal*, 3 (1929), 83–95.

Whatley, Christopher A., and Derek J. Patrick, *The Scots and the Union* (Edinburgh: Edinburgh University Press, 2006).

Whitaker, Lawrence, British Library, Diary of Lawrence Whitaker, Add. MS 31116, 253

Whyte, J. H., 'The North Erupts, and Ireland Enters Europe, 1968–72', in *A New History of Ireland*, ed. by J. R. Hill (Oxford: Oxford University Press, 2003).

Wilkinson, B., 'The Deposition of Richard II and the Accession of Henry IV', in *Historical Studies of the English Parliament*, ed. by E. B. Fryde and Edward Miller (London: Cambridge University Press, 1970).

Wilkinson, Bertie, ed., *The Creation of Medieval Parliaments* (New York: John Wiley & Sons, 1972).

Wilson, Ben, *Decency and Disorder* (London: Faber and Faber, 2007).

Wolfe, Eugene L., 'Creating Democracy's Good Losers: The Rise, Fall and Return of Parliamentary Disorder in Post-War Japan', *Government and Opposition*, 39 (2004), 55–79.

——, '"Into the Custody of the Serjeant at Arms": Inducing Parliamentary Attendance in Dublin and Westminster, 1690–1859', *Parliaments, Estates and Representation*, 38 (2018), 203–26.

Wood, Andy, *Riot, Rebellion and Popular Politics in Early Modern England* (Basingstoke: Palgrave, 2002).

Woolfe, B. P., 'Acts of Resumption in the Lancastrian Parliaments, 1399–1456', in *Historical Studies of the English Parliament*, ed. by E. B. Fryde and Edward Miller (London: Cambridge University Press, 1970).

Wyvill, Christopher, *A State of the Representation of the People of England on the Principles of Mr. Pitt in 1785* (York: W. Blanchard, 1793).

Young, John R., 'Charles I and the 1633 Parliament', in *The History of the Scottish Parliament*, ed. by Keith M. Brown and Alastair J. Mann (Edinburgh: Edinburgh University Press, 2005).

Zagorin, Perez, *The Court and the Country* (New York: Atheneum, 1969).

NOTES

What Is Parliamentary Violence?

1. It is unclear whether the duels that proved fatal to four other politicians were parliamentary in origin: William Brooke (1597); Charles Price (1645); Irish MP Edward Deane (1751); and Irish MP Richard Fitzgerald (1776).

2. Hunt, Giles, *The Duel: Castlereagh, Canning and Deadly Cabinet Rivalry* (London: I.B. Tauris, 2008).

3. Rosen, Andrew, *Rise up, Women: The Militant Campaign of the Women's Social and Political Union, 1903–1914* (London: Routledge & Kegan Paul, 1974). p. 243.

4. Gilmour, Ian, *Riot, Risings and Revolution: Governance and Violence in Eighteenth-Century England* (London: Pimlico, 1992). p. 271.

5. For example, the song 'Commons Brawl', by the rock band Jethro Tull, was inspired by events in the Thatcher era. 'Grave Disorder', an album of the British punk group The Damned, begins with former Speaker Bernard Weatherill intoning, 'I suspend the sitting, grave disorder having broken out.' The alternative band iLIKETRAINS's 2007 single 'Spencer Perceval/I am Murdered' commemorates the only British prime minister to be assassinated. The English punk band Angelic Upstart's 1986 single 'Brighton Bomb' celebrates an IRA attempt to kill another prime minister a century and a half later.

6. Paxman, Jeremy, *The English: A Portrait of a People* (London: Penguin, 1998). p. 247.

7. Langford, Paul, *Englishness Identified: Manners and Character, 1650–1850* (Oxford: Oxford University Press, 2000). pp. 43–6.

8. Neither will soon challenge the Tynwald for the title of the most tranquil assembly in the British Isles: the Manx body's sole episode of parliamentary violence occurred in 1237, when a conclave degenerated into a factional pitched battle that left at least three dead.

9. Rush, Michael, *Parliament Today* (Manchester: Manchester University Press, 2005). p. 313.

10. Macdonagh, Michael, *The Speaker of the House* (London: Methuen, 1914). p. 5.
11. *The New York Times*, 30 June 1923, p. 13.
12. *The Times*, 15 April 1988, p. 2.
13. Rogers, Robert, *Order! Order!: A Parliamentary Miscellany* (London: JR Books, 2009). p. 77.
14. *The Times*, 26 June 2013, p. 21.
15. *The Times*, 15 April 1998, p. 8.
16. *The Times*, 9 June 2009, p. 4.
17. O'Donnell, F. Hugh, *A History of the Irish Parliamentary Party*, vol. 1 (London: Longmans, Green, and Co., 1910). p. 103.
18. Macdonagh. p. 186.
19. Neale, J. E., *The Elizabethan House of Commons* (London: Jonathan Cape, 1949). pp. 352–3.
20. From an article in the March 1851 edition of 'Household Words,' quoted in Jennings, George Henry, *An Anecdotal History of the British Parliament* (London: Horace Cox, 1899). p. 587.
21. *The Times*, 15 February 1901, pp. 10, 12.
22. *The Guardian*, 1 June 1929, p. 22.
23. *The Times*, 17 June 2012, p. 21.
24. Jennings. p. 105.
25. In 1993, for example, Judith Chaplin died of a suspected blood clot following minor surgery. *The Times*, 20 February 1993, p. 1.
26. *The New York Times*, 16 September 1950, p. 8.
27. Wilson, Ben, *Decency and Disorder* (London: Faber and Faber, 2007).
28. Campion, Lord and T. G. B. Cocks, 'Sir Thomas Erskine May's Treatise on the Law, Privileges, Proceedings and Usage of Parliament' (London: Butterworth, 1950). p. 438.
29. *The Times*, 13 May 2009, p. 24.
30. *The Times*, 10 July 2013, p. 11. 31. Searle, G. R., *A New England?: Peace and War 1886–1918* (Oxford: Oxford University Press, 2004). p. 153.
32. *The New York Times*, 22 June 2019, p. A8.
33. Henning, B. D., *The House of Commons, 1660–1690*, vol. 3 (London: Secker and Warburg, 1983). p. 567.
34. The 18-year-old MP from Cheshire 'hurled a piece of tobacco-pipe' at a man he mistakenly thought was an acquaintance, an error that prompted an exchange first of words and then of challenges. Gurr, Andrew, *Playgoing in Shakespeare's London* (Cambridge: Cambridge University Press, 1987). pp. 192, 197.
35. The MP for Wiltshire 'virtually bought' Lady Ogle, a 14-year-old widow whose assets included a fine residence, 'but the marriage was never consummated, and she left him after a few months'. Henning, B. D., *The House of Commons, 1660–1690*, vol. 1 (London: Secker and Warburg, 1983). p. 617.
36. ibid. p. 530.
37. [anon], *The Life and Noble Character of Richard Thornhill, Esq.; Who Had the Misfortune to Kill Sir Cholmley Deering, Bart. Knight of the Shire for the*

County of Kent, in a Duel in Tuttle-Fields, on Wednesday the 9th of May, 1711 (London Richard Newcomb, 1711).

38. Cruickshanks, Eveline, Stuart Handley, and D. W. Hayton, *The House of Commons 1690–1715*, vol. 3 (London: Cambridge University Press, 2002). pp. 391–2.

39. Rudé, George, *The Crowd in History, 1730–1848* (New York: John Wiley & Sons, 1964). p. 145.

40. *The Times*, 2 March 1993, p. 3.

41. *The Times*, 22 June 2009, p. 21.

42. http://www.bbc.co.uk/news/uk-england-cambridgeshire-19038968

43. *The Times*, 26 May 2008, p. 8.

44. *The New York Times*, 5 June 1897, p. 7. *The Times*, 5 June 1897, p. 2.

45. *The Guardian*, 28 October 1912, p. 12.

46. Still another bomb was sent to a lawyer who worked for Celtic manager Neil Lennon. *The Times*, 21 April 2011, p. 9.

47. Dawson, Jane E. A., *Scotland Re-formed 1488–1587* (Edinburgh: Edinburgh University Press, 2007). p. 127.

48. Rait, Robert S., *The Parliaments of Scotland* (Glasgow: Maclehose, Jackson and Co., 1924). pp. 525–6(n).

49. The Journals of the House of Commons (hereafter JC), 267 vols. (London, 1802–2015), vol. 13, pp. 319, 321, 9 and 11 April 1700.

50. The Journals of the House of Commons of the Kingdom of Ireland, (hereafter JHOCKI), 19 vols. (Dublin, 1794–1800), vol. 2, p. 261, 19 December 1737.

51. JHOCKI, vol. 4, pp. 12 and 21, 7 October and 3 November 1731.

52. See, for example, JHOCKI, vol. 4, pp. 71 and 82, 5 October and 6 November 1733, vol. 5, p. 195 and 387, 23 November 1753 and 17 March 1756, and vol. 7, pp. 91 and 332, 18 December 1761 and 16 April 1764.

53. *The Guardian*, 14 January 1997, p. 7.

54. The most obvious exception is when parliamentarians are punished for mistreating those who work for them. An inquiry by Dame Laura Cox found that bullying, abuse and sexual harassment were widespread in the Commons. *The New York Times*, 16 October 2018, p. 6. The situation at the Independent Parliamentary Standards Authority, responsible for administering the expenses system for MPs, was so dire that those who worked there felt compelled to affix upon the office door the sort of plaintive sign familiar in places far removed from the corridors of power, 'Aggression to our staff will not be tolerated.' *The Times*, 22 May 2013, p. 23.

55. Sedgwick, Romney, *The House of Commons 1715–1754*, vol. 2 (London: Her Majesty's Stationery Office, 1970). p. 519.

56. Underdown, David, *Pride's Purge: Politics in the Puritan Revolution* (London: George Allen & Unwin, 1985). P. 222.

57. Quite a few parliamentarians have been the perpetrators rather than the victims of violence. See, for example, *The Guardian*, 9 December 1904, p. 8, 16 October 1911, p. 9, 6 November 1959, p. 4, 6 December 1976, p. 6, 26 October 1984,

p. 28, 1 April 1989, p. 24, 15 March 1990, p. 2, 13 August 1993, p. 5, and 6 August 1999, p. 5, *The Times*, 5 February 2008, p. 4, 5 June 2008, p. 4, December 19 2008, p. 31, and 6 May 2013, p. 4.

58. JC vol. 142, p. 552, 16 September 1887.
59. JC, vol. 143, pp. 50, 149, 221, 398, and 457, 20 February, 12 April, 14 May, 25 July and 6 November 1888.
60. *The New York Times*, 20 November 1920, p. 15.
61. This total is conservative, tabulating as a single incident both episodes in which multiple politicians are threatened serially (e.g. by a rampaging mob) and situations in which a parliamentarian is involved in connected events, as when a fistfight leads to a duel.
62. Gilmour. p. 5.
63. For a contrary view, however, see Pincus, Steve, *1688: The First Modern Revolution* (New Haven: Yale University Press, 2009).
64. Paul Seaward, Director of the History of Parliament Trust, makes an 'educated guess' that around 30,000 people have sat in the House of Commons over the centuries. (Personal communication of 29 July 2014 with Emma Peplow.) It would not be surprising if the historical membership of the House of Lords, combined with that of the other parliaments covered here, comprises a similar total. The number of recorded instances of violence, in short, is dwarfed by the quantity of parliamentarians.
65. To be sure, early parliaments met far less often and had far less power, both of which militated against violence.
66. Mackenzie, Kenneth, *The English Parliament* (Harmondsworth: Penguin, 1950), p. 43.
67. Rogers, Robert and Rhodri Walters, *How Parliament Works*, 6th edn (Harlow: Pearson, 2006). p. 14.

1 Childhood Trauma

1. Wilkinson, Bertie, 'The Creation of Medieval Parliaments' (New York: John Wiley & Sons, 1972). p. 1. Brown, Keith M. and Roland J. Tanner, 'Introduction: Parliament and Politics in Scotland, 1253–1560', in *The History of the Scottish Parliament*, ed. by Keith M. Brown and Roland J. Tanner (Edinburgh: Edinburgh University Press, 2004). p. 9. McQueen, Alison A. B., 'Parliament, the Guardians and John Balliol, 1284–1298', in *The History of the Scottish Parliament*, ed. by Keith M. Brown and Roland J. Tanner (Edinburgh: Edinburgh University Press, 2004). p. 32. McGrath, Charles Ivar, 'The Parliament of Ireland to 1800', in *A Short History of Parliament*, ed. by Clyve Jones (Woodbridge: Boydell Press, 2009). p. 321. Richardson, H. G. and G. O. Sayles, *The Irish Parliament in the Middle Ages* (Philadelphia: University of Pennsylvania Press, 1952). p. 61.
2. Thompson, Faith, *A Short History of Parliament, 1295–1642* (Minneapolis: University of Minnesota Press, 1953). p. 4.

3. Hindley, Geoffrey, *A Brief History of the Magna Carta* (London: Robinson, 2008); Maddicott, John, 'Origins and Beginnings to 1215', in *A Short History of Parliament*, ed. by Clyve Jones (Woodbridge: Boydell Press, 2009).

4. Field, John, *The Story of Parliament in the Palace of Westminster* (London: James & James, 2002). p. 26.

5. Treharne, R. F., 'The Nature of Parliament in the Reign of Henry III', in *Historical Studies of the English Parliament*, vol. 1, ed. by E. B. Fryde and Edward Miller (London: Cambridge University Press, 1970). p. 83.

6. Wilkinson. p. 97.

7. Calendar of Patent Rolls, Edward I, vol. 2, 1281–1291, (London: 1893). pp. 489, 517.

8. Richardson and Sayles. pp. 58–9.

9. Wilkinson, B., 'The Deposition of Richard II and the Accession of Henry IV', in *Historical Studies of the English Parliament*, vol. 1, ed. by E. B. Fryde and Edward Miller (London: Cambridge University Press, 1970).

10. Richardson and Sayles. pp. 274–5, 279. Quinn, D. B., 'The Hegemony of the Earls of Kildare, 1494–1520', in *A New History of Ireland*, vol. 2, ed. by Art Cosgrove (New York: Oxford University Press, 1993). pp. 642–3.

11. Mortimer, Ian, *The Greatest Traitor: The Life of Sir Roger Mortimer, Ruler of England, 1327–1330* (London: Pimlico, 2004). p. 204.

12. Thompson. p. 91.

13. Jennings. p. 6.

14. Plucknett, Theodore F. T., 'Parliament', in *Historical Studies of the English Parliament*, vol. 1, ed. by E. B. Fryde and Edward Miller (London: Cambridge University Press, 1970). p. 220.

15. Lydon, James, 'The Years of Crisis, 1254–1315', in *A New History of Ireland*, vol. 2, ed. by Art Cosgrove (New York: Oxford University Press, 1993). p. 203. Richardson and Sayles. p. 96.

16. Field. p. 50.

17. Ruff, Julius R., *Violence in Early Modern Europe* (Cambridge: Cambridge University Press, 2001). p. 130.

18. Stone, Lawrence, 'Interpersonal Violence in English Society 1300–1980', *Past and Present*, 101 (1983). p. 25.

19. Stater, Victor, *High Life, Low Morals* (London: Pimlico, 1999). p. 285.

20. Manchester, William, *A World Lit Only by Fire* (Boston: Little, Brown, 1992). p. 7.

21. Stone, Lawrence, *The Crisis of the Aristocracy, 1558–1641*, abridged edn (New York: Oxford University Press, 1967). pp. 108–9.

22. Thompson. p. 91.

23. Miller, Edward, 'Introduction', in *Historical Studies of the English Parliament*, vol. 1, ed. by E. B. Fryde and Edward Miller (London: Cambridge University Press, 1970). p. 7.

24. Edwards, J. G., 'The *Plena Potestas* of English Parliamentary Representatives', in *Historical Studies of the English Parliament,* vol. 1, ed. by E. B. Fryde and Edward Miller (London: Cambridge University Press, 1970).

25. Maddicott, J. R., 'Parliament and the Constituencies, 1272–1377', in *The English Parliament in the Middle Ages,* ed. by R. G. Davies and J. H. Denton (Manchester: Manchester University Press, 1981).

26. Kishlansky, Mark, 'The Emergence of Adversary Politics in the Long Parliament', *The Journal of Modern History,* 49 (1977).

27. Chris Given-Wilson (ed.), 'Richard II: Parliament of 1381, Text and Translation', in *The Parliament Rolls of Medieval England,* ed. C. Given-Wilson et al., item 4, CD-ROM. Scholarly Digital Editions, Leicester: 2005, vol. iii, p. 98.

28. Towson, Kris, '"Hearts Warped by Passion": The Percy–Gaunt Dispute of 1381', in *Fourteenth Century England,* ed. by W. M. Ormrod (Woodbridge: Boydell Press, 2004).

29. Richardson and Sayles. pp. 72–3.

30. Seymour Phillips (ed.), 'Edward II: Parliament of January 1316, Text and Translation, SC 9/20, 352, in *The Parliament Rolls of Medieval England,* ed. C. Given-Wilson et al., item 4, CD-ROM. Scholarly Digital Editions, Leicester: 2005.

31. Seymour Phillips (ed.), 'Edward III: Parliament of September 1331, Text and Translation, in *The Parliament Rolls of Medieval England,* ed. C. Given-Wilson et al., item 14, CD-ROM. Scholarly Digital Editions, Leicester: 2005.

32. Seymour Phillips (ed.), 'Edward III: Parliament of March 1332, Text and Translation, in *The Parliament Rolls of Medieval England,* ed. C. Given-Wilson et al., item 12, CD-ROM. Scholarly Digital Editions, Leicester: 2005.

33. Mortimer. p. 168.

34. Lydon. p. 279.

35. Chris Given-Wilson (ed.), 'Richard II: Parliament of February 1388, Introduction', in *The Parliament Rolls of Medieval England,* ed. C. Given-Wilson et al., item 4, CD-ROM. Scholarly Digital Editions, Leicester: 2005.

36. Denton, J. H., 'The Clergy and Parliament in the Thirteenth and Fourteenth Centuries', in *The English Parliament in the Middle Ages,* ed. by R. G. Davies and J. H. Denton (Manchester: Manchester University Press, 1981).

37. Spufford, Peter, *Origins of the English Parliament* (London: Longmans, 1967). p. 179.

38. Royle, Trevor, *Lancaster against York: The Wars of the Roses and the Foundation of Modern Britain* (Basingstoke: Palgrave Macmillan, 2008). p. 287.

39. Manchester. p. 36.

40. Lander, J. R., 'Attainder and Forfeiture, 1454–1509', in *Historical Studies of the English Parliament,* vol. 2, ed. by E. B. Fryde and Edward Miller (London: Cambridge University Press, 1970).

41. Edwards.

42. Roskell, J.S., 'Perspectives on English Parliamentary History', in *Historical Studies of the English Parliament,* vol. 2, ed. by E. B. Fryde and Edward Miller (London: Cambridge University Press, 1970). p. 296.

43. Woolfe, B. P., 'Acts of Resumption in the Lancastrian Parliaments, 1399–1456', in *Historical Studies of the English Parliament,* vol. 2, ed. by E. B. Fryde and Edward Miller (London: Cambridge University Press, 1970). p. 70.

44. Griffith, M. C., 'The Talbot–Ormond Struggle for Control of the Anglo–Irish Government, 1414–47', *Irish Historical Studies,* 2 (1941).

45. Henry F. Berry, ed., Statute Rolls of the Parliament of Ireland: Reign of King Henry VI, (Dublin: 1910). pp. xii, 711, 713.

46. Royle. pp. 32–3.

47. Field. p. 60.

48. Somerset Fry, Peter and Fiona, *A History of Ireland* (New York: Barnes & Noble, 1993). p. 95. Given-Wilson, C., 'Perrers, Alice (*d.* 1400/01)', *Oxford Dictionary of National Biography,* (Oxford: Oxford University Press, 2004) (hereafter *ODNB*).

49. Watt, J. A., 'The Anglo–Irish Colony under Strain, 1327–99', in *A New History of Ireland,* vol. 2, ed. by Art Cosgrove (New York: Oxford University Press, 1993). pp. 272–3. Martin, F. X., 'The Coming of Parliament', in *The Irish Parliamentary Tradition,* ed. by Brian Farrell (Dublin: Gill and Macmillan, 1973). pp. 51–4.

50. Thompson. pp. 100–7.

51. ibid. pp. 94–7.

52. Rogers and Walters. p. 45.

53. Mackenzie. p. 116.

54. Sir Thomas Tresham, a Lancastrian chosen as Speaker in 1459, was executed in 1471 for his persistent opposition to the Yorkist King Edward IV. William Catesby, who served as Speaker in 1484, suffered the same fate after the Battle of Bosworth the following year, evidently more for his close identification with the defeated Richard III than his activity in parliament. Sir Thomas More, Speaker in 1523, was killed in 1535 for persistent opposition (as Lord Chancellor) to Henry VIII's religious reforms. Both Sir Richard Empsom, Speaker in 1491–2, and Sir Edmund Dudley, Speaker in 1504, paid with their lives in 1510 for leading roles in the unpopular revenue-raising policies of Henry VII. The sixth Speaker presumably is Sir Robert Sheffield, who, while not executed, may have died in the Tower, having been imprisoned after a series of disputes with Cardinal Wolsey that began while he was presiding over the Commons from 1512–4.

55. Woolfe. p. 81.

56. Royle. p. 123.

57. Plucknett. p. 215.

58. Kleineke, Hannes, 'Parliamentarians at Law: Select Legal Proceedings of the Long Fifteenth Century Relating to Parliament', in *Parliamentary History: Texts & Studies,* ed. by Elaine Chalus (Chichester: Wiley-Blackwell, 2008). p. 4.

59. Given-Wilson, Chris, 'Richard II: Parliament of January 1397, Introduction, in *The Parliament Rolls of Medieval England,* ed. C. Given-Wilson et al. CD-ROM. Scholarly Digital Editions, Leicester: 2005.

60. Chafetz, Josh, *Democracy's Privileged Few: Legislative Privilege and Democratic Norms in the British and American Constitutions* (New Haven: Yale University Press, 2007). p. 69.

61. Pollard, A. F. and Nigel Ramsay, 'Yonge, Sir Thomas (*c*.1405–1477)', *ODNB*.

62. Summerson, Henry, 'Thorpe, Thomas (d. 1461)', *ODNB*.

63. MacIntosh, Gillian H. and Roland J. Tanner, 'Balancing Acts: The Crown and Parliament', in *The History of the Scottish Parliament*, ed. by Keith M. Brown and Alan R. MacDonald (Edinburgh: Edinburgh University Press, 2010). p. 8.

64. Godfrey, Mark A., 'Parliamentary and the Law', in *The History of the Scottish Parliament*, ed. by Keith M. Brown and Alan R. MacDonald (Edinburgh: Edinburgh University Press, 2010).

65. Goodare, Julian, 'The Parliament of Scotland to 1707', in *A Short History of Parliament*, ed. by Clyve Jones (Woodbridge: Boydell Press, 2009). pp. 301–3.

66. Penman, Michael, 'Parliament Lost – Parliament Regained?: The Three Estates in the Reign of David II, 1329–1371', in *The History of the Scottish Parliament*, ed. by Keith M. Brown and Roland J. Tanner (Edinburgh: Edinburgh University Press, 2004). p. 81.

67. Tanner, Roland, *The Late Medieval Scottish Parliament: Politics and the Three Estates, 1424–1488* (East Linton: Tuckwell Press, 2001). pp. 42–3.

68. ibid. p. 59.

69. Tanner, Roland, '"I Arest You, Sir, in the Name of the Three Astattes in Perlement": The Scottish Parliament and Resistance to the Crown in the Fifteenth Century', in *Social Attitudes and Political Structures in the Fifteenth Century*, ed. by Tim Thornton (Phoenix Mill: Sutton, 2000); Tanner. pp. 13–76.

70. Tanner. p. 86.

71. Brown, Michael, 'Public Authority and Factional Conflict: Crown, Parliament and Polity, 1424–1455', in *The History of the Scottish Parliament*, ed. by Keith M. Brown and Roland J. Tanner (Edinburgh: Edinburgh University Press, 2004). pp. 138–41.

72. MacIntosh and Tanner. p. 11.

73. Tanner. pp. 219–33.

74. Richardson and Sayles. p. 280.

2 Adolescent Challenges

1. Cam, H. M., 'The Legislators of Medieval England', in *Historical Studies of the English Parliament*, vol. 1, ed. by E. B. Fryde and Edward Miller (London: Cambridge University Press, 1970).

2. Brown, A. L., 'Parliament, C. 1377–1422', in *The English Parliament in the Middle Ages*, ed. by R. G. Davies and J. H. Denton (Manchester: Manchester University Press, 1981). p. 140.

3. Roskell. pp. 303–5.

4. Cavill, P. R., 'Debate and Dissent in Henry VII's Parliaments', *Parliamentary History*, 25 (2006).

5. Jennings. p. 559.
6. Kleineke. p. 22.
7. Rush. p. 34.
8. Neale. pp. 15, 143–9.
9. Neale, J. E., *Elizabeth I and Her Parliaments, 1559–1581* (New York: St. Martin's Press, 1958).pp. 17–8.
10. Jennings. pp. 71–2.
11. Payling, Simon, 'The House of Commons, 1307–1529', in *A Short History of Parliament*, ed. by Clyve Jones (Woodbridge: Boydell Press, 2009). p. 79.
12. Fryde, E. B., 'Introduction', in *Historical Studies of the English Parliament*, vol. 2, ed. by E. B. Fryde and Edward Miller (London: Cambridge University Press, 1970). p. 21.
13. Field. p. 70.
14. Hayes-McCoy, G. A., 'The Royal Supremacy and the Ecclesiastical Revolution, 1534–47', in *A New History of Ireland*, vol. 3, ed. by T. W. Moody, F. X. Martin, and F. J. Byrne (New York: Oxford University Press, 1993). pp. 56–60.
15. Russell, Conrad, *The Crisis of Parliaments: English History 1509–1660* (London: Oxford University Press, 1971). p. 116.
16. Chafetz. pp. 116–7. Thompson. pp. 154–5.
17. JC, vol. 1, pp. 6, 9. 21–4 January and 2 March 1549.
18. Russell. p. 141.
19. Jennings. pp. 14–5.
20. Hinton, R. W. K., 'The Decline of Parliamentary Government under Elizabeth I and the Early Stuarts', *Cambridge Historical Journal*, 13 (1957).
21. Graves, M. A. R., 'The Management of the Elizabethan House of Commons: The Council's "Men-of-Business"', *Parliamentary History*, 2 (1983).
22. Neale. *Elizabeth I*, p. 139.
23. ibid. pp. 152–7.
24. Treadwell, V., 'The Irish Parliament of 1569–71', *Proceedings of the Royal Irish Academy*, 65 (1966/1967). Falkiner, Caesar Litton, 'The Parliament of Ireland under the Tudor Sovereigns: Supplementary Paper', *Proceedings of the Royal Irish Academy*, 25 (1904/1905).
25. Neale. *Elizabeth I*, pp. 189–203.
26. Neale, J. E., 'Peter Wentworth: Part I', in *Historical Studies of the English Parliament*, ed. by E. B. Fryde and Edward Miller (London: Cambridge University Press, 1970). p. 250.
27. Neale, J. E., 'The Commons' Privilege of Free Speech in Parliament', in *Historical Studies of the English Parliament*, vol. 2, ed. by E. B. Fryde and Edward Miller (London: Cambridge University Press, 1970). p. 175.
28. Fryde.
29. Neale. *Elizabeth I*, pp. 253–61.
30. Neale. *Elizabethan Commons*, p. 417.
31. Hasler, P. W., *The House of Commons 1558–1603*, vol. 2 (London: Her Majesty's Stationary Office, 1981). pp. 240–2.

32. Neale. *Elizabeth I*, pp. 320–9, Neale. 'Wentworth', pp. 253–5.
33. Neale, J. E., *Elizabeth I and Her Parliaments, 1584–1601* (New York: St. Martin's Press, 1958). pp. 39–41, 48–9.
34. ibid. pp. 148–57.
35. ibid. pp. 164–75.
36. Keeler, Mary Frear, 'The Emergence of Standing Committees for Privileges and Returns', *Parliamentary History,* 1 (1982). Neale. p. 203.
37. Neale. *Elizabeth I*, pp. 252–6.
38. Neale. 'Wentworth'. Neale, *Elizabeth I*, pp. 257–63.
39. Neale. *Elizabeth I*, pp. 270–7.
40. ibid. pp. 278–9.
41. Neale. *Elizabethan Commons*, p. 387.
42. Neale. *Elizabeth I*, p. 32.
43. Mackenzie. p. 43.
44. Redlich, Josef, *The Procedure of the House of Commons: A Study of Its History and Present Form, Volume I* (London: Archibald Constable, 1908). p. 36.
45. 'Journal of the House of Commons: February 1589', in Simonds d'Ewes, *The Journals of all the Parliaments during the reign of Queen Elizabeth* (Shannon: 1682), pp. 428–441.
46. Edwards, Gonronwy, 'The Emergence of Majority Rule in the Procedure of the House of Commons', *Transactions of the Royal Historical Society,* 15 (1965).
47. Thompson. p. 187.
48. Field. p. 82.
49. Neale. *Elizabethan Commons*, p. 401.
50. Fraser, Antonia, *The Gunpowder Plot: Terror and Faith in 1605* (London: Phoenix, 1996).
51. Neale. p. 353. Field. p. 94.
52. Hunneyball, Paul M., 'The House of Commons, 1603–29', in *A Short History of Parliament,* ed. by Clyve Jones (Woodbridge: Boydell Press, 2009).
53. JC, vol. 1, pp. 335–6, 16 February 1607.
54. Clarke, Aiden, with R. Dudley Edwards, 'Pacification, Plantation, and the Catholic Question, 1603–23', in *A New History of Ireland,* vol. 3, ed. by T. W. Moody, F. X. Martin, and F. J. Byrne (New York: Oxford University Press, 1993). pp. 196–213.
55. McCavitt, John, *The Flight of the Earls* (Dublin: Gill & Macmillan, 2005). p. 192. Clarke. p. 214.
56. McCavitt. pp. 193–5. Clarke. pp. 214–6. McGrath. pp. 327–8.
57. JHOCKI, vol. 1, pp. 26, 30, 32–4, 4, 10, 18 November 1614.
58. Moody, T. W., 'The Irish Parliament under Elizabeth and James I: A General Survey', *Proceedings of the Royal Irish Academy,* 45 (1939). p. 62. Kearney, Hugh 'The Irish Parliament in the Early Seventeenth Century', in *The Irish Parliamentary Tradition,* ed. by Brian Farrell (Dublin: Gill and Macmillan, 1973). p. 94. JHOCKI, vol. 1, pp. 68–72, 3–5 May 1615.

59. Thompson. pp. 234–8. Hulme, Harold, 'The Winning of Freedom of Speech by the House of Commons', *American Historical Review,* 61 (1956).
60. Russell. p. 165.
61. JC, vol. 1, p. 483. 13 May 1614. Thrush, Andrew and John P. Ferris, *The House of Commons 1604–1629,* vol. 4 (Cambridge: Cambridge University Press, 2010). pp. 653–7.
62. Journal of the House of Lords (Hereafter JL), 249 vols. (London: 1802–2016), vol. 3, pp. 19–20. 16 February 1621.
63. JC, vol. 1, pp. 606, 611–3, 615–6. 3 and 7–9 May 1621. Jennings. p. 641.
64. Smuts, R. Malcolm, 'Howard, Thomas, fourteenth earl of Arundel, fourth earl of Surrey, and first earl of Norfolk,' *ODNB.*
65. JL, vol. 3, p. 674, 12 June 1626.
66. Underdown, David, *Revel, Riot and Rebellion: Popular Politics and Culture in England 1603–1660* (Oxford: Oxford University Press, 1985); Russell. p. 204.
67. Popofsky, Linda S., 'The Crisis over Tonnage and Poundage in Parliament in 1629', *Past and Present,* 126 (1990).
68. Bendix, Reinhard, *Kings or People: Power and the Mandate to Rule* (Berkeley: University of California Press, 1978). p. 306.
69. Lloyd, Selwyn, *Mr Speaker, Sir* (Exeter: A. Wheaton & Co., 1976). p. 42.
70. Macdonagh. pp. 207–10. Thrush and Ferris. vol. 4, pp. 271–9.
71. Fraser, Ian H. C., 'The Agitation in the Commons, 2 March 1629, and the Interrogation of the Leaders of the Anti-Court Group', *Bulletin of the Institute of Historical Research,* 30 (1957). p. 95.
72. Russell. pp. 309–10.
73. Brown, Keith M., 'The Reformation Parliament', in *The History of the Scottish Parliament,* ed. by Keith M. Brown and Roland J. Tanner (Edinburgh: Edinburgh University Press, 2004).
74. Dawson. p. 275.
75. Goodare. p. 313.
76. Dawson. p. 275.
77. Thanks to Alastair Mann for this observation.
78. MacDonald, Alan R., *The Burghs and Parliament in Scotland, C. 1550–1651* (Aldershot: Ashgate, 2007). pp. 160–5.
79. MacDonald, Alan R., 'The Third Estate: Parliament and the Burghs', in *The History of the Scottish Parliament,* ed. by Keith M. Brown and Alan R. MacDonald (Edinburgh: Edinburgh University Press, 2010). p. 112. Innes, Thomas, 'The Scottish Parliament: Its Symbolism and Its Ceremonial', *Juridical Review,* 44 (1932). The Register of the Privy Council of Scotland, vol. 1, pp. 604–5. Thanks to Julian Goodare for this reference.
80. Boyd, William K., ed., Calendar of the State Papers Relating to Scotland and Mary Queen of Scots, 1547–1603, (Edinburgh: 1915). vol. 9, p. 453. Calderwood, David, 'History of the Kirk of Scotland,' Thomson and Laing (eds), 8 vols. (Edinburgh: 1843–9). vol. 4, pp. 639–40.
81. MacDonald. *Burghs,* pp. 162–3.

82. Goodare, Julian Mark, 'Parliament and Society in Scotland, 1560–1603,' unpublished PhD Thesis, University of Edinburgh, 1989, pp. 518–21.

83. Dawson. p. 288.

84. MacDonald, Alan R., 'The Parliament of 1592: A Crisis Averted?', in *The History of the Scottish Parliament*, ed. by Keith M. Brown and Alastair J. Mann (Edinburgh: Edinburgh University Press, 2005). p. 63.

85. MacDonald. *Burghs*, p. 153.

86. Cameron, Annie I., ed., *Calendar of State Papers Relating to Scotland and Mary, Queen of Scots, 1547–1603*, vol. 11, (Edinburgh: 1936). p. 129. Thanks to Julian Goodare for this reference.

87. Brown, Keith M. and Alastair J. Mann, 'Introduction: Parliament and Politics in Scotland, 1567–1707', in *The History of the Scottish Parliament*, ed. by Keith M. Brown and Alastair J. Mann (Edinburgh: Edinburgh University Press, 2005). pp. 25–31.

88. McAlister, Kirsty F. and Roland J. Tanner, 'The First Estate: Parliament and the Church', in *The History of the Scottish Parliament*, ed. by Keith M. Brown and Alan R. MacDonald (Edinburgh: Edinburgh University Press, 2010). pp. 50–1.

89. Rait. pp. 408–9.

90. Young, John R., 'Charles I and the 1633 Parliament', in *The History of the Scottish Parliament*, ed. by Keith M. Brown and Alastair J. Mann (Edinburgh: Edinburgh University Press, 2005). pp. 128–35.

91. Moody, T. W., 'Introduction: Early Modern Ireland', in *A New History of Ireland*, vol. 3, ed. by T. W. Moody, F. X. Martin, and F. J. Byrne (New York: Oxford University Press, 1993). p. xlvii.

92. JHOCKI, vol. 1, pp. 122–3, 132–3. 4 and 14–5 November 1634. Clarke, Aiden, 'The Government of Wentworth, 1632–40', in *A New History of Ireland*, vol. 3, ed. by T. W. Moody, F. X. Martin, and F. J. Byrne (New York: Oxford University Press, 1993), pp. 247–8. Kearney, Hugh F., *Strafford in Ireland, 1633–41: A Study in Absolutism* (Manchester: Manchester University Press, 1956), pp. 250–1.

93. Clarke, Aidan, *The Old English in Ireland 1625–42* (Ithaca: Cornell University Press, 1966). p. 84. JHOCKI (G), vol. 1, p. 68, 30 July 1634.

94. JHOCKI, vol. 1, pp. 69–70, 1 August 1634. Ibid., p. 85. Thanks to Brid McGrath for this reference.

95. JHOCKI, vol. 1, pp. 86–7, 2–3 December 1634. Kearney. p. 59. Kearney. p. 98.

96. JHOCKI, vol. 1, p. 90, 12 December 1634.

97. Clarke. 'Government of Wentworth', p. 251.

3 *Uncivil Wars*

1. Zagorin, Perez, *The Court and the Country* (New York: Atheneum, 1969).

2. JL, vol. 4, pp. 88–9, 11 November 1640.

3. Clarke, Aiden, 'The Breakdown of Authority, 1640-41', in *A New History of Ireland*, vol. 3, ed. by T. W. Moody, F. X. Martin, and F. J. Byrne, (New York: Oxford University Press, 1993), p. 277.

4. JHOCKI, vol. 1, pp. 163–4, 9 November 1640. McCafferty, John, *The Reconstruction of the Church of Ireland: Bishop Bramhall and the Laudian Reforms, 1633–1641* (Cambridge University Press). pp. 210–1.

5. JHOCKI, vol. 1, pp. 172, 183, 207–8, 13 and 24 February and 17–8 May 1641.

6. JHOCKI, vol. 1, pp. 185 and 198, 27 February and 4 March 1641.

7. Field. pp. 88–9.

8. The word 'mob' is used to denote a potentially violent crowd.

9. Pearl, Valerie, *London and the Outbreak of the Puritan Revolution* (London: Oxford University Press, 1961), p. 196.

10. JC, vol. 2, p. 88. 18 February 1641.

11. Braddick, Michael, *God's Fury, England's Fire: A New History of the English Civil Wars* (London: Penguin, 2008), p. 135.

12. Manning, Brian, *The English People and the English Revolution* (Harmondsworth: Penguin, 1976), p. 22.

13. Pole, J. R., *The Gift of Government* (Athens, Georgia: University of Georgia Press, 1983), p. 101.

14. Pearl. p. 216.

15. Manning. p. 24.

16. ibid. pp. 26–8.

17. Those expelled were Henry Wilmot, Sir Hugh Pollard, William Ashburneham and Henry Percy. JC, vol. 2, 10 December 1641, p. 337. As the name implies, this plot was hardly unique. Two years later, another MP, Edmund Waller would be arrested for plotting to deliver London to the king's forces, by, among other things, kidnapping parliamentary leaders.

18. Manning. p. 27.

19. ibid. pp. 31–2.

20. Jennings. p. 80.

21. Russell. p. 338.

22. Braddick. p. 171.

23. Manning. pp. 63–4.

24. ibid. pp. 65–6. Lindley, Keith, *Popular Politics and Religion in Civil War London* (Aldershot: Scolar Press, 1997), p. 96.

25. Manning. pp. 68–72.

26. Lindley. pp. 99–101.

27. Manning, pp. 82–92. Lindley, pp. 106–7.

28. Pearl, p. 224.

29. Lindley, p. 109.

30. Manning, pp. 93–6.

31. ibid. pp. 97–99. Lindley, pp. 111–2.

32. Manning, p. 101.

33. Stevenson, David, *The Scottish Revolution, 1637–1644: The Triumph of the Covenanters* (New York: St. Martin's Press, 1973). pp. 237–9. Rait, p. 528.

34. Lindley. p. 118.

35. Coates, Willson Havelock, 'The Journal of Sir Simonds D'Ewes' (New Haven: Yale University Press, 1942). p. 348.

36. Lindley, pp. 120–2.
37. ibid. pp. 123–5.
38. ibid. p. 131.
39. Braddick, p. 184.
40. Manning, p. 126.
41. Pearl, p. 227.
42. Kishlansky.
43. The chart tabulates only interventions recorded in the journals, excluding others (e.g. by the Speaker, the King, or colleagues) that did not occupy parliamentary time.
44. JL, vol. 4, pp. 694 and 712, 2 and 11 April 1642.
45. JC, vol. 3, p. 352. 25 December 1643.
46. JC, vol. 2, p. 26. 11 November 1640.
47. JL, vol. 4, p. 293, 29 June 1641.
48. JL, vol. 4, p. 308, 12 July 1641.
49. Bawcutt, N. W., 'The Control and Censorship of Caroline Drama: The Records of Sir Henry Herbert, Master of the Revels 1623–73', (Oxford: Oxford University Press, 1996). pp. 9–11. JC, vol. 2, pp. 64 and 100, 6 January and 9 March 1641.
50. Thrush, Andrew and John P. Ferris, *The House of Commons 1604–1629*, vol. 6, (Cambridge: Cambridge University Press, 2010). p. 415.
51. JC, vol. 1, p. 892, 5 May 1628.
52. Cust, Richard, 'Honour and Politics in Early Stuart England: The Case of Beaumont V. Hastings', *Past and Present,* 149 (1995). p. 76.
53. Lassiter, John C., 'Defamation of Peers: The Rise and Decline of the Action for Scandalum Magnatum, 1497–1773', *The American Journal of Legal History,* 22 (1978).
54. Stone, pp. 117–8. Stater, p. 287. Russell, p. 175.
55. Goodwin, Gordon, and Peacey, J. T., 'Howard, Henry Frederick, fifteenth earl of Arundel, fifth earl of Surrey, and second earl of Norfolk (1608–1652), nobleman,' *ODNB.* 'Historical Collections: July 1641 (2 of 2)', in *Historical Collections of Private Passages of State: vol. 4: 1640–42* (London: 1721), pp. 333–357. Russell. p. 165.
56. JL, vol. 4, p. 355. 9 August 1641.
57. JC, vol. 2, p. 404. 31 January 1642.
58. JC, vol. 2, pp. 404–5, 467. 31 January and 5 March 1642.
59. Scally, John J., 'The Rise and Fall of the Covenanter Parliaments, 1639–51', in *The History of the Scottish Parliament,* ed. by Keith M. Brown and Alastair J. Mann (Edinburgh: Edinburgh University Press, 2005).
60. Mann, Alastair J., 'House Rules: Parliamentary Procedure', in *The History of the Scottish Parliament,* ed. by Keith M. Brown and Alan R. MacDonald (Edinburgh: Edinburgh University Press, 2010). p. 149.
61. 'Procedure: Articles agreed for ordering the house of parliament', 19 July 1641. https://www.rps.ac.uk. Thanks to Gillian MacIntosh for this reference.

62. JC, vol. 3, p. 387, 3 February 1644.

63. JL, vol. 6, p. 405, 1 February 1644.

64. JC, vol. 3, pp. 716–7, 6 December 1644.

65. JC, vol. 4, p. 125, 28 April 1645.

66. JL, vol. 8, pp. 328, 335, 338. 25, 28–9 May 1646.

67. JL, vol. 8, p. 612, 15 December 1646.

68. JL, vol. 9, pp. 110, 116–7, 30 March and 1 April 1647.

69. Jennings. p. 612.

70. Wroughton, John, 'Hungerford, Sir Edward (1596–1648)', *ODNB*.

71. JC, vol. 2, p. 981. 27 February 1643.

72. Personal communication from Alison Wall, 4 March 2009.

73. JC, vol. 3, pp. 106–7. 27 May 1643.

74. JC, vol. 3, p. 185. 28 July 1643.

75. JC, vol. 3, p. 51. 18 April 1643 and JL, vol. 6, pp. 10–1. 18–9 April 1643.

76. Barber, Sarah, 'Marten, Henry (1601/2–1680)', *ODNB*. Purkiss, Diane, *The English Civil War: A People's History* (London: Harper, 2006). p. 117.

77. JC, vol. 4, p. 188. 28 June 1645.

78. Underdown. p. 69. See also Kishlansky. p. 633. JC, vol. 4, p. 400, 8 January 1646.

79. Whitaker, Lawrence, British Library, Diary of Lawrence Whitaker, Add. MS 31116,253

80. JC, vol. 5, p. 133, 2 April 1647. Steinmetz, Andrew, *The Romance of Duelling*, vol. I (London: Chapman and Hall, 1868). p. 35. Jennings. p. 641.

81. JC, vol. 5, p. 198. 4 June 1647.

82. JC, vol. 5, p. 359. 16 November 1647.

83. JL, vol. 10, pp. 46, 78, and 125. 17 and 15 February and 21 March 1648.

84. Stevenson, David, *Revolution and Counter-Revolution in Scotland, 1644–1651* (Edinburgh: John Donald, 2003). pp. 84.

85. JC, vol. 7., 2 February 1659, pp. 596–7. See also Rutt, John Towill, (ed), 'The Diary of Thomas Burton Esq.', vol. 3, (London: H. Coburn, 1828). pp. 33–45.

86. Drake, George A., 'Percy, Algernon, tenth earl of Northumberland (1602–1668)', *ODNB*. See also JC, vol. 3, p. 51, 17 April 1643 and JL, vol. 6, p. 11, 19 April 1943.

87. Pearl, p. 272.

88. Purkiss, pp. 280–1.

89. Braddick, p. 481.

90. ibid. pp. 487–8. JC, vol. 5, p. 118, 19 March 1647.

91. Braddick, pp. 497–500.

92. Macdonagh, pp. 218–9.

93. ibid. pp. 219–20. Braddick. p. 501.

94. Underdown, p. 115.

95. ibid. pp. 143–58.

96. Purkiss. p. 550.

97. ibid. p. 555. Underdown, p. 185.

98. It has been calculated that at the time of the Purge, radicals constituted only 15% of the Commons' 471 active MPs, the majority of whom were imprisoned (9%), secluded (40%), or voluntarily stayed away from the Rump (18%). Underdown. pp. 208–20.

99. Purkiss, p. 508.

100. Rogers, p. 63. JC, vol. 7, p. 209, 4 November 1652.

101. Stevenson. *Revolution*, pp. 110–5, 175–6, Scally. p. 161.

102. Jennings, pp. 90–1.

103. Russell, p. 386.

104. ibid. p. 390.

105. Gaunt, Peter, 'Cromwell's First Purge? Exclusions and the First Protectorate Parliament', *Parliamentary History*, 6 (1987); Egloff, Carol S., 'The Search for a Cromwellian Settlement. Exclusions from the Second Protectorate Parliament. Part 1: The Process and Its Architects', *Parliamentary History*, 17 (1998); Egloff, Carol S., 'The Search for a Cromwellian Settlement. Exclusions from the Second Protectorate Parliament. Part 2: The Excluded Members and the Reactions to the Exclusion', *Parliamentary History*, 17 (1998); Roberts, Stephen K., 'The House of Commons, 1640–60', in *A Short History of Parliament*, ed. by Clyve Jones (Woodbridge: Boydell Press, 2009). p. 118.

106. Underdown. pp. 348–51.

107. Gaunt. p. 1.

108. Harris, Tim, *London Crowds in the Reign of Charles II* (Cambridge: Cambridge University Press, 1987). p. 49.

4 Restoration and Revolution

1. Pennington, D. H., 'A Seventeenth-Century Perspective', in *The English Parliament in the Middle Ages,* ed. by R. G. Davies and J. H. Denton (Manchester: Manchester University Press, 1981). p. 198.

2. Simms, J. G., 'The Restoration, 1660–85', in *A New History of Ireland,* vol. 3, ed. by T. W. Moody, F. X. Martin, and F. J. Byrne (New York: Oxford University Press, 1993). p. 423.

3. MacIntosh, Gillian H., 'Arise King John: Commisioner Lauderdale and Parliament in the Restoration Era', in *The History of the Scottish Parliament,* ed. by Keith M. Brown and Alastair J. Mann (Edinburgh: Edinburgh University Press, 2005).

4. Tweeddale's devotion to parliamentary free speech was, in any case, somewhat contingent, for several years later he interrupted a colleague to assert that the latter's extended oration was intolerable, particularly as it was intended to persuade the three estates not to comply with the royal will. Rait. pp. 521–2. John R. Young, 'Hay, John, first marquess of Tweeddale (1626–1697)', *ODNB*.

5. 'Act for settling the orders in the parliament house', 13 May 1662. https://www.rps.ac.uk

6. Rait. p. 428. 'Parliamentary Minutes', 5 and 10 July 1672, https://www.rps.ac.uk

7. Harris, Tim, *Restoration: Charles II and His Kingdoms, 1660–85* (London: Penguin, 2005). p. 59.

8. Wood, Andy, *Riot, Rebellion and Popular Politics in Early Modern England* (Basingstoke: Palgrave, 2002). pp. 175–185.

9. Pincus, Steve, '"Coffee Politicians Does Create": Coffeehouses and Restoration Political Culture', *The Journal of Modern History*, 67 (1995).

10. Porter, Stephen, 'Coventry, Sir John,' *ODNB*.

11. JC, vol. 9, pp. 188–9, 9–14 January 1671. Jennings. p. 41.

12. Brown, Keith M., 'Gentlemen & Thugs in 17th-Century Britain', *History Today*, 40 (1990). p. 30.

13. Peltonen, Markku, *The Duel in Early Modern England: Civility, Politeness and Honour* (Cambridge: Cambridge University Press, 2003). pp. 206–8.

14. JC, vol. 8, p. 286, 1 July 1661.

15. JC, vol. 8, pp. 328–9, 9–10 December 1661.

16. JC, vol. 8, pp. 389 and 391, 18 and 20 March 1662.

17. JC, vol. 8, pp. 421, 425, 427, 5, 9, and 12 May 1662.

18. JC, vol. 8, p. 429, 14 May 1662.

19. JHOCKI, vol. 1, p. 577, 13 September 1662.

20. JL, vol. 9, pp. 536–8, 543–7, 12, 18, 26–7 June and 1–2 July 1663.

21. JC, vol. 8, pp. 516–8, 3–4 July 1663.

22. Henning, B. D., *The House of Commons, 1660-1690*, vol. 3 (London: Secker and Warburg, 1983). p. 422.

23. Grey, Anchitell, 'Grey's Debates of the House of Commons' (London: T. Becket and P. A. de Hondt, 1769). vol. 1, 18 March 1668, p. 118.

24. Kelly, James, *'That Damn'd Thing Called Honour': Duelling in Ireland 1570–1860*, (Cork: Cork University Press, 1995). p. 30.

25. JL, vol. 12, pp. 18–9, 22. 26, 29, and 31 October 1666.

26. Samuel Pepys, Robert Latham and William G. Matthews (eds.), *The Diary of Samuel Pepys*, vol. VII-1666, (Berkeley: University of California Press, 2000). pp. 414–5.

27. JL, vol. 12, pp. 52–3, 55. 19 and 22 December 1666.

28. JL, vol. 12, pp. 272–7 and 562–3, 23–26 November 1669 and 21–2 March 1673.

29. JL, vol. 12, p. 423. 8 February 1671.

30. JL, vol. 12, p. 658. 14 April 1675.

31. Holland, Barbara, *Gentlemen's Blood: A History of Dueling from Swords at Dawn to Pistols at Dusk* (New York: Bloomsbury, 2003). p. 9.

32. Henning, vol. 3, p. 632.

33. ibid. p. 110.

34. ibid. p. 447.

35. Grey. vol. 3, pp. 128–30. The second source is *Marvell's Epistles* p. 47, cited in the above. Henning. vol. 3, p. 447. Jennings. pp. 34–40, 646.

36. JC, vol. 9, pp. 361–3, 369, 20, 22 and 25 October and 8 November, 1675. Grey. vol. 3, pp. 291–3 and 337–41.

37. Macdonagh, pp. 238–40.

38. JC, vol. 9, p. 480, 10 May 1678.

39. JL, vol. 13, p. 358, 14 November 1678.

40. JC, vol. 9, p. 543, 21 November 1678. Grey's Debates of the House of Commons, vol. 6, pp. 254–60, 21 November 1678.

41. JL, vol. 13, p. 384, 27 November 1678.

42. Eagles, Robin, 'The House of Lords, 1660–1707', in *A Short History of Parliament*, ed. by Clyve Jones (Woodbridge: Boydell Press, 2009). p. 67.

43. Corish, Patrick J., 'The Cromwellian Regime, 1650–60', in *A New History of Ireland*, vol. 3, ed. by T. W. Moody, F. X. Martin, and F. J. Byrne (New York: Oxford University Press, 1993). p. 375.

44. Harris. *Restoration*, p. 192.

45. Jennings, p. 98.

46. Henning, B. D., *The House of Commons, 1660–1690*, vol. 2 (London: Secker and Warburg, 1983), p. 392.

47. ibid. pp. 146, 604.

48. Ibid. p. 234. Halliday, Paul D., 'Williams, Sir William, first baronet,' *ODNB*.

49. Harris. *Restoration*, p. 356.

50. Rait, p. 86. Young, John R., 'Hamilton, John, second Lord Belhaven and Stenton (1656–1708)', *ODNB*.

51. Rait. pp. 524–5.

52. 'Complaint against the earl of Caithness heard', 15 September 1681. https://www.rps.ac.uk

53. Harris, Tim, *Revolution: The Great Crisis of the British Monarchy, 1685–1720* (London: Penguin, 2006). pp. 97–100

54. Mann, Alastair J., 'James VII, King of the Articles: Political Management and Parliamentary Failure', in *The History of the Scottish Parliament*, ed. by Keith M. Brown and Alastair J. Mann (Edinburgh: Edinburgh University Press, 2005). pp. 200–2.

55. Harris. *Revolution*, pp. 158–63.

56. Pincus. *1668*.

57. ibid. pp. 282–6. Sachise, William L., 'The Mob and the Revolution of 1688', *Journal of British Studies*, IV (1964).

58. Harris. *Revolution*, pp. 389–94.

59. Mackenzie, p. 38.

60. Kemp, Betty, *King and Commons 1660–1832*, (Greenwood Press, 1957). p. 7.

61. Seaward, Paul, 'The House of Commons, 1660–1707', in *A Short History of Parliament*, ed. by Clyve Jones (Woodbridge: Boydell Press, 2009). pp. 126–7.

62. Toland, John, *The Danger of Mercenary Parliaments* (London, 1698). p. 3.

63. Namier, Lewis, *England in the Age of the American Revolution* (Macmillan, 1961). p. 4.

64. Higley, John and Michael Burton, 'Elite Settlements and the Taming of Politics', *Government and Opposition*, 33 (1998).

65. McGrath; Simms, J. G., 'The Case of Ireland Stated', in *The Irish Parliamentary Tradition*, ed. by Brian Farrell (Dublin: Gill and Macmillan, 1973).

66. Pincus. *1668*, p. 301.

67. JC, vol. 10. pp. 70, 124. 279, 28 March, 7 May, 4 November, 1689. JL, vol. 14, pp. 232, 350, 3 June, 22 November, 1689.

68. JC, vol. 10, pp. 348, 354–5. March 21, 24, and 25 1690.

69. JL, vol. 14, pp. 527–8, 532, 540.

70. JC, vol. 10, p. 806. 7 February 1693. JL, vol. 15, p. 236. 18 February 1693.

71. JC, vol. 11, pp. 135–6, 331, 448, 22 March 1694, 2 May 1695 and 13 February 1696.

72. Cruickshanks, Eveline, Stuart Handley, and D. W. Hayton, *The House of Commons 1690–1715*, vol. 4 (London: Cambridge University Press, 2002). p. 379.

73. Hopkins, Paul, 'Fenwick, Sir John, third baronet (*c.*1644–1697)', *ODNB*. JC, vol. 11, p. 581, 9 November 1696.

74. Cruickshanks, Handley, and Hayton. p. 89.

75. JL, vol. 16, p. 378, 9 February 1699.

76. Cruickshanks, Eveline, Stuart Handley, and D. W. Hayton, *The House of Commons 1690–1715*, vol. 5 (London: Cambridge University Press, 2002). p. 363.

77. JC, vol. 13, p. 90, 21 December 1699.

78. JC, vol. 15, pp. 405–6, 17 November 1707.

79. JC, vol. 13, pp. 444, 540, 28 March and 14 May 1701; vol. 14, p. 115; 15 January 1703; vol. 15, p. 622, 20 March 1708; vol. 16, pp. 49, 288, 346 and 458, 16 December, 1708, 31 January and 4 March 1710, and 16 January 1711. JL, vol. 17, pp. 188, 248 and 524, 10 December, 1702, 19 January, 1703 and 24 March 1704; vol. 19, pp. 138, 745–6, 1 April, 1710, 5 July 1714.

80. JC, vol. 16, p. 562, 19 March 1711.

81. Cruickshanks, Eveline, Stuart Handley, and D. W. Hayton, *The House of Commons 1690-1715*, vol. 3, p. 684.

82. ibid. p. 1000.

83. Mackay, Charles, *Extraordinary Popular Delusions and the Madness of Crowds* (New York: Barnes & Noble, 1989 [1841]). pp. 680–1.

84. Handley, Stuart, 'Wrey, Sir Bourchier, fourth baronet (*c.*1653–1696)', *ODNB*.

85. Cruickshanks, Handley, and Hayton, vol. 3, p. 162.

86. Cruickshanks, Handley, and Hayton, vol. 5, p. 191.

87. Cruickshanks, Handley, and Hayton, vol. 4, p. 138.

88. Cruickshanks, Handley, and Hayton, vol. 5, p. 9.

89. ibid. p. 928.

90. Cruickshanks, Handley, and Hayton, vol. 3, p. 890.

91. [anon], *A True Account of What Passed at the Old-Bailey, May the 18th, 1711. Relating to the Tryal of Richard Thornhill, Esq; Indicted for the Murder of Sir Cholmley Deering, Bart.*, Second Edition Corrected edn (London: John Morphew, 1711). Cruickshanks, Handley, and Hayton, vol. 3, p. 874.

92. *The Works of Jonathan Swift* (Edinburgh: Archibald Constable, 1824), 'Journal to Stella,' p. 335.

93. Stater.

94. Mackay, p. 683.

95. Cruickshanks, Handley, and Hayton, vol. 3, p. 22.

96. Rait, p. 301.

97. Brown, Keith M., 'Party Politics and Parliament: Scotland's Last Election and Its Aftermath, 1702–3', in The History of the Scottish Parliament, ed. by Keith M. Brown and Alastair J. Mann (Edinburgh: Edinburgh University Press, 2005). p. 273.

98. Young, John R., 'Hamilton, John, second Lord Belhaven and Stenton (1656–1708)', ODNB. 'Procedure: Members pardoned,' 30 June 1703. https://www.rps.ac.uk

99. Rait. pp. 514–5. Patrick, Derek John, 'Stewart, Alexander, fifth Lord Blantyre (d. 1704)', ODNB. 'Procedure: Member disciplined,' 13 August 1703. https://www.rps.ac.uk

100. Stephen, Leslie and Lee, Sidney, eds. *Dictionary of National Biography* (New York: Macmillan, 1908), vol. 7, p. 295.

101. Robertson, John, 'Fletcher, Andrew, of Saltoun (1653?–1716)', ODNB.

102. Bowie, Karin, *Scottish Public Opinion and the Anglo–Scottish Union, 1699–1707* (Woodbridge: Boydell Press, 2007). pp. 34–5.

103. Rait. pp. 412–3.

104. Whatley, Christopher A. and Derek J. Patrick, *The Scots and the Union* (Edinburgh: Edinburgh University Press, 2006). pp. 9–10.

105. Bowie. p. 115.

106. ibid. p. 140.

107. ibid. p. 141.

108. ibid. p. 132.

109. ibid. p. 141.

110. Whatley and Patrick. pp. 277–8.

111. Bowie, p. 165.

112. JC, vol. 11, pp. 682–4, 29 January 1697.

113. JC, vol. 11, p. 749, 20 March 1697. Cruickshanks, Handley, and Hayton, col. 3, p. 253.

114. Gilmour, p. 50.

115. Simms, J. G., 'The Establishment of Protestant Ascendancy, 1691–1714', in A New History of Ireland, vol. 4, ed. by T. W. Moody and W. E. Vaughan (New York: Oxford University Press, 1986). p. 27.

116. Plumb, J. H., *The Growth of Political Stability in England 1675–1725* (Macmillan, 1967); Plumb, J. H., 'The Growth of the Electorate in England from 1600 to 1715', *Past and Present*, 45 (1969).

5 From Walpole to Wilkes

1. Shoemaker, Robert, *The London Mob: Violence and Disorder in Eighteenth-Century England* (London: Hambledon Continuum, 2004), p. 111.

2. Field. p. 139. JC, vol. 18, p. 653, 4 December 1717.

3. JHOCKI, vol. 3, p. 131, 17 September 1717.

4. Langford, Paul, 'The Eighteenth Century (1688–1789)', in *The Oxford History of Britain,* vol. 4, (Oxford: Oxford University Press, 1992). pp. 5–7.

5. Pearce, Edward, *The Great Man: Sir Robert Walpole: Scoundrel, Genius and Britain's First Prime Minister* (London: Pimlico, 2007). p. 207.

6. JC, vol. 18, p. 408, 21 March 1716; vol. 19, pp. 109–10, 21 February 1719. JL, vol. 21, p. 84, 2 March 1719. For the challenge, see JC, vol. 19, p. 129, 12 March 1719,

7. Robbins, Caroline, *The Eighteenth-Century Commonwealthman* (Cambridge: Harvard University Press, 1959). p. 272.

8. JC, vol. 19, p. 330, 5 April 1720. JC, vol. 21, p. 148, 3 May 1728. JC, vol. 21, p. 171, 20 May 1728. JC, vol. 21, p. 796, 11 February 1732. JC, vol. 22, p. 92, 16 March 1733. JC, vol. 24, p. 460, 8 March 1743. JC, vol. 25, p. 720, 7 February 1749. JC, vol. 25, p. 797, 16 March 1749. JC, vol. 26, p. 194, 24 April 1751. JL, vol. 28, 18 April 1753, p. 101. JL, vol. 29, 30 May 1753, p. 347. Sedgwick. pp. 21, 497.

9. JC, vol. 29, pp. 675, 976, 24 November 1763 and 22 March 1764; JL, vol. 31, 10 December 1766, p. 448; and JC, vol. 31, p. 618, 18 February 1768.

10. Sabine, Lorenzo, *Notes on Duels and Duelling* (Boston: Crosby, Nichols & Co., 1855)., p. 79.

11. Peltonen. pp. 211–2.

12. Sedgwick. pp. 435–6. Thomas, P.D.G., *The House of Commons in the Eighteenth Century* (Oxford: Oxford University Press, 1971). pp. 6–7.

13. Jennings. p. 112.

14. Foord, Archibald S., *His Majesty's Opposition* (New York: Oxford University Press, 1964). pp. 151–7.

15. Atherton, Herbert M., *Political Prints in the Age of Hogarth* (London: Oxford University Press, 1974). pp. 259–61.

16. Kramnick, Isaac, *Bolingbroke and His Circle* (Harvard University Press, 1968). Bolingbroke, 'A Dissertation Upon Parties', in *Works* (Philadelphia: Carey & Hart, 1841).

17. Browning, Reed, 'Hervey, John, second Baron Hervey of Ickworth (1696–1743)', *ODNB*.

18. Sedgwick. pp. 21, 497.

19. Rogers, Nicholas, *Whigs and Cities: Popular Politics in the Age of Walpole and Pitt* (Oxford: Oxford University Press, 1989). p. 54.

20. Rudé, George, *Hanoverian London, 1714–1808* (Berkeley: University of California Press, 1971). p. 151.

21. Jennings, p. 117.

22. Pearce, p. 312.

23. JC, vol. 22, p. 115, 12 April 1733.

24. Pearce, p. 313.

25. Rudé. *Hanoverian London,* p. 209.

26. ibid. p. 153.

27. ibid. p. 210.

28. Field, p. 37.
29. Hopton, Richard, *Pistols at Dawn: A History of Duelling* (London: Piatkus Books, 2007). pp. 215–6. Philip Woodfine, 'Walpole, Horatio, first Baron Walpole of Wolterton (1678–1757)', *ODNB*.
30. JC, vol. 24, p. 460, 8 March 1743.
31. Kelly, pp. 130–1. Jennings, pp. 652–3.
32. Kelly, pp. 128–9.
33. ibid. p. 69.
34. ibid. 106–12. Atherton. p. 60. *Gentleman's Magazine and Historical Review*, vol. 43, 1773, pp. 95–7. Gilchrist, James, *A Brief Display of the Origin and History of Ordeals...*, (London: Bulmer and Nicol, 1821), pp. 105–6.
35. McDowell, R. B., 'Colonial Nationalism and the Winning of Parliamentary Independence, 1760–82', in *A New History of Ireland*, vol. 4, ed. by T. W. Moody and W. E. Vaughan (New York: Oxford University Press, 1986)., p. 196.
36. Murphy, Sean, 'Charles Lucas and the Dublin Election of 1748–9', *Parliamentary History*, 2 (1983); McCracken, J. L., 'Protestant Ascendancy and the Rise of Colonial Nationalism, 1714–60', in *A New History of Ireland*, vol. 4, ed. by T. W. Moody and W. E. Vaughan (New York: Oxford University Press, 1986). p. 118. JHOCKI, vol. 5, p. 14, 16 October 1749.
37. Porritt, Edward and Annie G. Porritt, *The Unreformed House of Commons*, vol. 2 (Cambridge: Cambridge University Press, 1903). p. 438.
38. Murphy, Sean, 'The Dublin Anti-Union Riot of 3 December 1759', in *Parliament, Politics and People: Essays in Eighteenth-Century Irish History*, ed. by Gerard O'Brien (Blackrock: Irish Academic Press, 1989). pp. 50–4.
39. JHOCKI, vol. 6, pp. 155–6, 24 and 26 November 1759.
40. Murphy., pp. 54–6. Smyth, Jim, *The Men of No Property: Irish Radicals and Popular Politics in the Late Eighteenth Century* (New York: St. Martin's Press, 1992), p. 129. Jennings. p. 653.
41. Gilmour, p. 288.
42. ibid. p. 291.
43. Rogers, p. 122.
44. Rudé. *Hanoverian London*, p. 211.
45. Jennings, p. 120.
46. Rogers, p. 134.
47. Gilmour, p. 304.
48. Sainsbury, John, '"Cool Courage Should Always Mark Me": John Wilkes and Duelling', *Journal of the Canadian Historical Society*, 7 (1996), pp. 20–4. Cash, Arthur H., *John Wilkes: The Scandalous Father of Civil Liberties* (New Haven: Yale University Press, 2006), pp. 82–5.
49. Cash. pp. 98–100.
50. ibid. pp. 100–23. Rudé, George, *Wilkes and Liberty* (London: Oxford University Press, 1962), pp. 21–9.
51. Cash, pp. 138–40.
52. ibid. pp. 143–53.

Notes

53. ibid. p. 80, 153.
54. ibid. pp. 153–6, 167. Sainsbury, pp. 26–31. Gilmour, p. 309. Steinmetz, pp. 317–21. Edward Walford, 'Hyde Park', in *Old and New London:* Vol. 4 (London: Cassell, Petter & Gilpin, 1878), pp. 375–405.
55. Namier, Sir Lewis and John Brooke, *The House of Commons 1754–1790*, vol. 2 (London: Her Majesty's Stationary Office, 1964). p. 546. JC, vol. 29, p. 675, 24 November 1763.
56. Namier and Brooke, p. 528.
57. Cash. pp. 159–60.
58. ibid. p. 161.
59. Gilmour, pp. 253, 311. Stevenson, John, *Popular Disturbances in England, 1700–1832*, 2nd edn (London: Longman, 1992). pp. 83–4, 152. Langford, Paul, *A Polite and Commercial People: England 1727–1783* (London: Guild Publishing, 1989), p. 455.
60. Cash, pp. 196–8. Sainsbury, p. 32.
61. Cash, p. 223. Rudé, *Wilkes*, pp. 49–53.
62. Langford, p. 96. *The Scots Magazine*, vol. 32, 1770, p. 106.
63. Cash, p. 251.
64. ibid. p. 252. Rudé, *Wilkes*, pp. 57–65.
65. Cash, pp. 252–4. Rudé, *Wilkes*, pp. 68–73.
66. Cash. p. 254.
67. Harris, Bob, 'The House of Commons, 1701–1800', in *A Short History of Parliament*, ed. by Clyve Jones (Woodbridge: Boydell Press, 2009). p. 188.
68. Pole, J. R., *Political Representation in England and the Origin of the American Revolution* (New York: St. Martin's Press, 1966). p. 387.
69. See, for example, JC, vol. 21, p. 238, 26 February 1728 and vol. 29, p. 207, 3 March 1762.
70. Rudé, *Wilkes*, pp. 155–9.
71. JC, vol. 33, p. 285, 25 March 1771.
72. Rudé, *Wilkes*, pp. 162–4, Rudé, *Hanoverian London*, p. 218. Gilmour. p. 324.
73. Rudé, *Wilkes*, p. 165.
74. Hilton, Boyd, *A Mad, Bad, and Dangerous People?* (Oxford: Oxford University Press, 2006). p. 51.
75. Mackenzie. p. 61–2.
76. Langford. p. 721.

6 Heyday of the Fire Eaters

1. Rudé, *Hanoverian London*, pp. 219–20.
2. Langford. p. 550.
3. Stevenson. *Popular Disturbances*, pp. 95–6.
4. Gilmour. p. 349.
5. Stevenson. *Popular Disturbances*, p. 97.
6. Gilmour. p. 349.
7. ibid. p. 350.

8. Jennings. p. 52.
9. Gilmour. p. 350.
10. Stevenson. *Popular Disturbances*, p. 97.
11. Rudé, *Hanoverian London*, p. 50.
12. Stevenson. *Popular Disturbances*, p. 99.
13. Gilmour. p. 352.
14. Stevenson. *Popular Disturbances*, p. 100.
15. Gilmour. pp. 352–3.
16. Rudé, *Hanoverian London*, p. 222.
17. Stevenson. *Popular Disturbances*, p. 102.
18. Webb, R. K., *Modern England* (New York: Harper & Row, 1968), p. 94.
19. Langford. p. 721.
20. Gilmour. p. 340.
21. Rudé, *Hanoverian London*, pp. 226–7.
22. Gilmour. p. 370.
23. Hague, William, *William Pitt the Younger* (London: Harper Perennial, 2004), p. 166. Gilmour. p. 379. Stevenson. *Popular Disturbances*, p. 206.
24. Gilmour. p. 385.
25. ibid. p. 410. Hague. p. 370.
26. Gilmour. p. 410.
27. Stevenson. *Popular Disturbances*, p. 216.
28. Gilmour. p. 411. Stevenson. pp. 216–7.
29. Gilmour. p. 423. Stevenson. *Popular Disturbances*, p. 218.
30. Smyth. p. 132.
31. *The Scots Magazine*, vol. 41, Edinburgh, 1779, pp. 608–9. Smyth, pp. 121, 131–3.
32. ibid. pp. 136–7.
33. Smyth, James, 'Dublin's Political Underground in the 1790s', in *Parliament, Politics and People: Essays in Eighteenth-Century Irish History*, ed. by Gerard O'Brien (Blackrock: Irish Academic Press, 1989). pp. 137–8. Smyth, *Men of No Property*, pp. 128, 142, 149–50. McDowell, pp. 341–3.
34. Gilmour, p. 268.
35. Shoemaker, Robert B., 'The Taming of the Duel: Masculinity, Honour and Ritual Violence in London, 1660–1800', *The Historical Journal*, 45 (2002).
36. Kiernan, V. G., *The Duel in European History* (Oxford: Oxford University Press, 1989). pp. 59, 101.
37. *The Times*, 27 May 1789, p. 3.
38. Freeman, Joanne B., *Affairs of Honor: National Politics in the New Republic* (New Haven: Yale University Press, 2001). p. 180.
39. Kelly, pp. 104–5. Jennings. pp. 650–1.
40. Jennings, p. 650.
41. ibid. p. 166.
42. Shoemaker. *London Mob*, p. 263. *The Gentleman's Magazine and Historical Chronicle*, vol. 49, 1779, p. 610.

43. Fry, Michael, 'Fullarton, William, of Fullarton,' *ODNB*. Clarke, *The Georgian Era: Memoirs of the Most Eminent Persons Who Have Flourished in Great Britain*, vol. 1, (London: Vizetelly, Branston and co., 1832), p. 333.

44. Cannon, John, 'Petty, William, second earl of Shelburne and first marquess of Lansdowne (1737–1805)', *ODNB*.

45. Thomas, p. 7.

46. JC, vol. 36, p. 995, 26 May 1778.

47. JL, vol. 36, 3, 6, 16–7 November 1780, pp. 178, 188–91, 195–7.

48. JC, vol. 38, 22 June 1781, p. 535.

49. Jennings, pp. 134–5. Namier and Brooke, p. 53.

50. *The European Magazine and London Review*, vol. 13, January to June 1788, p. 442.

51. Namier, Sir Lewis and John Brooke, *The House of Commons 1754–1790*, vol. 3 (London: Her Majesty's Stationary Office, 1964), pp. 376–8.

52. Thorne, Roland, 'Maitland, James, eighth earl of Lauderdale (1759–1839)', *ODNB*.

53. *The Times*, 3 July 1792, p. 4.

54. O'Gorman, Frank, *The Emergence of the British Two-Party System 1760–1832*, (London: Edward Arnold, 1982), p. 31. Hilton. p. 94.

55. Hague. pp. 424–6. J.P. W. Ehrman and Anthony Smith, 'Pitt, William [known as Pitt the younger]', *ODNB*.

56. George, M. Dorothy, *English Political Caricature*, vol. 2 (London: Oxford University Press, 1959), p. 39.

57. Kiernan p. 190.

58. Hopton, p. 236.

59. *The Times*, 31 May 1798, p. 2 and 6 June 1798, p. 2.

60. Gatrell, Vic, *City of Laughter: Sex and Satire in Eighteenth Century London* (London: Atlantic Books, 2006). pp. 452–3.

61. Kelly. *Damn'd Thing*.

62. ibid. Hayton, D. W., 'Voters, Patrons and Parties: Parliamentary Elections in Ireland, C. 1692–1727', *Parliamentary History*, 24 (2005).

63. Porritt and Porritt, p. 414.

64. JHOCKI, vol. 9, pp. 401–2, 28 January 1778.

65. Kelly, James, 'Flood, Henry (1732–1791)', *ODNB*.

66. Kelly. *Damn'd Thing*, pp. 134–7.

67. Kelly, James, 'Parsons, Lawrence, second earl of Rosse (1758–1841)', *ODNB*.

68. Kelly. *Damn'd Thing*, p. 145. Fitzpatrick, Samuel A. Ossory, *Dublin: A Historical and Topographical Account of the City* (New York: E. P. Dutton and Co., 1907). p. 206.

69. *The Times*, 23 August 1785, p. 4.

70. *The Times*, 12 April 1790, p. 2. Kelly, James, 'Curran, John Philpot', *ODNB*.

71. McDowell, pp. 324–5. Kelly, pp. 203–5. *The Parliamentary Register, or History of the Proceedings and Debates of the House of Commons of Ireland*, vol. XII, (Dublin: P. Byrne and J. Moore, 1793). pp. 202, 232–3.

72. Wilkinson, David, 'Fitzwilliam, William Wentworth, second Earl Fitzwilliam in the peerage of Great Britain, and fourth Earl Fitzwilliam in the peerage of Ireland (1748–1833)', *ODNB*.

73. Johnston–Liik, E. M. 'Corry, Isaac (1753–1813)', *ODNB*.

74. *The Times*, 22 February 1800, p 3.

75. *Caledonian Mercury* (Edinburgh), 1 March, 1800.

76. Hunt, p. 44.

77. Jennings, p. 651.

78. A gallery would have to be set aside for the adjustment of parliamentary affairs of honour. 'The differences arising from a debate are to be decided the following day, before the Chaplain enters to read prayers. When they are over, he will be at hand, and at leisure to bury the dead.' Procedures also would have to be changed. Since Members could speak only once on a given question, they would be restricted to one duel on it as well. In committee, where speaking more than once per question was allowed, 'each member will be allowed to fight as often as he has spoken'. Peers, who could vote by proxy, would be allowed to fight duels in the same manner. *The Times*, 6 March 1800, p. 3.

7 *Reform or Revolution?*

1. Hopton. p. 231.

2. *The Times*, 25 January 1802, p. 3.

3. Thorne, R. G., *The House of Commons 1790–1820*, vol. 3 (London: Secker & Warburg, 1986), p. 95.

4. ibid., p. 260. This was not Brogden's first affair of honour. Almost a decade earlier the MP had been arrested to keep the peace, after a complaint that he intended to fight a duel as a result of a dispute 'respecting politics', that had arisen a few days earlier at a coffee house. *The Times*, 29 March 1798, p. 3.

5. Campbell, John, *Pistols at Dawn: Two Hundred Years of Political Rivalry, from Pitt and Fox to Blair and Brown* (London: Jonathan Cape, 2009), pp. 69, 73. Webster, C. K., H. Temperly, and E. Cooke, 'The Duel between Castlereagh and Canning in 1809', *Cambridge Historical Journal*, 3 (1929). *The Times*, 10 October 1809, p. 2. See also *The Times*, 2 October, 1809, p. 3.

6. Hunt, p. 154.

7. Thorne, R. G., *The House of Commons 1790–1820*, vol. 4 (London: Secker & Warburg, 1986). p. 848. JC, vol. 65, pp. 134, 136, 27 February and 1 March, 1810. Hansard HC Deb 27 February 1810, vol. 15, cc641–2.

8. JC, vol. 68, p. 410, 13 April 1813. The disagreement arose during discussion of the Irish Estimates. Kelly. Damn'd Thing, p. 242.

9. Thorne, vol. 3, p. 575. JC, vol. 70, p. 129, 1 March 1815.

10. Kelly, *Damn'd Thing*, pp. 243–4.

11. *The Times*, 9 September 1815, p. 3.

12. Kelly, *Damn'd Thing*, pp. 245–6.

13. *The Times*, 6 December 1815, p. 2.

14. McCord, James N., Jr., 'Politics and Honor in Early-Nineteenth-Century England: The Duke's Duel', *Huntington Library Quarterly*, 62 (2000), p. 95.

15. ibid. p. 100.

16. Houfe, Simon R., 'Buckingham Versus Bedford: The Kensington Duel', *Bedfordshire Magazine*, 9 (1964), pp. 225–6.

17. *The Times*, 3 May 1822, p. 6.

18. At issue, apparently, was O'Grady's inconsistency: he voted for an Irish tithes leasing bill and then, less than a week later, voting for an inquiry into the tithes. *The Times*, 6 July, 1822, p. 3. Fisher, D. R., *The House of Commons 1820–1832*, vol. 5 (Cambridge: Cambridge University Press, 2009), p. 396.

19. Fisher, ibid. p. 5. JC, vol. 77, p. 423, 12 July 1822.

20. Sieveking, A. Forbes, 'Duelling and Militarism', *Transactions of the Royal Historical Society*, 11 (1917). pp. 181–2, 'The Speeches of the Right Honourable George Canning: With a Memoir of his Life,' Roger Therry, ed., vol. 1, James Ridgway, London, 1836, pp. 135–7. HC Deb 17 April 1823 vol. 8 cc1070–106. JC, vol. 78, p 224, 17 April 1823. Jennings, pp. 233–4.

21. Thorne, R. G., *The House of Commons, 1790–1820*, vol. 1, London, Secker & Warburg, 1986, p. 421.

22. *The Gentleman's Magazine*, vol. 80, Part 1 (London: John Nichols and Son, 1810), pp. 376, 569–70.

23. Gatrell, p. 74.

24. Stevenson. *Popular Disturbances*, pp. 231–3. Hindley, pp. 299–300.

25. Baer, Marc, 'Burdett, Francis, fifth baronet', *ODNB*.

26. Rudé. *Crowd*, p. 90.

27. Jennings, pp. 284–5. JC, vol. 79, p. 483, 11 June 1824.

28. Linklater, Andro, *Why Spencer Perceval Had to Die* (New York: Walker & Co., 2012).

29. Thompson, E. P., *The Making of the English Working Class* (New York: Random House, 1963), p. 570.

30. JC, vol. 70, p. 144, 6 March 1815.

31. Stevenson. *Popular Disturbances*, p. 236.

32. Thorne, R. G., *The House of Commons 1790–1820*, vol. 5 (London: Secker & Warburg, 1986), pp. 278–96.

33. Stevenson. *Popular Disturbances*, pp. 237–8.

34. Stevenson, John, 'The Queen Caroline Affair', in *London in the Age of Reform*, ed. by John Stevenson (Oxford: Blackwell, 1977), p. 122.

35. ibid. p. 126.

36. Jennings, p. 186.

37. Stevenson. 'Queen Caroline', pp. 130–1.

38. Fisher, D. R., *The House of Commons 1820–1832*, vol. 2 (Cambridge: Cambridge University Press, 2009), p. 488.

39. Stevenson. Queen Caroline, p. 142.

40. Shoemaker. *London Mob*, p. 152.

41. Tilly, Charles, 'Parliamentarization of Popular Contention in Great Britain, 1758–1834', *Theory and Society*, 26 (1997). Tilly, Charles, *Popular Contention in Great Britain, 1758–1834* (Cambridge: Harvard University Press, 1995). Tilly, Charles, 'Contentious Repertoires in Great Britain, 1758–1834', *Social Science History*, 17 (1993).

42. Jupp, Peter, *The Governing of Britain, 1688–1848* (London: Routledge, 2006), pp. 251–2.

43. Stevenson. *Popular Disturbances*, p. 288.

44. Connolly, S. J., 'Union Government, 1812–23', in *A New History of Ireland*, vol. 5, ed. by W. E. Vaughan (Oxford: Oxford University Press, 1989), pp. 72–3.

45. Connolly, S. J., 'Mass Politics and Sectarian Conflict, 1823–30', in *A New History of Ireland*, vol. 5, ed. by W. E. Vaughan (Oxford: Oxford University Press, 1989), pp. 84–7, 98–9.

46. ibid. p. 103.

47. Hurd, Douglas, *Robert Peel* (London: Phoenix, 2007). pp. 120–2.

48. *The Times*, 23 March 1829, p. 5.

49. Baldick, Robert, *The Duel: A History of Duelling* (London: Chapman & Hall, 1965), pp. 104–5.

50. *The Times*, 24 March 1829, p. 2.

51. *The Times*, 31 March 1829, p. 4.

52. Fisher, D. R., *The House of Commons 1820–1832*, vol. 3 (Cambridge: Cambridge University Press, 2009), p. 691.

53. Davis, Richard P., 'O'Brien, William Smith', *ODNB*. Less than two years later, O'Brien would fight another political, though evidently not parliamentary, duel, with W. R. Mahon. Fisher, vol. 6, p. 309 and vol. 7, p. 149.

54. Cannon, John, *Parliamentary Reform, 1640–1832* (Cambridge: Cambridge U. Press, 1972). Veitch, George S., *The Genesis of Parliamentary Reform* (Archon Books, 1965). Foord, Archibald S., 'The Waning of "The Influence of the Crown"', *English Historical Review*, 62 (1947).

55. O'Farrell, John, *An Utterly Impartial History of Britain: Or 2000 Years of Upper-Class Idiots in Charge* (London: Doubleday, 2007), p. 302.

56. Wyvill, Christopher, *A State of the Representation of the People of England on the Principles of Mr. Pitt in 1785* (York: W. Blanchard, 1793).

57. Tilly. *Popular Contention*, p. 312.

58. Hamburger, Joseph, *James Mill and the Art of Revolution*, vol. 8 (New Haven: Yale University Press, 1963).

59. O'Gorman, Frank, *Voters, Patrons, and Parties: The Unreformed Electoral System of Hanoverian England 1734–1832* (Oxford: Oxford University Press, 1989), p. 310.

60. Evans, Eric J., *Political Parties in Britain: 1783–1867* (London: Methuen, 1985), p. 23.

61. Fraser, Antonia, *Perilous Question: The Drama of the Great Reform Bill 1832* (London: Weidenfeld & Nicolson, 2013), pp. 43–4.

62. George, p. 239.

63. Fraser, *Perilous Question*, pp. 106–8.
64. Hansard HL Deb 22 April 1831 vol. 3 cc1805–11.
65. Lloyd, E. M. and Heesom, A. J., 'Vane [Stewart], Charles William, third marquess of Londonderry (1778–1854)', *ODNB*.
66. *The Times*, 23 April 1831, p. 4.
67. Beckett, John, 'The Nottingham Reform Bill Riots of 1831', *Parliamentary History*, 24 (2005). Stevenson. p. 291. Gaunt, Richard, 'The Fourth Duke of Newcastle, the "Mob" and Election Contests in Nottinghamshire, 1818–1832', *Midland History*, 33 (2008), p. 198.
68. Fraser, *Perilous Question*, p. 166.
69. ibid. pp. 151–2. Hamburger, pp. 147–54. Fisher, vol. 5, p. 708.
70. Amey, Geoffrey, *City under Fire: The Bristol Riots and Aftermath* (Guildford: Lutterworth Press, 1979). p. 14.
71. Beckett, J. V., 'Aristocrats and Electoral Control in the East Midlands, 1660–1914', *Midland History*, 18 (1993), p. 77.
72. Fraser. *Perilous Question*, pp. 160–1.
73. ibid. pp. 170–2.
74. ibid. pp. 155, 173–4. Amey, p. 31.
75. Redlich, p. 139.
76. Fraser, *Perilous Question*, pp. 167–8.
77. Amey, pp. 100–1.
78. *The Times*, 3 February 1832, p. 2.
79. *The Times*, 4 February 1832, p. 2.
80. Fraser, p. 206.
81. Hilton, p. 426.
82. Fraser, *Perilous Question*, p. 265. *The Times*, 19 June 1832, p. 3. *The Manchester Guardian*, 23 June 1832, p. 2.

8 The Lull

1. McCord, pp. 89–90.
2. JL, vol. 64, pp. 387–9. 17 July 1832.
3. JC, vol. 89, 5 February 1834, pp. 9, 11. Jennings. p. 227.
4. JC, vol. 91, 10–13 June 1836, pp. 464, 466–8.
5. JC, vol. 91, 17 June 1836, pp. 484–5.
6. JC, vol. 92, 17 April 1837, p. 270.
7. MacDonagh, Oliver, 'Politics, 1830–45', in *A New History of Ireland*, vol. 5, ed. by W. E. Vaughan (Oxford: Oxford University Press, 1989), pp. 169, 185.
8. A. F. Pollard, 'Ruthven, Edward Southwell (1772?–1836)', rev. Peter Gray, *ODNB*.
9. Kelly, *Damn'd Thing*, p. 267.
10. *The Times*, 1 December 1835, p. 3.
11. *The Times*, 20 April 1835, p. 2.
12. This was not the first time the club found itself involved in an affair of honour. George 'Fighting' Fitzgerald, a notorious 'fire-eater', forced his way into

Brooks's by warning that, if blackballed, he would challenge each member of the committee. Simpson, Antony E., 'Dandelions on the Field of Honor: Dueling, the Middle Classes, and the Law in Nineteenth-Century England', *Criminal Justice History*, 9 (1988), p. 113.

13. *The Times*, 5 May 1835, p. 4. The duel was criticised not only because a son faced death for the actions of his father but also because O'Connell mistakenly fired before instructed to do so. However, instead of allowing Alvanley to fire in reply, or forcing O'Connell to fire his next shot in the air, the seconds allowed the principals to proceed as if O'Connell had not fired at all. See *The Times* 6 May 1835, p. 2, and 7 May 1835, p. 5. This led to further complaints a few years later, when O'Connell's second, who was seen to be primarily to blame for the violation of dueling protocol, received a valuable diplomatic posting. *The Times*, 16 March 1838, p. 4 and 23 March 1838, p. 4.

14. *The Times*, 6 May 1835, p. 3.

15. Temperly, Howard, 'The O'Connell–Stevenson Contretemps: A Reflection of the Anglo–American Slavery Issue', *The Journal of Negro History*, 47 (1962). *The Times*, 15 August 1838, p. 6, 30 October 1838, p. 5, and 26 December 1838, p. 5.

16. *The Times*, 15 June 1839, p. 6.

17. *The Times*, 30 August 1839.

18. *The Times*, 10 September 1839, p. 4.

19. *The Times*, 17 January 1840, p. 5. *Caledonian Mercury* (Edinburgh) 20 January 1840. Boase, G. C. and Matthew, H. C. G., 'Horsman, Edward', *ODNB*. Seitz, Don C., *Famous American Duels* (Freeport, NY: Books for Libraries, 1966 [1929]), p. 16.

20. Kent, Charles and Matthew, H. C. G. Matthew, 'Berkeley, Craven Fitzhardinge (1805–1855)', *ODNB*.

21. Simpson. pp. 137–9.

22. See, for example, *The Times*, 29 February 1844, p. 4, 4 March 1844, p. 6 and 16 November 1825, p. 2.

23. Steinmetz. p. 39.

24. Dabhoiwala, Faramerz, 'The Construction of Honour, Reputation and Status in Late Seventeenth- and Early Eighteenth-Century England', *Transactions of the Royal Historical Society*, 6 (1996), pp. 212–3. Shoemaker, *London Mob*, pp. 60–75.

25. Kiernan, p. 120.

26. Banks, Stephen, 'Killing with Courtesy: The English Duelist, 1785–1845', *Journal of British Studies*, 47 (2008). p. 544.

27. Simpson, p. 140.

28. Shoemaker. *London Mob*, p. 174.

29. Emsley, Clive, *Hard Men: The English and Violence since 1750* (London: Hambledon Continuum, 2005), pp. 12, 75.

30. The help, particularly if possessing darker pigmentation, also may have been an exception: in mid-Victorian India, hotels reportedly felt compelled to post signs stating, 'Gentlemen are earnestly requested not to strike the servants'.

Cunningham, Hugh, *The Challenge of Democracy* (Harlow: Longman, 2001), p. 184. Yet even this suggests that upper-class behaviour once condoned had become unacceptable.

31. Banks, pp. 549–50.

32. *The Times*, 10 March 1786, p. 3, and 22 September 1790, p. 2. Gilmour. p. 276.

33. *The Times*, 6 October 1841, p. 4.

34. *The Times*, 28 July 1806, p. 3, and 30 July 1806, p. 3.

35. Landale, James, *Duel: A True Story of Death and Honour* (Edinburgh: Canongate, 2005), pp. 271–2.

36. Holland, p. 74.

37. LaVaque-Manty, Mika, 'Dueling for Equality: Masculine Honor and the Modern Politics of Dignity', *Political Theory*, 34 (2006).

38. *The Times*, 24 March 1835, pp. 3–4.

39. *The Times*, 21 November 1835, p. 5. See also, *The Manchester Guardian*, 28 November, 1835, p. 2.

40. *The Times*, 9 September 1841, p. 4 and 10 September 1841, p. 5.

41. *The Times*, 17 June 1845, p. 4.

42. *The Times*, 4 July 1845, p. 5.

43. *The Times*, 23 June 1845, p. 7.

44. Hurd, p. 361.

45. Hansard HC Deb 24 April 1846, vol. 85, cc980–1022.

46. Monypenny, William Flaville, *The Life of Benjamin Disraeli*, vol. 2 (London: John Murray, 1912), p. 379.

47. Hansard HC Deb 08 June 1846 vol. 87 cc129–94.

48. Hurd, p. 366.

49. *The Times*, 18 August 1846, p. 7.

50. HC Deb 13 April 1848 vol. 98 cc284–301. JC, vol. 103, pp. 442–3, 13 April 1848.

51. *The Times*, 19 December 1850, p. 5.

52. Macdonagh. *Speaker*, pp. 311–2. JC, vol. 117, 24 February 1862, p. 64. Hansard HC Deb 24 February 1862 vol. 165 cc617–26.

53. JC, vol. 132, 11 April 1877, pp. 144–5.

54. JC, vol. 136, 1 February 1881, p. 50.

55. Jenkins, Roy, *Churchill* (London: Pan Macmillan, 2001). p. 93.

56. *The New York Times*, 18 February 1912, p. C5.

57. *The New York Times*, 20 March 1914, p. 12 and November 2 1920, p. 18.

58. *The Times*, 8 July 1935, p. 13.

59. JC, vol. 101, pp. 582–3, 602–3, 757, 768, 28–30 April and 22, 25 May 1846.

60. The Commons was forced to adjourn over 100 times for want of members in the 1830s, 1840s, 1860s, 1870s and 1880s but reached this total in only one other decade, the 1790s.

61. Wolfe, Eugene L., '"Into the Custody of the Serjeant at Arms": Inducing Parliamentary Attendance in Dublin and Westminster, 1690–1859', *Parliaments, Estates and Representation*, 38 (2018).

62. Thompson, E. P., *Customs in Common: Studies in Traditional Popular Culture*, (The New Press, 1993). Critchley, T. A., *The Conquest of Violence: Order and Liberty in Britain* (London: Constable, 1970).

63. Jupp, pp. 255, 262.

64. Stevenson. *Popular Disturbances*, p. 299.

65. Webb, pp. 268–9.

66. Hurd, pp. 249–57.

67. The assassin, Daniel MacNaghton, was delusional – his trial would lead to the establishment of 'MacNaghton Rules' as the standard for acquittal due to insanity. Though his mistake was not surprising in an era before photography (not to mention television) made politicians widely recognizable: Drummond was seen frequently with Peel, and had been leaving his residence when shot.

68. Hurd, pp. 299–300.

69. Hilton, p. 619.

70. *The Manchester Guardian*, 3 May 1848, p. 3.

71. HC Deb 08 June 1852 vol. 122 cc273–4 and 09 June 1852 vol. 122 cc367–73. JC, vol. 107, pp. 227–9, 292, 301–2, 8–10, 14, 16 June 1852. Jennings. p. 582.

72. Aldous, Richard, *The Lion and the Unicorn: Gladstone Vs Disraeli* (London: Pimlico, 2006), pp. 73–4.

73. Harrison, Brian, 'The Sunday Trading Riots of 1855', *The Historical Journal*, 8 (1965). Critchley, p. 146. Cowie, Leonard W., 'Grosvenor, Robert, first Baron Ebury (1801–1893)', *ODNB*. Hansard, HC Deb 2 July 1855, vol. 139 cc 368–71.

74. Aldous, p. 167.

75. Cunningham, pp. 68–9. Campbell, pp. 113–5.

76. Aldous, pp. 281–2. Hawkins, Angus, *British Party Politics, 1852–1886* (London: Macmillan, 1998). p. 203.

77. Jennings, pp. 59, 205–6.

78. Grey, Victor and Aspey, Melanie, 'Rothschild, Lionel Nathan de, Baron de Rothschild in the nobility of the Austrian empire (1808–1879)', *ODNB*. Interestingly, while the Commons prevented Rothschild from taking his seat, it allowed him to play a prominent role in negotiations with the Lords over the 1858 Oaths Bill. Jennings, p. 586.

79. HC Deb 18 July 1851 vol. 118 cc979–86. JC, vol. 106, 21 July 1851, pp. 380–1. HC Deb 28 July 1851 vol. 118 cc1573–94.

80. *The Times*, 24 June 1880, p. 11.

81. JC, vol. 135, pp. 228, 233–6, 241, 21–4 June 1880. *The Times*, 24 June 1880, p. 11.

82. JC, vol. 136, 27 April 1881, p. 199.

83. *The Times*, 4 August 1881, p. 8.

84. *The Times*, 4 August 1881, p. 9.

85. *The Manchester Guardian*, 24 June 1880, p. 5.

86. JC, vol. 139, 11 February 1884, pp. 40–1.

87. Royle, Edward, 'Bradlaugh, Charles (1833–1891)', *ODNB*. Jennings, pp. 589–97.

88. *The New York Times*, 24 November 1960, p. 12.

89. JC vol. 216, 8 May 1961, p. 221.

90. *The New York Times*, 25 August 1963, p. SM18.

91. Among those excluded for criminal convictions have been O'Donovan Rossa and John Mitchell, elected for Tipperary in 1869 and 1875, respectively, and Bobby Sands, returned for Fermanagh and South Tyrone in 1981.

9 Irish Home Rule

1. Farrell, Brian, 'The Paradox of Irish Politics', in *The Irish Parliamentary Tradition,* ed. by Brian Farrell (Dublin: Gill and Macmillan, 1973), p. 23.

2. Hansard, HL Deb 10 August 1871, vol. 208, cc1254–6. JL, vol. 103, p. 629, 10 August 1871. Hansard, HL Deb 17 June 1872, vol. 211, cc1800–45. JL, vol. 104, p. 381, 17 June 1872. There may be a third instance. Page 27 of the index of the JL for 1943–4 to 1952–3 indicates that the asperity Standing Order was read on 9 July 1883, but this is not recorded in either Hansard or the JL for that date.

3. Cox, Gary W., *The Efficient Secret...* (New York: Cambridge University Press, 1987). Hanham, H. J., 'Opposition Techniques in British Politics (1867–1914)', *Government and Opposition,* 2 (1966). O'Gorman; Hawkins; Salmon, Philip, 'The House of Commons, 1801–1911', in *A Short History of Parliament,* ed. by Clyve Jones (Woodbridge: Boydell Press, 2009). Beer, Samuel H., *Modern British Politics,* 3rd edn (London: Faber and Faber, 1982).

4. Redlich, pp. 64–5. Dion, Douglas, *Turning the Legislative Thumbscrews: Minority Rights and Procedural Change in Legislative Politics* (Ann Arbor: University of Michigan Press, 1997).

5. Macdonagh. *Speaker*, pp. 200–1.

6. Porritt, Edward, 'Amendments in House of Commons Procedure since 1880: The Aims and Tendencies of the Newer Standing Orders', *American Political Science Review,* 2 (1908). p. 517. Porritt, Edward and Annie G. Porritt, *The Unreformed House of Commons,* vol. 1 (Cambridge: Cambridge University Press, 1903), pp. 543–4. Russell, p. 165.

7. *The Times,* 23 July 1875, p. 9. *The New York Times,* 4 August 1875, p. 4.

8. Ensor, R. C. K., *England, 1870–1914* (Oxford: Clarendon Press, 1936), p. 37.

9. Between 1837 and 1878 no fewer than seven parliamentary committees investigated procedural changes that would have reduced the opportunities for obstruction, but they shied away from making any but the most minor alterations to the rules. Porritt, 'Amendments', pp. 519–21.

10. Comerford, R. V., 'Isaac Butt and the Home Rule Party, 1870–77', in *A New History of Ireland,* vol. 6, ed. by W. E. Vaughan (Oxford: Oxford University Press, 1989), p. 24.

11. Thornley, David, 'The Irish Home Rule Party and Parliamentary Obstruction, 1874–87', *Irish Historical Studies,* 12 (1960).

12. O'Donnell, p. 248.

13. Jellinek, Georg, 'Parliamentary Obstruction', *Political Science Quarterly,* 19 (1904). p. 580.
14. JC, vol. 132, p. 375, 25 July 1877.
15. JC, vol. 132, pp. 383–4, 27–8 July 1877.
16. *The New York Times*, 2 August 1877, p. 5.
17. Ensor, pp. 56–7, 72–3. Webb, pp. 360–1.
18. JC, vol. 136, p. 31, 25 January 1881.
19. *The New York Times*, 11 February 1881, p. 5.
20. It also elicited not-quite-violent retribution against those seen to be keeping MPs from their beds. 'The spectacle of Joseph Gillies Biggar asleep in a corner of the Library aroused in some supporters of the Government a desire to consult the heaviest books in bulk and weight that they could find, and by a strange mischance these mighty tomes always slipped from their hands and fell with a crash close to the slumbering arch-obstructionist.' Macdonagh, *Speaker*, p. 319.
21. Although it was unprecedented for the Speaker to end debate in this manner, by the mid nineteenth century, MPs collectively were doing the same thing, using 'inarticulate noises' to drown out any speaker to whom they did not wish to listen. Jennings, p. 633. See, for example, *The New York Times*, 1 April 1872.
22. *The New York Times*, 3 February 1881.
23. He also might have pointed out that the prime minister had been on the other side of the obstructionist debate: in an effort to filibuster the 1857 Divorce Bill, Gladstone made 27 speeches in a single day, as a result of which one clause of the legislation occupied the House for ten hours. Thornley, p. 42.
24. *The Times*, 4 February 1881, p. 6. See also JC, vol. 136, pp. 55–7, 3 February 1881.
25. Redlich, p. 161.
26. See for example, *The New York Times*, 24 October, 1902, p. 7 and 26 October, 1902, p. 4.
27. Webb, p. 361.
28. Hughes, Edward, 'The Changes in Parliamentary Procedure, 1880–1882', in *Essays Presented to Sir Lewis Namier,* ed. by Richard Pares and A. J. P. Taylor (London: Macmillan, 1956), pp. 287–319. 306.
29. Field, pp. 219–20.
30. *The New York Times*, 19 November 1882, p. 3.
31. Hanham, p. 47.
32. Rush, Michael, *The Role of the Member of Parliament since 1868: From Gentlemen to Players*, (Oxford: Oxford University Press, 2001), p. 69.
33. Redlich, pp. 180–1. Ensor, pp. 178–9.
34. *The New York Times*, 11 May 1887, p. 1.
35. *The Times*, 23 February 1883, p. 9 and 23 December 1916, p. 9. JC, vol. 138, p. 44, 22 February 1883.
36. JC, vol. 138, pp. 232 and 238, 31 May and 1 June 1883.
37. New York Times, 16 April 1887, p. 1.

38. HC Deb 28 February 1889 vol 333 cc603–83. *The Manchester Guardian,* 1 March 1889, p. 6.

39. Field, pp. 223–4.

40. *The New York Times,* 9 August 1889, p. 5.

41. Burleigh, Michael, *Blood and Rage: A Cultural History of Terrorism,* (London: Harper, 2009). pp. 2–11. Ensor. pp. 54–6, 116. Comerford, R. V., 'Gladstone's First Irish Enterprise, 1864–70', in *A New History of Ireland,* vol. 5, ed. by W. E. Vaughan, (Oxford: Oxford University Press, 1989), pp. 439–41, 449.

42. *The Times,* 5 February 1881, p. 10.

43. *The New York Times,* 23 February 1881, p. 3.

44. Ensor, p. 75.

45. Comerford, R. V., 'The Land War and the Politics of Distress, 1877-82', in *A New History of Ireland,* vol. 6, ed. by W. E. Vaughan (Oxford: Oxford University Press, 1989), p. 50.

46. O'Donnell, F. Hugh, *A History of the Irish Parliamentary Party,* vol. 2 (London: Longmans, Green, and Co., 1910), pp. 122, 131.

47. Burleigh, pp. 13–7.

48. *The New York Times,* 25 January 1885, p. 1.

49. *The New York Times,* 25 January 1885, p. 2.

50. Ensor, p. 96.

51. O'Donnell, vol. 2, p. 222.

52. *The Manchester Guardian,* 28 December, 1887, p. 5.

53. *The New York Times,* 24 January 1899, p. 6.

54. Ensor, p. 181.

55. Richter, Donald C., *Riotous Victorians* (Athens, Ohio: Ohio University Press, 1981). p. 146. This episode foreshadowed the Troubles ahead not only because it was dubbed 'Bloody Sunday' and pitted a parliamentarian against the police but also due to O'Brien's reaction to being treated like a common criminal: he embarked 'upon an act of voluntary constipation'. Concerned, Dublin Castle sought regular reports of his bowel movements, 'a "crisis" only ended when the prison doctor smuggled a laxative into the prisoner's food'. Searle, p. 155. A century later, other Irish nationalists would respond to similar treatment by adopting an approach at the opposite end of the incontinence spectrum from O'Brien's: the 'dirty' protest.

56. Berrington, Hugh, 'Partisanship and Dissidence in the Nineteenth-Century House of Commons', *Parliamentary Affairs,* 21 (1968).

57. *The New York Times,* 9 May 1893, p. 5.

58. *The New York Times,* May 18 1893, p. 5.

59. *The New York Times,* 28 July 1893, p. 1. The newspaper's correspondent apparently witnessed the incident first-hand, from the gallery. The correspondent for *The Times,* by contrast, evidently was in the lobby, so that paper's account, on 28 July, p. 6, is an exercise in multivocality, a jumble of conflicting, Rashamon-like, accounts of who did what to whom. Another eye witness

account suggests that peacemakers outnumbered actual combatants, even if the exploits of the latter received more attention. Macdonagh, *Speaker*, pp. 350–1.

60. It certainly did not help that Liberal Unionists (in opposition) were sitting with their former Liberal colleagues on the government benches while Irish nationalists (who supported the government) were sitting on the opposition benches to underline their independence, a situation Gladstone professed beyond his ability to alter. Searle. p. 168. *The New York Times*, 1 August 1893, p. 8. Hansard HC Deb 31 July 1893 vol. 15 cc886–7

61. Quoted in *The New York Times*, 29 July 1893, p. 2. See also *The Times*, 1 August 1893, p. 7.

62. *The New York Times*, 29 July 1893, p. 4 and 30 July 1893, p. 1.

63. Lyons, F. S. L., *The Irish Parliamentary Party, 1890–1910* (Westport, Connecticut: Greenwood Press, 1974), pp. 67–99, 236.

64. Hansard HC Deb 5 March 1901, vol. 90, cc592–696. The suspension of one of these MPs, Jeremiah Jordon, subsequently was lifted after he claimed that he had not refused to participate in the division. JC vol. 156, 5 and 7 March, 1901, pp. 62, 65.

65. *The New York Times*, 6 March 1901, p. 1.

66. *The New York Times*, 7 March 1901, p. 2.

67. Hansard HC Deb 7 March 1901, vol. 90, cc845–992. *The New York Times*, 8 March 1901, p. 1.

68. *The New York Times*, 21 March 1902, p. 1, *The Times*, 21 March 1902, p. 7. See also Hansard HC Deb 20 March 1902, vol. 105, cc565–661.

69. HC Deb 07 May 1902 vol. 107 cc1020–53. *The New York Times*, 8 May 1902, p. 8.

70. *The New York Times*, 17 October 1902, p. 6.

71. Parliamentary disorder also may have encouraged similar behaviour in other fora. In October 1908, for example, the London County Council was first suspended and then adjourned, as an attempt to eject a disorderly Labour member turned violent. *The Manchester Guardian*, 14 October, 1908, p. 3.

72. Macdonagh, *Speaker*, pp. 363–4.

73. Jenkins, p. 93.

74. *The New York Times*, 7 July 1904, p. 7. *The Times*, 7 July 1904, p. 6.

75. *The New York Times*, 23 May 1905, p. 4.

76. *The New York Times*, 24 May 1905, pp. 6, 8.

77. Porritt, 'Amendments', p. 526.

78. Jenkins, Roy, *Mr Balfour's Poodle* (London: William Collins, 1968). pp. 80–5.

79. Dennis, Alfred L. P., 'The Parliament Act of 1911', *American Political Science Review*, 6 (1912).

80. Jenkins. *Poodle*, p. 263.

81. Webb, pp. 469–70.

82. *The Times*, 15 April, 1910, p. 9.

83. *The New York Times*, 11 March 1911, p. 5.

84. *The Manchester Guardian*, 6 April 1911, pp. 8, 10.

85. HC Deb 05 April 1911 vol. 23 cc2349–51. *The Times*, 6 April 1911, p. 8.

86. *The Times*, 25 July 1911, pp. 8 and 12. *The New York Times*, 25 July 1911, p. 1. JC vol. 166, p. 351, 24 July 1911. Jenkins. *Poodle*, pp. 230–2.

87. Hansard HC Deb 27 July 1911, vol. 28, cc1801–5.

88. *The New York Times*, 28 July 1911, p. 5.

89. *The Times*, 9 June 1890, p. 10. See also *The Daily Telegraph*, 19 July 1890, p. 3.

90. du Parcq, Herbert, *Life of David Lloyd George*, vol. II (London: Caxton, 1912). pp. 224–5. Morgan, Austen, *J. Ramsay Macdonald* (Manchester: Manchester University Press, 1987), p. 27.

91. *The Times*, 8 March 1900, p. 10.

92. *The Manchester Guardian*, 12 April 1900, p. 6. du Parcq. pp. 226–7.

93. Ibid. pp. 292–6. *The New York Times*, 19 December 1901, p. 1. *The Manchester Guardian*, 19 December 1901.

94. It was not just disorder at home that was disdained; by the early twentieth century violence in defence of empire also increasingly was rejected. Ferguson, Naill, *Empire: How Britain Made the Modern World*,(London: Penguin, 2003), p. 334.

10 Sectarians, Soldiers and Suffragettes

1. Field, p. 171.

2. Cunningham, pp. 76, 219–20.

3. Rosen, p. 13.

4. ibid. pp. 80–2. *The New York Times*, 26 April (p. 1) and 24 October (p. 6) 1906, 12 February (p. 4) and 14 & 29 October (both p. 1) 1908, and 19 February (p. 4) and 20 June (p. 1) 1909. *The Manchester Guardian*, 25 October 1906, p. 7.

5. *The New York Times*, 1 July 1908, p. 4.

6. *The New York Times*, 2 July 1908, p. 4.

7. Mayhall, Laura E. Nym, *The Militant Suffrage Movement: Citizenship and Resistance in Britain, 1860–1930* (New York: Oxford University Press, 2003), pp. 50–1.

8. Rosen, 122–3.

9. *The New York Times*, 7 October 1909, p. 8.

10. www.theguardian.com/uk/2006/sep/29/gender.women.

11. Jenkins, *Churchill*, pp. 109, 185–6.

12. *The New York Times*, 14 November 1909, p. C3.

13. *The New York Times*, 25 November 1909, p. 1. *The Manchester Guardian*, 25 November 1909, p. 10.

14. Jenkins. *Poodle*, p. 108.

15. *The New York Times*, 17 December 1909, p. 3.

16. Rosen, p. 129.

17. Hansard HC Deb 12 July 1910 vol. 19 cc207–333.

18. *The New York Times*, 19 November 1910, p. 3.

19. *The New York Times*, 23 November 1910, p. 3.

20. *The New York Times*, 27 November 1910, p. 1.

21. Hansard HC Deb 5 May 1911, vol. 25 cc738–809.
22. Mayhall, pp. 96–7.
23. *The New York Times*, 9 February 1912, p. 1.
24. *The Manchester Guardian*, 5 March 1912, p. 6.
25. Rosen, pp. 157–61.
26. *The New York Times*, 15 June 1912, p. 1.
27. *The New York Times*, 27 June 1912, p. 5.
28. *The New York Times*, 29 June 1912, p. 5.
29. *The Manchester Guardian*, 20 July 1912, p. 9.
30. *The New York Times*, 21 July 1912, p. C1.
31. *The New York Times*, 19 July 1912, p. 5.
32. *The New York Times*, 12 September 1912, p. 1.
33. *The New York Times*, 23 September 1912, p. 4.
34. *The New York Times*, 5 November 1912.
35. *The New York Times*, 1 December 1912, p. 1.
36. *The New York Times*, 28 January 1912.
37. *The New York Times*, 14 July 1912, p. 1. *The Times*, 15 July 1912, p. 7.
38. *The Manchester Guardian*, 20 July 1912, p. 8.
39. *The New York Times*, 21 July 1912, p. C1.
40. Lawrence, Jon, *Electing Our Masters: The Hustings in British Politics from Hogarth to Blair* (Oxford: Oxford University Press, 2009), p. 85.
41. *The New York Times*, 23 September 1912, p. 4.
42. Mayhall, pp. 107–15.
43. *The New York Times*, 30 January 1913, pp. 1, 4.
44. *The New York Times*, 20 February 1913, pp. 1, 3.
45. *The New York Times*, 26 April 1914, p. SM3.
46. *The New York Times*, 16 April 1913, p. 3.
47. *The Manchester Guardian*, 8 May 1913, p. 8.
48. *The Times*, 12 June 1913, p. 8.
49. *The Times*, 12 July 1913, p. 5.
50. *The New York Times*, 29 August 1913, p. 1.
51. *The New York Times*, 2 November 1913, p. C3.
52. *The New York Times*, 15 November 1913, p. 5.
53. *The New York Times*, 20 January 1914, p. 5.
54. Rosen, p. 222.
55. *The Times*, 13 February 1914, p. 8.
56. *The New York Times*, 19 February 1914, p. 4.
57. *The Manchester Guardian*, 5 March 1914, p. 9.
58. *The New York Times*, 15 March 1914, p. 31.
59. *The New York Times*, 28 October 1913, p. 6.
60. See *The Times Higher Education Supplement*, 26 January 2007. Bearman, C. J., 'Confronting the Suffragette Mythology', in *BBC History*, (2007), pp. 14–8. Bearman, C. J., 'An Examination of Suffragette Violence', *English Historical Review*, 120 (2005), pp. 368–9.

61. Ensor, p. 398. Searle. pp. 464, 468. For a claim that the prospects for women's suffrage improved in 1913–4 because of or despite the efforts of the militants, see Marr, Andrew, *The Making of Modern Britain* (London: Pan, 2009), p. 178.

62. Searle, p. 467. As Liberal Harold Cawley told the Commons in 1913, 'It may be right to yield to the violence of the many, but I am perfectly certain that it is bad policy to yield to the violence of the very few.' Hansard, HC Deb 6 May 1913, vol. 52 cc1887–2005.

63. *The Times*, 19 May 1915, p. 8 and 3 January 1936, p. 17. See also *The New York Times*, 19 May 1915, p. 1.

64. Smith, Jeremy, 'Bluff, Bluster and Brinkmanship: Andrew Bonar Law and the Third Home Rule Bill', *The Historical Journal*, 36 (1993). Cunningham, pp. 208–9. Searle, p. 434.

65. Jenkins. *Churchill*, pp. 234–6. *The Manchester Guardian*, 9 February 1912, p. 7

66. *The Manchester Guardian*, 9 February 1912, p. 7.

67. Hansard HC Deb 13 November 1912, vol. 43, cc2003–54.

68. *The Times*, 14 November 1912, p. 6. *The New York Times*, 14 November 1912, p. 1.

69. *The Times*, 19 November 1912, p. 10.

70. *The Manchester Guardian*, 19 November 1912, p. 8.

71. *The New York Times*, 2 April 1913, p. 5.

72. *The New York Times*, 20 March 1914, p. 2.

73. *The Times*, 22 May 1914, p. 8. *The New York Times*, 22 May 1914, p. 8.

74. The MP for Westmeath North was expelled from the Irish Nationalist Party in 1909. Two years later, he was suspended from the Commons for a week for publishing a letter (written by another MP) calling into question the Speaker's impartiality. Lysaght, D. R. O'Connor, 'Ginnell, Laurence (*bap.* 1852, *d.* 1923)', *ODNB*. HC Deb 20 February 1911 vol. 21 cc1553–86. HC Deb 08 May 1916 vol. 82 cc284–5.

75. JC vol. 171, 27 July 1916, p. 155. Hansard HC Deb 27 July 1916, vol. 84, cc1859–62. *The Times*, 28 July 1916, p. 10.

76. *The New York Times*, 26 July 1917, p. 4.

77. *The New York Times*, 27 July 1917, p. 3. JC vol. 172, 26 July 1917, p. 171.

78. Lyons, F. S. L., 'The New Nationalism, 1916–18', in *A New History of Ireland*, vol. 6, ed. by W. E. Vaughan (Oxford: Oxford University Press, 1989), pp. 226–40. Farrell, p. 208.

79. Hopkinson, Michael, 'Civil War and Aftermath, 1922–4', in *A New History of Ireland*, vol. 7, ed. by J. R. Hill (Oxford: Oxford University Press, 2003), p. 44.

80. During the Irish civil war all ministers, with the exception of the Minister of Defence, were 'forced to live in their government offices for fear of assassination'. Ibid. p. 45. On 7 December 1922 Deputy Sean Hales, a supporter of the Anglo–Irish Treaty, was killed, and Deputy Speaker Padraic O Maille was wounded while walking to the Dáil. The next day, four imprisoned anti-treaty leaders were executed to discourage further attacks on politicians. Five years later, Minister for Justice Kevin O'Higgins, who had signed the execution

orders, was assassinated while on his way to Mass. Bardon, Jonathan and Dermot Keogh, 'Ireland, 1921–84', in *A New History of Ireland*, vol. 7, ed. by J. R. Hill (Oxford: Oxford University Press, 2003), pp. lxx–i.

81. Lyons, F. S. L., 'The War of Independence, 1919-21', in *A New History of Ireland*, vol. 6, ed. by W. E. Vaughan (Oxford: Oxford University Press, 1989), p. 247.

82. *The New York Times*, 2 November 1920, p. 18.

83. *The Times*, 23 November 1920, p. 12.

84. Hansard HC Deb 22 November 1920, vol. 135, cc38–43. *The New York Times*, 23 November 1920, pp. 1–2.

85. Marr, pp. 188, 261.

86. Middlemas, Robert Keith, *The Clydesiders* (London: Hutchinson, 1965). pp. 71–2.

87. *The Times*, 30 November 1915, p. 15.

88. *The New York Times*, 12 November 1916, p. 2. *The Manchester Guardian*, 13 November 1916, p. 5.

89. *The New York Times*, 10 January 1917, p. 2. *The Manchester Guardian*, 10 January 1917, p. 5.

90. *The New York Times*, 11 January 1917, p. 1.

91. *The New York Times*, 11 August 1917, pp. 1, 3.

92. *The Manchester Guardian*, 2 September 1918, p. 8.

93. He had created a sensation by winning election in 1916 on a platform critical of the country's air defence efforts. He followed this up with a McCarthyesque claim that the Germans had a 'Black Book' containing the names of tens of thousands of influential British 'perverts' and that the Kaiser's men were seeking to lure British men into homosexual acts. Only slightly less outrageous was his assertion that airpower should be used indiscriminately against civilians, although by the end of the war the Royal Air Force had been created to put this doctrine into practice. *The New York Times*, 11 March 1916, p. 3. Marr, p. 290. Taylor, A. J. P., *English History 1914–1945* (London: Book Club Associates, 1965), p. 44.

94. *The New York Times*, 27 July 1917, p. 1. See also *The Argus* (Melbourne), 28 July (p. 19) and 2 August (p. 7).

95. Hansard HC Deb 1 July 1918, vol. 107, cc1410–2.

96. JC vol. 173, 1 July 1918, p. 141.

97. *The Times*, 2 July 1918, p. 10.

98. Hosking, Geoffrey and Anthony King, 'Radicals and Whigs in the British Liberal Party, 1906–1914', in *The History of Parliamentary Behavior*, ed. by William O. Aydelotte (Princeton: Princeton University Press, 1977).

99. Pugh, Martin, *The Making of Modern British Politics 1867–1939* (Oxford: Blackwell, 1982), p. 156. Searle, p. 468.

11 The Clydesiders

1. Schmitt, Carl, *The Crisis of Parliamentary Democracy* (Cambridge: MIT Press, 1985 [1923]).

2. Loewenberg, Gerhard, 'The Influence of Parliamentary Behavior on Regime Stability', *Comparative Politics*, 3 (1971).

3. Stevenson, John and Chris Cook, *The Slump: Society and Politics During the Depression* (London: Quartet Books, 1977), p. 265.

4. Practical considerations also were a factor: the party's trade-union paymasters demanded respectability and Commons sittings extended by disorder could cause Labour MPs to have to return home via taxi rather than train, an expense many could ill afford. Jennings, Ivor, *Parliament*, 2nd edn (Cambridge: Cambridge University Press, 1957 [1939]), p. 166. Pugh, p. 271.

5. Middlemas, pp. 44–5.

6. JC vol. 163, 15 October 1908, p. 403. *The Times*, 16 October, 1908, p. 8. Hansard HC Deb 16 October 1908, vol. 194, cc614–34. *The New York Times*, 17 October 1908, p. 5.

7. Morgan, p. 47.

8. *The New York Times*, 15 December 1922, p. 18.

9. Marquand, David, *Ramsay Macdonald* (London: Richard Cohen Books, 1997), p. 288.

10. Webb, p. 466.

11. *The Times*, 16 February 1923, p. 6.

12. *The New York Times*, 12 April 1923, p. 3.

13. *The Times*, 12 April 1923, p. 12. Marquand. p. 290.

14. *The New York Times*, 12 April 1923, pp. 1, 3. JC vol. 178, 11 April 1923, p. 88. Due to a scanning error, Hansard's online account of this incident is recorded as taking place five years after it actually transpired. See, Hansard, HC Deb 11 April 1928 vol. 162 cc1264–6.

15. *The Times*, 16 May 1923, p. 14. JC vol. 178, 15 May 1923, p. 156.

16. Brown, Gordon, *Maxton* (Glasgow: Collins/Fontana, 1986), p. 114.

17. JC vol. 178, 27 June 1923, p. 237.

18. *The Times*, 28 June 1923, p. 14.

19. Brown. p. 152.

20. *The New York Times*, 28 June 1923, p. 19.

21. Brown, p. 143. The Times, 29 June 1923, p. 16.

22. *The Times*, 30 July 1923, p. 10.

23. Brown, p. 138.

24. *The Times*, 31 July 1923, p. 10. See also Middlemas. pp. 130–1.

25. Field, p. 241.

26. Brown, p. 156.

27. *The Times*, 10 April 1924, p. 14.

28. *The New York Times*, 11 April 1924, p. 5.

29. Brown, p. 156.

30. *The Times*, 10 May 1924, p. 12. Hansard HC Deb 9 May 1924, vol. 173, cc789–874.

31. *The Times*, 6 March, 1925, p. 8.

32. Time, 16 March, 19, 1925, see http://www.time.com/time/magazine/ article/0,9171,720007,00.html *The Times*, 6 March, 1925, p. 8. Hansard HC Deb 5 March 1925, vol. 181, cc707–14.

33. *The Times*, 6 March 1925, p. 14.

34. *The Times*, 10 March 1925, p. 14.

35. *The New York Times*, 13 February 1925, pp. 1, 8.

36. Taylor, p. 250.

37. Marquand, pp. 392–5, 416.

38. Hansard HC Deb 25 June 1926, vol. 197, cc699–778. *The Times*, 26 June 1926, p. 9. Hansard HC Deb 1 July 1926, vol. 197, cc1359–475. *The New York Times*, 2 July 1926, p. 4.

39. *The New York Times*, 30 June 1926, p. 3.

40. Hansard HC Deb 1 July 1926, vol. 197, cc1359–475. *The New York Times*, 2 July 1926, p. 4.

41. *The Times*, 9 July 1926, p. 9.

42. *The New York Times*, 9 July 1926, p. 3.

43. *The New York Times*, 10 July 1926, p. 4.

44. *The New York Times*, 15 August 1926, p. SM3.

45. JC vol. 182, 16 November 1927, pp. 328–9.

46. *The New York Times*, 17 November 1927, p. 1.

47. Toye, Richard, '"Perfectly Parliamentary"? The Labour Party and the House of Commons in the Inter-War Years', *Twentieth Century British History*, 25 (2014), pp. 17–9.

48. Middlemas, pp. 236–46. Brown, pp. 206–7.

49. *The New York Times*, 18 July 1930, p. 1.

50. It eventually would be carried 260 to 26. Hansard HC Deb 17 July 1930, vol. 241, cc1462–9.

51. A rather dissimilar involuntary adjournment almost happened in 1943, when an assistant Serjeant-at-Arms mistakenly removed the mace at the end of a committee meeting. Although members shouted, 'Come back,' it was too late. 'Attendants, seeing the mace being removed, gave the time-honored shout, "Who goes home?" and the electricians began to switch off the lights.' However, the mace was soon retrieved, allowing the House to finish its business. *The New York Times*, 2 April 1943, p. 11.

52. *The New York Times*, July 18 1930, p. 1.

53. *The Times*, 18 July 1930, p. 14. JC vol. 185, 17 July 1930, p. 454. *The New York Times*, 24 July 1930, p. 2.

54. *The New York Times*, 28 November 1930, p. 1.

55. *The New York Times*, 29 November 1930, p. 9.

56. *The Times*, 27 November 1930, p. 8. Winterton's behaviour conformed to family tradition: his ancestor had been ennobled by Charles II after being forced to resign from the Commons for 'confounded, quarrelsome impudence'. *Time Magazine*, 8 December 1930.

57. Hansard HC Deb 2 July 1931, vol. 254, cc1465–71.

58. *The New York Times*, 3 July 1931, p. 1.
59. JC vol. 186, 2 July 1931, p. 333.
60. *Time Magazine*, 13 July 1931.
61. *The Times*, 3 July 1931, p. 14.
62. *The Times*, 7 July 1931, p. 8. JC vol. 186, 6 July 1931, p. 338. *The New York Times*, 4 July 1931, p. 9.
63. Taylor. pp. 295, 354. Pugh. p. 264.
64. *The New York Times*, 12 September 1931, p. 8. It is hard to tell what Astor said that was so provocative. See Hansard HC Deb 11 September 1931, vol. 256, cc419–90.
65. *The New York Times*, 22 November 1933, p. 1.
66. *The New York Times*, 2 December 1933, p. 7.
67. Brown. p. 256.
68. *The Manchester Guardian*, 28 June 1934, p. 12.
69. *The Manchester Guardian*, 16 October 1934, p. 12.
70. *The Times*, 24 July 1936, p. 8. JC vol. 191, 22–3 July 1936, pp. 341–2. Hansard HC Deb 22 July 1936, vol. 315, cc473–941.
71. *The New York Times*, 24 July 1936, p. 2.
72. *The Times*, 5 April 1938, p. 8. *The New York Times*, 5 April 1938, p. 15.

12 Fading Post-War Comity

1. Beer. Clarke, Peter, *Hope and Glory: Britain 1900–2000*, Second edn (London: Penguin, 2004), p. 441.
2. Beer, Samuel H., *Britain against Itself* (London: Faber and Faber, 1982). Searing, Donald D., 'Rules of the Game in Britain: Can Politicians Be Trusted?', *American Political Science Review*, 76 (1982). Toye. pp. 25–8.
3. The chart excludes three incidents in which grave disorder was externally generated: twice because objects were thrown from the public gallery and once owing to the misbehaviour of the lights, not the Members. On the latter, see Hansard, HC Deb 24 November 1927, vol 210, cc2117.
4. There were at least two instances in which MPs disagreed with the Speaker's ruling that grave disorder prevailed. See Hansard, HC Deb 9 February 1961 vol. 634 cc642–53 and Hansard, HC Deb 13 February 1961, vol. 634 cc938–1019. More frequently, the presiding officer declined to invoke the relevant standing order despite considerable upheaval on the floor. See *The Times*, 4 March 1947, p. 4. *The New York Times*, 2 February 1965, p. 1. *The Times*, 9 March 1966, p. 10. Hansard HC Deb 18 November 1976, vol. 919, cc1565–6.
5. *The New York Times*, 29 July 1943, p. 10.
6. *Time Magazine*, 9 August 1943.
7. *The Times*, 30 July 1943, p. 8.
8. *The Times*, 6 April 1949, p. 4.
9. Lloyd, p. 62.
10. *The Times*, 22 June 1951, p. 4. Hansard HC Deb 21 June 1951, vol. 489, cc746–833.

11. Jenkins, p. 838.
12. Webb, p. 574.
13. *The Times*, 28 December 1989, p. 12.
14. Hansard, HC Deb, 1 November 1956, vol. 558, cc1619–30. *The New York Times*, 2 November 1956, p. 1.
15. Field, pp. 266–7.
16. *The Times*, 9 February 1961, pp. 5, 12. Hansard HC Deb 8 February 1961, vol. 634, cc591–2. JC vol. 216, 8 February 1961, p. 98.
17. When the sitting resumed, questions about whether it had been properly suspended soon led to a decision to adjourn. *The Times*, 7 December 1961, p. 14. Hansard HC Deb 6 December 1961, vol. 650, cc1399–500. JC vol. 217, 6 December 1961, p. 55.
18. *The New York Times*, 8 February 1965, p. 2.
19. *The Times*, 4 February 1965, p. 6.
20. *The Times*, 3 February 1965, p. 10.
21. Norton, Philip, *Dissension in the House of Commons, 1974–1979* (Oxford: Oxford University Press, 1980).
22. Although it is often asserted that extended sittings tend to be disorderly, this is far from always the case as long as those on the opposition benches feel they have had a chance to have their say. For example, commenting on a 22-hour sitting devoted to Army estimates in March 1954, the Times observed, 'Seldom has an all-night sitting generated so little excitement or acerbity,' a lack of pyrotechnics attributed to the absence of any attempt to closure the debate. *The Times*, 13 March 1954, p. 6.
23. Heffer, Eric S., *The Class Struggle in Parliament* (London: Victor Gollancz, 1973), pp. 222–3.
24. Lloyd. pp. 66–8.
25. Marquand, David, *Britain since 1918* (London: Phoenix, 2008), p. 246.
26. Heffer, p. 225.
27. *The Times*, 26 January 1971, p. 1. Hansard HC Deb 25 January 1971, vol. 810, cc37–290. JC vol. 226, 25 January 1971, p. 216.
28. HC Deb 28 January 1971 vol. 810 cc880–7.
29. *The Times*, 29 January 1971, p. 6, and 30 January 1971, p. 21. Lloyd. p. 101.
30. *The Times*, 30 January 1971, p. 21.
31. Lloyd, p. 148.
32. *The Times*, 21 January 1972, p. 7. Hansard HC Deb 20 January 1972, vol. 829, cc660–1.
33. Hansard HC Deb 20 January 1972, vol. 829, cc660–1.
34. *The Times*, 18 February 1972, p. 1.
35. Lloyd, p. 64.
36. Hansard, HC Deb 13 March 1972, vol. 833, cc120–73.
37. *The Times*, 14 March 1972, p. 1.
38. *The Guardian*, 14 March 1972, p. 1.
39. *The Times*, 26 January 1973, p. 2.

40. *The Times*, 5 March 1975, p. 1. Hansard HC Deb 4 March 1975, vol. 887, cc1270–6.

41. *The Guardian*, 25 March 1975, p. 32.

42. Two decades later the shoe was on the other foot as the Tories provoked similar accusations of unfair play, but no disorder, when they won a vote after 'pairing' three of their MPs with three each from Labour and the Liberal Democrats. *The Independent*, 18 December 1996.

43. *The Times*, 28 May 1976, p. 1. *The New York Times*, 29 May 1976, p. 2. Hansard HC Deb 27 May 1976, vol. 912, cc767–8.

44. *The Times*, 7 February 1947, p. 2 and 11 February 1947, p. 8.

45. *The Times*, 25 May, 1949, p. 4.

46. *Time Magazine*, 5 February 1951, p. 19. *The Times*, 29 January, 1951, p. 4.

47. Robinton, Madeline R., 'Parliamentary Privilege and Political Morality in Britain, 1939–1957', *Political Science Quarterly*, 73 (1958), p. 190. *The Times*, 28 November 1956, p. 6.

48. *The Times*, 22 February 1958, p. 6.

49. *The Times*, 25 February 1958, p. 8.

50. *The Times*, 19 July 1958, p. 10.

51. *The Telegraph*, 14 April 2008.

52. Critchley.

53. Clutterbuck, Richard, *Britain in Agony: The Growth of Political Violence* (London: Faber and Faber, 1978).

54. Beer, p. 143.

55. *The Guardian*, 29 October 1967, p. 1.

56. *The Times*, 4 May 1968, p. 1. Straw, Jack, *Last Man Standing* (London: Macmillan, 2012), p. 73.

57. *The Guardian*, 9 November 1968, p. 1.

58. *The Guardian*, 17 May 1969, p. 4.

59. Her son subsequently helped the former PM research his memoirs. *The Times*, 19 July 2005.

60. *Time Magazine*, 31 January 1972.

61. *The Times*, 11 November 1972, p. 1 and 18 November 1972, p. 1. *The New York Times*, 18 November 1972, p. 9.

62. Bright, Martin, 'Look Back in Anger,' *The Observer*, 3 February 2002.

63. *The Guardian*, 6 November 1976, p. 4.

64. *The Guardian*, 15 July 1977, p. 1.

13 Ulster's Troubles

1. Webb, pp. 493–4.

2. Dixon, Paul, *Northern Ireland: The Politics of War and Peace*, 2nd edn (Basingstoke: Palgrave Macmillan, 2008), p. 340.

3. *The New York Times*, 23 May 1922, p. 1.

4. Barton, Brian, 'Northern Ireland, 1920–25', in *A New History of Ireland,* vol. 7, ed. by J. R. Hill (Oxford: Oxford University Press, 2003), pp. 178–9. Cottrell, Peter, *The Irish Civil War 1922–23* (Oxford: Osprey, 2008), pp. 67–8.

5. Burleigh, p. 23.

6. Taylor, p. 188. Hopkinson. pp. 22–3.

7. Barton, pp. 189–95. Barton, Brian, 'Northern Irleand, 1925-39', in *A New History of Ireland,* vol. 7, p. 223.

8. Barton. 1925-39, p. 201. Walker, Graham, 'The Northern Ireland Parliament and Assembly at Stormont', in *A Short History of Parliament,* ed. by Clyve Jones (Woodbridge: Boydell Press, 2009), pp. 345–7.

9. *The Times,* 23 November 1928, p. 9. *The New York Times,* 23 November 1928, p. 4.

10. *The Times,* 1 October 1932, p. 7.

11. Dixon, pp. 74–5.

12. *The Times,* 13 July 1967, p. 3.

13. *The Times,* 21 May 1968, p. 1.

14. Whyte, J. H., 'The North Erupts, and Ireland Enters Europe, 1968–72', in *A New History of Ireland,* vol. 7, ed. by J. R. Hill (Oxford: Oxford University Press, 2003), p. 326.

15. Coogan, Tim Pat, *The Troubles: Ireland's Ordeal 1966–1995 and the Search for Peace* (London: Hutchinson, 1995), p. 62. Whyte, p. 327.

16. Coogan, p. 75.

17. *The New York Times,* 27 June 1970, p. 1.

18. JC vol. 226, 23 July 1970, p. 68.

19. *The Times,* 24 July 1970, p. 1.

20. *The New York Times,* 25 July 1970, p. 20. *The Guardian,* 25 July 1970, p. 16.

21. Coogan, pp. 138–9.

22. ibid. p. 112.

23. *Time Magazine,* 27 December 1971.

24. Whyte, pp. 341–2.

25. *The Guardian,* 15 December 1971, p. 1.

26. *The Guardian,* 1 February 1972, p. 1. *The Times,* 1 February 1972, p. 1.

27. Lloyd, pp. 69–70.

28. *The Times,* 1 February 1972, p. 1.

29. *The Guardian,* 26 February 1972, p. 1. *The Times,* 26 February 1972, p. 1.

30. *The Guardian,* 27 June 1973, p. 1.

31. *The Guardian,* 8 June 1974, p. 22. Fox may have been killed not for his political activities but because he interrupted an IRA arms raid on the house of his fiancée's parents. *The Guardian,* 21 May 1974, p. 6.

32. *The Times,* 18 June 1974, p. 1. *The Guardian,* 18 June 1974.

33. Coogan, pp. 157–65.

34. *The Times,* 1 August 1973, pp. 1–2. *The Guardian,* 1 August 1973, p. 1 and 2 August 1973, p. 20.

35. Coogan, p. 166.

36. *The Times*, 6 December 1973, p. 1. *The New York Times*, 6 December 1973, p. 14.

37. *The Times*, 23 January 1974, pp. 1–2. *The New York Times*, 23 January 1974, p. 5.

38. *The Times*, 24 January 1974, p. 1.

39. Dixon, p. 190.

40. Molyneaux speculated that the target of the attack had been another passenger, Chief Constable of Northern Ireland James Flanagan, who was traveling to London to receive an award, but the Royal Ulster Constabulary dismissed the latter's presence on the aircraft as 'pure coincidence'. *The Times*, 24 July 1974, p. 1.

41. *The Times*, 24 October 1974, p. 1.

42. *The Times*, 19 April 1977, p. 1.

43. *The Guardian*, 6 May 1977, p. 2.

44. Dixon, pp. 162, 176.

45. *The Guardian*, 7 July 1978, p. 1. JC, vol. 234, 6 July 1978, p. 438.

46. Just as Republican gunmen had sought to provoke the British army in the hopes that the ensuing repression would rally Catholics to the nationalist cause, it is possible that an assassination that could increase the chances of election of a hardline prime minister could, paradoxically, have benefitted the cause espoused by terrorists. In any case, whether this was the intention or not, Thatcher's election, and especially her intransigent response to the 1981 hunger strikes, did much to boost Republican support.

47. *The Guardian*, 17 January 1981.

48. Coogan, pp. 234–7. Arthur, Paul, 'Northern Ireland, 1972–84', in *A New History of Ireland,* vol. 7, ed. by J. R. Hill (Oxford: Oxford University Press, 2003), p. 421.

49. Dixon, p. 46.

50. Hansard HC Deb 16 November 1981, vol. 13, cc23–9. *The Times*, 17 November 1981, pp. 1, 24.

51. *The Guardian*, 12 October 1988, p. 24.

52. *The Guardian*, 23 September 1982, p. 3.

53. *The Guardian*, 15 March 1984, p. 1.

54. The British government has denied repeated claims that its security forces cooperated with loyalist paramilitaries. Still, the quick apprehension of Adams's assailants (and those of McAliskey and her husband) by soldiers who supposedly just happened to be in the area has led to claims that the loyalists were in fact set up by British security. Coogan. p. 289.

55. *The Guardian*, 13 October 1984, p. 1.

56. Coogan, p. 337.

57. Dixon, pp. 184–7.

58. *The Los Angeles Times*, 21 November 1985. Seawright was imprisoned for nine months for his part in the incident. *The Guardian*, 3 October 1986, p. 2. Previously, he had been expelled from the DUP for calling for the incineration of Catholics

who refused to sing the National Anthem. Following Seawright's assassination in November 1987, the Ulster Volunteer Force claimed him as a member.

59. Coogan, p. 184.
60. *The Times*, 13 June 1990, p. 1 and 14 June 1990, pp. 1 and 3.
61. *The Times*, 26 June 1990, p. 1.
62. *The Los Angeles Times*, 31 July 1990.
63. Thatcher, Margaret, *The Downing Street Years* (London: HarperCollins, 1993). p. 414.
64. *The Times*, 8 February 1991, p. 1.
65. Hayes, Burnadette C and Ian McAllister, 'Sowing Dragon's Teeth: Public Support for Political Violence and Paramilitarism in Northern Ireland', *Political Studies*, 49 (2001).
66. Stone previously had been imprisoned for the 1988 murder of three people at an IRA funeral, an attack he later admitted was an attempt to assassinate Adams and McGuinness. *The Independent*, 25 November 2006.
67. *The Times*, November 15 2008, p. 8. *The Times*, 9 December 2008, p. 20.
68. *The Times*, 8 December 2012, p. 4.
69. *The New York Times*, 30 October 2013, p. A8.
70. This is true even without including the 1979 IRA assassination of Lord Montbattan, who seems to have been targeted not for his parliamentary activities but because he was a member of the royal family.
71. Coogan, p. 293.

14 Custard's First Stand

1. Riddell, Peter, *Honest Opportunism* (London: Indigo, 1996).
2. Rush, pp. 185, 285–6. Seaward. pp. 293–4. Rush. pp. 35, 63, 126–8.
3. Norton, Philip, 'The Changing Face of the British House of Commons in the 1980s', *Legislative Studies Quarterly*, 5 (1980).
4. Straw, p. 141.
5. Judge, David, 'Disorder in the House of Commons', *Public Law* (1985). pp. 370–1.
6. Blackburn, R. W., 'Unparliamentary Language', *The Political Quarterly*, 56 (1985).
7. Judge, David, 'Disorder in the "Frustration" Parliaments of Thatcherite Britain', *Political Studies*, 40 (1992). Searing.
8. *The Times*, 14 November 1980, pp. 1, 6. Hansard HC Deb 13 November 1980, vol. 992, cc763–70.
9. *The Times*, 2 September 1982, p. 1.
10. *The Guardian*, 28 February 1984, p. 23.
11. *The Times*, 23 November 1984, p. 4.
12. *The Times*, 22 November 1984, p. 1. Hansard, HC Deb 21 Nov 1984, vol. 68, cc 385–6.
13. Hansard, HC Deb 17 Jan 1985, vol 71 cc 525–6. *The Times*, 18 January 1985, pp. 1, 4.

14. *The Times*, 26 November 1987, p. 4.
15. *The Times*, 12 January 1988, p. 1.
16. Hansard, HC Deb 15 March 1988, vol. 129, cc1006–13. *The Times*, 16 March 1988, pp. 1, 32.
17. *The Guardian*, 20 April 1988, p. 1. Hansard, HC Deb 20 April 1988, vol. 131, cc934–60.
18. Hansard, HC Deb 20 April 1988, vol. 131, cc934–60.
19. *The Times*, 16 December 1988, p. 12. Judge. p. 542.
20. *The Times*, 15 March 1990, p. 9. Hansard HC Deb 13 March 1990, vol. 169, cc461–2. *The Guardian*, 15 March 1990, p. 6.
21. *The Times*, 4 July 1990, pp. 1, 9. Hansard, HC Deb 3 July, 1990, vol. 175, cc859–67. Judge. 'Frustration', p. 542.
22. Armitage, Faith, 'Peace and Quiet in the British House of Commons, 1990–2010', *Democratization*, 20 (2013).
23. *The Times*, 18 December 1992, p. 2. Hansard HC Deb 17 December 1992, vol. 216, cc579–88. JC, vol. 249, 17 December 1992, p. 332.
24. Marr, Andrew, *A History of Modern Britain* (London: Pan Macmillan, 2007), pp. 392–5.
25. *The Times*, 14 March 1981, p. 3.
26. *The Guardian*, 4 August 1982, p. 1.
27. *The Guardian*, 15 January 1983, p. 2.
28. *The Times*, 8 February 1983, p. 1.
29. *The Guardian*, 16 November 1983, p. 1.
30. *The Guardian*, 14 February 1985, p. 1.
31. *The Guardian*, 2 March 1985, p. 30.
32. *The Guardian*, 9 November 1985, p. 1.
33. *The Guardian*, 15 February 1986, p. 4.
34. *The Times*, 3 February 1988, p. 1 and 5 February 1988, p. 1.
35. *The Times*, 27 February 1993, p. 9.
36. *The Guardian*, 25 July 1994, p. 1.
37. *The Independent*, 16 April 1995.
38. *The Independent*, 17 April 1996.
39. *The Guardian*, 13 June 1996, p. 2.
40. *The Guardian*, 4 December 1996, p. 2.
41. Redlich, p. 211. Crewe, Emma, *Lords of Parliament: Manners, Rituals and Politics* (Manchester: Manchester University Press, 2005). Jones, Clyve, 'Dissent and Protest in the House of Lords, 1641–1998: An Attempt to Reconstruct the Procedures Involved in Entering a Protest into the Journals of the House of Lords', *Parliamentary History*, 27 (2008).
42. Dorey, Peter, 'The House of Lords since 1949', in *A Short History of Parliament*, ed. by Clyve Jones (Woodbridge: Boydell Press, 2009).
43. Hansard, HL Deb 2 May 1950, vol. 167, cc3–53. JL, vol. 182, 2 May 1950, p. 90.
44. Hansard, HL Deb 10 May 1966, vol. 274, cc600–52.

45. Hansard, HL Deb 11 June 1980, vol. 410, cc452–528. JL, vol. 213, 11 June 1980, p. 1065.

46. Brazier, Rodney, *Constitutional Practice: The Foundations of British Government*, 3rd edn (Oxford: Oxford University Press, 1999). pp. 245, 249.

47. Hansard, HL Deb 10 March 1998, vol. 587, cc139–96.

48. http://news.bbc.co.uk/1/hl/uk_politics/486551.stm.

49. *The Independent*, 5 November 1999.

50. *The Times*, 13 March 2001, p. 14 and 14 March 2001, p. 16. Hansard, HC Deb 9 March 2001, vol 364, cc526–31.

51. *The Independent*, 15 October 2005.

52. *The Telegraph*, 6 December 2001. *The Times*, 6 December 2001, p. 12.

53. *The Times*, 10 November 2005, pp. 6–7. *The Daily Telegraph*, 10 November 2005, p. 4.

54. *The Mail on Sunday*, 12 February 2006.

55. http://www.dailymail.co.uk/debate/article-1117982/QUENTIN-LETTS-MP-John-McDonnell-suspended-cheers-admiring-kingdom.html

56. *The Times*, 12 May 2010, p. 9.

57. *The Times*, 12 July 2012, p. 7.

58. *The Times*, 24 February 2012, p. 19.

59. *The Times*, 15 March 2013, p. 4.

60. *The Times*, 13 February 1982, p. 1.

61. *The Guardian*, 23 March 2000, p. 7.

62. *The Guardian*, 12 February 2000, p. 22.

63. *The Times*, 23 June 2003, p. 6.

64. *The Times*, 22 March 2005, p. 6.

65. http://www.bbc.co.uk/news/uk-politics-21783379

66. *The Times*, 15 May 2010, p. 3, 23 May 2010, p. 6, and 6 November 2010, p. 11.

67. *The New York Times*, 23 March 2017, p. A1 and 24 March, p. A9.

68. Phillips, Melanie, *Londonistan* (New York: Encounter, 2006), p. 198.

69. *The Guardian*, 3 February 2000, p. 5.

70. *The Independent*, 28 April 2000.

71. *The Telegraph*, 4 April 2001.

72. *The Scotsman*, 6 March 2001. *The Guardian*, 6 March 2001, p. 10.

73. Http:news.bbc.co.uk/1/hi/wales/1369404.stm

74. *The Telegraph*, 20 May 2004. www.telegraph.co.uk/news/uknews/1462319/purple-flour-bomb-hits-Blair.html.

75. *The Daily Telegraph*, 16 September 2004.

76. *The Times*, 16 October 2011, p. 19.

77. *The Times*, 20 November 2004, p. 3.

78. *The Guardian*, 7 February 2006.

79. *The Times*, 27 June 2006, p. 12.

80. *The Telegraph*, 24 October 2008.

81. *The Times*, 7 March 2009, p. 3.

82. www.telegraph.co.uk/comment/columnists/philipjohnston/4950796/you-cant-go-bananas-over-a-bit-of-custard.html.

83. *The Times*, 1 December 2009. p. 24.

84. *The Times*, 11 November 2010, pp. 1, 6–7. More than 100 academics subsequently signed an open letter castigating the organizers of the demonstration for deploring the violence. *The Times*, 12 November 2010, pp. 1, 14–5.

85. *The Times*, 25 November 2010, pp. 4–5 and 26 November 2010, p. 7.

86. *The Times*, 7 December 2010, p. 21.

87. *The Times*, 10 December 2010, pp. 1, 3–5.

88. *The Times*, 6 February 2011, p. 1.

89. www.bbc.com/news/uk-politics-14209268

90. *The Times*, 17 July 2011, p. 2.

91. *The Times*, 26 August 2011, p. 28. http://www.telegraph.co.uk/news/politics/nick-clegg/8723466/Nick-Clegg-attacked-with-blue-paint.html

92. *The Times*, 26 August 2011, p. 26. http://www.telegraph.co.uk/news/uknews/crime/8723583/Louise-Mensch-man-59-held-over-email-threats-to-Torys-MPs-children.html

93. *The Sunday Times*, 3 February 2013, p. 8.

94. Latham professed surprise that she listed as the top target on the website given that all she had done is support the government line that a limited experimental badger cull should be carried out to ascertain if this curbed the spread of bovine tuberculosis. *The Sunday Times*, 9 June 2013, p. 17.

95. http://www.theguardian.com/technology/2013/jul/30/police-death-threats-stella-creasy-twitter

96. Oral evidence to Parliament's Joint Committee on Human Rights, inquiry into Democracy, Free Speech and Freedom of Association (HC 1890), 24 April 2019, pp. 4–5.

97. *The New York Times*, 17 March 2018, p. A10. Seven months later David Parnham pleaded guilty to 14 charges, including soliciting murder, in connection with the campaign. *The New York Times*, 15 October 2018, p. A5.

98. *The New York Times*, 31 August 2014, p. 11.

99. Garnett, Mark, *From Anger to Apathy: The Study of Politics, Society and Popular Culture in Britain since 1975* (London: Vintage, 2007), pp. 371–5.

100. The killer, who has a history of espousing extreme right-wing beliefs, was sentenced to life imprisonment for Cox's murder. *The New York Times*, 24 November 2016, p. A13.

101. *The Guardian*, 12 July and 19 October 2016.

102. *The New York Times*, 10 December 2018.

103. The New York Times, 29 January 2019, p. A6.

104. https://www.express.co.uk/news/uk/1095486/brexit-news-jeremy-corbyn-egg-finsbury-park-mosque-john-murphy-second-referendum

105. *The New York Times*, 7 October 2016, p. A3. http://www.telegraph.co.uk/news/2016/10/08/ukip-mep-steven-woolfe-says-injuries-prove-he-was-attacked-by-pa/

W(h)ither Parliamentary Violence?

1. Stone. p. 32.

2. Langford. p. 148.

3. It may be no coincidence that in the US, which enjoyed a more democratic franchise from the start, duels were employed more often as a political weapon. Freeman, Joanne B., 'Dueling as Politics: Reinterpreting the Burr–Hamilton Duel', *William and Mary Quarterly,* 53 (1996); Freeman, *Affairs.*

4. Pitkin, Hanna Fenichel, *The Concept of Representation* (Berkeley: University of California Press, 1976). p. 237.

5. Heffer, p. 223.

6. As a proportion of total parliamentary violence, that involving outsiders did increase, from 21% in the 1700s, to 30% in the 1800s, 65% in the 1900s and 75% in the first decades of the 2000s.

7. Critchley. p. 208.

8. Oral evidence to Parliament's Joint Committee on Human Rights, inquiry into Democracy, Free Speech and Freedom of Association (HC 1890), 24 April 2019, pp. 5–6, 13.

9. *The New York Times*, 2 May 2019, p. A8.

10. *The Times*, 16 May 2008, p. 21.

11. *The Times*, 17 March 2008, p. 27, 5 April 2010, p. 8, 2 May 2011, p. 7, 13 July 2011, p. 6, 10 September 2011, p. 23, 1 April 2013, p. 6.

12. *The Times*, 10 January 2008, p. 30. 3 March 2008, p. 4, 18 August 2008, p. 17, 12 December 2008, p. 24.

13. *The Times*, 24 December 2012, p. 14.

14. *The Times*, 2 December 2008, p. 4, 8 May 2010, p. 40, 9 August 2010, p. 15.

15. *The Times*, 7 December 2008, pp. 1, 3.

16. http://www.mailonsunday.co.uk/pages/live/articles/news/news.html?in_article_id=511553&in_page_id=1770.

17. *The Times*, 8 June 2010, p. 4.

18. *The Times*, 21 August 2009, p. 4, 22 February 2010, pp. 1–2, 6–7, 26 August 2010, p. 9, 22 May 2013, p. 23. *The New York Times*, 31 October 2017, p. A4.

19. Ilie, Cornelia, 'Gendering Confrontational Rhetoric: Discursive Disorder in the British and Swedish Parliaments', *Democratization,* 20 (2013).

20. Riddell, pp. 137–9.

21. *The Times*, 4 June, 2011, p. 19. *The Sunday Times*, 3 February 2013, p. 11.

22. A panel of medical experts argued that free or subsidized alcohol in Westminster Palace posed not only long-term health risks but also undermined the ability of MPs to do their jobs. During a 2010 budget vote, some MPs 'were so drunk they stumbled through the lobbies, with others hardly able to stand'. One Tory, the aptly named Mark Reckless, reportedly was so inebriated he was unable to vote. *The Times*, 9 October 2011, pp. 1–2, 20.

23. If parliamentary violence continues at its present pace – 47 incidents from 2000 through early 2019 – there will be 247 episodes by the end of 2099, a total substantially higher than the 209 in the 1900s.

24. Wolfe, Eugene L., 'Creating Democracy's Good Losers: The Rise, Fall and Return of Parliamentary Disorder in Post-War Japan', *Government and Opposition,* 39 (2004).

INDEX